AGENTS WITHOUT EMPIRE

Agents without Empire

MOBILITY AND RACE-MAKING
IN SIXTEENTH-CENTURY FRANCE

Antónia Szabari

FORDHAM UNIVERSITY PRESS   NEW YORK 2024

Fordham University Press gratefully acknowledges financial assistance
and support provided for the publication of this book by the University
of Southern California.

Copyright © 2024 Fordham University Press

All rights reserved. No part of this publication may be reproduced, stored
in a retrieval system, or transmitted in any form or by any means—electronic,
mechanical, photocopy, recording, or any other—except for brief quotations
in printed reviews, without the prior permission of the publisher.

Fordham University Press has no responsibility for the persistence or
accuracy of URLs for external or third-party Internet websites referred to
in this publication and does not guarantee that any content on such websites
is, or will remain, accurate or appropriate.

Fordham University Press also publishes its books in a variety of electronic
formats. Some content that appears in print may not be available in
electronic books.

Visit us online at www.fordhampress.com.

Library of Congress Cataloging-in-Publication Data available
online at https://catalog.loc.gov.

Printed in the United States of America
26 25 24   5 4 3 2 1
First edition

For Alice and Felix

Contents

PREFACE ix

Introduction: French Agents in the Ottoman Empire 1

1 Big Appetite and Rabelais's Multiracial Empires 29

2 Bird-Man 2, Female Androgyne, and Other Speculative Transformations 60

3 Snake Women of the East: Staging Freedom and Invisible Unfreedoms 89

4 Nicolas de Nicolay's Empire of Ink 121

5 Distancology and Universalizing French Masculinity 160

Coda: Race and Self-Discovery 189

ACKNOWLEDGMENTS 197

NOTES 199

WORKS CITED 249

INDEX 269

Preface

What constitutes race in sixteenth-century France? This is the question that motivates the following introduction, five chapters, and coda. If we are to answer this question, we must first put it into context. The modern notion of race is closely tied to histories of European colonial power, settler colonies in the so-called New World, the slave trade, enslavement and its justification by racist ideologies, and the reliance on slave labor in the plantation economy. To address the sixteenth-century French context, however, we need to ask what race is *before* the rise of the French empire, during a period in which France had made only a handful of small-scale, unsuccessful, or short-lived attempts to establish colonies. This is a question that does not regularly come up and may even require justification within sixteenth-century French studies, where a strong distinction is still maintained between the modern notion of race and a different, seemingly unrelated application of the term "race" that is specific to the fifteenth through seventeenth centuries.[1] Race in its modern sense is also often ignored in sixteenth-century literary studies, even though symbols and narratives of cultural others, empire, enslavement, skin color, and non-Christians and non-Europeans became prominent in French culture in the period. These narratives serve as testimonials to the fact that the French encountered people they perceived as different from them and assigned special status to these people. The French, especially those among educated populations, were literate in reading the markers of race. They reflected on and made claims to naturalize their own belonging to the group of Christian, French, European, and, by extension, White and free men. They distinguished between their own mobile selves and the racialized identities of others. This book shows some of the ways in which they achieved this.

Studies of sixteenth-century French culture have largely treated the racializing language and images in the archives of diplomacy and spying on the Ottomans and related literary texts as anomalous, positioning them as leftovers of bygone medieval habits of the mind that are somehow separate from the questions to be asked in literary and cultural studies. In new historicist accounts of early modern French literature concerning the non-European world, certain French authors have become canonical points of reference. These "heroes,"[2] including François Rabelais (ca. 1494–1553), Michel de Montaigne (1533–1592), Pierre Belon (1517–1564), and André Thevet (ca. 1516–1590), have been celebrated for their flexible worldviews, empathy, and interest in the difference of non-French cultures both inside and outside of Europe. As a result, this period in French cultural history has come to be valued as an exceptional era of cultural opening toward others. The present study shows that such a celebration is, at the very least, problematic. My aim is to ask what this peculiar corpus can do to help us understand the role played by race in the constructions of protocolonial French male subjectivity in sixteenth-century literary and diplomatic cultures. I hope to shift the attention away from the question of how cultural or ethnic others were encountered and represented from a French- and Eurocentric perspective to instead spotlight the selves that were being dynamically constructed as agential and mobile by way of turning to others.[3] French humanist authors like Rabelais, Belon, Guillaume Postel, Étienne Jodelle, Joachin du Bellay, and Montaigne push the humanist practice of locating examples for powerful, morally oriented action beyond classical and biblical sources and look to the validity of the actions of others outside the Christian humanist canon—but this cosmopolitan turn demands its own analysis.

It is well known that Renaissance culture, by virtue of its belief in the idea that man is the measure of all things, gave an empowering role to the individual (or, in modern terms, to agency). Classically inflected notions of agency were available to men in Renaissance culture, and this male bias or "manism" of humanism has been amply documented.[4] But how does race factor into this culture of empowerment? How are non-French, non-Christian, or non-White subjects coded as non-agential vis-à-vis humanism? And how do such codings relate to descriptions of White French men as empowered or agential? What kinds of dialogues and interactions were possible between these two groups? In *Agents without Empire*, I show that, before the rise of the French colonial empire in the seventeenth century, medieval eschatological categories of race were recast through perceptions of the material world of the Ottoman Empire that were made accessible, in a sudden and entirely unprecedented manner, to agents of the French crown. These agents were minor diplomatic actors (always male) who served the French ruling elite in its alliance with the Sublime

Porte. Most of the aforementioned authors were also agents of the French ruling elite, which gave them a mixed status. Despite being instruments of a master's will, they were also repeatedly required to enact their own agency in delicate situations. Politically and existentially without control and placed in a contingent realm of actions, they looked to others as models for their own desired agency. I devote special attention to the fact that these actors went beyond classically inflected models of male and Christian agency and, indeed, even beyond human agency itself. French agents encountered people of different ethnicities, faiths, and skin colors in the Ottoman Empire, which allowed them to rethink medieval stereotypes about non-French and non-Christian others. However, they also extended their modeling of action to include material aggregates, animals, and other nonhuman entities. In the eyes of the French, the Ottoman Empire was a vast realm of powerful military, economic, natural, and cultural resources, diverse ethnic groups, animals, plants, and minerals; it was a veritable world in the world. It is for this reason, along with the corresponding abundance of French documents about the Ottoman Empire, that I chose to discuss race in this context rather than in that of the New World. That said, many of the insights in *Agents without Empire* are also valid in the context of the New World, especially the fact that agential selves were created through a turn, or what Sara Ahmed has called an "orientation," toward others.[5] Ahmed's critical postcolonial, feminist phenomenology inspires me to ask what it means to understand others through one's own male, empowered, mobile French body—one which is shaped by service while also using such perceptions of others to bolster the sense of self. One of the ways I show this is by emphasizing the continuity between images of itinerant men in the Ottoman Empire and the emerging figure of the New World "cannibal" to whose figure Montaigne devoted an essay, setting it up to become a walking signifier of seemingly universal moral values from which European (male) readers drew most benefit.

Developing a critical concept of race in sixteenth-century France also allows me to attend to the ambiguities, the acts of violence, and the aspirations that characterize these sixteenth-century moments and to make connections with future forms of colonialism. Empire thus has two meanings in this book, both of which I subject to ongoing analysis. One is empirical and concrete, pertaining to the historical yet largely unsuccessful process of the French state's colonial empire-building in the sixteenth century. The other looks to the universalist fantasies and unrealizable utopias called upon by agents to counterbalance their vulnerable positions and low status as they found themselves enmeshed within an expansionist French state over which they had little or no control. *Agents without Empire* offers a view of the accidents and existential uncertainties that attended the emergence of hegemonic French Christian (mostly Catholic) male subjectivity, as well as the cracks and fissures in this self as they become visible in diplomatic archives and some hypercanonical literary texts.[6] The aim of this book is to reverse our usual focus by showing that these minor texts written by agents reveal racializing perspectives that are *also* established as a steady component in literary texts whose authors have gained much greater visibility. Finally, if we are to consider the racializing aspects of French and European male agency, we must also question how we have been reading the symbols of race in this culture up until this point and be attentive to the limits of our own literacy in being able to read what early modern readers and writers understood as race terms. In short, the book questions the very perspective from which we read French Renaissance culture and the empowered individual that produces and consumes it. This questioning is necessary if we are to open up new avenues of thought from which to continue reading the literary sixteenth century.[7]

AGENTS WITHOUT EMPIRE

Introduction: French Agents in the Ottoman Empire

Polite to a fault with foreigners, the French courtier never stops treating them with a certain tone of superiority ("ne se défait jamais avec eux d'un certain ton de supériorité") inspired by his own good opinion of himself and the extreme splendor of the court. This attitude is a small compensation for the pliability ("souplesse") that he is obliged to maintain toward his own master.
—JOSÉPHINE DE MONBART, *LETTRES TAHITIENNES* (1784)

If the New World fed dreams, what was the Old World reality that whetted the appetite for them?
—TONI MORRISON, *PLAYING IN THE DARK* (1992)

The Entwining of Race and Agency

The chapter "Of the Origin and Antiquity of the Great Pantagruel," which explains the genealogy of the eponymous folkloric giant featured in the novel *Pantagruel* (published ca. 1531–1532), takes us into the thick of emerging notions of race in the first third of the sixteenth century.[1] The humanist author, François Rabelais, both uses and subverts the received meaning of the contemporary term "race" in such a way that it becomes entwined with agency. Many races of giants were born, tells the fictive narrator Alcofrybas, when Cain's fratricide caused the earth to become saturated with Abel's blood and produce medlars ("mesles") so large that three of them filled a bushel. These medlars were attractive to the eye and pleasing to the palate, but accidents happened to those who ate the sweet winter fruit in large quantities: Different parts of their bodies ballooned in unexpected protuberances of growth. Some grew in the stomach (i.e., the comic Mardi-Gras "saint" Pansart and an imaginary giant jokingly named "Mardigras"), some in the back (becoming hunchbacks), some in the virile member (i.e., Priapus), some in the thigh, some in the nose, some in the ears, some in the eyes, and yet some, like Pantagruel's ancestors, in their whole body. Pantagruel's bloodline (or medlar line) in Rabelais's telling includes Atlas, Alexander the Great, Sisyphus, Hercules, and Fierabras, all legendary giants and popular historical figures. The narrator remains sympathetic to all these overeaters of medlars while also revealing the dangers inherent to their consumption—and, indeed, some fare better than others. Even though this comic tale of generation by accidental growth and protuberance can be seen as parodying serious Greek, Arab, Hebrew, and Christian genealogies, it also makes important claims about the differences of bodies while rethinking notions of alimentation and health. Sweet and desirable to the taste, the medlars contain apparent similarities to the apple in the biblical story of Adam and Eve—but their consumption in *Pantagruel* is, by contrast, not prohibited by any moral authority. Recalling the intoxication of the Old Testament patriarch Noah, the narrator notes that medlars are similar to wine in this respect: Their consumption carries both risks and benefits for the health of the body. With this substitution of medlars for grapes, Alcofrybas distances himself from the story of Noah's intoxication and its negative consequences: Noah's shameful nudity and the racializing interpretations of the patriarch's oft-misquoted curse on Ham.[2] The medlars spring forth from the blood of Abel spilled over the earth, allowing everyone to be generated from this "just" blood.[3] Their efficacy is not tied to a curse but to their material abundance and power to alter bodies, which, nonetheless, introduces uncertainties in the story. The capacity for moral agency, which is tied to the Hebrew-Christian virtue of love and transmitted by way of Abel's spilled blood, is then distributed over the whole earth thanks to the fortuitous transformation of the blood into fruit sap—and the bodies that emerge from the consumption of the juicy, powerful medlars also come to benefit from—or suffer under—different accidents.

This fictional genealogy provides a good starting point for the discussion of protocolonial notions of race in France because Alcofrybas uses race in a sense specific to the fifteenth and sixteenth centuries while also parodying this usage and thus allowing it to take on supplementary significance. Before the eighteenth century, the term "race" was used to denote a bloodline that constituted a family or dynasty through the transmission of physical and moral characteristics. The modern notion of race and the early modern term "race" (French "race" and "razza," both derived perhaps from the Italian "razza") have the same etymology but distinct meanings. Although speculative etymologies suggest links to the Latin *radix* ("root") and the Arabic *ra's* ("head, beginning, origin"), the word's origins remain obscure. Arlette Jouanna begins her magisterial doctoral thesis (published in 1976) on the notion of "race" in sixteenth-century France with the insight that the existence of natural differences between human beings was generally accepted in this period and that, moreover, "race" was used to fix people's rank and place in society.[4] The most privileged "race," nobility, was defined by *lignée* (similar to the modern term "pedigree," which derives from the *pied de grue,* or "foot of crane," a forked sign used to designate descent in old genealogical charts). The lignée was the bloodline that defined noble families and marked the noble caste as separate from all others. However, the sixteenth-century concept of "race" was not all about predeterminism by birth. In his contribution to the discussion of pre-biological, nature-based conceptions of difference, Pierre Boulle argues that "race" became a loaded term in the fifteenth and sixteenth centuries because of the rise of a new nobility, which necessitated definitions that both restricted this status and allowed for ways of acquiring it. Boulle shows that the French "race" emerged in the late fifteenth century to distinguish between old noble bloodlines—which were deemed to carry valuable qualities—and the newly minted nobility created by royal grants.[5] Boulle highlights a specific meaning of "race" in the sixteenth and seventeenth centuries as denoting pre-excellence made possible by both a hereditary transmission of blood and a noble upbringing.[6] Nobility, in this sense, consisted of a set of qualities generated in noble men and women analogously to those produced in noble animals used for war and the hunt. Rabelais's tale about the medlars and the generation of races of giants, however, further destabilizes the continuity of race ensured in early modern French society through bloodline, marriage, and education by tying it to accidents of nature and violent events. It opens race up to definitions through matters other than noble blood (especially as blood, the legally codified marker of nobility in medieval Europe, becomes fruit sap) and creates the fiction of more or less excellent races generated in the contingent realm of nature.

Rabelais's tale indicates a changing sense and significance of race beyond its role in defining social caste. Race becomes more pliable because of its connection with the physical world, but also more intense because of its connection to moral agency. The tale contests the standard notion of "race" as a bloodline, for it substitutes those considered to have less symbolic or social power for those who hold socially sanctioned positions of agency—that is Pantagruel for the prince, and fruit juice for blood. My reading here diverges from established interpretations of Rabelais's novels as humanist fictions dealing with ideal government. Such readings emphasize that both Pantagruel and Rabelais's other giant princes, Gargantua and Grandgousier, embody Christian moral values that operate in line with the humanist thought of Desiderius Erasmus (ca. 1466–1536).[7] While I am not debating that Rabelais was a Christian humanist, I underscore that his fiction is implanted in the physicality of the body. It creates agencies of appetite. Race is a function of these differentiated bodies and agencies. Even his giant princes act horizontally, through friendship and sharing meals, rather than vertically. In their relations to others, their size telescopes, and the instability of the humoral body and its proneness to growth and shrinking provide them with a mobile, rather than absolute, perspective. His characters do not sublimate all forms of appetite or self-interest to the interests of the state, and his fictions of agency diverge from rationalist state ideologies.[8]

The story about medlars and giant bodies tells us that, unlike the consumption of wine that separated Christians and Muslims, the consumption of this fruit brought them together. Alcofrybas's mixed Muslim-Christian genealogy, moreover, was written while the French crown's alliance with the Sublime Porte was well underway. And, at least occasionally, Rabelais himself served the French monarchy as an agent—albeit not in the Ottoman Empire, but in the greater Mediterranean region—and had a great interest in this diplomatic relationship that redefined who was friend or foe. Alcofrybas rewrites medieval narratives about self and other by naming Fierabras, a legendary Saracen who appears as the enemy of Christian knights in medieval romance literature (rather than Olivier, the companion of Roland and defeater of Fierabras) among Pantagruel's ancestors. Pantagruel, his father, Gargantua, and his grandfather Grandgousier stem from a lineage running from the invented giant Chalbroth to the Saracen Fierabras. They can count the imaginary Saracen giant, Gafaffre (featured in a thirteenth-century epic poem), among their ancestors, thereby defying medieval religious and geopolitical conceptions of race that separate Muslim "Saracens" from Christian "Europeans." Alcofrybas—whose faux-Arabic name is to be noted—tells us that the moral ability to treat others charitably, the value upheld in the New Testament, was given to everyone on Earth and that there is no moral distinction between Christians and Muslims concerning their ability to respond to the ethical demands of brotherly love. And yet, even though all races ultimately emerge because of the blood spilled by Abel, with the medlars functioning as intermediaries, all bodies are not equal under the accidents of nature and alimentary processes. These accidental differences lead, in turn, to physical, moral, and, in sixteenth-century terms, racial differences. Pantagruel's race is distinguished from those of other giants, and these differences are marked by discernible bodily features. While all differences are due to nature's capacity for change through accidents without the intervention of a divine or transcendent power, agency does emerge as a constant that gives shape from within to matter in flux. By indexing the capacity for social bonds in people of different ethnicities and religions to a uniform nature, Alcofrybas's gesture levels moral differences, abolishes certain ontological differences that were deeply rooted in the medieval history of France, and also creates new, protocolonial ones. From the outset of what would grow into a multivolume novel about war, diplomacy, travel, and exploration, Rabelais indexes bodily and moral differences to a nature prone to accidents—specifically, violent passions, bleeding bodies, turgid fruit, and (animal) appetite. These instances of physical matter, blood, fruit, and appetite reveal the importance of the humoral body that is embedded in a larger cosmic material realm. The hemispheric fruits of the *neflier* serve as reminders that all things consist of humors, circulation, and growth—and, in this story, humoral bodies grow like medlars as they develop protrusions ("enflure"[9]) and obey a logic of both vegetal and animal bodies. Here, we are not just dealing with individual bodies but also their extensions, through eating and food, in a cosmic nature. Rabelais's giants nonetheless represent body types that fall into two groups: those whose bodies are disproportionate and those whose are proportionate, beautiful, and complete bodies. The accidental shapes of the resulting bodies are described and sorted through categories of harmony and disharmony, with the latter bordering on monstrosity such that Pantagruel's race comes from the only line of giants that grew proportionately and harmoniously in all parts of the body. However, the other giant races similarly bear the mark of the medlars and Abel's blood, as well as that of the plasticity of the physical world.[10] Their monstrosity is ambivalent, and Alcofrybas's story seems to introduce divisions at much the same time as it asks readers to contemplate similarities and alliances. The famous Renaissance diversity of nature is here combined with the practical undecidability of these other races, bodies, and physiognomies. Rabelais's pre-WWII Dutch illustrator, Henk Henriët, was especially attentive to the plasticity of human and animal physiognomy in Rabelais. As such, his sketches serve as muted commentaries on the variability of bodies (see Figure 1).

Pantagruel's appearance indicates the health and wholeness of the body and the larger sociopolitical world. The ancient Hippocratic-Galenic model, inflected as it is by an implicitly Aristotelian bias toward wholeness and rationality, perceives the body to be an unstable flux of humors that is stabilized by the corporeal distillation of a thin material and spiritual substance (the putative fifth and most perfect element or the "quintessence"). According to this model, appetite is the first step in a chain of events that sees the consumed substance transformed into humors that become progressively more refined, proceeding from unstable flux to rarefied spiritual matter. Alcofrybas, as a self-described "abstractor of quintessence," claims to be an agent of this transformation and

Figure 1

hence the embodiment of bodily and spiritual excellence. He is the agent of agency, the image of the self emerging from flux (see Figure 2). Alcofrybas thus takes on the task of producing agencies similar to those exercised by Pantagruel, albeit in a more writerly but no less exuberant mode, with the medlars and matter also playing a role in this genesis. If we transform the question of Pantagruel's responsibility—which is ethical in orientation—into that of agency—which is ethical *and* political in orientation— then we must begin with the bodily differences between Pantagruel and the other races of giants whose bodies grew disproportionately. The agency of Pantagruel and his race has to do with restituting this whole, after the spilled blood of Abel—but, in this process, the story leaves open the question about the role of the other races, which are characterized by excessive passions leading to disproportionate growth. Rabelais's fiction thus invents a new model of agency—one that can be tested by accidents and manifest itself across the geographic, religious, and cultural boundaries drawn by the Crusades in medieval Europe. Visibility and testing by accidents together make up this new form of agency that enlists the holistic perspective of humoral medicine and the appetitive body, which, through this same appetite, becomes boundless and stands in mimetic relation to the material world it consumes. If "origin" is synonymous with "nation" (Lat.

Figure 2

"natio," i.e., birth, origin), then Pantagruel also shows how the body of France can be made beautiful and whole by fortuitous alliances that rewrite medieval history. The tale tells readers that healthy bodies, including political bodies, are not made by laws (including dietary restrictions in Christianity, like the divine command not to eat the apple growing on the tree of knowledge in the biblical Garden of Eden or the rules of Lent in Catholic Europe). Nor are they made by divine creation. Rather, they are made by vagaries of vegetal growth, violent events that disrupt the social and political order, and whims of appetite—but that also have the potential to make this realm whole, possibly on a large scale. Such a disruption (or, according to the hopes of the ruling elite, restoration) was exemplified by the French crown's alliance with the Sublime Porte, which was preceded by what French humanists perceived to be another "violence," here perpetrated by Spain against France. More broadly, Alcyfrobas's genealogy reorientates the readers toward the physical world and away from a medieval clash of civilizations.

Rabelais's tale alters the classical notion of virtuous action by distributing it among the giants, their appetites, and the fruit. To be sure, the fourth-century BCE philosopher and polymath Aristotle did not exclude subconscious, involuntary acts like blushing and breathing or acts based on desire ("epithumía") of children and animals from the category of actions. And yet his definition of virtuous action, as described in the *Nicomachian Ethics*, which provides the basis of Western notions of agency, is defined as purposeful action based on a choice or decision ("haíresis") that is autonomous, rational, and free of constraint.[11] This action can be controlled by the individual from beginning to end.[12] Aristotle distinguishes virtue from disposition and courageous action from excessive fearlessness, which he associates with non-Greeks like the Celts, thus introducing ethnic bias into his philosophy of action. One of the most famous (and infamous, from the perspective of religious authorities) Renaissance texts, Giovanni Pico della Mirandola's *Oration on the Dignity of Man* (written in 1486), rewrote the medieval ontological order, the Great Chain of Being, by designating the adult, male human being the only being confined by no bounds. Pico della Mirandola thus claims that educated humanist men raise themselves up through the ontological hierarchy, which is divided into a sensual lower part and a rational upper part, to become philosophers—or angels. Pico della Mirandola's text thus effectively differentiates between ontological status or rank of human beings ("dignity") based on education and especially esoteric learning that endow one with agency.[13] Like the Italian humanist, Rabelais's Alcofrybas also resorts to a process of abstracting moral agency. But this alchemy takes place in the body of Pantagruel with the participation of nourishment, the medlars, which act as intermediaries to Panurge to redeem the world from the hostility of Cain's act. Yet, as Rabelais extends the notion of agency to the nonhuman realm of fruit, he also restricts it to those bodies marked by harmony and beauty (although agencies of disharmony also act in this fictional tale). In one possible reading, Pantagruel's race is in possession of the most human, most rational form of agency, as is evinced by his beautiful, proportionate body in which the humors are kept in check from overabundance. Is it the case, then, that Pantagruel comes to save *all* the bodies, enacting a privileged agency from which a new world grows and to which this new world is rendered subordinate? Or, alternatively, is he to share this agency with material others: the fruits of nature, blood, and other humors, and the perpetrators of violence? I believe there is some ambiguity here that allows for Pantagruel to live in a physical world of ontological ambiguity, while the tale leaves us to ponder these questions that have such political and geopolitical resonance in the context of sixteenth-century Europe. But, most importantly, it creates some uncertainty about Pantagruel's capacity for stabilizing the flux of an animate nature and human emotional violence. Alcofrybas extends agency beyond the human individual in ways that reject the exceptionality of rational human agency as it appears in most Western metaphysics, beginning with Aristotle. But it is also by tying agency to nature that he makes moral and racial differences. In contemporary terms to which I will return later, Rabelais's giants are hybrids generated by the agency of people, humors, plants, spilled blood, and sweet juice, as well as scriptural exemplars, medieval romances, and the printing press. This hybridity allows them to acquire agency away from that associated with the blood-based nobility of aristocracy and the spiritual caste of the clergy. Rabelais's dynasty of giants exists on an equal ontological footing with its subjects, bound and molded by the same appetite, and serves as a model of action and imitation rather than a representation of divine will. Their agency, which allies itself with that of human and nonhuman others, I suggest, was an attractive attitude in those situations where spaces of agency were imagined as distinct from the political actors claiming to represent divine powers. In political realms organized by pressures from masters, kings, and emperors, it helped carve out spaces of autonomy for those with mixed status.

Rabelais's tale about enmity and reconciliation rewrites what Geraldine Heng has described as medieval racializing categories, or the relations between races defined by biblical narrative, popular beliefs, collective memory, and art and literature in the European Middle Ages. In her book *The Invention of Race in the European Middle Ages,* Heng advocates for using the term race instead of "otherness" and "difference" broadly and comprehensively in medieval Europe, questioning the consensus that the concept of race was born out of modern colonial science.[14] Heng also contests prevalent modernist articulations of race theory that take the biological body and the intricate taxonomies of nineteenth-century symbolic regimes as their privileged reference point. Against these definitions of race as the product of modernity, she defines race transhistorically and discursively,[15] positioning it as a "strategic essentialism" for demarcating people through differences "to distribute positions and powers differentially to human groups."[16] Heng shows that race-making took place in medieval Europe along the axes of cartography, religion, and skin color. Following the work of art historians and cultural historians, she situates the emergence of the European subject in the thirteenth through fifteenth centuries.[17] This insight relies on significant and exemplary cultural and political events such as the emergence of white as a perceived skin color of European Christians,[18] the use of the senses to racialize Jews in medieval England, and competition for religious domination between Christianity and Islam, which contributed to the prevalent use of the term "Saracen" in Europe. These medieval stereotypes of race-making, as charted by Heng, were alive in sixteenth-century European culture, which was at the time in the throes of redefining its own Christian identity. However, changes were also underway because of geopolitical shifts, the Reformation, humanism, and the emergence of centralized rivalrous states in Europe. In the Middle Ages, and going back to the Church Fathers, Arabs, or Saracens (also called Ishmaelites), were reputed in Latin Europe to stem from Ishmael, the son of Sara's Egyptian slave Hagar. Heng links this to Genesis 16:10, which, "prophesying that descendants of Ishmael would be an uncountable multitude, now seemed to describe not merely Islamic Arab tribes but a growing and dispersed population of all kinds of Muslims whose numbers were, indeed, becoming uncountable."[19] Alcofrybas scrambles this division between Saracen-slaying French Crusaders and Saracens by making Gargantua and Pantagruel stem from a race of multiethnic giants and also shifts the agent of rebellion from Ishmael to Cain's fratricide. Medieval Europe associated Ishmael and the rebellious nature attributed to him to the expansion of Islam starting in the seventh century. Islam became a global empire in the Middle Ages—though this fact did not become apparent to the Europeans until the thirteenth or even fourteenth centuries, after which, and even more so after the Ottoman conquest of Constantinople in 1453, they saw "Saracens," "Arabs," and, later, also "Turks" as a primary threat. The proliferative materiality attributed to Ishmael's descendants in medieval racializing narratives is reattributed in Alcofrybas's genealogy to material nature, along with ontological ambiguity. Pantagruel comes to heal the discord created by fratricide, but rebelliousness in this framing is no longer an attribute of faith or a product of eschatological design; instead, it is a direct correlate of the distortion and disharmony of bodies. The abundance and productivity that offer the potential of rebellion also mark Pantagruel's proportionate yet excessive body. Ontological differences are not solely based on political or religious boundaries but also on perceived similarities—notably, those between French and Saracen bodies—and differences. This perception represents a significant shift from the most extreme medieval wholesale understanding of Muslims, conceived for the battlefield not as human bodies but rather as agents of eschatological evil, to understanding of agency as embodied and manifested in visible corporeal differences.[20]

Another axis of critical race theory's intervention in precolonial Europe has been the examination of the discursive power of humanism to construct the human as a restrictive category masquerading as one that is universal. In her 2003 essay, "Unsettling the Coloniality of Being/Power/Truth/Freedom,"[21] Sylvia Wynter sketches a broad genealogy of race-making in European culture, identifying epistemic shifts that occur in the Middle Ages, the early modern period, and modernity. Humanism, for Wynter, is placed somewhere around the midway point of such a genealogy. Wynter's work, which draws on a transhistorical archive, ties European race-making to the "overrepresentation of Man," whose two iterations (sometimes called Man 1 and Man 2) are medieval Christian and early modern humanist in their formations. In both instances, the overrepresentation of culturally produced Man creates the conditions for coloniality to institute itself by claiming universality for European culture's particular and parochial self-definition, as well as for the Western ethnoclass, all the while excluding broader humanity from the category of Man. In Wynter's genealogy, colonial difference is first instituted by the separation between celibate churchmen (Man 1) and marrying laymen in the Christian Middle Ages. Here, the idea of enslavement appears as the legacy of the Adamic fall indexed to the sinful flesh, earth, and, geographically, the Torrid Zones (classified as incapable of supporting civilized life) and the Atlantic Ocean (thought to be incapable of supporting a landmass and life). Secular, rational Man (Man 2), meanwhile, relies upon a new idea of enslavement linked to the passions and desires of the body (following Michel Foucault's anti-sensualist genealogy of modernity[22]). Man 2 required the sublimation of interests particular to those of the state and common good as a new "behavior-motivating 'plan of human salvation.'"[23] Wynter takes Pico della Mirandola's *Oration* as paradigmatic of the new Man 2. By designating Man as the only being capable of moving up or down the hierarchical ladder, Pico della Mirandola's rewriting of the medieval ontological order "meant that the primary behavior-motivating goal, rather than that of seeking salvation in the *civitas dei*, was now that of adhering to the goal of the *civitas saecularis*, the goal, that is, of seeking to ensure the stability, order, and territorial expansion of the state in a competitive rivalry with other European states."[24] "Unsettling the Coloniality of Being/Power/Truth/Freedom" locates a major genealogical shift in the fifteenth and sixteenth centuries and traces the distinction between human and nonhuman (the former imperially reserved for the Western ethnoclass and instituted by the intellectual elite) while also formulating a demand for a new concept of the human independent of this colonial divide. Reading Wynter's genealogy of race-making and her demand for new notions of the human from the angle of sixteenth-century France, we can open a line of inquiry into the modalities for sublimating personal interests and the desires of the body to the interests of the state. Notably, as agents of the state, the authors under examination here did not simply or fully sublimate their interests (or suppress their passions). In more than one way, they consumed the world. Beyond the discursive category of Man 2, White, Christian, male selves were constituted not only from the vantage point of controlling the appetite but also in response to the pressures of service to their own state. Moreover, given the geopolitical advantage wielded over France by the Spanish and the Ottoman Empires (each of which harbored its own universalist claims[25]), the specificities of race-making in France differed from those of the Spanish and Ottoman context.[26] In sixteenth-century France, the categories that racialize non-French and non-Europeans came into effect *before* France had acquired the colonies with administrations run from France and plantation regimes.[27] French humanists and royal apologists developed arguments about other people based not on the need to justify colonizing them in the New World but on the need to justify the French crown's alliance with the Ottoman Empire. Wynter discusses the sixteenth-century dispute that transpired between the humanist and royal apologist Ginés de Sepúlveda (1494–1573) and the missionary priest Bartolomé de las Casas (1484–1566) regarding the status of Indigenous peoples of the Americas in the Spanish Empire, highlighting the opposition between raciocentric and theocratic notions of the human—and the fact that each regards Indigenous peoples as inferior.[28] However, Wynter's anti-sensualist schema does not allow us to account for the sensualist claims or the incredible moral claims to self-empowerment, self-enrichment, freedom to enjoy nature's abundance, and mobility acquired in foreign lands that allowed Frenchmen in the sixteenth century to assert their racial superiority over the inhabitants of foreign lands.

In the following five chapters and coda, I examine the visual and discursive formations that contribute to racializing practices in a cultural domain traversed by powerful political forces. In Chapter 1, "Big Appetite and Rabelais's Multiracial Empires," I analyze Rabelais's letters and his fiction of a Christian empire built through the courteous treatment of North African pirates—namely, by "sating their hunger." This utopian community with Muslim Turkish others, however, is put to the test by the racializing fault lines of the same fictions of agency that underpin it. I explore Rabelais's dietary utopias, which are also dietary racisms, through fictions of the agency of appetite. In Chapter 2, "Bird-Man 2, Female Androgyne, and Other Speculative Transformations," I examine speculative visions in which agents, including Pierre Belon and Guillaume Postel, transgress the boundaries of their French selves to become animal and queer selves in the observations of articulations (in Bruno Latour's sense of the term) of the physical world. These boundary crossings require ruse, sartorial performances, changes of clothing, and immersion in experiences of water, as well as the pleasures of gender-transgressing experiences. In Chapter 3, "Snake Women of the East: Staging Freedom and Invisible Unfreedoms," I explore the power of orientation in two Orientalist tragedies, Étienne Jodelle's 1533 *Cléopâtre captive* and Jean de la Péruse's *Médée* (which debuted in the same year), as esoteric performances of animal, serpent-like agencies. The staging of two Orientalist plays coincides with claims made by the French elite that French soil is free, initiating a tradition that defines French freedom in contrast with the unfreedom of slaves. I interrogate theater as a medium that allows the audience to visualize themselves through the bodies of others conjured up on stage. In Chapter 4, "Nicolas de Nicolay's Empire of Ink," the agent emerges as a mobile body whose stable autonomy is guaranteed by habits of seeing in a world that must appear as unstable and chaotic. I analyze Nicolay's popular travel book *Navigations et Pérégrinations* (1567), which is filled with hostile depictions of people living in and around the Ottoman Empire. I examine the illustrations included in the book as a way of training the inner eye of cosmopolitan European readers to experience the viewing of intimate, savage, erotic, and hypersexualized bodies as ennobling for them while also teaching them categories of the colonizable. This is also one of the first illustrated books in sixteenth-century France in which differences in skin color are made visible. In Chapter 5, "Distancology and Universalizing French Masculinity," I examine Michel de Montaigne's literal and imagined conversations with animals and non-French others side by side with his letters and reports from the French embassy in Constantinople. I argue that Montaigne was a distancologist, if there ever was such an occupation, and strove to define how far or close others were from him, which is made possible by a series of gestures and embodied acts such as undressing, testing the body, and managing the weight of his own mixed agency, all of which he subjects to countless descriptions in *The Essays*. In a coda, "Race and Self-Discovery," I review the critical moments of self-discovery that chance meetings with, for example, French-speaking dervishes, Ottomans, and enslaved Black people incite in the travel account of Jean Palerne. What does it mean to discover oneself through these experiences?

French Cosmopolitanism

In the remainder of this Introduction, I situate this emerging agential racism in two contexts specific to sixteenth-century France: the broad cultural turn to the ideology and symbols of cosmopolitanism and the distribution of agency to non-French and even nonhuman bodies. The idea that accidents of nature, including appetites and fluxes of humors, can lead to agency was, of course, fundamentally opposed to the French monarchy's understanding and presentation of state power, which often relied on Platonic and Christian notions of transcendence. The politics of the early modern state was marked by a wariness of contingency allegorized as "fortune." During Rabelais's lifetime and beyond, the French monarchy practiced a realpolitik that aimed at increasing its territory and influence within Europe, including the Low Countries and Eastern Europe, as well as the Mediterranean region, including North Africa. To achieve this, it allied itself with the Sublime Porte and various officials and commoners of the Ottoman Empire, along with other foreign actors. While the strategic plans of the French crown in its negotiations with the Sublime Porte do not constitute my main subject here, they are nevertheless an important part of the background against which I have formulated my analysis of cosmopolitan culture and agents. De Lamar Jensen has called the French maneuvering in the Ottoman Empire a "diplomacy of survival" because it served France in counterbalancing Spain's power and influence. He also emphasizes the lasting importance of this politics—beyond the largely unsuccessful military campaigns—in developing economic and trade relations between the two states.[29] However, while trade was a secondary concern in the sixteenth century,[30] the crown used its alliance with the Sublime Porte throughout the century and beyond to expand its territory, control its population by liberating enslaved French and Christian people, attempt to resettle (mostly Protestant) French people in Eastern Europe in lands under Ottoman influence, and extend its control over Christian Churches in the East. Humanist apologists of the French crown often adopted the Stoic criticism of ethnocentrism, along with the critique of imperialism in the name of humanity (from the Latin *humanitas*), to attack the Holy Roman Empire and resorted to examples of interreligious alliances from the Old Testament to legitimate the French alliance with the Ottoman Empire—but Stoicism and religious visionary thinking were also a source of agents' own constructions of autonomy, as we shall see later. These "spin doctors" (in modern jargon) of the French crown repeatedly claimed that Spain unjustly occupied French territories, notably Genoa and Naples, so the French court justly sought an alliance with a non-Christian power for the purpose of self-defense.[31] Their legalist arguments allowed the crown to build on an extra-European commercial relationship with Muslim states from the Middle Ages. The medieval history of these agreements needs to be kept in mind because it constituted previous exemplars of French presence in the Eastern Mediterranean. A commercial agreement dating back to 1332–1334 with the Mameluk rulers of Egypt,[32] which was renewed after the Ottoman conquest of Cairo in 1517 and again by Sultan Suleiman I in 1528, served as legal precedent for the alliance. Francis I's secret envoy, Antonio Rincón, negotiated additional protections for Christians living in Jerusalem during his mission in 1528–1529. Rincón was dispatched again in 1532 to try and dissuade (unsuccessfully) the sultan from attacking Hungary.[33] The first negotiations with admiral Hayreddin Pasha (1466?–1546), also called "Hayreddin Barbarossa" in Europe, in 1533 culminated when Francis I appointed the first resident ambassador to the Sublime Porte, Jean de la Forest (ambassador from 1534 to his death of the plague in 1537), who negotiated a joint military campaign against Spain for the year 1537. De la Forest also concluded the first official state-to-state treaty in 1536 (in terms of Ottoman state bureaucracy, it was an *ahidnâme* or a unilateral granting of rights to French subjects by the sultan), according to which the French maintained their former right to trade in the Levant and expanded it to the Ottoman Empire.[34] French subjects had the right to trade without additional taxation, were allowed to practice their faith, were protected from prejudicial lawsuits, and, according to Article 13, had the right to reclaim captives, fugitives, and the victims of shipwrecks. In addition, French ships held a favored status in the Ottoman-controlled waters of the Mediterranean.[35] Besides a series of joint military campaigns against Spain in the Mediterranean in the 1530s and the 1540s, in 1543, French and Ottoman ships laid siege to Nice and, subsequently, the Ottoman navy wintered in Toulon. During the Ottoman campaign in Hungary in 1543–1544, French artillery soldiers participated in the Ottoman army.

Beginning with the inception of this alliance in 1525 and continuing through its renewals in 1569 and 1581, the court's politics of diplomacy was repeatedly cast in terms borrowed from Roman Stoic cosmopolitanism and biblical teachings about the universal reach of Christianity. In 1525, after Francis I was captured and imprisoned by Charles V, Francis I's mother, Louise de Savoy, wrote a letter to Sultan Suleiman I—Emperor Charles V being their common enemy—to ask for his help. In her letter, she addressed the sultan suppliantly as "Great Caesar," thus acknowledging his right as the inheritor of the Byzantine Empire.[36] As a Christian monarch, Francis I treated Suleiman I as the New Testament recommends treating Caesar, as a legitimate authority within his realm.[37] In 1535, Francis I made the claim to Pope Paul III that his alliance with the Sublime Porte was justifiable in view of advancing the unity of humankind in its entirety rather than simply the unity of Christianity.[38] In evoking the "unity of humankind," he also evoked natural rationality as a common denominator outside of faith. Through his ambassadors and agents, Francis I forged a relation with Suleiman I, in which he consistently accepted his authority and state as legitimate. In the same year, Francis I instructed his ambassador, de la Forest, to transmit the message to Suleiman I that the French king appreciated his "goodwill, estimation, great affection, humanity, and liberality" and to reassure him that he would "always be his kind brother and friend in all matters as long as they do not offend Christian faith."[39] The Valois court followed the rationalist and universalist spirit of ancient Roman cosmopolitan ideas and legal precedents. By *de jure* not distinguishing between people of different religious faiths or ethnic origins and instead relying on the notion of *humanitas*, which was synonymous with civilized, gentle, educated manners and seen, according to Paul Veyne, as "an internal modification of the individual human being but at the same time an extension of human ascendancy over the external world," the Roman Empire was able to integrate non-Romans, to a point.[40] Roman Stoic philosophers who incorporated less acceptable philosophical traditions (notably, authority-defying Cynic cosmopolitanism[41]) provided less ethnocentric, moralized versions of universalism because they believed that virtue alone created differences among people—and virtue could be attained by anyone regardless of social, ethnic, or educational differences. Veyne argues that the Stoics' cosmopolitan rational morality still excluded those deemed to be without virtue from this community of *humanitas*.[42] Early Christianity, with its transnational universalist aspirations, appropriated and transformed Roman cosmopolitan ideas, especially with recourse to the evangelical rule, "render therefore onto Caesar the things which are Caesar's and onto God the things that are God's" (Matthew 22:21). In this analogy, the Christian world-city ("the things that are God's") exists side by side with the local (Roman) authority, with the former recognizing the legitimacy of the latter. Legal constructs such as natural law also served the interests of a universalist, or "catholic," Church. In the Middle Ages, Christian theologians incorporated the Roman idea of natural law and attributed rationality to non-Christians; for example, Thomas of Aquinas did not condemn Islamic states because, according to natural law, they were just as legitimate as Christian states.[43] The cosmopolitan ideas and attitudes inherited from ancient and medieval traditions have raised serious questions about the beneficiaries unto whom these traditions conferred power and affluence.[44] Although the cosmopolitanism of the French crown put an end to France's participation in various anti-Ottoman alliances and crusading (which had turned almost entirely nominal by the sixteenth century, anyway), it nonetheless came after the period of high medieval Crusades that replaced the legalist Roman model of empire with a militant Christian one.[45] This new empire has been described by scholars as "a *medieval* version of European colonial experiments" based on faith and the sword.[46] The Crusades were instrumental in shifting the economic balance toward Europe by boosting European manufacturing that was often reliant on materials exported by the Levant, bringing exotic wares to Europe, and turning European Christians that settled in Jerusalem into Orientals.

The cosmopolitan aspirations that appeared through the 1530s court documents did not disappear throughout the century. Rather, they spread outside the court and made possible colonizing attitudes, which is what Wynter calls the originary "colonial divide" of considering some humans as lesser, and what the eighteenth-century expat writer Joséphine de Monbart calls the "tone of superiority" of the courtier toward non-Europeans, non-French, and people of color.[47] These attitudes targeted Turks, Africans, and Eastern Europeans. Rendering the non-French world governable, according to Christian Platonic or Stoic universalist models, gave justification to the undertakings of the court, which was often able to idealize its actions as "peacemaking" in the zones of confrontation between the Ottoman Empire and Christian Europe and position itself accordingly as a protector of Christians there. With the politics of repression against French Protestants intensifying under the reign of Henri II (1547–1559) and serving to radicalize religious differences, the Valois turned increasingly toward Christian (mainly Catholic) self-definition, while a similarly pious turn characterized the rule of Suleiman I in the Ottoman Empire from the 1550s onward.[48] The turn to increasing control over religion did not, however, put a stop to the alliance, which served the interest of both states; in fact, the use of the alliance to centralize the French state intensified. Cosmopolitanism encouraged a flexible attitude that looked beyond religious differences. To the genealogy of modern secularism, Talal Asad adds humanism as an ideology that helped master several goals of the early modern state—namely, the control of the increasingly mobile poor, arbitration between hostile religious factions, and the regulation of commercial and military expansion beyond Europe.[49] It was a cosmopolitan humanism that helped extend these state powers beyond France's borders. Notably, France used its influence in the Ottoman Empire to negotiate privileges in trade and the liberation of French slaves. Gillian Weiss shows that, around 1550, the French project of "liberating slaves from North Africa changed from an expression of Christian charity to a method of state building and, eventually, a rationale for imperial expansion."[50] Although incremental, by the end of the sixteenth and the beginning of the seventeenth centuries, the efforts of the French state were concretized into a set of diplomatic privileges. These included increased protections for enslaved French subjects in the North African states, protection of Christian churches, protector status for Christian nations in the Eastern Mediterranean, the ascension of Henri, Duke of Anjou, to the Polish throne in 1573 (which he abandoned for the French throne in the next year), the project (never actualized) of resettling French Protestants in Moldavia, and permission from the Sublime Porte to use direct diplomatic or military interventions to achieve the liberation of French subjects in North Africa.[51] The French crown not only gained privileges that facilitated travel, negotiations, and commerce in the Ottoman Empire, but, through the alliance, it also had the opportunity to remake itself as an imperial power controlling people who lived far away.

French aristocratic families liked to showcase their cosmopolitan culture by engaging the service of non-French people, especially North Africans and Eastern Europeans. Symbolically speaking, the French court evoked the Roman Empire as the image of imperialism and the forebear of the Spanish and Holy Roman Empires and incorporated foreigners who had been historically opposed to the Roman Empire. Cosmopolitanism and images of a cosmos moved by its own rationality or animacy as found in Stoic and Epicurean cosmologies, and even the animal gods of Egyptian religion, vaguely evoked, served to reinforce the power of the Valois monarchy and the role of France in ruling over distant people. Thus, the playwright Étienne Jodelle (1532–1573) celebrates Cleopatra, the late queen of the Egyptian empire, for her ability to resist Octavian Caesar by bringing about her own death through a bodily alchemy of passions in 1553. Three years later, in 1556, Catherine de Médicis has the Italian play *Sophonisbe*, about the eponymous Numidian heroine who thwarts the plans of the Roman general Scipio to marry her by poisoning herself, performed on the occasion of a double wedding at the court. These examples (which I discuss in Chapter 3) point to the incorporation of select, idealized, or acceptable foreigners, non-Christians, and non-Europeans at the court. They also point beyond a fashion of exotic costumes and persons to the countless people of color and captured persons who were used to give a cosmopolitan hue to contemporary courtly ceremonies, as well as to the many foreigners from non-Christian lands outside Europe who served the Valois and other elite families through diplomatic or domestic duties.

Stoic universalism proved popular as the dominant way of thinking about the non-Christian world until 1572, when, in the wake of the Massacre of Saint Bartholomew's Day, French Calvinist pamphleteers reviled the French king as another Nero and the Roman Stoic philosopher Seneca as his helper. Stoic universalism was critiqued because it failed to create an inclusive polity for French Protestants despite the crown's (uneven) attempts to mediate between opposing religious factions.[52] Among European Protestant intellectuals such as Alberico Gentili (1552–1608)[53] and Hugo Grotius (1583–1645), who spent time in exile in France because of disputes within the Dutch Calvinist Church, the sense of disillusionment with the idealized prince led to the creation of a legal framework of European diplomacy in which the protection of diplomats did not depend on the goodwill of individual princes. French Protestants served the king on diplomatic missions throughout the sixteenth century, often in the hopes of serving both the monarchy and the Protestant community simultaneously. Examples included Claude du Bourg, Nicolas de Touteville (reputed as Francis I's natural son), Charles de Téligny (Gaspard de Coligny's future son-in-law), Guillaume de Grandchamp (seigneur of Grantrie at the Porte in 1566 and 1567, who proposed the settlement of German and French Protestants in Moldavia and briefly and unsuccessfully negotiated a marriage between Marguerite de Valois and the Transylvanian Prince John Sigismund Zápolya, as well as negotiating Ottoman naval support for the Protestant Prince of Condé), and Philippe Fresne-Canaye (the young Protestant aristocrat and diplomat in training who was a mere extra in the negotiations of François Noailles with Selim's court in the early 1570s). Cosmopolitanism provided a universalist Stoic frame of civilized rationality, or the Christian frame of charity that served the French crown—in which, ultimately, Protestants and other religious dissenters did not find their place. In *Agents without Empire*, I also examine how various authors shadowed the cosmopolitan ideology of the Valois court and how some of them reflected on those instances in which they differed from it in attempts to develop their own spaces of freedom and autonomy.

Mixed Agency and the Self as Other

The most straightforward articulation of the anxieties evinced by young courtiers in the middle of the sixteenth century, as well as their claims of autonomy and agency, can be found in the treatise *De la servitude volontaire*, a precocious text written in defense of freedom from tyranny. The book was to remain unpublished in the lifetime of its author, the Bordeaux magistrate and humanist writer Étienne de la Boétie (1530–1563). It was appropriated by French Huguenots in the sixteenth century as a justification to resist a tyrant and in the modern era as a foundational text of liberalism, but in the sixteenth century, the text was mostly hidden because a generation of authors and editors, notably de la Boétie's friend Montaigne, chose not to publish its rebellious words. Here, I zoom in on the extraordinary role granted to the will in de la Boétie's definition of servitude, which he describes as the complete molding of the body of the courtier—including that of feet, hands, eyes, and ears, as well as his future thoughts and wishes, his will—to the will of another, the master. He writes,

> ... the tyrant sees to it that those close to him flatter and lie to seek his favor: they not only have to do what he tells them, but they must anticipate even his thoughts. Their task is not simply to obey him; they have

to please, and they must break themselves apart, torture themselves, kill themselves, find his pleasure to be their pleasure ("quils se plaisent de son plaisir"), let his taste take the place of theirs, alter their facial expression, rid themselves of their natural manners, watch his every word, his voice, his gestures, his eyes, so that they have no eye, foot, or hand that is not continually on the lookout, to espy his will and discover his thoughts ("quils n'aient œil, ni pied, ni main que tout ne soit au guet pour espier ses volontés, et pour descouvrir ses pensées"). [. . .] What condition is more miserable than living like this, without anything to claim as one's own, depending on someone else for one's ease, one's liberty, one's body, and one's life?"[54]

Quite aside from reiterating the classical critique of tyranny, de la Boétie here considers servitude a loss of autonomy that amounts to psychological humiliation and physical torture, a total bodily and mental submission. The courtier must find the pleasure of the tyrant to be his own pleasure, and he must also espy and unwaveringly represent the master's will (the more specific meaning of "pleasure" here). As de la Boétie sees it, courtiers are agents without any agency of their own, with servitude being a slippery slope of self-subjugation that leads to a total loss of autonomy. In fact, de la Boétie's description of the boundless and collective nature of subjugation in the political realm resembles Rabelais's image of Panurge's sheep who follow each other and jump unquestioningly to their demise from the ship into the sea. In this framing, the will's consent to servitude metaphorically enslaves the people (or turns them into herd animals, in Rabelais's rendering) by gradually putting to sleep both their will to freedom and their consciousness of the condition of servitude itself. De la Boétie, then, does not define freedom as the lack of constraint but as the result of perfecting human nature by awakening the will from its accustomed state of slumber and bewitchment that is produced and naturalized in relations of service. De la Boétie follows the anti-sensualist tradition of Stoicism, in which the unfree are bound by either their passions (their will to servitude) or the passions (will or "pleasure") of another who fully controls and masters them.[55] In his treatise, women, animals, and slaves briefly appear to offer themselves up as mirror images to reflect the profound servitude that is experienced by the courtier. In the sixteenth century, the slave and the condition of slavery were often evoked as metaphors for describing the condition of service regarded as a burden. The poet Joachim du Bellay, the young but impoverished scion of the illustrious du Bellay family who served in the household of his cousin Jean du Bellay, a cardinal and diplomat to Henri II at the Vatican, likens the service through which he, as his cousin's servant, earns a living to the unfreedom of serfs, prisoners, galley slaves, message carriers, and stage actors.[56] In doing so, the poet du Bellay relies on the literal and metaphorical meanings of "slave" ("esclave"), which denotes a range of concepts in the French language, from Slavs to subordination in love.[57] These images of unfreedom and enslavement, which are perhaps a little exaggerated coming from the pen of someone who served as the superintendent of his influential cousin in a city known for its luxurious ways, reveal a characteristically French male anxiety about the loss of agency. To drive home this message regarding the effects of servitude on agency, the poet du Bellay even describes Jean du Bellay as an "actor." He implies that both diplomats, who represent the will of their prince, and actors, who—to recall the words of Hamlet—act in a "dream of passion," are induced by the will or ambitions of others (the master and the character in the play) into a quasi-sleeping state with limited or no agency of their own.[58] In sixteenth-century France, where slaves represented the farthest spectrum of the human will's tyrannical domination by masters, transgressive animality figured as a site of resistance for the desired malleability of the self. For du Bellay, for example, the freedom of being able to write a hymn about a "small cat"[59] and the fluid movement of the Tiber formed one of the only ways to escape the relentless impositions of another's will and "humor" as entailed by service.[60] Rabelais's fictional heroes stop to think—if only tactically—about the other agencies surrounding them. Constantly projecting the nightmare scenario of the loss of human autonomy, humanists looked outside the human realm to turn to the transgressive potential of the physical world, animals, marginalized or exotic human beings, plants, minerals, and the cosmos.

In the aftermath of de la Boétie's treatise, instead of the Stoic idea of awakening the individual will (which would have amounted to disobedience and outright rebellion in political terms), courtiers and servants of the ruling elite made use of expanding their agency by appealing to the alliance of others outside the social and political life of the court. They did this by projecting themselves onto more powerful material aggregates or exotic, non-European actors who were non-Christian but could be made to conform to universalized Christian moral values. The historian Robert Mandou argues that, from the mid-sixteenth century, French aristocrats, under the pressure of increasing absolutism in the royal government, developed claims for their exercise of power independent of that of the crown by articulating arguments about the purity of blood.[61] Similar claims of agency by lesser or disgraced nobility and aspiring commoners ("routiers") were based on the capacities of the natural body to transgress limits in an affective, cosmopolitan (if not cosmic), and sometimes mystical context. To those who could not make claims to noble blood, there remained the examples of fruit sap, animals, forces and aggregates of nonliving nature, larger-than-life actors, and other exemplary human and nonhuman agencies supplied by the vast Ottoman Empire. This allowed for greater mobility and transgression, such as the autonomy of self-determination outside the norm embodied, for example, by Rabelais's giants walking through cities they have outgrown and thus made perceptible the vision of a world, a community, an empire: one that was cosmopolitan in scope, and organized around specific values and agencies.

On speculative visions that shadow the French court's political ambitions, a case in point is the pamphlet *Apolygye*,[62] written by François Sagon in 1544 to justify the alliance of Francis I with the Sublime Porte. In this text, the author responds to the Spanish criticisms of Francis I's joint military campaigns with the Ottomans by comparing the Turks to the Samaritan who helps a Jewish wayfarer abandoned by thieves in the New Testament "Gospel according to Luke." In Sagon's allegorical retelling of the parable, the thieves represent Emperor Charles V, while the priest and the Levite, who ignore the beaten and wounded traveler, represent the Roman Catholics (whose church needed reform, according to the author). The Samaritan becomes the figure of the religious other—Sagon calls him a "stranger from far away" ("estranger lointain")—who takes pity on the traveler and stands in for the French monarch, abandoned by his Christian neighbors. Charity (or compassion) is extended to the Ottomans ("the Turk") who allegedly came to "heal," "in the sign of the crescent moon," France, whose king was being held in Spanish captivity after the battle of Pavia in 1525. Sagon presents the Samaritan and the Jewish victim as strangers who nonetheless help one another through "communication": a term that, like its Latin original, means the sharing of things and information and becomes a code word for diplomatic negotiations and military cooperation. Sagon thus projects the Hebrew-Christian virtues of grace, pity, gentleness ("douceur"), and mercy ("misericorde") onto the Turks. Moreover, by arguing that God resembles no one, but that one must nonetheless love Him just as one must love one's neighbor, Sagon suggests that the absolute otherness of God allows Christians to feel love for non-Christians. The negative definition of the divine ("resembles no one"), to which Montaigne will also resort a few decades later, offers a model of the other in this evangelical (that is, reform-minded, emphasizing faith rather than knowledge as the relation to the divine) booklet. Sagon's text does not only extend compassion but also the capacity for compassion specifically to Muslim Ottomans (and the sultan). His vision differs from the imperialist-absolutist, top-down models of communities of compassion that circulated in the seventeenth century with the king as "Compassioner-in-Chief."[63] Reform-minded subjects of the French crown, like Sagon and Rabelais, did sense the community-building potential of compassion or fellow feeling, but their imagined communities of compassion also entail the expansion of Christianity to the East. Sagon's reference to the Samaritan is not only a biblical reference but also an Orientalist one. During his first stay in the Levant in 1536 and 1537, the Orientalist and agent of Francis I, Guillaume Postel (1510–1581), purchased a Samaritan manuscript that became part of the royal library.[64] The French, who defined themselves as cosmopolitan (as Postel did), viewed the Orient from a universalist Christian perspective, but their idiosyncratic, phantasmatic universalisms clashed with the authorities they served. Arguments for inclusion were often made with the implicit assumption of an unknown or yet-to-come empire, like Sagon's unknowable God, that would be supple enough to accommodate non-Christians and extend Christianity over the East. Postel, a syncretic millenarist Catholic visionary with a spiritual ambition to create a utopian Christian empire that transcended the French (or indeed any) monarchy's political boundaries, was also numbered among the humanists and writers in France who spread the belief that France was destined to conquer the Ottoman Empire.[65]

In these visions, one imagines oneself as other by way of analogy to outsiders of Christian Europe and France while also being capable of infusing new moral values into old selves. This self-as-other also coincides with the ancient philosophical thought of the Cynics that were disseminated through anecdotes. In the early sixteenth century, Erasmus wove strands of the philosophy-as-lifestyle perspective espoused by the Cynics with his own interpretations of the Stoics, Homer, and the New Testament. The Rotterdam humanist thereby solidified sporadic identifications between the various walking ascetics in antiquity into a form of Christian Cynicism as an ascetic, moral ideal predicated upon the rejection of wealth and an unflinching disrespect of authorities.[66] In Christian humanist accounts, the Cynics' rejection of possessions and social norms was interpreted according to the ascetic practices of the early Church fathers, and even their doglike animality was translated into moral action.[67] Erasmus compares the teachings of the New Testament to the teachings of Socrates, Diogenes, and Epictetus in the Preface to his 1516 Latin edition. The collective examples of these wise "pagan" men serve to correct the political world of interests ("greed"). Earlier, in the 1501 "Handbook of the Christian Soldier," Erasmus extends the exemplarity of the Cynics to non-European wandering philosophers by inciting readers to follow the "Brahmans, Cynics, and Stoics" in fixing "the dogmas of your sect deeply within your soul."[68] These examples are colored by an Orientalism that attributes a lost or desired autonomy to select representatives of ancient and Eastern cultures whose teachings have been reduced to gestures and aphorisms. Guillaume Postel and Nicolas de Nicolay, two French authors, political servants, and agents of the monarchy, make a distinct reference to the Cynics by calling themselves "cosmopolitan," citing the rare ancient Greek noun ("kosmopolites") whose first documented use was made by Diogenes Laertius in his account of the life of Diogenes the Cynic.[69] With that said, many French authors, notably Rabelais and Montaigne, were similarly inspired by Diogenes's example. Humanists tended to respond to Cynic acts such as rejecting norms, indexing morality to natural needs including defecation, hunger, and libido, and questioning authority by translating them into universals (according to the logic of the reception of Cynics analyzed by Michel Foucault, which I discuss in Chapter 1). The universalizing of the Cynics anticipates the Western myth of the "great forest" in the so-called New World as the space of subjectivities existing outside of politics and history. Citing Alain Badiou, Serge Gruzinski argues: "It is hard to avoid fantasizing about this timeless world. The Amazon is often invoked when couching indigenous creativity in terms of survival, when conceiving of mankind in general as 'the symptom of a troubling conservatism' in a manner so abstract that it overlooks the uniqueness of specific situations."[70] In other words, concrete experiences allow for recuperation through universalizing fantasies. This universalizing of the "wild man" began with mythological exemplars like "Pan" and "Priapus," was continued by Ottoman ones like the "dervish," and was helped by way of its serialization in descriptions, visual depictions, and the print medium in the French and European Renaissance.

While I consider the historical fact of concrete animals, I also uncover animality as the organizing notion of a holistic yet distributed cosmic agency that incorporates both cohesion and instability, agency and its disintegration. Chiara Thumiger describes the ontological bias of ancient Greek and Roman holism to animate and animal life: "The most direct instance of ontological holism is the biological notion according to which a defining quality of animate life, and especially of animal (and human) embodied life, is that it forms a whole that can only be properly understood as a living system, not as a mere conglomerate of parts that mechanically suffice to determine life."[71] Animality also implies embodied and material animacy and transgression. Animals are defined, in Greek antiquity and beyond (notably in Aristotle's fourth-century BCE treatise *Peri psuchēs* [*On the Soul*, Lat. *De anima*]), through appetite and movement toward a telos (food, etc.). Animals consume the material environment, and this completes them insofar as hunger is seen as a source of incompleteness, illness, and death. Meanwhile, nourishment and the movement it comprises involve them in a contingent *physis* that renders them prone to accidents, as evinced by Rabelais's races of giants. Because animals move toward something external, their movement is also transgressive. The animal is both a figure of immersion in the material world and of transgression toward an outside, the transcendental. I use animality capaciously to include the idea of *anima mundi* inherited from pre-Socratic hylozoism and Plato's *Timaeus*,[72] as well as Aristotelian and early modern natural histories and Stoic and Epicurean cosmologies that see the universe as both animate and as an animal—in addition to seeing it as capable, as the sixteenth-century poets of the Pléiade group underscore, of both making and destroying empires. My use of the term is rooted, too, in Hippocratic and Galenic medicine and alchemy, esoteric discourses, and Renaissance reconstructions of paganism, each of which is engaged in defining the animacy of matter, material being, and universalism. While modern or new materialisms are "ontologically egalitarian," the old materialisms that explore the animacy and animality of matter and its agency skew toward a holistic ontology in which the agency of nonhuman matter and accidents gains positive value at times.[73] Contemporary ecological thought tends to be decidedly anti-holistic, as is evinced, for example, by Latour's critique of views of the world articulated from "without." These contemporary projects about the distribution of agency rely on historically determined commitments to maintaining agency as something that is not exclusively human, such that, as Lois McNay puts it, "agency is regarded not as the exclusive property of humans but rather as an ever-changing set of potentialities immanent within the energetic and uncontainable dynamics of material existence."[74] My goal in tracing these holistic old materialisms is to put them into conversation with new materialisms. Within such contemporary new materialisms—as is exemplified in the work of such thinkers as Donna Haraway, Jane Bennett, and Mel Y. Chen—the instability of matter represents an ontological value because of its ability to resist anthropocentric, ableist, capitalist, and Anthropo- and Plantationocene definitions of matter as an inert object of manipulation and exploitation, thereby countering "old imperialism" and "neoimperialisms."[75] In contrast to contemporary new materialisms that take on feminist, queer, and anti-colonial agendas, the fascination with matter exhibited within old materialisms was more ambivalent and tended to be organized around opposing ontological poles. Matter was viewed as both dangerous and redemptive—or, to evoke Rebecca Zorach's characterization of Renaissance nature, as an excess that was both threatening and productive.[76] Zorach reminds us that the starting point of most early modern conceptions of matter is the Aristotelian duality of matter and form, in which the masculine form denotes agency over passive, shapeless, female substance and its productivity in both nature and art. "Chaotic matter is controlled and ordered by form, a relationship modeled explicitly (in Aristotle) on that of artisan and product. [However,] matter sometimes threatens to get out of control, to produce on its own. In an alternative view of matter and form, matter might attract and engender more matter, as if it possesses its own volition and agency."[77] Zorach's examples of generative matter getting "out of control" are the spilling of ink in the use ornament of the so-called School of Fontainebleau and the proliferation of cheap reproductive print, which was both desired and seen as a threat. I suggest that such excessive agencies of matter were also found in the Ottoman Empire, seen as the material world. The Ottoman Empire represents to agents alternately fascinating and threatening excesses, spiritual purity and corruption; it amounts to the military ambitions and resources with which to counter Spain's expansion, at the same time as it is seen to harbor unmeasurable greed, rich natural resources, wild, uncivilized *physis*, the cultural refinement of a powerful civilization, and the artful dissimulation of the elite. Old materialisms can complicate and question the new materialist tendency to favor ontological leveling by revealing that ideas of distributed agency coexisted with the development of asymmetrical relations that define the (early) modern colonial world order.

Travel in the Ottoman Empire became a dramatic test of agency, given that the Ottoman Empire was a powerful civilization in which agents harbored anxieties about the pressures of sovereign laws and unknown customs. In these enactments of agency, agents made the human both animal and plastic, to use a concept developed by Catherine Malabou. Building on Georg Wilhelm Friedrich Hegel's eighteenth-century *Phenomenology of the Spirit*, Malabou uses "plasticity" to define the possibility of giving (and receiving) form, change, and "alterity without transcendence."[78] Plasticity makes possible both habit and subservience to habit—as well as the explosion and discontinuities of form. This plasticity of the human also includes, in the sixteenth century, the susceptibility of the will to pressure, which, in the anti-sensualist tradition, was associated with negative meanings of the animal. In *Becoming Human*, through an analysis of Toni Morrison's *Beloved* and a consideration of the broader context of anti-Black discourse in the US and elsewhere, Zakiyyah Iman Jackson presents a critical perspective on human plasticity for which "the slave is the discursive-material site that must contend with the demand for seemingly infinite malleability, demand whose limits are set merely by the tyrannies of will and imagination."[79] Blackness or blackening humanity, Iman Jackson argues, is the necessary site for constructing "the human" and "the animal" as "positions in a highly unstable and indeterminate relational hierarchy."[80] In the sixteenth century, anxieties about the loss of agency—which included the frequent conflation of service with servitude and slavery—came to be the site that allowed for the coupling of service with transgressive mobility, existential and cosmopolitan animality, and agency. Slavery, however, emerged as an arena of literary, visual, and legal definition owing to the "free soil principle" (the legal fiction of the absence of slaves on French soil that I discuss in Chapter 3) and the many artistic representations that gained popularity among the elite and even became a tool for defining Frenchness.

The agents' preoccupation with the plasticity of their humanity and that of others—with animality and animacy revealing the plasticity of the human—created the conditions for seeing those they encountered in the Ottoman Empire as pertaining to "nature" or humoral bodies, abstracted from culture and history. While sixteenth-century France was far from homogeneous in terms of ethnic, linguistic, or religious makeup, it was in the Ottoman Empire that French agents became especially aware of ethnical, cultural, and religious diversity and people with different skin colors, body types, or features. This awareness allowed them to emphasize their own bodily and cultural homogeneity against the background of these differences. Moreover, differences came to be interpreted according to a dynamic scale of agency, whose category was articulated around opposing but unstable poles such as freedom and servitude, the self as other and othering, agential and abject animality, and empowering and unruly plasticity. Race in sixteenth-century France was a mobile but powerful notion tying together the selves that drew from it privilege and visibility and those that were othered through it in a hard-wearing bind. And the Ottoman Empire existed as an imaginary space of nature and matter, which was seized and used by agents to increase their autonomy during travel. Then in their writings, and, finally, when diplomacy slowed and came under increased state control and institutionalization by the end of the century, it continued to exert its power in the fictional, narrative selves that it inspired. For educated, elite male authors, the Ottoman Empire became an unlikely but powerful space of self-reinvention. These selves that emerged from reflections on the otherness of others, and from the effects of racism on the selves that reinvented it, were those selves in the Old World that whetted the appetite for that of the New by defining the human as a plastic medium and a site from which to reflect on agency. The universal selves, Rabelais's doglike Panurge, Montaigne's "naked" self, and the mystical, transgender, trans-species transformations described by agents are ways of searching for communities in which to find a place for oneself. However, they are also openings into an ideology of empire in which some seek mobility and autonomy from the pressures of servitude, while others become racialized.

1
Big Appetite and Rabelais's Multiracial Empires

Tucked away in François Rabelais's chronologically second novel, *Gargantua* (first printed in Lyon ca. 1534–1535), there is a short tale that describes the parleying between Grandgousier, king of Utopia, and Alpharbal, king of Canarre. This tale not only alludes to the geographic areas and diplomatic rituals involved in the French–Ottoman relations at the time but, as a fictional reworking of alliance-making that offers both a utopia of reconciliation and a possible scenario of French imperial rule over foreign populations, it provides us with a good starting point from which to tell the story of constructions of moral agency and race in sixteenth-century France. My analysis revolves around, on the one hand, the courteous, good-humored attitude (embodied by Grandgousier) that is supposed to resolve conflicts—and, on the other hand, the sense of appetite that various actors share in the story. Additionally, I focus on the tensions in the tale between the Christian cosmopolitan ideology of the French court and the agency that is granted to the Canarrians, especially their pirate king, Alpharbal. This short episode is largely overshadowed within critical literature by the frame story that narrates a squabble between Picrochole's bakers of the round sweet-and-spicy bread (the *fouace*) and Grandgousier's grape farmers and its subsequent escalation into war. The handful of critics who pay attention to this episode have proposed interpretations that recuperate generosity as either the manifestation of an older gift economy (Davis[1]) or as evocative of a Christian Stoic moral philosophy that offers an alternative to the ruthless logic of political necessity (Céard et al.[2]). I argue, however, that Grandgousier does politics, not despite but with the help of humoral bodies—in particular, by redirecting the Canarrians' enormous appetite such that he both redeems and debases them. The result is that, even though Grandgousier and the Canarrians both possess boundless appetites, the fiction grants the former just rule over the latter. I discuss the different ways Rabelais's fiction binds racial distinctions to the vagaries of appetite, and—by examining the mixed agency of Alcofrybas Nasier—I reflect on how Rabelais saw autonomy in broader terms as the extension of the mobile physical and animal body.

Rabelais's Transnational Humoral Body Politic

Chapter 50 of *Gargantua* relates the aftermath of the Utopians' victory over the army of their choleric neighbor, Picrochole. Grandgousier's only son, Prince Gargantua, rises to speak and eloquently tells the story of how the former Utopian kings, his ancestors, strove to "erect trophies and monuments" commemorating their victories in the "hearts" of the vanquished people, rather than in "mute" inscriptions in arcs, columns, and pyramids. Gargantua praises the power of capturing the hearts and minds of the enemy, exhibiting an attitude that hovers between manipulative strategy deployed toward the enemy population and reconciliatory tactics to achieve peaceful coexistence. Gargantua then points to a past example of generosity: his father Grandgousier's exceptionally humane treatment of the defeated pirate king, Alpharbal.

> All this hemisphere has been filled with the praise and congratulations that you and your fathers offered when Alpharbal, king of Canarre, not sated with his good fortunes ("non assovy de ses fortunes"), furiously invaded the region of Aunis, practicing piracy in all the Armorican Islands and adjacent regions. He was captured and vanquished in a set naval battle by my father, whom God keep and protect. But what then? Whereas other kings and emperors, indeed those who call themselves Catholics, would have treated him miserably, imprisoned him in harsh conditions, and placed excessive ransom on him, he treated him courteously, lodged him amiably with him in his palace, and with incredible kindness sent him back with a safe conduct, laden with gifts, laden with favors, laden with all services of friendship ("chargé de toutes offices d'amytié").[3]

In the frame story, Grandgousier declares that he intends to follow the example of Christ instead of that of ancient warrior heroes. This declaration anticipates Grandgousier's jaunty generosity with Alpharbal and his unceremonious rejection of legal and diplomatic conventions. At the same time, his brisk, theatrical performance also riddles his loud and clear profession of Christian exemplarity with ambiguities.[4] The episode can be read as a reflection on humanist ideas about the nature of justice and the ideal of reconciling Christian morality with the state's needs to defend itself—both of which were problems that Desiderius Erasmus of Rotterdam (ca. 1466–1536) and Guillaume Budé (1467–1540), two thinkers that Rabelais very much admired, also attempted to resolve in their numerous tracts. Budé, for example, equates charity with natural goodness, making social harmony the goal of legal practice. For him, true justice cannot be resumed by codified law. In this episode, Grandgousier chooses charitable action over legal treaties. If Budé emphasizes the importance of acting and interpreting the Scriptures in ways that—as Claude la Charité shows—optimize action for joyfulness, then Grandgousier's actions, which become more exaggerated at each turn, are examples of what Budé would consider lessons of love.[5] The actions of the body in Rabelais are no longer solely defined by Christian rites, although they remain compatible with Christian values.

The parleying between Grandgousier and Alpharbal hinges on the physicality of the exchange, which begins with Grandgousier showering Alpharbal in gestures of hospitality and courtesy. Grandgousier's encounter with Alpharbal unfolds through a quick succession of actions and reactions, including Alpharbal's movements and the Canarrians' reactions to them. Alpharbal's concrete actions—he "returned to his lands," he "expounded"—contribute to the instantaneous reaction of the Canarrians, their decree, and their unanimous consent:

> What came of it? He, back in his lands, assembled all the princes and estates of his kingdom, expounded to them the humanity ("leur exposa l'humanité") he had found in us, and asked them to deliberate on this in such a way that the world would find it an example, as in us it had been of honorable graciousness ("de gracieuseté honeste"), so in them it would be in gracious honorability ("de honesteté gracieuse"). There it was decreed by unanimous consent ("par consentment unanime") that they would offer up their entire lands, domains, and kingdoms, to do with at our free will ("selon nostre arbitre").[6]

The Canarrians decide "unanimously" to give their kingdom to Grandgousier. As we saw in the Introduction, Francis I evoked a Stoic naturalist interpretation of morality to justify his alliance with the Ottomans to Pope Clement VII. This idea that natural reason renders every person sociable will reappear in the work of Protestant jurist Hugo Grotius (1583–1645), who, in "On the Law of War and Peace" (published in Latin in Paris in 1625), reworked Cicero's moral law by eliminating references to positive theology and stating that natural morality is grounded in "Sociability . . ., this care of maintaining Society in a Manner conformable to the Light of human Understanding."[7] While this natural will to transcend self-interest is taken for granted by both Christian humanists and, in the next century, the theorists of professional diplomacy, it receives additional prompting from the irrational gestures of Grandgousier in the tale of Grandgousier and Alpharbal. The Canarrians' sudden turn to peaceful life agrees with Budé's notion of natural goodness, but the dynamism of their transformation can only be explained through the wild choreography of actions that transpire between Grandgousier, Alpharbal, and the Canarrians themselves. The quick succession of actions leaves little space for the characters to interpret one another's gestures (there is no time for complex, Erasmian levels of interpretation), and their responses—especially given the sudden nature of their reactions—seem to follow directly from the (lower) movements of their bodies rather than from deliberation. This makes the Canarrians' decision to give away their realm and all their possessions seem impulsive and, if we consider the final effect, imprudent. It is Grandgousier's first courteous act that transforms the Canarrians from hungry pirates into subjects that are conscious of sociable, moral sentiments. However, the story intensifies the logic of generosity such that, as Grandgousier makes more and more extravagant gestures, the Canarrians respond to his actions with more and more extravagant actions in kind. The story grants moral agency to the Canarrians, who are asked to deliberate on the example of good-natured sociability. But their agency remains ambiguous and reactive or secondary to the actions of Grandgousier and Alpharbal (in this order) while also being crucial to the story's resolution. Moreover, Grandgousier succeeds in redirecting the Canarrians' hunger toward a natural morality (and submission) *with the help of* Alpharbal, who is the king of the Canarrians but becomes Grandgousier's ally and friend. Alpharbal extends the scope of these gestures by returning to his people and demonstrating his willingness to explain to them the charitable, humane treatment he received from Grandgousier. The Canarrians reciprocate and imitate Grandgousier's gestures thanks to Alpharbal's intervention, and it is Alpharbal whom they send back with eight great vessels laden with "not only the treasures of his house and kingly line but almost the whole country."[8] It is implied that Alpharbal, prompted by Grandgousier's generosity, acts as a mediator between Grandgousier and the Canarrians, which reveals Alpharbal's personal bond with Grandgousier. Alpharbal, the king of the Canarrians no less, thus becomes the de facto agent of Grandgousier. Outside of Grandgousier's gestures and Alpharbal's legwork, it is their bond, rather than any legal means or treaties, that creates the new alliance that forms the basis for a utopian realm of love and friendship (or colonial empire, depending on the reader's perspective). Because their alliance is personal, it is difficult to read the story as a humanist desire to subordinate self-interest to the interests of the state. After all, Rabelais's fiction repeatedly channels a feeling of distrust toward state bureaucracy and religious institutions (including dietary restrictions imposed by the latter) and actively rebels against the leveling effect of the law. Grandgousier anticipates the Chiquanous episode of the *Quart livre* (1552), in which the seigneur Basché loses his privileges in the royal system of justice and threatens to exile and ally himself with the sultan.[9] The story of Grandgousier and Alpharbal similarly dreams up a swerve from the legalist understandings of the political realm, pivoting instead toward personal bonds and alliances that transgress religious and institutional boundaries. However, these alliances in Rabelais's fiction take on the ability to organize larger communities that operate on universal principles—the presumed one of appetite and the humoral body—and take on imperial traits.

The Canarrians exhibit an irrational bend toward a sense of servitude. However, Grandgousier rejects all the gestures of service and self-subjection they perform within the legal framework of diplomacy and even theatrically throws the ratified contract into the fire:

> Once arrived, [Alpharbal] wanted to kiss my said father's feet; the act was judged unworthy ("fut estimé indigne") and was not tolerated, but he was embraced sociably. He offered his presents, which were not accepted, for seeming excessive. He offered both himself and his offspring as agent and voluntary servant ("se donna mancipe et serf volontaire"), which was rejected for not seeming equitable. He yielded, by the decree of the estate, his lands and kingdom, offering the transaction signed, sealed, and ratified by all those who should perform it; this was totally refused, and the contracts cast into the fire.[10]

Grandgousier replaces the legal contract and the ceremonies of political treaty-making with embodied performance, which culminates in lamentation and crying prompted by the natural goodness of his former enemy[11]:

> The end was that my said father began to lament for pity and weep copiously, considering the free goodwill and simplicity ("franc vouloir et simplicité") of the Canarrians, and, by exquisite words and fitting sayings, he played down the good turn he had done them, saying he had done them no good that was worth even a button, and, if he had shown them any decency, he was bound to do so.[12]

Because they fall outside the legal framework, Grandgousier's acts prompt the Canarrians to make of themselves voluntary perpetual tributaries and to oblige themselves to deliver unto Grandgousier two million pieces of gold, an amount that they agree—voluntarily—to increase every year. The Canarrians' voluntary actions of self-subjection bespeak an inner transformation from unassuaged appetite to choosing voluntary goodness in the form of servitude that also acts as a means of redemption. Having been liberated by Grandgousier from both the bondage of the law and the tyranny of their former unsated hunger through this final act of submission unreservedly given, the Canarrians are now free, even as—or especially as—tributaries of Grandgousier. Yet, the end of the tale makes it clear that the Canarrians continue to act on impulse. And, as I will continue to show, they are moreover racialized and defined as lesser in a hierarchy created by a humoral politics that hinges on appetite throughout this tale.

Gargantua's anecdote thus attributes grandiose agency to his father, Grandgousier, who, we are told, transforms the Canarrians from an army driven by a relentless appetite for booty into gentle and governable subjects by way of using and domesticating their appetite. Emmanuel Naya and others have shown that humoral medicine plays a large role in both the composition of Rabelais's fictions and the development of his characters, and this story is no exception.[13] The oversize presence of the humoral body here and elsewhere in Rabelais's fiction stems from the author's intimate familiarity with Galenic medicine, which was based on the works of the second-century Greek doctor and philosopher Aelius Galénus (or "Galen of Pergamon"), who lived in the Roman Empire. Emmanuelle Lacore-Martin shows that Rabelais's fiction repeatedly reveals the mechanisms of the humoral body and its relation to the immaterial soul that stems from the humoral body.[14] In Galenic theory, animal spirits are weightless, invisible entities distilled from nutrients first absorbed by the liver that are then transported to the left ventricle of the heart and carried as vital spirits by the carotid arteries to the brain, where they are mixed with inhaled air in the cerebral ventricles or moved through the "wonderful net," a plexus of blood vessels, to become animal spirits stored in the brain. Animal spirits provide a schema that links the material and immaterial dimensions of the human being, tying the intellect to the material processes of the body in a way that radically differs from the more familiar (to us) mind-body dualism associated with the seventeenth-century thought of René Descartes. According to Lacore-Martin, "For Rabelais, the relationship between the soul and the body is essential and organic; feeding the body is, quite literally, feeding the soul (. . .)."[15] Within this system, the Christian notion of the "immortal soul" can be thought of as a product distilled from physical nourishment through the intermediary of material humors, a process that reintroduces human ontological transcendence and the bias against inert matter in accordance with Aristotelian metaphysics. Rabelais's fiction seeks to contain the humoral body's inherent instability by presenting it as capable of stabilizing itself by distilling the values taught by

Christ. And, as the abstractor of quintessence, Rabelais's fictional narrator Alcofrybas Nasier claims to practice this art. Rabelais's fiction repeatedly stages the political effects of certain sudden emotions, which, in contradistinction to processes of rational deliberation, uniformly account for the actions of the Canarrians: "Instinctive, immediate emotions like anger, fear, or indeed joy are always associated in Rabelais's fiction with a loosening movement in specific locations within the lower body; and, while these movements may result in undignified situations for the individual concerned, they are, nonetheless, presented positively because of the beneficial purging of the body that they afford, letting aggravating substances flow out of the body and thereby reinstating the humoral balance that is key to its health."[16] However, this balancing of humors is biased in a way that privileges French male bodies. For example, in the notable Chapter 5 of *Gargantua*, "How Gargantua Was Born in a Very Strange Fashion," Rabelais writes that Gargantua was born through the left ear of his mother, Gargamelle, after she released a large quantity of feces. From this, we can deduce that it was the release of the feces that allowed Gargantua to begin his ascent, after having been released from the cotyledons (from the Greek *kotúlē*, "cup," "bowl") of the womb in which he received his first nourishment, moving inside the vena cava through the diaphragm and up to the left shoulder and the left ear.[17] Gargantua is born out of the purging of the maternal body, and he exits this body as a Christian prince by the left ear rather than a lower opening of the body. By contrast, in Chapter 27 of *Pantagruel*, Rabelais's first novel, Pantagruel's failure of humoral self-mastery results in the birth of "little men and women" who are born from Pantagruel's obstructed farts. These men, along with their perpetual war with the cranes, reference the legendary African "Pigmies" known to Rabelais from descriptions by Homer and Pliny the Elder.[18] There is an inversion within Pantagruel, whose obstructed farts upset the balance of humors in his body and threaten to impede the development of animal spirits until they are purged and materialize as men and women with stunted stature.[19] Here, Rabelais's fiction of unstable humoral bodies that need improvement and are at risk of illness projects the consequences of the imbalanced body onto a geographically distant, mythical Africa. The differences in the humoral processes result in differences analogous to the differences in the various races of giants described by Alcofrybas, which we saw in the Introduction.

Scholars have also pointed to the fact that the category of pigmies constituted a racial slur in this period. Evidence suggests that pigmies served in humanist discourse as an identifier of Black Africans enslaved in Europe through the Portuguese slave trade, which spilled over into Spain and other European countries. Imtiaz Habib analyzes the commentary advanced by

English humanist Thomas More on the "Spanish escort" accompanying Princess Catherine of Aragon on her entry to London in 1501, which consisted of slaves and maids of honor, as "hunchbacked, barefoot, undersized pigmies from Ethiopia."[20] Habib argues that pigmies in this context is a term of ridicule, along with "hunchback" and "barefoot," deployed not necessarily to denote an ethnic or geographic origin but rather smallness of stature, and that these adjectives could designate the "black female youths" forming part of the princess's retinue. "Overall, that this negative marking of black people comes from someone [who] will become one of England's most famous Humanist philosophers is starkly indicative of how even European high philosophy will be complicit in the marking down of black people and the negative interpretation of blackness in early modern Anglo-European political and cultural history."[21] Rabelais, whose *Gargantua* is a nod to More's 1516 book best known by its short title *Utopia*, signals in the earlier *Pantagruel* that Black persons only have a marginal existence in the body politic, while in *Gargantua*, tamed pirates are welcome only after they have stabilized their unstable hunger by subjecting themselves to a Christian prince. More's demeaning description of Africans also recalls the disproportionate shape of some of the races in the genealogy of Pantagruel that I discussed in the Introduction. We realize that the "little men and women" in Rabelais's comic ontological fiction are unfortunate examples of stunted growth that correlates with excesses in other parts of the body, as indicated by their alleged bellicose nature directed at the cranes. Just as Alcofrybas's genealogy explains bodily differences as being produced by humoral differences that culminate in moral ones, descriptions of the excessive or stunted growth of the body or specific body parts were often deployed as a mode of racialization in the sixteenth century. In evoking the hypersexualized body, facial features with prominent lips or noses, and hunchbacks where an overgrowth in one part of the body implies stunted growth in another (all of which are elements of sixteenth-century representations of race), Alcofrybas's genealogy both parodies and confirms such representations. Alcofrybas presents a comic version of a generalized stereotype of the Black that occurs, notably, in Albrecht Dürer's *Four Books on Proportion*[22] (first published in German in 1528 and in French in 1557) (see Figure 3). Here, the artist examines a series of proportional head types based, allegedly, on the study and observation of hundreds of men and women, and in which the Black (not noted) appears with a "round" nose and large lips as two departures from the proportional mean. These divergences from an unnamed norm, or "protrusions," make visible the agency of matter as it comes to imply possibilities of bodily autonomy or revolt against the hierarchical structures of French and European social and political order.

PROPORTION DE L'HOMME.　　LIVRE III.　　85

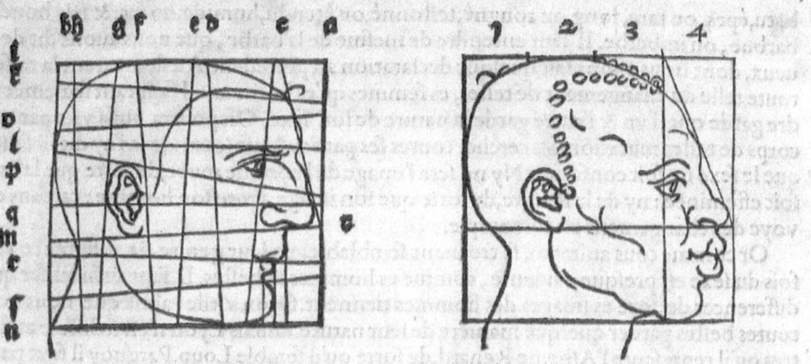

Il reste que nous parlions du changement des effigies de front, & de leurs variations. Mais pour autant que la raison de remuer les croisieres, de toutes les effigies de pourfil est de mesme de celles de front: c'est donc pour cest heure temps perdu de parler des varietés des croisieres. Tant seulement vous veux ie bien auertir que les croisieres peuuent estre toutes biesées, ou en partie en celle de front. Les faces de vray sont aussi bien torces, comme quand vn coté du quarre est raualé, & l'autre eleué. Poursuyuons donques le propos des perpendiculaires: lesquelles comme suyuant nostre doctrine elles soient notées dedans les cotés a.b. des lettres I.g.c.d.e.f.h. k. & qu'elles notent les principales parties, comme le front, les yeux, le nés, les oreilles, la bouche, & le menton, elles peuuent chacune, ou partie, ou bien toutes estre remuées de leur lieu: de sorte que comme plus elles seront distantes, de tant plus grande sera la largeur: & plus proches, de tant plus sera elle moindre: Mais encor sont elles pourtraites de sorte, que quasi elles s'assemblent par le haut: & semblent au dessous s'entrefuir, & au contraire.

On les pourtrait aussi panchantes, & lors elles ne tirent plus à plomb, estans ou biesantes, ou courbes. Touchant ceste raison tu trouueras en la forme exprimée, le front s'élargir, ou reserrer: & entre les angles des yeux des petis espaces grandelets, ou étroits, & entre eux, interualles plus grans, ou plus reserrés. Les yeux aussi pourront estre notés d'inegale grandeur, & lieu, & les paupieres, & sourcils. Tu verras aussi à l'vn le nés aggrandi, à l'autre retiré haut, ou bas: le mesmes encores droit, & aussi courbe: amoncelé, ou agu: plein, ou noueux, étroit iusques aux narilles, elles estans ouuertes. Ou bien au contraire, au dessus d'elles fort élargi, elles estans fort serrées. Nous pourrons dire le semblable de l'étendue, ou resserrement de la bouche, menton, & machoueres. Et de chacune partie qui au dessus sera reserrée & au dessous étendue, & au contraire. Par ceste voye donques d'inegaleté les faces sont pourtraites bossues, ou torses, & étranges en plusieurs sortes, comme d'vne bouche étroite, ou grande, à leures courbes, grosses, petites, grandes, ou bien inegales, machoueres amples, reserrées, agues, mouces, d'vne iointe apparente, ou non. Toutes lesquelles choses & diuersités vn studieux lecteur, & experimenté deura exprimer, dont il pourra découurir beaucoup de choses admirables, qui y sont cachées. Il n'est rien si certain, que ceux qui ont la cognoissance de la difformité, & laidure, pourront facilement entendre ce qui leur est à cuiter en vne entreprinse d'vn ouurage de bonne grace. Il est de vray necessaire que comme plus quelqu'vn fuira la difformité, de tant plus approchera il de la beauté. Celuy à qui ces choses seront manifestes entendra facilement, & appertement comment vne chose est differente d'vne autre, & la raison est: que non seulement auiendra necessairement es plates peintures, mais aussi es ouurages taillés, & burinés. Lesquels celuy qui entreprendra ignorant ceste raison (combien qu'il face quelque chose proportionnée, & egale:) ce sera toutesfois d'auanture, & non d'art.

Mais reuenons à nostre propos. La face apparoit autre assise sur vn col long, & gresle, & autre sur vn court, & gros. Outreplus il faut prendre garde aux lineamens de la face, lesquels aux vns sont grans, & pleins d'yeux, de nés, & menton, aux autres menus, & pressés. Les faces aussi apparoissent autres si la teste est cheuelue, ou rase, ou à poil crespelu, ou ab-

p iij

Figure 3

What happens when the humoral fabrication of Christian values reintroduces ontological transcendence *after* the fact of ontologically leveling all bodies to the fluidity of the humors? Does Rabelais's fiction draw up scenarios in which a community that is not concretely Christian behaves like Christians ought to (i.e., the Canarrians), while other communities become degraded as a side effect of this alimentary process (i.e., the "little men and women")? The Canarrians hail from North Africa and the Canary Islands, which is directly evoked by their name. Indeed, Rabelais's choice of a name that references the Canary Islands may have to do with a sense of national pride, for a Norman aristocrat and adventurer, Jean de Béthencourt, conquered the islands as a vassal of the Castilian king Henry III in 1402. The Canarrians' geographic location references important sites of piracy and the slave trade that were carried out on both sides of the Mediterranean—by Berbers, Jews, and Arabs on the African side, and Genoese, Aragonese, and Portuguese on the European side—in the Middle Ages and the fifteenth century.[23] Their self-organizing autonomy also extended into the sixteenth century in spite of, or in collaboration with, the Ottoman and Spanish Empires that vied for control of the two sides of the Mediterranean. On the African side, there existed the so-called pirate republics of the Maghreb, and, on the European side, Spanish, Portuguese, and Genoese privateers and merchants, as well as the Knights of St. John who were housed on the island of Malta after 1530. The North African pirate states in Algeria, Tunisia, and Morocco were made up of Berbers, Arabs, and many renegade Europeans, and they resisted the push of the Portuguese and the Spanish into the African continent.[24] The slave trade—the capture of people and their sale—is left conspicuously unmentioned in Rabelais's tale of the Canarrians. Rabelais narrates an alliance with the Canarrians, who are seen as desirable allies because of the autonomy and wealth they derive from their appetite. However, he also relegates them to the ontologically nether regions of an unsated appetite that they are incapable of satisfying of their own accord without Grandgousier's acts of generosity. Because the implicit hierarchy of the Galenic humoral body converges with an Aristotelian hierarchy of matter and form, Grandgousier's government over the Canarrians also affords him the rational and spiritual upper hand. The animals gifted by the Canarrians embody the lower passions, for (female) monkeys ("Guenons") and parrots have been noted since antiquity for their propensity for imitating humans.[25] The smaller animals, meanwhile—that is, the tropical civets, genets, and porcupines—suggest appetite, stealth, and secrecy.[26] These animals signal the appetitive bodies of the Canarrians, their endless hunger. It is the immense appetite of the Canarrians that leads them to possess such enormous wealth. This appetite, which is the driving force of the story, is also ambiguous: the same desire to satisfy their appetite that drives them to capture booty is that which drives them to subject themselves to Grandgousier and his redemptive design. The Canarrians are accepted into Grandgousier's kingdom insofar as it does not contain any laws, not as full members, but as always marked by their all-too-great desire for material things or subjection. This integration contrasts with the production of "degrees of conditional acceptance" for Black African persons like the medieval Black saint famed within Europe, St. Maurice. In her description of this figure, Geraldine Heng shows that, in this instance, the medieval European identification with "the other" is an identification with oneself, as is reflected in the other's most praiseworthy qualities: "virtue, courtliness, chivalry, prowess, wealth, and, more rarely, Christianity."[27] Rabelais's political fiction does not grant partial values to non-Christian North Africans. Instead, it assumes that they can be transformed into subjects in a Christian realm as part of the process of perfecting the humoral body. Meanwhile, other human humoral bodies, such as those of Black Africans, are relegated to a lesser existence of endless warring with their avian enemies. Here, animality has to do with the holistic model of the humoral body that is capable not only of encompassing animated bodies and their dietetic regimes, but also of constituting universalist body politics. Owing to this holistic view, Rabelais's fiction projects a cosmopolitan kingdom that operates by first rejecting the racializing stereotypes Heng describes in the name of a universal human nature while also reintroducing ontological gradations by evoking the differentiated agency of matter. It does not make assumptions about preexisting French blood, as later colonial administrators would do beginning in the seventeenth century. Instead, it attributes different degrees of perfection and agency to different ways of managing the instability of humoral processes. It defines Frenchness through a moral agency tied to a "healthy" appetite that trumps the ability to sublimate the passions. While Aristotle considers legitimate political power to consist in power over free men that serves their common good, as opposed to a despotic rule that seeks only its own interest, Rabelais's Pantagruel and Gargantua exert pressure over natural bodies that are both inclined to be ruled by appetite and capable of freedom through the right use of appetite. This is the crux of the matter: Rabelais's fictions extend the circle of the "well-born" beyond nobility, to all estates, but they also tie the distribution of agency to optimized physical bodies rather than to legal rights, thereby extending the need to transform others whose bodies are not optimal. The hedonistic and transgressive mastery of the body may not be the privilege of one particular social group or class, but its distribution is skewed toward those gendered male and their bonds. It confers privileges that imitate those of nobility and, while it can certainly serve as a tool to attack the status quo, more often than not it also confirms racial biases and social hierarchies.

Rabelais did not imagine communities forming from the bottom up simply from the will of the people. Rather, he viewed such formations as resulting from the work of moral agents: abstractors of quintessence, who come from any part of society, are latter-day Cynics, and rely on affective, humoral bonds with others, including princes. Pantagruel famously discerns the nobility of Panurge without any evidence other than a gut feeling inspired by Panurge's physiognomy. When Pantagruel meets Panurge in Chapter 9, the narrator describes Panurge as "a man of handsome stature and elegant in every bodily feature"[28] but also as emaciated and looking like someone who has escaped from the dogs or like an apple picker from the Perche region (known for its apples and apple cider). Pantagruel questions this description by pointing out: "Do you see that man coming along the Charanton Bridge road? 'Pon my word, he is poor only in fortune, for from his physiognomy I assure you that Nature brought him forth from some rich and noble line ("de riche et noble lignée"), but the accidents that happen to the adventurous ("gens curieux") have reduced him to such penury and indigence."[29] While Pantagruel identifies Panurge as a natural product of "a rich and noble line," it turns out that they are both French from the Touraine region and thus possess corporeal and facial features that the French came to associate with their own distinctive shape. This chance meeting initiates a veritable bromance between these two persons of ostensibly very different social status, allowing Panurge to become not only Pantagruel's lackey but also his quasi-equal in speech and actions. This ennobling of Panurge is not only the result of his loyalty but also, perhaps, his role as a comic but loyal informant who reports back to his master.[30] Does Panurge's excellent physiognomy arise in the eyes of Pantagruel because he discerns in the impoverished traveler the loyal agent even before speaking with him, or does the fact that Panurge looks like him (and comes from the same region) render him attractive? Rabelais's novels abound in satirizing representations directed at certain groups; not only are those who prescribe the Lent (the Catholic Church), represent Catholic imperialism (Spain), or are members of Genevan Calvinist leadership described as having certain visibly unpleasant corporeal characteristics, but so, too, are Muslims and Africans. His fiction makes visible corporeal differences and creates corporeal subjects whose agency is defined by their visible bodies, with characteristics distributed along a scale between beautiful and ugly. There have been many appropriations and reappropriations of the work of Rabelais by Protestant editors during the Wars of Religion and by seventeenth-century libertines who appreciated his difficult, erudite, and sharp wit, and these reappropriations—as French *gauloiseries*, as a carnival for the poor, as lessons in evangelical humanism, and as an example of post-structural modernism[31]—align Rabelais's fiction with different communities of readers. My reading differs by highlighting simultaneously utopian and imperialist aspects of Rabelais's imagined communities. The friendships of Grandgousier and Alpharbal, on the one hand, and Pantagruel and Panurge, on the other, show the personal way powerful alliances are imagined in Rabelais's fiction. Neither is a friendship between equals but between master and agent. Carla Freccero calls the friendship between Pantagruel and Panurge queer,[32] for it perverts the patriarchal normative ideal of filial piety and relies on a bond that recalls Eve Kosofsky Sedgwick's notion of homosocial desire.[33] This homosocial quality of Rabelais's political imagination makes it possible for these fictions to transgress religious norms and national boundaries (insofar as Rabelais imagines a bond between a Utopian prince whose culture is Christian and French and a Mediterranean pirate king who, as I will argue, is Muslim). In *Gargantuan Polity*, drawing on political theories of the "common good" and especially Claude de Seyssel's *La grant monarchie de France* (1518), Michael Randall argues that Rabelais creates ideal humanist political fictions in which the oversize and often vulgar body of the giant Grandgousier, who revels in eating and drinking with his subjects, as well as that of his son, Gargantua, reveal them as imperfect kings that are made of the same "stuff" as their subjects. The giants' power is conferred accordingly by the consent of their subjects through a form of "distributed sovereignty" in which they are expected to promote the common good.[34] However, while Grandgousier and other Rabelaisian princes are indeed made of the same stuff—the humoral body—as other subjects, not all appetitive bodies are wholesome. And, more importantly, these giants do not eat with just anyone; those with whom they do eat often are, or become (as is the case with the Canarrians), their subjects. Their superior and well-managed appetites tend to define what is wholesome and universal about appetite, for eating together imposes ideas on others of what it means to eat well.

As with the parleying of Grandgousier with Alpharbal, we can detect in the encounter between Panurge and Pantagruel categories like masculinity, nationality, ableism, and autonomy that set the pair on an equal footing despite their persisting cultural differences. Scholars have noted that Panurge, who, in another episode, cruelly humiliates the "haughty" Parisian lady who rejects his sexual advances, excludes women from the bond that exists only in its homosociality.[35] By contrast, saving the Canarrians is possible because there is a certain congruence between Grandgousier's (French) male aristocratic values and those of the Canarrians. The story implies that the Canarrians act out of honor and to avoid shame, eager to prove that they are "son[s] reputedly of a good mother."[36] They value their honor (a characteristic of nobility), possess money and valuables, and make decisions about their body politic in an assembly. They live in patriarchal societies that recognize the importance of controlling women and women's sexuality. We may wonder if Rabelais's tale resolves the tensions between the origin of their wealth, how they generate it, their piracy (including, in all verisimilitude, the plunder of goods and the sale of people), and their political values (such as autonomy and patriarchy). Rabelais's political community is universalist and imperialist, for it is premised on the universality not just of the capacity for sociability but also that of appetite. It represents a speculative political community with parameters that do not fully coincide with Valois politics or those of the French nation. Instead, it is based on building communities of autonomous agents that resist hegemonic institutional pressures from the Catholic and Protestant Churches as well as the crown while relying on exclusively male bonds (which Rabelais tentatively imagines crossing geographic and religious boundaries) and establishing a racially skewed hierarchy of agency that assumes the possibility of perfection through constant and sudden transformations.

Pan and Agents in the Mediterranean

The French crown's alliance with the Sublime Porte was euphemistically called "friendship" ("amitié"), which reflects the belief that a common goal, or affective bond, existed between the two. In reality, the French politics of diplomacy in the Ottoman Empire was largely transactional and considered the interests of the Sublime Porte, even though the rhetoric of diplomatic writing contained frequent vilifications of these interests as "greed" owing to distrust or self-justification. The spatial dimensions of the encounter between Alpharbal and the Canarrians coincide with the zones of contact between agents of the French court and the Sublime Porte in the Mediterranean region. The pirate king Alpharbal, meanwhile, evokes Hayreddin Pasha (1466?–1546), or "Barbarossa" ("Red Beard"), as he was commonly called in Europe, and his Maghreb empire. It has been noted that Alpharbal's name is a distortion of the Carthaginian general Hannibal.[37] However, it also echoes that of Hayreddin Pasha. In diplomatic documents, such as in the instructions of the first resident ambassador to Constantinople, Jean de la Forest, the Frenchman wrote Hayreddin Pasha's name as "Haradin." Rabelais likely plays with both names—Hannibal and Haradin—in coining the name Alpharbal. Moreover, Alpharbal contains the faux-Arabic article "al," imitating "al-Dīn," a common suffix (meaning "of the Creed") that appears in Hayreddin Pasha's Arabic name. Rabelais's authorial sobriquet "Alcofrybas Nasier" employed in the 1542 edition of *Gargantua* works similarly. Many parallels can be drawn with the real-life negotiations with the Ottomans in the parley scene between Grandgousier and Alpharbal. Hayreddin Pasha was a North African corsair originally from the island of Lesbos, who achieved the sovereignty of Algiers from Spain and, after being named fourth pasha of the Ottoman Empire in 1533, actively sought an alliance with the Valois. There were many contacts between the French and the Ottoman-allied territories of North Africa in the early 1530s. In the spring of 1533, Captain Pierre de Piton was sent to Fez, ostensibly to buy exotic animals and to liberate officers of the king, but also to carry out a secret mandate to obtain authorization for French ships (both merchant and naval) to anchor in the port of Fez.[38] Hayreddin Pasha sent an envoy to Francis I, and in July 1533, this resulted in the first public reception of an envoy of a Muslim state in Marseille. Francis I also met with him in Puy. The envoy liberated Christian prisoners and brought exotic animals, including the "lion of Barbarossa," Hayreddin Pasha's most famous gift, which was regifted to Pope Clement VII a few months later. On February 11, 1534, Antonio Rincón, an agent of Francis I who had a particularly close bond with the king,[39] embarked for Constantinople. He followed his Ottoman counterpart, the grand vizier Ibrahim Pasha, Sultan Suleiman I's childhood friend and close advisor, to Aleppo and discussed the plan for conquering and dividing up Italy. Hayreddin Pasha conquered Tunis on August 16, 1534, from its pro-Spanish local ruler and sent twelve envoys to Francis I. They arrived in Marseille on October 14, 1534, met with Francis I in Châtellerault in November, and accompanied the king to Paris. This meeting led to a three-year-long truce between Hayreddin Pasha and Francis I.[40] The publication of *Gargantua* landed between the fall of 1534 and the spring of 1535. Even more important than the question of dating *Gargantua*, which has sparked debates,[41] is the fact that Rabelaisian fiction functioned as a super-disseminator grafted on systems like the printing press, fairs, networks of news carrying, and early journals and newspapers. The real-world meetings between the French and Hayreddin Pasha, especially the truce that concluded in November 1534, are repeated and reworked in fiction through the peaceful resolution achieved without legal documents between Grandgousier and Alpharbal. Rabelais's tale reveals that the performative, ceremonial aspect of French–Ottoman diplomatic relations was crucial in the 1530s and continued to have relative importance through the 1550s. Francis I sent his personal friends, or at least aristocrats loyal to him personally, including Rincón, de la Forest, and Gabriel de Luels d'Aramon (d. ca. 1553), to the Sublime Porte. In sixteenth-century France, it was not uncommon to think of the military ambitions of the Ottomans as useful for the French insofar as they weakened Spain. In his account of the life of

Antoine Escalin des Aimars (1516–1578), otherwise known as Captain Polin de la Garge, a soldier of Francis I (and, later, captain of the king's galleys), the seigneur of Brantôme describes Polin as being the master of "Barbarossa" owing to the sultan's command to Hayreddin Pasha to obey the French captain.[42] The assumption (or presumption) that Ottoman military interests could be redirected for the benefit of France (officially, Christianity) and that Ottoman interests could be made to coincide with the court's military ambitions through French mastery of Ottoman "appetite" thanks to extraordinary agents like the "great" Captain Polin is mirrored in the story of Grandgousier and the Canarrians.

Accounts of both ad hoc and planned meetings between the agents of the two courts also reveal the importance of ceremonies in building trust. In an eyewitness account ("oculaire intelligence") for the French court, Jean de Véga, a sailor from Marseille employed by the court, describes the naval journey of the French mission on Betrand d'Ornesan, Baron of Saint-Blancard's ship, which departed from Marseille on August 15, 1537, to sail along the shore of North Africa to their uncertain meeting point with the Ottoman naval ships (which they found near Avlonas). De Véga's account is replete with descriptions of ceremonies and repetitive rituals that create social bonds between members of different groups. He describes the encounters between the French crew and the people along the North African coastline as occasions for the spontaneous exchange of greetings, foodstuffs, weapons, and information—and it is the success or failure of these exchanges that often determines the identity of a friend versus that of an enemy. During the French galleys' first landing in Tunis at the Cape Bon (the northernmost point of Sharīk Peninsula south of Tunis), the French, in de Véga's account, are greeted by friendly, pro-French envoys, including a "Moor" (a generic term that could be applied to different ethnic groups of North Africa or Muslims) who boards the ship "all naked" carrying small birds as gifts, and is given a mantel ("berne"); a red, tight-fitting jacket ("un gergault de drap rouge"); a shirt; a cap; and some money. The next day they proceed to Hammamet, where Hayreddin Pasha keeps a garrison but where inhabitants are divided between Spain and the Ottomans. Once they have verified that those meeting them are friends (they see a familiar Moor from the previous day), the French purchase water and food, while the inhabitants bring bread and fruits to their galley. Saint-Blancard gives twelve *écus* to the one who brings the presents and, when asked to sound his cannon, he gives two cannonades to frighten the "Alarbes" (denoting "Arab," this term carried connotations of hostility). The fleet proceeds to Sousse, then Monastir, where they meet a great number of "Moors and Turks" on horseback and on foot wearing Ottoman insignia. The French greet them by raising the king's banners, and the Ottomans reciprocate with a series of gunshots ("escopeterie") and equestrian racing and vaulting ("courreries et volteries de cheveulx"). The Baron sends an envoy and translator named Dimittre to the town captain, who sends back bread, sheep, cattle, and fruits to the Baron, and the Baron reciprocates the gift by giving twelve *écus* and two coats to the carrier. The captain boards their galley and greets the Baron with a French bow ("faist la reverence"), recognizing the Baron from having seen him in Algiers. The captain asks for more gunpowder, and the Baron grants it to him. They write a message to Hayreddin Pasha and send it with a "Turk" who comes to their ship. These accounts also reveal that non-French, Ottoman, and North African agents were involved in the mission of the crown. For example, near Tunis, the French crew are greeted by pro-Spanish Moors and their translators ("zagaies"), who turn hostile when they spot a man wearing a long, Turkish-style mustache and beard, a Turkish hat, and boots under French-style clothing.[43] Ceremonies of greeting, especially on the ad hoc and lower levels further away from the courts, rely on the similarities that shape the lives of the French and the Ottomans. These reciprocal, repetitive ceremonies, and the importance of the social bonds to which they give rise, indicate that there were attempts in the 1530s by agents of both the Sublime Porte and the French crown to mobilize cultural practices, bodily performance, and a theater of diplomacy to cement relations and a sense of understanding between the two parties. In this context, Rabelais's account of Grandgousier and Alpharbal's parleying, free of legal constraints, represents a very optimistic tale about the success of diplomatic rituals in creating a sense of belonging, trust, and common purpose. We can thus see in Grandgousier's and Alpharbal's bodily gestures and shared rituals an anticipation of the theater of diplomacy that was later cultivated by the French monarchy in the seventeenth century, with representations of the crown's acts, as well as those of other nations, taking the form of court ballet and other lavish spectacles.[44]

Rabelais's fiction of a harmony of wills may have been inspired both by his experiences of similar rituals of making contact with Ottomans in southern France and news reports about the Ottomans. The author's poorly documented life gives us only a few glimpses into how he came into contact with the world of high politics. Rabelais lived in the household of his patron, Bishop Jean du Bellay, in Rome[45] at the time when du Bellay was the king's ambassador extraordinaire at the Holy See (January–May 1534) and was tasked with dissuading Pope Clement VII and the College of Cardinals from excommunicating Henry VIII for annulling his marriage to Catherine of Aragon. In the 1534 Preface to his translation of Bartolomeo Marliani's *Topographia antiquae Romae*, Rabelais showers du Bellay with lavish praise, stating that he considers seeing du Bellay in Rome a more special privilege than seeing the city of Rome itself.[46]

Describing him as a truth-sayer or (in Greek) *parrhesiastes*,[47] which evokes a similarity to the Cynics known for their unrestrained speaking of truth to power,[48] Rabelais shows Jean du Bellay as willing to disregard decorum in speaking with freedom, thus discrediting institutions whose hold is seen as despotic, such as the Conclave of Cardinals. Rabelais, in turn, earns the dubious honor of being called "my Pantagruel," a humanist wise man and a comic figure interloping in the serious world of politics, in the cardinal's letters. This shifting of political agency to rebellious acts contrasts with the "exercise in the politics of prudence" that the aristocrat and prelate du Bellay reveals in his correspondence.[49] During his second trip to Rome as du Bellay's secretary, which lasted from August 1535 to his departure in April 1536 (at which time Rabelais witnessed the Emperor's ceremonial entry into the city[50]), the author wrote letters, three of which remain extant, to his patron Geoffroy d'Estissac, abbot of Maillezais. These communications suggest his avid interest in the news and his views about the Ottomans. In a letter dated December 30, 1535, Rabelais reports on things he personally observed and read in pamphlets circulating in the eternal city: the preparations for Charles V's entry to Rome; the Persian victory over the Ottoman army at Khoi near Tabriz and Bitlis; and the arrival of the French ambassador Claude Dodieu de Vély, who was coming from Charles V's court.[51] Rabelais even speculates that the Persian casualties were greater than de Vély had reported, testifying to his capacity for fabricating political scenarios. He also compares the failed Ottoman strategy of splitting up the army and sending them to fight on two fronts to Francis I's decision to send his ally John Stuart, Duke of Albany, to Naples before the battle of Pavia. He suggests that Francis I and Suleiman I made the same mistakes, emphasizing how persons living in different cultures were similarly prone to making rash or biased decisions (Rabelais was so fond of this idea that, in *Gargantua*, Picrochole also chooses this weak strategy of splitting his forces). The emperor, de Vély presumably reports, still harbors fears of an imminent Ottoman attack on Sicily. Rabelais hastens to reassure his correspondent that he does not believe this will happen and pokes fun at those who use similar predictions to justify claiming more tithes. Because Francis I himself received tithes from the pope in 1534 and 1535 to defend the coast of Italy from pirates,[52] Rabelais's opposition to the princely use of ecclesiastic revenues collected from peasants to consolidate their territory indicates, once again, the distance between his imagined alliance and the actual projects of the French state. Rabelais makes a few special mentions of Hayreddin Pasha in his letters, noting that, after the defeat of the Ottoman army by the Persians, "Barbarossa" took his fleet to protect Constantinople and "avowed, invoking his benevolent gods ('dict par ses bons Dieux'), that this [defeat] is negligible compared to the great power of the

Turks."[53] He portrays Islam as the religion of "benevolent gods," comparable to or compatible with benevolence to Christian values. In a letter dated January 28, 1536, Rabelais again reports on Persian victories over the Ottoman army in Bitlis and reassures d'Estissac (wrongly[54]) that the Ottomans hastened to respond with a counterattack "of the most furious kind ever seen" and, after burning and devastating a great area in "Mesopotamia," drove "the Sophy" (i.e., the Persian shah) behind the Tauris mountains. He also reports that Hayreddin Pasha is still in Constantinople but left garrisons in the Algerian port city Annaba and Algiers. Finally, he reports having sent his correspondent a portrait of Barbarossa (now lost) along with a map of Tunis and its surroundings.[55] Should we see Rabelais's account of the fierceness of the "Turk" as a pejorative image of barbarism, as a simple reminder of the savagery of warfare in general, or, yet again, as a reassuring gesture pertaining to the strength of the French ally even to the point of overstating the military strength of the Ottomans? After all, the devastation he (exaggeratedly) ascribes to the Ottoman army can be seen as the manifestation of the victory of those who fight justly (in self-defense, as Hayreddin Pasha presumably did in Rabelais's view after the Spanish capture of Tunis, by protecting Annaba, Algiers, and Constantinople). Rabelais's fictional character, the fierce monk Frère Jean des Entommeures, fights to defend the grapes of his monastery from the marauding soldiers of Picrochole with the same savagery. For reasons of the shared values I discussed earlier, the admiration of the fierce "pirates" of North Africa was not uncommon in educated and elite French society. Portraits of Hayreddin Pasha were circulated and collected in these networks, including the likeness first published by the Lyonese printer Guillaume Rouillé in 1553 (see Figure 4). However, Rabelais consistently takes issue with representations of the Ottomans that depict them as menacing intruders who threaten the integrity of the land. Rabelais's representation of the Canarrians as capable of peaceful alliance agrees with his disapproval of joining together papal and royal power against the Ottomans by the allocation of tithes to crusading. Rabelais draws attention to the common interests and characteristics between the French and the Ottomans, each of whom he views from a non-state perspective. Accordingly, "his" Ottomans, portraited either in his letters, often through the acts of Hayreddin Pasha, or in his fiction, through the fictional figure of Alpharbal, do not possess qualities of innate evil or religious error. Marie-Luce Demonet suggests, moreover, that Rabelais harbored a fondness for the islands of Hyères because he came in contact with Ottomans there. Located not far from Toulon, these islands formed a site of intercultural encounters in the name of both piracy and alliance, existing as a place outside the law where the French king suspended his jurisdiction and gave clemency and freedom to convicts willing

PROMPTV. DES MEDALLES 241

BARBEROVSSE Roy d'Algiers, né de mere Chrestiḗne, fut contraint en sa ieunesse, par poureté & necessité, porter vendre des formages & autres semblables cas, en Espaigne, pour viure de ceste petite trafique. puis apres se mit à brigander sus mer, ou il s'enrichit: si que ayant ramasé vn tas de larrons & brigans de mer comme luy, & toute sorte de meschans gens, abandonnez & sans adueu, print d'assault & de surprise le royaume d'Algiers, qui est en la Mauritanie, que lon appelle à present Barbarie. Depuis il se ioignit auec le grād Turc, & feit maintes guerres sus mer, en quoy la fortune luy fauorisa. Il endōmagea fort l'Espaigne: chassa le Roy de Tunis hors de son royaume: qui toutesfois peu apres y fut remis par Charles cinqieme. Aussi sa puissance n'estoit pas assez grāde pour soustenir l'effort dudit Emp. Charles: car il n'auoit peuple riche, ny belliqueux & ne tenoit pas grand cas auec Algiers: ains sa plus grande puissance venoit de l'appuy du Turc. Voyez les Chron. de Iouio & Gazzo.

MVLEASEM estant dechacé de son royaume de Tunis par Barberousse, fut remis en iceluy par Charles cinqieme, l'an 1535. & permit que lon y preschast nostre S. Foy. Or l'an 1541. iceluy Emp. ioint auec ledit Muleasem, s'efforça en vain de chacer Barberousse hors de son royaume d'Algiers. Car ayant sous ceste intention trauersé la mer, & desia asiegé bonne partie de la ville, se leua subit vne grande & horrible tempeste, meslee de grandes pluyes & vents. Ainsi les Algeriens prenans à leur auantage ceste occasion du temps qui combatoit pour eux, sortirent, & se ruerent si bien sus leurs ennemis ia batus, & à demy vaincus de la tempeste, que l'Emp. fut contraint se retirer auec grande perte de ses gens, & de ses galeres. cela fut au commencement du moys d'Octobre audit an. Voyez Gazzo & Paulo Iouio.

q q

Figure 4

to live there.[56] On the frontispiece of the 1546 first editions of the *Tiers livre*, Rabelais claims to be a monk of the Hyères islands, thereby tying himself to the particular geographic area in which much of the contact between the French and the Ottomans was taking place in the 1530s and early 1540s. Drawing attention to a large number of Mediterranean toponyms, especially those hailing from the southeast of France, that populate the *Tiers livre* and the *Quart livre*, Demonet argues that Rabelais must have spent time on the islands, possibly as the king's agent—a hypothesis that she supports by pointing out the Sorbonne's recognition of Rabelais as a Master of Requests of the king in 1543. The special laws of these borderlands were at odds with the strict boundary-setting of the modern state.

In the early 1540s, Rabelais is known to have lived in the household of Guillaume du Bellay, knight of Langey, and worked as his personal physician while du Bellay served as governor of Piedmont until the time of his death in January 1543. While in Turin, Rabelais exchanged letters on rare plants and the length of pregnancies with Guillaume Pellicier, the French ambassador in Venice. In his description of Guillaume du Bellay's death, embedded as it is within an account that straddles the genres of memoir, fiction, and humanist essay, Rabelais provides a superb image of agency *in* (but not quite *of*) the body and agency as animal. In the *Quart livre*, the fourth installation of Rabelais's adventure novels, the narrator belatedly reports the death of du Bellay, propagandist to Francis I, negotiator with the Protestant princes of Germany, and late patron to Rabelais (Chapter 27). Directly thereafter, the narrator recounts the mythical event of the death of the ancient god Pan in a retelling of an anecdote from Plutarch's "The Obsolescence of Oracles" (Chapter 28). The two deaths are supposed to be interpreted as a pair, and both are described as being accompanied by natural and mysterious "signs."[57] This pairing of the powerful French aristocrat and elite diplomat of French kings with the half-goat Pan has long puzzled critics and does not fit neatly with Christian humanist readings of Rabelais's fictions. By placing the two deaths and their circumstances in parallel, Rabelais frames du Bellay as the double of Pan, the latter of which is, in turn, defined doubly by his divinity and animality, with the two appearing coextensively in his (partly) human body. Although this pairing may seem to bring du Bellay "down" to the level of the lower body, it is, in fact, *elevating* his agency through plastic humanity as animality. "Pan" is the Greek word for "all," evoking the cosmos, and suggests that this relation is defined by the agent's embracing of a totality figured as nature. The animality of the body opens up a cosmic, cosmopolitan agency based on the mobility of the body and its ability to know the world.

Evoking the death of Guillaume du Bellay side by side with the death of Pan can be situated amid the long history of the *sōma*, or a unified body marked by its limits, including skin, hair, and death. However, instead of turning to Rabelais as a physician and the melancholic subject of memory,[58] the narrative pivots to address the animal agency of du Bellay himself. By comparing an agent of Francis I with Pan, Rabelais extends the body of medicine and moral philosophy into an additional dimension in which the pagan bucolic deity and its obscene animality reveal a forceful and sensitive, even hedonistic, relation of matter and material bodies to the world. This animality of natural bodies requires nuancing in view of the values and interests they serve and sometimes fail to serve. Rabelais transforms du Bellay through Pan's goatlike lower body and places him in the mountains covered with woods, situated amid the secret routes taken by diplomats, envoys, and spies when they wanted to steer clear of open roads and waterways. This scene claims unique agency for du Bellay at much the same time as it makes assumptions about the savagery of the world. One anecdote, in particular, helps us to interpret this curious image. According to Guillaume du Bellay's brother, Martin du Bellay, Emperor Charles V came to France in 1541 and met "fraternally" with Francis I, promising safe conduct for the king's envoys through his lands and making everyone believe that he would stand by his promise, "except a few people who knew the humors and disposition of the emperor to be such as to allow himself, whether by deceit or some other means, to reach his goals based entirely on ambition."[59] Martin du Bellay describes his brother Guillaume, who was in Turin at the time, as the sole one to recognize the intentions of Charles V and understand that his ally the condottiero Alfonso d'Avalos, Marquis of Vasto, placed people to ambush Francis I's envoys, Antonio Rincón and Cesar Fregoso, who were dispatched to the Sublime Porte and Venice respectively. Guillaume recommended they take a safer, longer route leading to Venice through the Alps instead of the shorter but more exposed one on the river Po. When the envoys declined his suggestion, he persuaded them to leave their papers with him. Guillaume du Bellay sent these papers to the French ambassador Guillaume Pellicier (1490–1568) in Venice in a separate dispatch, whence they reached Constantinople. Rincón and Fregoso were murdered while traveling on a barque on the Po. Unable to prevent the assassination, du Bellay nonetheless prevented the leak of sensitive information contained in the documents.[60]

In depicting Guillaume du Bellay as Pan, Rabelais echoes the sentiments of Martin du Bellay, who presents his brother as one who knew the humors of Charles V and garnered insights into the concealed intentions of his master's political opponent while also cultivating valuable knowledge of secret forest routes. This kind of extensive sensitive knowledge of the physical world, extending from human affections to sylvan landscapes, allows du Bellay to navigate a deceptive world in which a fraternal bond conceals raw ambition, and a river route becomes the site for an ambush. Pan's obscene body also genders du Bellay as masculine, and this dominant masculinity hinges on his mastery over powerful political actors (including the emperor).[61] Furthermore, Pan introduces a geographic drift away from the roads of trade and diplomacy that connected cities, looking instead toward the mountains and the woods, the Mediterranean and the East. The category of the "savage" (with the French *savage* deriving from the Latin *sylvus* or "forest") was used throughout the sixteenth century to designate both the Mediterranean, which they saw as a coveted territory, and extra-European territory. It was also deployed to evade speaking about Ottoman institutions, the Ottoman Empire, and, increasingly, Native Americans, all of which were, at some point, described as being outside the *polis*.

Panurge and Dietary Racism

Panurge is Rabelais's figure of the agent, and readers are cued to this by Pantagruel's description of him as an adventurous or "curious" man. In medieval and early modern French usage, the word *curiosité* meant both "curiosity" and "extreme carefulness," which became associated with the trouble taken by the powerful to engage in spying on others. Panurge's mobility and his ability to establish bonds over social and cultural boundaries come to the fore in the story of his captivity in and escape from Constantinople, which is narrated in Chapter 14 of *Pantagruel*. The story is famously told by Panurge directly to Pantagruel and thus closes the circle of the bond that ties them together. Although this literary tall tale has received much attention within Rabelais scholarship, it is still worth recounting. Panurge tells us that he partook in the failed siege of Mytilene, the capital city of the island of Lesbos under Ottoman rule, which was, in reality, unsuccessfully besieged by a group of French, Venetian, papal, and Spanish crusaders in 1501. After being captured by Turks and refusing to convert, Panurge narrates how he was taken to the house of a pasha in Constantinople and promptly put on the spit to be roasted by a roast chef, who added pieces of bacon to season his emaciated and dry body. According to his increasingly far-fetched account, Panurge escaped by throwing an ember into the lap of the roast chef—causing the man's penis to burn and his testicles to become scorched—and then setting fire to the straw in the pasha's palace, which, in turn, caused the pasha to impale the roast chef, effectively turning him from chef into food. As the fire spread to the city, Panurge claims, he successfully appealed to the sympathy of the locals, who pitied him and threw water on him. Meanwhile, a Corinthian woman (a designation intended as a thinly concealed euphemism for a prostitute) gave him plums that are known aphrodisiacs, and a "vile little Turk" with a hump tried to nibble the pieces of bacon hanging from his waist, but Panurge slapped him on the fingers. Panurge also claims that the fire burnt and shortened his virile member, which now hangs only as low as his knees, and cured his sciatica, which is a known symptom of syphilis. The story ends with a pack of dogs smelling the bacon and attacking Panurge, who stops to look back at the burning city (figured in this gesture as the biblical Sodom) and saves himself by throwing the bacon at them.

This burlesque story has received detailed analysis from critics wanting to ascertain insights into Rabelais's views of the Ottomans. Notably, Timothy Hampton shows that Panurge's tale reveals the limits of an imagined community based on the Christian ideal of love, as exemplified by the moral arguments made by Erasmus in his four tracts that weigh in on the Turkish question.[62] Ranging chronologically from "War Is Sweet to Those Who Have Not Tried It" (1515) to "On the Turkish War" (1530),[63] these tracts see Erasmus arguing that Christians ought to wage war against Turks only in self-defense, and should otherwise practice Christian values—including love—even toward Turks. [64] The story, Hampton points out, ends by literalizing the common slurs used in Christian France and repeated by Panurge in his story—namely, that Turks are "lecherous" ("paillards Turcqs") and "treacherous dogs" ("traistres chiens"). First, these offensive epithets are turned into actual things, as is exemplified by the bed of straw ("paillasse") on which Panurge finds himself in captivity, with his body "the wretched half-roasted flesh" ("paillard chair demi-rosti") on the spit, and, finally, the literal dogs chasing him at the end of the story. Hampton suggests that the presence of bacon, although it was not consumed by Muslims, anticipates the emergence of the dogs who chase Panurge to get to it at the end of the story: "For the various layers of signification at work in the depiction of the bacon, all operate within the context of the most obvious and outrageous irony in Panurge's story. This is the fact that Turks do not eat bacon, which is forbidden them for religious reasons. Only dogs eat bacon—or, more precisely, Turks only eat bacon when they have been turned into dogs."[65] If bacon, standing in for the flesh, the penis, and a parody of charity itself, momentarily resolves hostilities here, it is only at the price of effacing the humanity of the Turks. Thus, the racializing metaphors—including the epithet "dog," which is used in the old French *Song of Roland* to denote Muslims[66]— are literalized in the tale, with the "treacherous dogs" turned into the literal dogs (and maybe literal Muslims, if we follow Hampton) who chase Panurge and eat his bacon. Medieval slurs portrayed Muslims as "dogs" or "black dogs," distortions of the name of the Prophet Muhammad, implying that Muslims prayed to the devil. In Christian theology, the "flesh" and desire are often vilified as sinful, seen as the consequence of the fall and an appetite in need of chastising. And this metaphysical sinfulness of the flesh often came to be denoted by metaphors of Blackness, analyzed by Cord J. Whitaker as "shimmering" tropes.[67] Here, however, the Turk's desire and appetite are no longer metaphorical, no longer interpreted from a spiritual perspective; instead, they denote literal appetite housed in the natural body, just as the dogs also become literal in the story.

For Hampton, the Turks remain the limit against which French identity can be defined. Pascale Barthe, in a subsequent reading, also emphasizes this limit, but she argues that it functions as a place of passage. Barthe highlights the odd and foreign qualities of Panurge, who is French only "under the guise of worldly polyglotism."[68] She argues that Panurge's tall, emaciated body, lovingly compared by the narrator to a salt herring ("comme un haran soret"[69]), brings into relief a body that travels much like a food that is recognized as nonlocal, yet is not quite seen as exotic. "In Chapter 14, the *routisserie* is the boundary that separates but also potentially connects life and death, Christianity and Islam."[70] Barthe speaks of the limit as a passage that is rhetorical, just as, for Hampton, the limit is represented by tropes that become literalized. Both attest to the idea of qualities and objects being transferred from Panurge to the Turks and vice versa. While the pasha initially sets out to roast and eat Panurge, by the end, it is Panurge who ends up roasting *him*—and the roast chef, who starts out by turning Panurge on the spit, is the one who ends up taking his place on the spit wielded by the pasha. The pasha and Panurge begin to share physical characteristics—for example, they both resemble salt herrings—and culinary preferences.[71]

In her reading of the tale, Barthe zooms in on representations of dietary habits that function as anthropological markers, suggesting, for example, that there is a link between the spit upon which Panurge is being roasted in Constantinople and the stake at which Protestants were burned in France.[72] Her reading emphasizes that the transgression from what is considered civilized into the arena of the *un*civilized is globally and interculturally recognized in early modern Europe and that other nations—principally, the Turkic and American Indigenous peoples—were added to the list of exemplary cannibals in the late Middle Ages. Anthropophagy in Homer and Hesiod represents the absence of justice and humanity, and Barthe makes the case for this division returning in ever-shifting configurations in the global early modern world.[73] Barthe considers "cannibal" to be a relative term of dietary transgression capable of endlessly shifting boundaries between cultures. I agree with Barthe that Rabelais considers appetite transgressive and a means of crossing cultural boundaries. However, although transgressions break down boundaries, certain foods, notably wine and the taking of human flesh for food, nonetheless function to damn the Turks. As a neologism created by Christopher Columbus, "cannibal" was originally contrived on the basis of mishearings of the name of American Caribes and ended up mislabeling the peoples of the Americas by imposing an identity upon them that would be subsequently instrumentalized to define the continent itself.[74] Although Panurge does reverse the direction of who is being burned on the spit (first he, then the Turkish roast chef), he never quite settles down to eating from the meat; instead, he uses this colonial instance of labeling in his depiction of "Turks," marking them with an appetite that imposes on them a failed agency and calls for Panurge to redeem them.

Panurge is also careful to point out that Turks do not drink wine. In fact, the appetite of the Turks becomes a way for Panurge to correct their allegedly stunted bodies, caused by their dietary bans on wine and bacon that, in the racializing logic of the story, results in a too-great avidity for human flesh. Panurge does not simply dehumanize the Turks by revealing their animality (via their canine appetite for bacon), for animality is both ambivalent and agential in Rabelais's fiction. Like the tale of the friendship between Grandgousier and Alpharbal, Panurge's story also asserts that only someone who can feed the Turks can domesticate them; here, a role taken on by Panurge himself. It is the recognition of Panurge's very special body, its animality and its extreme plasticity, that helps us to understand his dual function as one who both crosses and maintains boundaries. By roasting Panurge on the spit, the Turks treat him as food, all-too willingly mistaking him for the salt herring that he resembles in appearance.[75] Panurge thus passes from being a martyr, a role he enacts for a short time, to food, and then instigator of hunger for allegedly wholesome things (like bacon). It is through his role as an agent transforming the appetites of others that his actions in Constantinople take shape. In a way, Panurge's mission is to show the universality of the animal as an index for the category of the human, and the appetite as an index for moral agency, thereby delineating friends from foes and even deciding on the very boundaries between human beings and animals. The dogs at the end of the story correspond to the truth that all humanity is defined by appetite, which is called upon to flatten cultural differences, while the right and wrong use of appetite works to reinstall them as differences of moral agency. This emphasis on an all-powerful and solely natural need—that is, redemption by appetite alone—helps Panurge to insert himself into the social fabric in Constantinople (or its fictional version, at least) and to cause it to fray by challenging the pasha's authority and appealing to people's sympathy and love. Panurge narrates how the moment the roast chef's penis and scrota become scorched, the chef unties him, intending to throw him into the fire. The roast chef calls his master through the window to come and put out the fire, but, in a mockingly burlesque fashion, the master—who has been walking nearby in the company of pashas and muftis ("Baschatz et Musaffiz")—arrives for dubious reasons ("to come to our aid and to take the jewelry"),[76] pulls out the spit to which Panurge was tied, and drives it into the roast chef's body. He thrusts it through the third lobe of his liver, the diaphragm, the pericardium, and the dorsal spine, thus killing the roast chef effectively by blocking the upward movement of humors from the liver to the brain. As Panurge is fleeing in the burning city, the Corinthian woman who helps him illustrates the free reign she gives to her libido as she throws water on him. The "vile little Turk" ("villain petit Turq bossu par devant"[77]), whose appetite for bacon momentarily halts Panurge in his escape from the fire, is depicted as having a hump "in the front," which represents a priapic growth and implies, in turn, a stunted growth or unsated appetite in other parts of the body; one that, assumedly, he is attempting to resolve by way of stealing the bacon. Panurge's story naturalizes the hunger for bacon and universalizes appetite in such a way that the characters fall into categories of being hypersexualized (the Corinthian woman), avidly hungry and greedy for bacon (the "vile little Turk"), or forever stunted in the growth and movement of the humors (the roast chef). Panurge is set free thanks to the chaos of these appetites, each serving him in his escape from and destruction of the city. Meanwhile, the satire is aimed at the pasha ("mon villain Bascahz"[78]) whose house burned down and whom Panurge offers to assist in his suicide attempt by hanging and smoking him, like a salt herring, over a slow fire. In a rather simplified gesture, Panurge's tale declares the stunted appetite of his captors—as evinced by their aversion to pork, resulting in anthropophagy, and the refusal to drink wine—to stem from a lack of humoral health, which is restored by the dogs that appear like latter-day Cynics, revealing that a true moral compass can be provided only by a healthy appetite. In depicting the "Turks" in this way, Rabelais is exporting his political agenda and theological vision of human autonomy from laws and antiauthoritarianism to a foreign culture, formulating a gesture of desired universal validity that proves to be (unsurprisingly) parochial.

The dogs that chase Panurge are incarnations of the Cynics, those exemplary Greek philosophers who lived in the public eye and took dogs as their model. In his 1983–1984 lectures at the Collège de France, Michel Foucault describes ancient Cynic thought as a form of alethurgic discourse whose subject constitutes itself as the producer of truth by insistently referencing the animal body. Cynicism, as a philosophy that was marginalized throughout antiquity, did not survive through texts or teachings; instead, it endured as an attitude carried out in many variations by its different practitioners.[79] Foucault finds its late avatars in medieval Christian asceticism, revolutionary militantism in the nineteenth century, artistic life in modernism, and existentialism in modern philosophy.[80] He notes that animality gains a positive value in Cynic philosophy by becoming a model that functions as the limit to human need: what animals can do without is not a legitimate human need. This tenet is exemplified in countless anecdotes, including the snail carrying its house on its back or Diogenes living in a barrel. According to the Cynics, having too many needs implies a lack of liberty and self-mastery. Cynic moral philosophy, moreover, dictates that animality be taken up in front of those mindful of societal norms as an exercise and challenge and thrown in their face as a scandal. True life consists in following a logos that is indexed to nature. And there can only be true life as an other life,[81] thereby doubling the body's opacity and potential resistance to the mind, for "[a]nimality was always, more or less, a point of repulsion for the constitution of man as a rational and human being."[82] Foucault notes one other element that was uniquely attached to the Cynics in the anecdotes that circulated about their lives: the slogan "alter, change the value of currency" (in Greek, "parakharattein to nomisma").[83] Linked sometimes to a pejorative meaning, that of the dishonest falsification of money (in some anecdotes, carried out by Diogenes's father; in others, by Diogenes himself), and other times to a more positive meaning, that of taking wealth away from the rich, distributing it among the poor, or, metaphorically, of privileging one's authentic self over what one passes for ("know yourself"),[84] this slogan reveals the necessity of breaking rules and laws (with "nomisma," "currency" and "nomos," "law" being related) to uncover that which is natural and authentic about the self. Foucault's description of Cynic teachings leads to him pinpointing a paradox:

> But you can see that there is a very strange paradox here, since, on the one hand, we have seen Cynicism described as a very particular form of life, on the fringe of institutions, laws, and recognized social groups: the Cynic is someone truly on the fringes of society who moves around society itself without being acceptable or taken in. The Cynic is driven out; he wanders. And at the same time Cynicism appears as the universal core of philosophy. Cynicism is at the heart of philosophy and the Cynic moves around society without being admitted to it. An interesting paradox. We get the impression that people of the Imperial, and even late Imperial period, who were interested in philosophy, had a double attitude towards Cynicism. On the one hand, there is an attempt to distinguish and eliminate a certain form of Cynic practice. And on the other hand, there is an effort to extract from this Cynic practice, or from other philosophical practices, some kind of core

which was recognized as the essence, the specific, pure essence of Cynicism itself.[85]

Cynicism, which had few theoretical texts, could be easily universalized by extending its moral "core" beyond the distinction between Greek civilization and barbarism. As moral thought, it was also deemed practicable by any, even though the practices of the Cynics themselves were strongly censored and critiqued. Erasmus and other Christian humanists found Cynicism, alongside other popular philosophies, to be useful in terms of thinking about extending the moral scope of Christianity. They were able to draw a line connecting Christ and Diogenes, or Christ and the Brahmans, while also following the attitudes of Roman philosophers and writers that exclude and marginalize subversive conduct. Cynics presented a "shortcut" to virtue, going by way of action rather than discourse,[86] which could be put to work in the service of Christian morality, seen as universal at its core. As "[t]he Cynic moves around society without being admitted to it," such acting allows for a simplified schema, based on animality, for universalizing the human while also admitting to its plasticity and mobility. The Renaissance revivals of Cynic acting bring new complications into the simple schema of Christian scandal—but they, too, obey a universalizing logic, and they, too, are subject to the logic of early modern capitalism and consumption.[87] The boundary-crossing that is a source of pleasure both in this story of animal agencies, and in Rebecca Zorach's example of monstrous and overgrown forms in Renaissance art "does not constitute a space liberated from political concerns."[88] Panurge's other is the dog—and sometimes the cat.[89] And this relation to animality allows him to "circulate" in society and in the world outside France, and to impose universalized forms of French values.

As Gérard Defaux has argued in his classical study *Pantagruel et les sophistes*, Panurge's knowledge of the world coincides with the sensitive knowledge of the ancient Greek Sophists, which was famously rejected by Plato via Socrates.[90] Rabelais's political tales are decidedly anti-Platonic not only because of the importance they place on the lower body (from which moral sentiments can be abstracted) but also because the sensitive self, the animal self, and its resistance to the mind elevates personal bias into moral agency. In *Our Emotional Make-Up*, the philosopher of science Vinciane Despret[91] excavates a long history of objectifying emotions going back as far as Plato's *Republic*, in which the human soul is seen as the miniature model of the entire political realm. Plato describes the soul as tripartite, located in three places in the body: the intellect in the head, courage and anger in the chest or heart ("thumós"), and passion or lustful desire ("páthos") in the abdomen. The intellect directs the emotions, but courage (or anger) assists it in the form of noble emotions. According to this Socratic-Platonic heroic model, the emotions represent the wild, subversive force that needs to be contained and controlled by the intellect—and, when necessary, by the courageous force of noble emotions acting in service of the intellect. The soul is born out of its defense against the passions and its defenses are doubled by the polis, governed by a philosopher king who relies on brave warriors to suppress the irrational mob. Aristotle, a student of Plato, translated his teacher's political model and its explanation of the power of the intellect over the emotions into a discussion of slavery, suggesting that the soul naturally rules over the body and that those in whom the bodily aspect is dominant are natural slaves.[92] However, anti-Platonic models like those presented in Rabelais's tales represent an insurrection within this rationalist body politics—up to a point—by showing that emotions also carry with them the possibility of assembling hierarchies between the shifting terms of emotions and control by way of reapplying agency, often in the guise of critique. In his tale of captivity and escape, Panurge crudely arrogates the prince's gesture of generosity while revealing that the political realm (including princely power) relies upon agents that cross boundaries, including both political boundaries and those that separate so-called base and noble emotions.

Another fictional voyage to the Ottoman Empire is narrated by Alcofrybas Nasier, the pseudonym under which Rabelais published *Pantagruel*. This name is not only an anagram of François Rabelais, but also one that associates him with Arabic culture and a large nose. In Chapter 32, Alcofrybas climbs into Pantagruel's mouth to take refuge from the rain and describes what he sees there: the inhabitants, whom he names "Gorgias" (both after "gorge" and the Sophist by the same name), and the land, a vast space consisting of "twenty-five kingdoms without the deserts and a large stretch of sea" that recalls the Ottoman Empire with its sanjaks, deserts, and coastal territories. Barthe zooms in on the unassuming appearance of a flock of pigeons in this chapter. Living inside the fictional giant king's cavernous mouth, the pigeons fly between this space and the outside world. Barthe argues that these birds recall the carrier pigeons utilized to carry messages, predominantly in the Arab world, in the sixteenth century.[93] Indeed, Pierre Belon reports that Egyptian, Cretan, and Cypriot sailors used pigeons to send messages of their arrival from home and would habitually see columbaria situated on top of houses in Paphlagonia (North Central Anatolia).[94] Alcofrybas encounters a nonchalant peasant planting cabbage, whom Pauline Goul has identified as an avatar of Diogenes the Cynic.[95] Diogenes claimed to be a citizen of the cosmos, rather than of Sinop, the town on the southern shore of the Black Sea where he lived and which was part of the Ottoman Empire in the sixteenth century. Rabelais thus places him in an imaginary land that maps not only onto the Ottoman Empire but also onto the human mouth and gorge. When asked why he sells his cabbages at the market, the peasant responds, in a characteristically provocative manner, that not everyone can have balls as large as millstones, and ordinary people, too, need to eat. The appearance of the good-natured Cynic signals both a particular geographic location—Anatolia—and a universal attitude that indexes the human to natural needs and appetite. In Panurge's tale, the narrator claims to smoke the pasha after driving a spit through his "throat" ("gargamelle"[96]) and thus quite literally shoves this schema of Cynic morality down his throat. This episode also refers to yet another throat. When Alcofrybas emerges from Pantagruel's mouth and stands in front of his colossal master, Pantagruel asks him not just what he saw, "But (he said) where did you then shit?" ("Voire mais (dist il) où chioys tu?"). Alcofrybas's provocative answer, "In your throat, sir," calls attention to the power difference figured by the enormous gorge and the superior appetite that defines the monarch's power vis-à-vis his subjects, while also leveling the difference with the scatological joke.[97] The transgressive animal subjectivity of the servant Alcofrybas, who moves freely in and out of Pantagruel's mouth and defecates as he likes, all the while carrying messages or information—indeed, acting as a pigeon—is revealed in this casual remark that perverts the norm and questions the authority of the prince. This is the paradox of Rabelais's agents: Although they presume to discern inner qualities based on the physiognomies of other bodies and regard the world as an extension of their own mobile, appetitive bodies, they also find themselves ensconced within hierarchical structures in which they seek their own autonomy through transgressive performance.

2

Bird-Man 2, Female Androgyne, and Other Speculative Transformations

The title of Philip John Usher's "Walking East in the Renaissance" underscores the salience of embodied action in French accounts of traveling to and in the Ottoman Empire. In this article, Usher reminds readers of the role played by anxieties about the self in accounts of French voyagers, both real and imagined, moving into and around the East. These travelers, he shows, project their fears onto the other and exemplify the rhetorical logic in which "that which is not wanted is written onto the Other."[1] For example, the Franciscan Henri Castella, a French pilgrim who traveled to Jerusalem in 1600, advised others to pretend they were deaf and mute to avoid submerging themselves in the physical space of the Ottoman Empire as much as possible.[2] Usher argues that many pilgrims carefully masked their anxiety regarding the culture of the other, which they saw as directly threatening to the unique state of mind they were trying to achieve, by describing the Muslim other as seeking to transgress his own laws. This is manifested, for example, in representations that show Muslim subjects drinking wine or, spuriously, as we saw in Rabelais's fictional tale, by eating bacon. In sharp contrast to Castella's vigilance, the cosmopolitan agents whose writing I explore in this chapter—Pierre Belon (1517–1564), Guillaume Postel (1510–1581), and Bertrand de la Borderie (ca. 1507)—indulge, by their own accounts, in mundane pleasures in the Ottoman Empire such as eating and sharing food, changing clothes, enjoying sights and sounds, getting naked, taking baths, walking, and associating with others. All these activities entail opening the orifices of the body to experience pleasures that, themselves, become politically inflicted. In this chapter, I show that conceptions of superior agency did not (only) stem from cultural anxiety or eschatological distrust of the other but rather from positive experiences of enjoyment and the specific pleasures of sweet and gentle things, of which agents became connoisseurs. I examine how two modes of writing—natural history and Christian mystic and Kabbalist theology—allowed agents and authors to reconfigure these experiences, such that they were framed not as dangers to a bound self, but rather as utopian modes of transgression and transformation in view of a greater totality (nature or god). These agents and authors were attuned to the instability of flows of bodies and the *physis*, as well as the humors and movements of animals and people. They also understood the possibilities of reversal within such a system and aimed at bartering positions for living with these possibilities. Agents saw both themselves and others as appetitive bodies, as physical bodies, or as "flesh" (in the case of Postel), and thus as similar to animal and human others—some of whom they saw as transmogrified into the positions of meaningful barterers. Belon and Postel were agents and writers with different ideological commitments. Belon was an ambitious, partly self-taught natural historian and an orthodox Catholic who opposed the Reformation, while Postel was a self-taught Orientalist and a provocative visionary who, despite also being a Catholic in the period of the Reformation, considered the papacy to be illegitimate and built visions of a new, universal Christian community. Both Belon and Postel came from modest, indeed poor, backgrounds. And both tended to see in the sciences they studied (natural history and theology, respectively) the power to have an impact on scholars and society as a whole. In what follows, I zoom in on the power structures, racializing impulses, and dystopias inherent to the utopias that these two agents imagined.

Mediterranean Articulations

Pierre Belon, the natural historian and spy who traveled in the Ottoman Empire between 1546 and 1549, published his *L'histoire de la nature des oyseaux* in 1555. In this text, he relates Francis I's habit of sleeping with the cub of a lion or a snow leopard on his bed, "like peasants do with their domestic animals" ("quelque animal privé") in order to tame them.[3] Belon also describes the king's aviary, which was built in the park around the Château of Fontainebleau. Birds came there to nest, incubate their eggs, and raise their chicks, he writes, and the king tamed visiting herons by forcing them to enter through a tunnel.[4] Belon calls Francis I a "matchless subduer of all things animate."[5] And, he goes on to explain, "The work of forcing nature seems to have something of the divine to it."[6]

Belon, who probably spied on the Ottomans on behalf of his French patrons, thus pays lip service to the French court's ambition of exercising dominion over physical nature and, particularly, over living or animate matter. His anecdote about the French king bespeaks a double ambition of imitating the force of nature, as is embodied by prey animals such as the Felidae and the herons, and "forcing nature" or redirecting the law of the kingdom back onto nature.[7] Despite their socially modest status, peasants are exemplary here because they enjoy the privilege of a close relation with the animals that they keep and handle. Training and bonding with the "noble races" of animals (i.e., horses bred for aristocrats, hunting dogs, and hunting birds) were traditionally reserved for princes and aristocrats in early modern Europe and the great medieval empires of the Eurasian peninsula. It was also the princes and aristocrats that were the recipients of exotic and "difficult" animals as gifts from Asia, Africa, and the New World. Hunting created the conditions for an intimate relationship between the elite and their dogs and horses that permitted one to look "beyond their otherness,"[8] but even these noble and much-loved companion animals were seen to require discipline and control.[9] Dwelling within this ambivalent place between intimacy and domination, Belon grants the peasant the privilege of being able to move into roles that are not properly his—a position that is rivaled only by the king, who bonds with and possesses large cats and water birds (and imitates peasants if he so wishes). Amid the traditional praise of quasi-divine royal power, Belon inserts his own, different yet similar, position: He, too, sees himself in animals such as migratory birds, and he, too, can imitate the clever tricks of Mediterranean peasants and coastal peoples. As a natural historian sent on a mission to the Ottoman Empire,[10] Belon was afforded a privilege that few others could attain: that of crossing interspecies and geographical boundaries. This position is exemplified by his transplanting of large deciduous trees, such as the Oriental plane, and of evergreen coniferous species, such as cypress and pine trees, back to France.[11] Ilana Zinguer calls Belon's natural historical work a Rabelaisian project,[12] corresponding to the advice Gargantua gives his son Pantagruel in Chapter 7 of *Pantagruel* to study all the fish in the rivers, lakes, and seas; all birds, trees, and bushes; all fruits in the forests; all plants in the fields; all metals and minerals; and all the precious stones of the South and the Orient. Similarly, Alexandra Merle shows that Belon mainly considered nature a self-moving, autonomous force rather than a place where an inscrutable transcendental cause was at work, following the medieval tradition rooted in Aristotelian-Thomist physics as opposed to an Augustinian, transcendentalist one.[13] According to this model, rationality was manifest in the concrete operation of the *physis* in agreement with Aristotle's famous hylomorphism, in which form is imprinted upon matter like a seal on wax.[14] Knowledge, while rational, was only attainable through the medium of the senses.[15] In Thomist theology, the rationality of Aristotelian inclinations of material things was seen as mechanical and countered the spontaneity and freedom of the spiritual.[16] And yet Belon, much like Rabelais, distinguished himself from the strict rationalism espoused by Aristotelian and Thomist philosophy. He noticed and promoted material nature as an autonomous realm, in which he recognized the mechanical set of motions exhibited by matter as well as the free ones pertaining to the spirit. In his preface to the reader in *L'histoire des oyseaux*, Belon describes the natural world as a realm in which nature "in its pleasure" assigns to each one of its "animated" works a duty,[17] which recalls the Thomist view of inclinations—with the exception that Belon names nature, rather than divine reason, as the chief distributor of tasks. Belon also sees an analogy between nature and the human social and political order. For sixteenth-century readers, the expression "nature's pleasure" evoked the formula "For this is our pleasure" ("Car tel est nostre plaisir"), which was first instituted by Louis XI (1423–1483) to denote an instance of the king's absolute power and routinely used in legal documents like royal decrees thereafter. The expression recognizes that, while kings were to observe the common good, their will, sanctioned by divine power, was absolute—that is, literally, "untied" from any obligation to the law or the interests of others in the body politic.[18] Belon thinks of nature as a regime of absolute government in which nature's absolute satisfaction, rather than the good of each creature, is the final directive. Nature assigns duties that serve its own pleasure and are not subject to discussion. Nature's absolute pleasure leads to a politics of nature in which various agencies, nonetheless, can obtain different pleasures for themselves. In Belon's description, nature is a separate realm of autonomy and sovereignty that imitates the political realm of the human *polis*. Although kings can exert force on nature or the material realm, the latter is no less autonomous—and, in its autonomy, it models royal power itself. Nature has agency; it is not dead or inert, as in the seventeenth-century rationalist model associated with the philosopher and mathematician René Descartes. Nor is it fully mechanical, as it is seen in an orthodox Aristotelian-Thomist model. Moreover, Belon views both the Aristotelian nested model and the Thomist hierarchical model of nature as existing in a fragmented state, branching into separate flows of strategically or tactically deployed forces or movements, where either greater force or greater intelligence holds command over the lesser one. In the sixteenth century, it was not uncommon to attribute spirit (noble sentiments and intelligence), seen as a fine substance distilled from their humors, to animals, as was the case of horses, whose noble spirit was evinced by their ability to be dressed to move to music.[19] This idealization of animals as noble while also being material contributes to what I call *animality*, the intertwining of a dangerous fluidity and the possibility of transcendence in bodies—and this ambiguous animality is set, accordingly, in the service of national and racial politics of nature.

Belon often describes nature as a domain in which appetites act upon one another sinuously and reversibly, generating pleasure as the fortuitous outcome of the one rising above the other and manifesting itself as spirit, intelligence, or cunning agency. In this nature, power and agency are dynamic; they come down to the directionality of consumption, the relative position of appetite, and the question of who becomes the prey of whom. Belon's *Observations*, published in 1553 and containing his descriptions of various regions of the Ottoman Empire, abound in stories of appetite and consumption that require some sort of ruse or reversal of who eats whom, and who captures whom. For example, while observing the vultures ("vautour"), eagles ("aigle"), and falcons ("faucon") in Crete, Belon notes that, instead of building their nests on trees like other birds, they affix them to the bottom of the cliffs protruding over the sea in out-of-reach places. Local peasants use long ropes to descend from the top of the nest (or send down their children), capture the birds, and climb back up the rope. The vultures steal the peasants' lambs, kids (baby goats), and hares. Meanwhile, the peasants reverse such predatory acts through this ruse that allows them to capture the vultures from their nests, skin them, and sell them for the manufacture of expensive articles: the feathers to arrow makers and the skin to tanners.[20] Belon's description of the competitive relationship between the vultures and the bird-like Cretan peasants reveals this exchange to be animated by the peasants' imitative desire, as the peasants learn to outsmart the vultures and make away with the booty. Belon also participates in this deadly game, albeit at a remove, by observing it from his position aboard a boat that affords him visual mastery over the entire scene. He imitates the peasants by finding access (in this case, ocular) to the situation that is otherwise hidden from the eye—but he also imitates the vultures by visually swooping in from the water to capture the scene through observation.

From the seventeenth century on, natural historians became agents of empire. The colonial violence instituted by the transportation and transfer of plants to different parts of the world destroyed ecosystems and imposed monocultures in colonial gardens, as well as kick-started the accelerated movement of living bodies across the globe. Ambassadors, agents, and other knowledge collectors in the sixteenth century, including Belon, did some of the groundwork by gathering knowledge about foreign faunas and floras. However, they did not (yet) impose universalizing taxonomies—or, at least, not with the same efficacy as later taxonomists. The agents' desire for freedom from hegemonic powers, which they had to navigate alongside their work in service of these same powers, necessitated much malleability. This renders their visions difficult to interpret from the vantage point of centuries. Belon sought freedom, a spiritual transformation premised upon the Aristotelian-Thomist model. This informed his observations, which also implicate the observer in the search for freedom and status. Imitative rivalry—as exemplified by Francis I with the lion and the Cretan peasants with the vultures—was seen as a model of mastery that could grant autonomy and agency to various actors in the metaphorical kingdom of nature without recourse to the hierarchy of later taxonomies, such as Carl Linnaeus's eighteenth-century *Systema naturae* (1735). The term "observation" appeared in the sixteenth century in association with medical skepticism and denoted the practice of collecting particulars intended for daily observation in fields as diverse as astronomy, medicine, anatomy, and travel writing.[21] Belon emphasizes the singularity of each observation, which stems from the unique humoral constitution of the observer in the process of observation: "The spirits and feelings ('les esprits et les affections') of different human beings are so different from one another that, among several people who are voyaging together in some country, it would be rather difficult to find two who are interested in observing the same thing."[22] Understood in this way, observation involves the humoral body ("the spirits and feelings") of the observer, his physical presence near the observable things, his position relative to the observed thing, and the point from which he observes physically (from a boat or a ship, walking in a desert, having access to the products of a market, or inspecting a mine, etc.). The observer thus directly participates in imitative rivalry, even as he often aims to maintain a certain distance and protection from others' appetites or aggression. Observation implies some distance, which is necessary for sight, as well as an intention or a turning-to that is either embodied or phenomenological in orientation. Belon's efforts to correct the descriptions of ancient Greek and Latin natural history, to better these writings on the natural world, should not be seen as mere attempts to capture the object in question. We should also pay attention to Belon's constant efforts to position himself, to ready his "spirits and feelings," to minimize the aggression directed at him, and to maximize his pleasure by being in the right place and turning to the thing itself.

In his *Observations* and, later, in *L'histoire des oyseaux*, Belon reveals and charts the migratory movements of birds—little understood at the time—between regions of Europe and across the Mediterranean, between Europe and North Africa.[23] He debunks, for example, the common belief that turtle doves hide and shed or eat their feathers during the colder months by observing them in Egypt in the winter—feathers and all.[24] He similarly debunks the popular idea that other birds, including black and red kits, cranes, swallows, and those commonly called *milans* in France, hide in the winter and come out in the spring. While navigating from Rhodes to Alexandria in Egypt, Belon remarks that quails alight on the ship to interrupt their southbound migration: "This made me certain that quails migrate, for I had seen them before in the spring while passing by the island of Zante, formerly known as Zakynthos, on my way to the Morea, also called Negroponte."[25] Catching the birds in the act of migration—describing their confident and routine comings and goings between distant locations, their ability to cover large distances, and their capacity for orienting themselves in different cultural and political spaces—is once again suggestive of a cosmopolitical agency that Belon claims for himself as he wrestles with a series of Greek toponyms to describe his and the birds' movements in the Mediterranean.

Belon's illustration of the similarities between bird and human skeletons in the same book consists of an image of a human skeleton ("Portraict de l'amas des os humain") and an image of a bird skeleton ("Portraict des os de l'oyseau"),[26] with each "heap" of bones ("amas") depicted hanging from a hook in the air. This illustration indicates that the similar disposition of the bones of each creature is made possible not only by the Aristotelian method of analogical classification (where beak and nose, wings and forelimbs are each other's analogies) but also by the suppleness of the human skeleton, in that having the arms spread to the sides, the digits of the hands and the feet elongated, and the head turned sideways allows it to assume a bird-like appearance (see Figures 5a and 5b). Aristotle defined analogy as discovering the new through the familiar—for example, by using the human body to describe the physical world. Here, however, the other—that is, the bird—returns to redefine the familiar. According to Tom Conley, who is inspired by Gilles Deleuze's anthro-ornithology in which the bird limits and undoes the binary of human and animal, the bird defines the boundaries of the human by also extending it into an animal dimension and delineating its "cardinal and corporeal bearing" in the flows of the physical world, the elements, and the humors.[27] Conley emphasizes the affinities that sixteenth-century French poetic selves felt with the dynamic hylomorphic movements of animals and the immanent flows of *physis*, rather than with the distanced, rationalist Cartesian epistemologies of science and binocular vision. Thanks to his understanding of bird migration, compounded with the association of his own transitory place and movement in the Mediterranean with that of birds, Belon did indeed come to identify as a "bird" himself, albeit in a manner that might be seen as conferring more advantages onto the human than the avian part of the analogy. The skeletal double portrait implies that birds, too, have human-like characteristics—but to see this necessitates killing and skinning them, and then hanging them or their skeleton on a hook. By contrast, Belon's Bird-Man represents an increase in human agency by extending into animality. This is Bird-Man 2, to evoke Sylvia Wynter's Man 2: the transfiguration of the human into a free eye in the midst of the

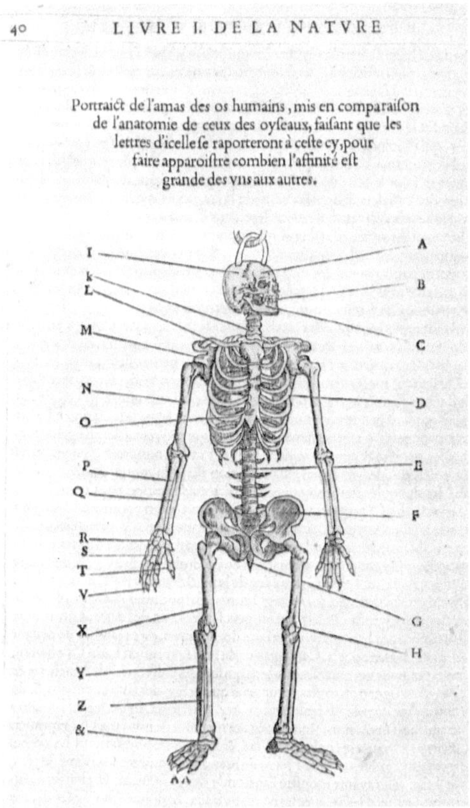

OTHER SPECULATIVE TRANSFORMATIONS

Figure 5a

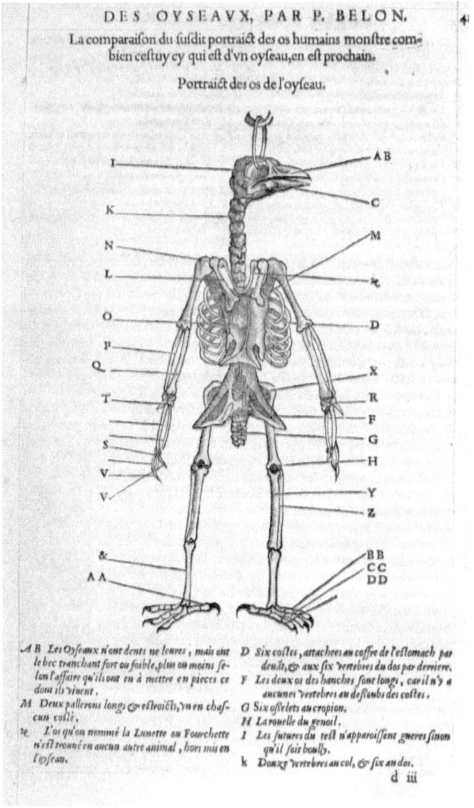

Figure 5b

mechanical movements of matter. One colored illustration in *L'histoire des oyseaux* contrasts this bird-agency, pictured as an eagle (identified by Belon in ancient Greek as *mórphnos* and in French as *gersault*), to a diminished agency represented by its dark-skinned handler, whose partially depicted body reveals a face disfigured by warts and a protruding tongue with a fly buzzing over it (see Figure 6).

In his reading of Alfred Hitchcock's eco-horror film *The Birds* (1963), Deleuze occasionally uses the figure of the bird, "an ordinary seagull" that swoops down on a man in a boat on the water in California's Edenic Sonoma county (a space that has cultivated a distinctly Mediterranean image) and wounds him, to transform "a peaceful whole of humanized nature" into three separate "fluxes": human, bird, and water. In this reading, "an entirely bird-centered Nature" is "turned against Man in infinite anticipation."[28] For Deleuze,

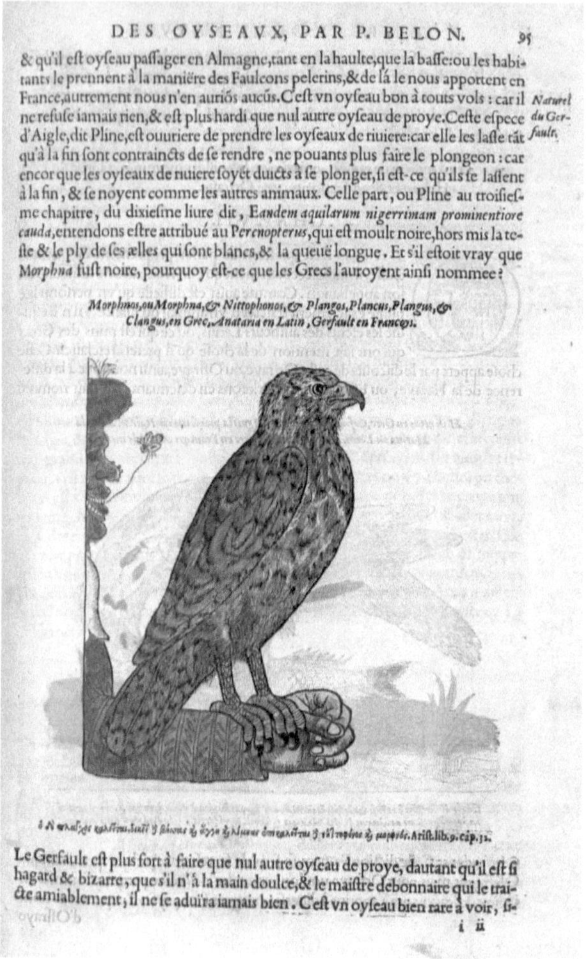

DES OYSEAVX, PAR P. BELON. 95

& qu'il eſt oyſeau paſſager en Almagne,tant en la haulte,que la baſſe:ou les habitants le prennent à la manière des Faulcons pelerins,& de lá le nous apportent en France,autrement nous n'en auriōs aucūs.C'eſt vn oyſeau bon à touts vols : car il ne refuſe iamais rien,& eſt plus hardi que nul autre oyſeau de proye.Ceſte eſpece d'Aigle,dit Pline,eſt ouuriere de prendre les oyſeaux de riuiere:car elle les laſſe tāt qu'à la fin ſont contraincts de ſe rendre , ne pouants plus faire le plongeon : car encor que les oyſeaux de riuiere ſoyēt duicts à ſe plonger,ſi eſt-ce qu'ils ſe laſſent à la fin , & ſe noyent comme les autres animaux. Celle part , ou Pline au troiſieſme chapitre , du dixieſme liure dit , *Eandem aquilarum nigerrimam prominentiore cauda*,entendons eſtre attribué au *Percnopterus*,qui eſt moult noire,hors mis la teſte & le ply de ſes ælles qui ſont blancs,& la queuë longue . Et s'il eſtoit vray que *Morphna* fuſt noire, pourquoy eſt-ce que les Grecs l'auroyent ainſi nommee? *Naturel du Gerfault.*

Morphnos,ou Morphna,& Nittophonos,& Plangos,Plancus,Plangus,& Clangus,en Grec,Anataria en Latin ,Gerfault en Françoys.

Le Gerfault eſt plus fort à faire que nul autre oyſeau de proye, dautant qu'il eſt ſi hagard & bizarre , que s'il n'à la main doulce,& le maiſtre debonnaire qui le traicte amiablement, il ne ſe aduïra iamais bien . C'eſt vn oyſeau bien rare à voir, ſi-

i ii

Figure 6

the camera is the non-human consciousness, which can assume the place of the animal, the inhuman, or the superhuman, and fractures humanized nature. That visual economy of the shot that turns *anthrōpos* against *ornīs*, creating an "uncertain relationship" in which bartered truces are violated now and again, plays out differently in Belon's descriptions. Much like the camera-eye, it is Belon, the observer, that directs the shots—but he does so in such a way that the fractured fluxes that attack Man come from actors in the Ottoman Empire, including pirates, animals, tempests on the sea, Ottoman authorities, and other great forces. Meanwhile, Belon looks for a mobile eye that invariably reveals the barterers of this truce: those who maintain the course among the flows in an unfamiliar world that is not centered on them. Frédéric Tinguely argues that French travelers who authored books about the Ottoman Empire in the sixteenth century regularly had recourse to a rhetorical trick of writing from the perspective of the "disembodied eye" that could transgress the boundaries enforced by Ottoman laws.[29] Similarly to the camera-eye, the observer's moving eye (while not exactly disembodied) moves and swoops in a way that breaks up the Ottoman Empire into separate flows and tactics. Birds, in this respect, represent the plasticity of the human, its cosmopolitan and mobile nature, and Belon reveals the birdlike qualities of human beings to reveal the ethereal values of the spirit.

It is not only bird migration but also other qualities of the natural world that orient the observer toward the East and the South. For example, Belon notes that the animals of Egypt—donkeys, buffalos, camels, horses, cattle, and sheep—are large.[30] This not only makes them remarkable, but it also makes their appetite apparent. It is this orientation toward nature that, as Sara Ahmed has argued, is constitutive of Orientalism, in which the Orient becomes the extension of the Western self.[31] As they veer toward birds and other animals and people in the Ottoman Empire, agents are defined doubly: They diverge from hierarchies of monarchical and imperial rule, but they also anticipate rather queer Western male orientations and the investment in transgressive, animal subjectivity. In Belon's descriptions of the fauna, flora, and people of Egypt, appetitive bodies come to be transvalued according to their mobility and ability to consume, as well as the pleasure afforded by these activities. He describes how the fishermen of the Nile make use of the gular pouches of pelicans, which allow them to catch and hold large quantities of fish.[32] While traveling by boat on the Nile, Belon and his companions amused themselves by throwing bread in the river for the Egyptian boys, who proved to be great swimmers, to fish out.[33] In comparing the boys who jump into the Nile to retrieve the bread to little ducks, Belon also acknowledges how the boys vie with the fish. However, the observer's pleasure, which is derived from observing the other's pleasure, implies yet another community: the readers of Belon's book, who can identify with those throwing bread into the river to observe the boys' efforts to fish them out, articulated as a collective "we" on the boat or around the book. This pleasure at a remove, a pleasure of the swooping movement of the eye, is what Belon calls "curiosity": a kind of profit that Belon seeks to distinguish from the profit of merchants by showing that it pertains to spiritual, instead of material, gain. Curiosity drives the natural historian and is considered ennobling since, unlike commerce, the pursuit of activities unrelated to making a living is a privilege afforded to aristocrats. Curiosity is rewarded by way of pleasure as its "profit."³⁴ In the description of the Egyptian boys, the pleasure is distributed between the boys and the observers (including Belon)—but not equally so. Here, Bruno Latour's notion of articulation comes to our aid in describing the politics of pleasures of agents. Latour maintains in his theory of actants that all actors are ontologically equal. Yet they establish political hierarchies because actants exert power on each other: "Every actant decides who will speak and when. There are those it lets speak, those on behalf of whom it speaks, those it addresses. Finally, there are also those who are made silent or who are allowed to communicate by gesture or symptoms alone."³⁵ Latour's articulation, which assumes that all actants are inherently weak and forced to rely on other actants, can describe the development of exerting power in situations whereby actants are not inherently socially powerful, as is the case for the agents discussed in this book. Egyptian boys are allowed to communicate by gesture alone—and that which they communicate, the universality of appetite and the mobility of the body, helps to increase the agency of the one who entices them and writes about them, as well as those who read the description. Amid the pleasure generated by curiosity, we can discern a reference to the "pleasure" that is the mark of sovereign will. This pleasure is the mark of spirituality and freedom that the observer exercises *over* the boys whose hunger he exploits to entice them to swim for food. We can discern in it the unidirectional gaze of the Western observer, but we should also not miss the visionary desire for a spiritual community underpinned by the mobile, curious, appetitive body.

Dániel Margócsy highlights Belon's abiding interest in snails and shelled mollusks and his curious (mis)identification of the *purpura*, or rock snail, a marine mollusk, as a marine version of the terrestrial snail with spikes on its shell.³⁶ Belon's interest in the resemblances and analogies between terrestrial snails and marine mollusks is not just some structural epistemological limit (as Michel Foucault argues in *The Archeology of Knowledge*) but rather reveals Belon's belief in the ability of essentially the same animal to dwell in all parts of the globe thanks to the protective shell it carries. It is also by virtue of its shell that this little mollusk becomes, for Belon, the figure of nature's pleasure. According to Belon's speculative zoology, the *purpura*'s enshelled movement in different parts of the world, as well as its movements in and out of its shell through an opening, are like the migration of birds between warm and colder climates; the minimal movement of the eyes provides freedom and mobility. Belon turns with fascination to those who can barter spaces of autonomy when forces turn against them. And, while the utopian possibilities of becoming-snail—that is, of being able to inhabit multiple elements and parts of the world and touch the world while avoiding harm—represent open-ended opportunities compared to the restricted nature of social norms or state interests, this articulation leaves those described not only mute but also susceptible to ontological devaluation. The Egyptian boys' hunger, like the Canarrians' appetite, appears less spiritual than Belon's cosmopolitan appetite for knowledge.

Belon considers moving around in the natural world to be a pleasure of a more transient kind, as well as a learning experience. Like the Cretan peasants, shelled mollusks, and birds, Belon transgresses species and spatial boundaries, often grasping for opportunities just as he grasps for plants. In one humorous anecdote, he relates a fortuitous interaction in which a powerful attack by plant toxins brings out the best in an inter-ethnic group of men. While spending time in the village of Livadochori on the island of Lemnos on a hot August day, Belon describes pulling the roots of a plant he calls *chameleon noir* up from the ground to dissect them. Those around him, Greeks and Turks, become curious and begin to imitate him, so they all work and sweat, touch their faces, and experience the "force and virtue" of the plant through an itchy and painful rash that everyone develops. When Belon apologizes for not knowing in advance about the power of these plants, they all laugh it off.[37] The haphazard grabbing of these roots and the men's willingness to imitate each other result in spontaneous cheer, effecting a moment of agreeable ad hoc sociability. This anecdote represents a utopian resolution of an "attack" through laughter that is characteristic of Rabelais's novels, working as the intimation of a peaceful, civil, habitable world to come. This distributed pleasure remains on the horizon as a utopian political ideal, like Grandgousier's kingdom of sated appetites.

As we saw in the previous chapter, curiosity also has the connotation of taking excessive care, as in spying—and Belon's text reveals a spy's awareness of his own embeddedness in unfamiliar and more powerful systems. Belon uses *mētis*, the practical wisdom or cunning deployed by those who find themselves at a disadvantage, either naturally (e.g., strength) or structurally (e.g., social status), in a given situation and seek to reverse it.[38] He is oriented toward animals that are mobile and weak human actors who tactically employ—or, to use a term theorized by Michel de Certeau, "metaphorize"—elements of imposed systems.[39] Belon looks at members of social groups with lesser status as extensions of himself and uses them as models to conduct his affairs "on the territory of the other"—that is, the codified and hierarchical society of the Ottoman Empire. Belon remarks on the spying networks and communication systems that the coastal peoples of the Mediterranean set up to ward off or protect themselves from piracy. Observers were mounted on top of mountains and on islands to keep a lookout, and when pirate ships were observed, these "spies" ("les espions") set fires to signal to each other. During the day, the fires were not visible from a distance, so they burned things that produced smoke and set multiple fires to signal multiple ships.[40] These warning systems aimed at reversing the power of surprise attacks and can be seen as a synecdoche of French agents in the Ottoman Empire, a spying operation nested inside a diplomatic mission in which individual agents were tasked with keeping an eye on an ally that was deemed untrustworthy. Belon, quick to change perspective, discerns the same cunning intelligence of the weak in piracy, which he describes as the last resort of the sort of poor men who have "a little barque or frigate, or a badly equipped brigantine," a compass ("bussolo"), a few light guns, sea biscuits, oil, honey, salt, onions, and water in tubs, which allow them to cook simple meals in the sun, sail for a month at a time, and make a modest profit.[41] Belon then changes perspective again and describes piracy as "the plague" and a "public menace" that "obliges people on land [near the coast] to watch out for them on the sea and observe them."[42] Historians have considered whether Belon was employed as a spy[43] on behalf of the crown and his patron, André Tournon (that is, until Belon was murdered under unknown circumstances in 1565). Given how broadly the French ruling elite relied on the services of those with whom they had a clientele relation, including using them for diplomatic and informal spying or message-carrying missions, the likelihood of Belon serving as a spy is considerable. Belon had powerful patrons, and when he found himself "in their hands" (that is, the hands of pirates) in the Mediterranean, an experience of which he does not divulge any specifics, he was ransomed by the cardinal and diplomat Georges d'Armagnac (1501–1585).[44] Belon's attitude toward pirates mimics the attitude of Grandgousier to the Canarrians—namely that, although pirates are dangerous, they can be managed by articulation through the enaction of a superior agency over them. Belon's nonchalant way of acknowledging his own captivity, a marked shift from the accounts of European captives of Ottoman slavery, implies, once again, that he believed in the plasticity of both his own agency and that of the French. It suggests that French agency was thought to be the opposite of the abject plasticity of captive and unfree people, for whom Belon offers a model of agency in the Mediterranean coastal villagers. These coastal communities present strategies that become the model and justification of French actions in the Mediterranean insofar as the observer abstracts from the circumstances of these communities, the actual lives that are disrupted, for better or (often) for worse. This plasticity relies on the naturalizing of appetite and the ontological leveling made possible by abstracting humoral and animal bodies from culture and institutions, which allows Belon and other agents to imagine scenarios in which they make themselves at home in the Ottoman Empire—albeit at a remove from its cultural and social realities.

Sartorial, Trans-Species, and Transgender Transformations

In the sixteenth century, clothing was socially and even legally codified, but French agents preferred to see it as indifferent, or *adiaphora*: envelopes for the body to protect itself as needed and to facilitate its movement and orientation toward other things. They accepted changing clothes as convenient because it granted them the privilege of mobility, and they sought to model their identities as French Christian men on other things, especially able and mobile bodies. It is in sartorial terms that Panurge, Rabelais's roguish character, defines the difference between Christian Frenchmen and Muslim Turks in the *Tiers livre* (1546). He praises the *braguette* (the triangular piece of cloth attached to the front of men's hose and called "codpiece" in English) as "the most noble piece of a warrior's armor" and goes on to claim that "the Turks are not properly armed because they are forbidden to wear codpieces by law."[45] This striking claim emasculates the Turks, as Panurge promotes the codpiece as the symbol of masculinity.[46] However, unlike in Rabelais's earlier book *Pantagruel*, Panurge here no longer praises the *braguette* and sheds his own. "Cease the war and let the reign of togas commence!,"[47] declares Panurge, riffing on Cicero. He dons long Roman-style habits to stop being a soldier and ready himself for marriage. Like Panurge, travelers also conceived of dressing in (similarly flowy) Oriental habits as a practical way of conforming to the Ottoman sartorial regime, avoiding conflicts, and symbolizing their cosmopolitan mobility. The long habit was not just a traveler's garb; it embodied an inner habitus in the world, a specific way of being in the body such that one did not have to be too visible or subject to manipulation by others. Nor did one have to be defined by sartorial rules. By changing habits, Panurge essentially declares that masculinity is performative and subject to destabilization. His toga allows him to perform gender in a specific way: within marriage, in a peaceful relation of husband to wife. Unsurprisingly, this performative gesture of taking off the codpiece is followed by anxiety about marriage, which shows that Panurge is not entirely done with his crisis of masculinity. Putting on long habits became a sign of cosmopolitan mobility, a gendered privilege, and a means of both signaling a specific kind of openness toward others who are culturally different and dampening the importance of religious or geographic identity. It also signaled a performance of the self defined as masculine yet androgynous, French yet cosmopolitan. Frenchmen traveling in the Ottoman Empire had to subject themselves to Ottoman laws (including sartorial ones[48]), but they reinterpreted their sartorial transformation as a sign of their autonomy. Belon confirms that traveling alone, in the company of just a dragoman and dressed "in their fashion," renders the trip practicable everywhere except for the deserts and borderlands.[49] If done right, wearing Levantine clothing was inoffensive for the most part precisely because it placed the wearer inside the jurisdiction of the legal, moral, and cultural codes of the Ottoman Empire. Nonetheless, French travelers tended to pass quickly over their own clothed bodies in their writings, for moving around in the Ottoman Empire was a temporary end—and wearing long habits could be seen as scandalous by French readers, many of whom were untouched by the cosmopolitanism that was fashionable at the courts of French and European aristocrats. Long habits indicated agents' movements within spaces that belonged to foreign sovereign powers—following Ottoman laws but serving the French monarch, receiving privileges granted by the capitulation between Suleiman I and Francis I or Henri II, and gaining practical benefits by way of blending in. Clothing was one way of verifying identity in the early modern Mediterranean, and in the Ottoman Empire, distinctions were made among Muslims, "Franks" (Western Christians), and the non-Muslim inhabitants of the Ottoman Empire (including Jews, Orthodox Christians, Roma, etc.).[50] While languages and papers were of little avail, given that so few inhabitants of the Ottoman Empire were familiar with Western European customs, clothes and outer insignia worn on the body were especially important. The agents' willing immersion was not just a pragmatic choice but a conscious rejection of an earlier identification with knightly militantism and crusading. When it comes to clothing as an integument affording protection and allowing for greater mobility and agency, Belon lingers on how some women in the Ottoman Empire also manipulated sartorial rules to their advantage. He explains that Turkish women, whose main occupation is needlework, either sell their products with the help of Jewish women who take them to the marketplace or carry their wares to the market after putting "a veil in front of their face, through which they can see and when they want to speak, they only need to lift the veil as if it were the vizier of a heaume."[51] Belon also describes Turkish women who dress in silk clothes (the most luxurious fabric in the early modern world) but cover them up with a white linen overcoat to obey the law of modesty and roll up or pull up the overclothing to make the silk clothing visible. Thus, even if their sleeves are "tight and long, so that their hands are covered," they can still reveal the luxury textile underneath.[52] Here Belon bends Ottoman social hierarchy to his own use. In Ottoman culture, appearing in public was not only regulated by laws (like the Sharia) but also by a social value system, and elite members of Ottoman society benefited from being able to appear with a retinue or send others instead of them on errands. Leslie Peirce notes, "When men and women of the elites went into public areas, their choice slaves would perform a retinue escorting them, the purpose of which was to broadcast the family's social standing and sometimes its political importance." The designation *muhaddere* (honorable, of sound reputation) did not have to do with following religious laws, but with women not showing themselves publicly to males outside their immediate family, which allowed this social honor to be attained by Jewish and Christian as well Muslim women.[53] Ottomans relied on a retinue of servants, many of them household slaves, to signal their status. Belon comments in particular on those of a lower status who either used surrogates or disguised their identity to gain access to public spaces in an effort to show and protect their status. From his perspective, women have lesser mobility than men, but Turkish women assert their autonomy by relying on servants or surrogates (for example, Jewish women). Agents often looked to examples in social groups outside of the Ottoman male elite as models for their own agency. Beyond the logic of exemplarity and imitation, these models were imbued with the universalized values of mobility, ruse, and transgression, which allowed agents to discern a momentary alliance and commonality with them (even as they understood little of their actual situation). French agents similarly treated themselves as protected and secret, autonomous and yet vulnerable to the gazes to which they were exposed. They also embraced the performative aspects of the self, such as the ambiguities of identity provided by clothing and the exemplary models of agency they collected in the Ottoman Empire. The ease with which they crossed gender lines in their identification bespeaks masculine privilege and a hierarchical relation to less free others. They used the sartorial laws to protect an inner "free" self and used the services of those deemed inferior—fixers, information providers, translators—to the same end. Belon reads the acts of Turkish women as if they were his own doubles, such that their noted use of the veil as a vizier (of a heaume) not only crosses gender boundaries but also reveals the transposition of an embattled identity onto the realm of ruse and clothing in a field of fractured forces and flows, thereby drawing attention to a terrain without a center.

During the time agents were able to change their clothes from the breeches that were customary for men in France to the long robes worn by the Ottomans and enjoy the mobility granted by their openness to changing clothing, they cultivated a sense that the human body was marked by differences in a manner similar to that of animal bodies, which provided a comforting source of identity. One of the agents that, somewhat unusually, acknowledged feeling some anxiety about changing into long, Levantine clothes was the poet Bertrand de la Borderie, who was part of the Baron of Saint-Blancard's mission in the summer of 1537.[54] He documents his trip, especially his impressions of Greece and Constantinople, in his long, erotic-geographic poem addressed to a lady, *Discours du voyage à Constantinoble, envoyé à une damoyselle françoyse* ["The Story of a Voyage to Constantinoble, Epistle Sent to a Young French Lady"] (1542).[55]

Borderie describes his movements in the Ottoman Empire through the poetic simile of a young goshawk ("le jeune Autour") flying away from the nest and continuing "from branch to branch around him" ("de branche en branche tout autour").[56] This erratic flight is disquieting insofar as it gradually distances him from the political center ("the nest") that is the French court and its familiar culture:

> And alone it must learn to fly,
> Alone to eat, alone to find consolation:
> Just as I, young in age and spirit,
> Must err on a long pilgrimage,
> And, far from friends, neighbors, and family,
> Travel in strange-looking lands,
> Forget the forest where I was born,
> And adopt new customs, clothes, and language.[57]

The poem describes the young goshawk leaving its territory, encountering foreign birdsong, and finding it disorienting, just as Borderie finds foreign languages and customs disorienting. While the bird is disoriented by foreign bird song ("ramage"), it is the forest itself, a vertiginous sylvan space of branches that represents the decentered space of the Ottoman Empire, that makes possible its free movement. As a boundless but peaceful realm existing outside of human passions (i.e., political interests), the forest becomes a model for autonomous human action and movement free from the constraints of service—with the implication that the poet's "young spirit" can be tested and mature within it. The image of the Ottoman Empire as a forest becomes more concrete if we recall that the name of the French ambassador who played a capital role in establishing a diplomatic alliance between France and the Ottoman Empire is Jean *de la Forest*. This imaginary sylvan space also symbolizes the French court's justification of its politics of diplomacy and military alliance with the Sublime Porte as a peacemaking mission in the Mediterranean, as is repeatedly broadcast by Borderie in the poem.[58]

The vertigo and disorientation caused by both the sylvan space and the encounter with foreign languages and customs are interrupted by a beneficial turn of events in the appearance of Ottoman travelers who look at Borderie and whose recognition of his foreignness lead him to a reaffirmation of the humoral, animal certainty of the self. While describing a voyage alone with two janissaries and a translator by land toward Constantinople, Borderie describes encountering foreign villages, small towns, and Ottoman travelers:

> Different habitations, towns, and villages,
> Unknown places, appear in front of our eyes ("s'offrent à noz visages"):

Voyaging Turks recognize and feel well
That, to judge from my face ("me voir à ma mine"),
I am not of their kind ("de leur naturelle origine").
They understand well that the costume that I wear
With my heart does not agree.⁵⁹

Deprived of the familiar breeches and other external markers of an emerging national and cultural identity,⁶⁰ the poet can nonetheless derive relief from being looked at by others that are different from him because his face reveals to them his "true" self. Yet this true self (the heart, the interior) is dependent on the exterior. Although the foreign language(s) and clothes may make the poet feel disoriented, the gaze of others and his face as seen by these others allows Borderie to feel more comfortable in his skin. The term "face" or "facial features" ("mine") is etymologically linked to a bird's beak and is conceptualized as a hardening or solidification of the humors of the body according to Galenic science (similar to the skin and other natural protective layers of human and animal bodies). The beak also takes on a taxonomic or signifying function in the breeding and observation of birds. In *L'histoire des oyseaux*, Belon notes the cosmopolitan nature of the goshawk, referencing "certain books of falconry" to suggest that Persian goshawks are superior to those from Greece, while the poorest performers are those that hail from Africa. He explains, too, that most goshawks in France come from either the forests in Germany or the forest of Ardennes in contemporary Belgium (see Figure 7). As a foreign "Bird-Man," Borderie feels best when he is conscious of being behind the hardened humoral skin that gives him a separate identity as he enters the culturally foreign space of Thrace. This metaphor of hardened, no longer fluid skin saves his self from merging with the new environment while allowing the poet to look at the things around him as he goes from "branch to branch." It is not by accident that Rabelais's character Panurge is described as birdlike; he has a "slightly aquiline nose" that is small and curved like an eagle's beak and reveals his keen sense for prey.⁶¹ The natural, humoral distinction manifested in the face and nose (or beak) becomes the natural site of difference and also of a pedigree, as the aquiline nose, attributed by the Hellenist essayist Plutarch to Marc Antony, was emerging as the mark of Europeanness.⁶² It serves as a shield to protect the self and a protrusion to indicate an orientation toward non-French and non-European others.

Borderie's poem indicates that French agents thought about the skin as the natural envelope of the body (analogously to clothes), which made possible their immersion in the culture of the baths of the Ottoman Empire. Bathing in public baths challenged accepted views of the vulnerability of the skin in Aristotelian physics and Galenic medicine, as well as in the medicine of medieval through

> DES OYSEAVX, PAR P. BELON. III
>
> pont est cy faicte mention. Il est frequent en Egypte : mais rare ailleurs. Car mes-
> memét lon n'en voit aussi bien peu en Syrië. Vray est qu'en auons aussi veu iusques
> en Caramanië, qui toutesfois nous sembla chose rare:desquels en auôs obserué de
> diuerses couleurs. Laurêt Valle traduisant Herodote l'à nommé en Latin Accipi-
> ter Aegyptius, du Grec Hierax d'Herodote: car au douziesme liure en Euterpe dit,
> que quiconques tuoit Ibis, & le Sacre Egyptien, encores qu'il ne le pensast faire, la   *Loy d'E-*
> loy par necesité le condamnoit à mourir. Et pour entendre la raison, fault sça-   *gypte con-*
> *tre ceux*
> *qui tuoyët*
>   *Hierax en Grec, Accipiter Aegyptini en Latin,*   *l'Ibis, ou*
>   *Sacre d'Egypte en Francoys.*   *le Sacre :*
> *& la rai-*
> *son de la*
> *loy.*
>
> uoir qu'il mâge les Serpêts d'Egypte. Parquoy quand ils en trouuoyent vn mort,
> comme aussi vn Ibis, ils auoyent soing de le mettre en sepulture, & le confire, tout
> ainsi côme ils faisoyent plusieurs autres bestes qu'ils auoyent en reueréce, & prin-
> cipalement celles qui estoyent dediees à quelque Dieu. Si aucun en veult sçauoir
> la maniere, lise ce qu'en auons escrit en vn liure intitulé *De seruato funere*, ou *De*
> *medicato cadauere.*
>
> Iz iiii

Figure 7

seventeenth-century Europe.[63] It was ill-viewed in France but commonly practiced in Switzerland, Germany, the Mediterranean, and Northern Europe. According to early modern science, the role of clothing was to cover and protect the body from the weather, hot or cold, and from other substances that were able to penetrate it. Throughout this long period in which knowledge about the body was defined by humoral medicine, the skin was seen as a porous envelope that held together the otherwise squishy internal organs and guaranteed the wholeness of the body without actually being part of it—similar to a fishing net holding the catch, an image that was popularized by Plato. Before the eighteenth century, the skin was considered a non-organ, an ambiguous but permeable boundary of the body. It was seen to operate as part of an open system in which fluids move through envelopes, both around the organs and around the body, in a nested way to lose or gain balance. As the first line of defense, it became the figure of "self-possession" and carried the danger of invasion or disease. It was a system in which purgation was to be done carefully and closure was always recommended to achieve stability, wholeness, and health. Humoral medicine, starting with Hippocrates, continuing with Galen, and developing throughout the Middle Ages and the early modern period, saw the skin as an indicator—the original meaning of "complexion," literally a weaving together of humors—of the humoral makeup of the body. Later, from the mid-sixteenth century onward, the English word "complexion" began to denote the skin or appearance as an indicator of the overall health of the body as well as, sometimes, its internal (i.e., moral) qualities. Although they represented a dangerous invasion of the body's porous barrier, the baths in the Ottoman Empire incited a great deal of interest among travelers. This enthusiasm was largely because the travelers saw them as vestiges of ancient Roman and Greek culture, but it was also because bathing produced sensations of pleasure in the body's protective layer of skin. For example, Belon makes an exception from his generally pejorative depictions of Ottoman culture to observe that it is the bathing culture of the Turks, more than any other nation, that best resembles that of the ancient Greeks and Romans (Belon puts the Germans and the Swiss second place). In their descriptions of the men's baths, French agents like André Thevet and Belon overlook the specific Islamic call for cleanliness that defined the hammams they attended (as is evidenced by the lack of pools, for example)[64] and largely fail to note that these are sites governed by both civil and religious laws.[65] In their accounts of such scenes, agents anchor their experiences in the Roman culture of bathing. They emphasize the foreignness of the skin as the outer shell of the body that is ready to be put to the test: to suffer a direct, albeit playful and pleasurable, attack at the hands of the bath slaves. The removal of hair, the trimming of the beard, and the depilation of the private parts help create a smooth skin that can withstand the onslaught of massaging, scrubbing, grating, and shaving. The beard is not removed, but trimmed, being a sign of masculinity in both the Ottoman Empire and France. While Belon makes sure that the bathing men, in their passivity, do not surrender their private parts ("les parties honteuses") to the manipulations of the male slaves, Thevet's image suggests that bathing is a pleasant experience—but that there is also potential danger that lurks in the surrender. A woodcut image in Thevet's *Cosmographie de Levant* (1544) depicts the men's baths in Tripoli, Lebanon, and shows men's languishing, powerless bodies handled and ushered through curtains and half-closed doors by vigorous servants (see Figure 8). Belon lingers on the bath slave's invigorating pressures

194   COSMOGRAPHIE

de Hongrie, de Transsiluanie & d'Afrique) qui soient de resistence : si que toute sa puissance ne consiste qu'en grand nombre de soudars, encores mal duits & tres mal propres aus armes. Mais vrayment ce que ie trouue beau, & de fort bonne grace dens Tripoli , & par toutes autres viles & bourgades de Turquie , ce sont les Beins grans & spacieus , la plus

part

Figure 8

on the body, especially the muscles. He describes the first part of bathing as a playful wrestling match, which reaffirms the body's strength by putting it to the test. Bathing is a pleasure that also assures the boundaries of the self as body, and these boundaries are not hard and defensive (closing the pores), but soft and hedonistic.

In *De la Republique des Turcs* (1560), Guillaume Postel, the most enthusiastic reviewer of Turkish baths, describes bathing as the pleasant experience of abandoning oneself to the "attack" on the body and skin that is carried out by the *kesici*, the washer:

> First arrives a large-bodied valet who makes you lie down on the floor and works all your limbs, rubbing all your muscles so well, cracking all your joints, so that I believe that if someone has the worst possible exhaustion, he would be cured, and I believe that the reason for this massage is the fact that Turks sleep on hard surfaces. Once you have been well rubbed and you have sweated to your contentment, your companion attacks you with a piece of cotton canvas, cloth, or serge folded up, instead of the *strigil* ("étrille") of the ancients, scrubbing and cleaning your body in a wonderous fashion. Then you are lathered with the use of [soap and] clear water, you lie down in a stone basin with two faucets of cold and hot water, which you mix and temper to your pleasure in a handsome silver bowl, from which you pour the water on your body as you wish. Then comes the pumice stone for scrubbing the bottoms of your feet. The beard, the hair, including in your armpits, are well scrubbed. For below, they give you a razor or a potion ("philotre") which epilates the area in an instant, and you apply an ointment to prevent it from burning the skin ("de peur qu'il ne s'ecorche").[66]

Postel's description seems to hover between the personal and the impersonal. It carefully combines references to the invigorating experience of bathing with references to the "tempered" quality of the bath; the water is neither too hot nor too cold, and the skin is both scrubbed and merely imbued with the depilatory cream, suggesting that a dangerous attack on the skin has been averted. Postel mentions that the use of the depilatory cream carries with it the risk of burning the skin. The verb *écorcher* refers to vegetal tegument—that is, *écorce* (bark, peel)—and suggests the lurking danger that the container that keeps the body whole could be eaten away if the depilatory substance stayed on for too long. While Postel evokes this danger, he does so to put the reader at ease. The passive abandonment to the virile "attack" itself becomes a form of access to a pleasure in which the self is reborn. Belon and Thevet describe bathing as a vigorous exercise that requires a measure of resistance. They use bathing to describe a phenomenology of the masculine, cosmopolitan self, constituted through experiences of risk and the institution of boundaries at the same time. This desire is both transgressive and liberating with respect to French and Christian norms, thereby enabling fantasies of a hegemonic French Christian "common good": a sweetness and a pleasure with material, utopian, and imperial dimensions.

Postel evokes the time of de la Forest's embassy in Constantinople in the winter of 1535 to 1536 and describes his pleasant experiences sharing meals with different members of Ottoman society.[67] These pleasures are unique to Postel, who was a humanist, a self-taught Orientalist and Christian Kabbalist, and an unparalleled speculative visionary in an era that had no shortage of self-appointed visionaries. He was born, in the village La Dolérie in Normandy, into poverty, which was exacerbated by the loss of his parents to the plague at the age of eight. Forced to work as a preceptor, agricultural worker, and domestic servant at the Collège Saint Barbe in Paris in his youth, he nonetheless studied voraciously; so much so that, according to his own autobiographic accounts, he often forgot to eat while studying. His modern editor, Jacques Rollet, interprets this bulimic desire for books as a way of purging the self through consuming knowledge and confusing the father (especially the spiritual one) with sustenance.[68] Postel learned Hebrew from a Portuguese Jew in Paris, studied with clandestine and syncretic Islamic prophets in the Ottoman Empire, and was inspired by visionaries in Venice, where he spent two-and-a-half years from late 1546 to the summer of 1549. By virtue of his characteristic "dualism" (as described by his intellectual biographer William Bouwsma), Postel could privilege both doctrines of Roman Catholicism and mystical thinking originating in different traditions such as the Kabbalah, Christian Churches in Asia, Islamic mysticism,[69] and female mysticism. It was during his second stay in Venice that Postel, who became an ordained priest in Rome in 1544, came to identify a fifty-year-old female visionary named Mother Giovanna (or Jeanne) as his spiritual leader, accepting her as the Messiah and Jesus Christ come again in a female body and seeing her as a "substantial" Second Eve made from Christ's actual flesh. Following her death ca. 1551, Postel claimed to be her reincarnation or "substantial son," born of Giovanna and her mystical spouse, Jesus, identical to them in the flesh—but without the divine nature. According to Postel's Joachimite messianic theology, Giovanna embodied Jesus's "inferior," "feminine" half, the *animus* and *anima* (but not *mens* and *spiritus* in theological terms). As with many religious leaders from humble backgrounds who followed self-appointed missions, Postel was not only a scholar; he also sought to transform society. He wanted to create a utopian

Christian empire composed of eclectic pieces from Eastern Christianity, Judaism, mysticism, and Islam that transcended the order of the Ottoman Empire but that also, ultimately, did not fit well with French and European institutions and political realities.[70] Like the Jesuits (by whom he was rejected), Postel extended ecclesiastical concerns to the scale of the entire known world. Islam, and the territories under Islamic rule, held strategic importance in his vision, as he believed that Islam was instrumental in achieving world peace. Ultimately, Postel also relied on the Western tradition of studying Islam that was initiated in the Middle Ages, which often made it into an object of knowledge by reducing it to generalizing stereotypes. Postel cites the derisive biographies of the Prophet and mocks citations of hadiths, sayings attributed to Muhammad or his followers.[71] The French court sent Postel along to accompany de la Forest, who was to negotiate the first joint Franco-Ottoman military campaign of 1537 and conclude the first official treaty in 1536. Postel returned to the Levant in 1549 on a pilgrim ship, looking for manuscripts, including Arabic and Aramaic translations of the New Testament and the Kabbalah, and planning to work on an Arabic translation of the Bible. His book on the Ottoman Empire, *De la Republique des Turcs*, presents events from both trips as well as Postel's unorthodox spiritual views. Despite his search through various parts of the world, Postel does not fully fit the melancholic mold of Western masculinity analyzed by Michel de Certeau, for he finds the utopian father in the flesh, and the female or androgynous flesh at that.[72] Like Belon, Postel uses pleasure to create or claim access to a visionary community.

The pleasures coalesce around events of eating and sharing meals, including a wedding banquet in Istanbul, the official reception of de la Forest's French embassy at the Sublime Porte, and the hospitality of semi-nomadic people in Anatolia. Postel describes the banquet at the men's quarters during a wedding ceremony as a sensory feast, during which nonnormative gendering allows him to experience pleasure and feel at home within the visionary no-place of his utopia. He calls the music of the harp players "sweet" ("douce") and palatable. He describes the dance of the *köçek*, or dancing boys dressed as girls ("hommes-femmes"), and the *çengī*, or harp players: young girls hired to play music and dance at private banquets.[73] The boy-girl dancers and the girl harp players are both androgynous in Postel's description, and his account focuses on the sweetness of the ambivalent gender of the *çengī*:

> ... the tallest and most beautiful one [of the *çengī*] stands up to dance in their manner, taking off her ("son") headscarf and gold bonnet, and picks up a turban, which is a headpiece for men, and then gestures, without words, representing the emotions of love so vividly

that describing it to men who cannot see it would excite more desire than pleasure.⁷⁴

Postel describes the tantalizing, erotic dance of the *çengī*, who takes on the role of the young male seducer, inviting men with her/their gaze and a handkerchief to dance, while another *çengī* kneels on the floor, beats the rhythm with her/their knees, and plays the harp placed between the thighs. The body is revealed here to be supple (in ways that are both acrobatic and erotic), and the performance is gender bending, not only an object of desire but also a means of acting out desire. Postel also wonders whether women enjoy a similar festivity in their separate quarters and guesses, from hearsay, that they do. Postel's interpretation of this sonorous and visual feast does not fully coincide with the patriarchal erotic culture described by Andrews and Kalpaklı as a binary culture of active and passive sexual roles,⁷⁵ in which the active role always falls to adult men while the passive role can be given to women as well as young men. Instead of seeing them as passive objects of sexual desire, Postel is fascinated by the androgyny of the dancers, and he finds sweetness in the experience that defies the binary of active and passive roles that was the norm in Ottoman and European erotic cultures alike. According to his messianic theology, the female Messiah, representing the lower part of Christ (animus/anima), the sinful flesh, was necessary for redemption, as was the union of this female Messiah with Christ. It was a process of exchanging souls, a "spiritual alchemy" that began with Jesus and Giovanna, and was then to be extended to all of mankind, starting with Postel as the first to be transformed.⁷⁶ Thus the spiritual regeneration of mankind was to continue — and, ultimately, this was the new universal community described by Postel in the Preface to *De la Republique des Turcs*, which was addressed to the French king Henri II to appeal for his patronage and support.

When looking at the *köçek* or "hommes-femmes" and the acrobatic, strong, and supple *çengī*, Postel has recourse to a spiritual countertradition that valorizes nonbinary sex as a divine and human ideal. This tradition includes the idea of an androgyne Adam, which attributes a state of undifferentiation as a sign of spiritual purity to the first man of the Scriptures.⁷⁷ Recognized similarly was the "alchemical Jesus" of the Renaissance, believed to be capable of transformation as well as transmuting objects, and the mystical dual gender of God that Postel discovered in the person of Mother Giovanna and also in the *Zohar*, a Hebrew manuscript that he obtained from the Venetian editor Daniel Bomberg.⁷⁸ Postel, much like other Christian Kabbalists, starting with Giovanni Pico della Mirandola, believed that the Kabbalah was entirely congruous with Christian teachings. It is this transgender identity of the divine (and ultimately of Postel himself) that Postel rediscovers, using his "kabbalistic speculative creativity,"[79] when editing his memoirs about the Ottoman Empire.[80] Postel presents androgynous Turks, if not as successive reincarnations of Christ, definitely as intimations of the Restitution (that is, the return of Christ in the flesh) through transformations that usher in a new Christian empire, all the while pandering to the ambitions of the French court. Postel's pleasure in the consumption of melodious sounds and the visual sight of the dancers thus also presents a glimpse into a spiritual utopia. This gentleness, for him, is the hallmark of the divine—but it is also pleasant and seductive to the "flesh." However, this utopian moment and other similar ones occur in concrete places and situations in which Postel engages in a gentle movement: one that generates pleasure and desire and eschews violence with the Ottomans, all the while linking the gentleness and sweetness that he finds in the Ottoman Empire with fantasies of empire and domination. Postel is often praised for being the traveler who speaks out about the values of civilization and culture in the Ottoman Empire; for being the traveler who respects what he sees as the civilized elements of the Ottoman Empire. And this recognition of the civilization and gentleness of the other, including the sweetness of the sounds of the banquet and the orderliness and tastiness of the food, comes with potential for both him and a French Empire. Anne Dufourmantelle analyzes the etymology of the French word *douceur* (sweetness, gentleness) by relating it first to the Greek word *proates*, which means "gentleness" or "kindness" and evokes in St. Paul the "spirit of gentleness" necessary for the establishment of community and, secondly, to the paired Greek word *praos*, meaning "good-naturedness." She links it, too, to the three Latin words *mites* (good-naturedness, meekness, fertility of the earth, ripeness, and tenderness for fruit), *suavitas* (intellectual or spiritual gentleness), and *dulcis* (melodiousness of sound, beauty of a thing, and sweetness of food). Gentleness implies a delicate dance with the presumed animality of the other, in which both parties are capable of gentleness.[81] In Greek and Latin culture, gentleness is strongly associated with living together, and hence with politics and community. It is also associated with civilization as that which tempers, and it is opposed to the fierceness and cruelty required of warfare. Postel thought of himself as the embodiment of Christian tradition, and those people and experiences he considers pleasant or "sweet" in the Ottoman Empire, similarly to Rabelais's sated Canarrians, constitute intimations of a Christian society to come in accordance with Postel's own Christian-Kabbalist creative speculations.

While Postel's visionary experiences with the Ottomans reveal his strong propensity to "read[] his whim into reality,"[82] he did not find all social contexts in the Ottoman Empire to correspond to his spiritual vision; nor, for that matter, to his whim. After describing the scene of the wedding banquet, Postel transitions to the official reception of the French embassy at the Sublime Porte.[83] Here, the quantity of meat served with rice in countless porcelain plates, the clothes worn by Suleiman I's court, the discipline exhibited by the Ottomans (the motionless standing of guards despite the great cold), and the effectiveness of the supervision make it a magnificent event, the image of imperial order, even if it deviates from French customs. However, on one point, Postel's description is telling. While the retinue of the French ambassador, seated at low tables separate from the ones where members of the Sublime Porte are seated, can enjoy the meats (mutton and poultry) even though the table is laid on the ground and set with wooden spoons instead of silverware, they declare themselves unable to eat the sweets unless wine is also served alongside. Wine, and the trouble of not having it with the meal, marks the religious and cultural difference of the French, for whom wine is of spiritual significance. It serves as a cultural boundary separating Christian and Muslim, French and Ottoman, selves, such that the lack of wine results in a kind of spiritual indigestion and the failure of tasting sweetness.

As Postel sees and amply explains in *De la Republique des Turcs*, Islam is a bad, corrupt law, which nonetheless allows for some precepts or doctrines of the true religion to be preserved in parts of Asia, Africa, and Southern Europe. The indigestion described by Postel associates Islam with illness despite the orderliness he also observes. In twelfth-century Europe, Islam was spiritualized at much the same time as it was maligned as a heresy, and the Prophet Muhammad was depicted as a trickster who used magic and deception to carry out miracles. Postel cites many of these stories that were circulating in medieval Europe, which attributed animality and deceitfulness to the Prophet, along with illness (epilepsy) and addiction (drunkenness). This imperial model of incorporation (with the "good" empire of the Valois king incorporating the "bad" law of Islam, alongside those of other civilizations and cultures outside of Christianity) defines Postel's imperialist imaginary.[84] The psychosomatic indigestion caused by the lack of wine is counterbalanced by Postel's great enjoyment of the rest of the meal, the orderliness of which proves to be the counterpart of the previous banquet: a desire to return to lawfulness and order, a total empire.

In a third instance of sharing food, the Anatolian house at which Postel stays during his travels becomes the site of an encounter that symbolizes this utopian experience of leveling differences:

> When I was traveling in Anatolia and I was forced to linger at my dwelling for a long time because of a storm, these Turks came into my tent, just as confidently as they would have gone into theirs, and without

saying anything except for *salem alec* [sic], "God protect you," they sat down or came up to the fire. Being shocked by this familiarity, I asked them *me sizumedat sugle varmec dahe evea, bouguzel ioctur* [sic], which is to say, "What kind of custom is yours, to enter in this way in strange houses?" They all responded to me by saying: *Corcma cardasch, bisum edat suyle varbiz bizdam corcmessis* [sic], which is to say, "my friend, or, my brother, don't be afraid. Our custom is such: we are not afraid of one another."[85]

Postel attributes the custom of hospitality to these Anatolian people, distinguishing between poorer "simple" Turks and the Ottoman elite, the overwhelming majority of which were not born as Turks and were educated in Ottoman culture, a sophisticated amalgam of Turkish, Persian, and Arabic that was most likely out of Postel's comprehension. Much like other agents, notably Belon and Rabelais's fictional Pantagruel, Postel finds that the people on the margins of Ottoman society are more "like" him. The simple Turk in his everyday life also corresponds to the androgynous gendering, evinced by the wearing of long unisex costumes, that Postel favors and that takes on a meaning within his own visionary theology:

> Now whoever wants safely to converse with them must first put on a long habit, of any color, in the manner of the country, then an adventurer's hat ("un bonnet dasap ou auanturier"), which is a tall hat made of wool, with earflaps cut on the sides so that they hang down to the shoulders, which both Turks and Christians, indifferently, are allowed to wear. Then let him travel over the country, if he can speak Slav, or Greek, or Turkish—for these languages are the ones spoken in all of Turkey until Karaman or Silicia, where people begin to speak Arabic dialects, while Classical Arabic is understood in all of Turkey, Tartary, Persia, Syria, Egypt, Barbary, and India because of the tradition of the Quran and Islamic law in these regions.[86]

Postel recommends the long habit, which, as he notes elsewhere, is unisex—both men and women wear loose, long habits and ankle boots[87]—and a nondescript hat worn by Turks as well as by foreigners. Postel goes on to sharpen the satirizing power of simply clothed Turks by explaining that "they especially distrust codpieces" because of their jealousy in thinking that "such a great stable houses a great horse."[88] Postel reminds his readers of the boundaries of the Anatolian male self and uses it to debunk French performances of masculinity, playing one masculinity out against another to relativize the power of the latter, familiar French one. The male traveler who gives up Western-style clothes disarms the competitive masculinity ("jealousy") of the Turkish men.

It is also to be noted that Postel calls the chastity belt worn by women in Turkey a *braguette* (the same word as "codpiece" in French). The notion of competitive masculinity is complemented by the image of female desire that requires male mastery (by way of the chastity belt), yet that remains in competition with it.[89] He reports that these "simple Turks" wear the same simple clothing for a long time and make fun of Europeans for changing their clothes often and for tearing them up once they are bored with them, calling them "foolish and cantankerous" ("*dely & maschara*: qui est a dire fols & acariastres").[90] This reversal of roles from the perspective of the "simple Turk" reflects Postel's actual position: his precarious status and his elevation from deep poverty to the standing of a learned humanist and an agent of the monarch, combined with his audacious attempts to shock and self-aggrandize, which led several times to his falling from the graces of the French monarch and to condemnations that he only narrowly escaped. In emphasizing his own familiarity with the world of semi-nomadic Anatolians, Postel presents himself as a seasoned traveler who is not so far from the "salt-herring" exemplified by Panurge, looking to assert his own status through his familiarity with strangers. His editor in Basel, Jean Oporin (aka Johannes Herbst), called Postel a "Ulysses polytropos."[91] The sympathetic description of Anatolian culture evokes, in a nutshell, Postel's grand project of universal concord. This was first presented in his book *De Orbis terrae concordia* (first published in Basel in 1543), which delegates to the French monarch the task of conquering the Holy Land and converting the Islamic inhabitants to Christianity. Like Rabelais's Utopia, Postel's spiritual empire was made with the help of ruses of the affective kind and rooted in the ability to find common cause with others. Furthermore, like Rabelais's fictional kingdoms, his imperial fantasies similarly failed to coincide with the political calculations of church and state.

Carla Freccero remarks that Panurge embodies queerness through his deviations from paternalist norms, which transpired alongside his conformism to cosmopolitanism, or moral imperialism.[92] These wayward movements, much like Postel's messianic visions, offer us a glimpse into queer utopias that were never fully claimed as such. Rabelais and Postel, in particular, create utopias that were indefinite, impossible, and infinitely delayed.[93] These utopias were created through species-based and cultural boundary crossings as well as scandalous performances of agencies that, while pandering to royal visions and ambitions, also represented deviations from the monarchy's law and order. At the same time, they also projected spiritual transformations that elevated a French and cosmopolitan agency above the fray of projected flows and forces in a fractured and decentered *physis*.

3
Snake Women of the East: Staging Freedom and Invisible Unfreedoms

" ... of the entire Orient, the captive remains" ("les despouilles captives")."

—JOACHIM DU BELLAY

The humanist lawyer Étienne Pasquier (1529–1615) describes the enthrallment of the audience when *Cléopâtre captive*, a tragedy about the death of the legendary Egyptian queen, was performed "to an applauding audience" at the Collège de Boncourt in February 1553.[1] Situated in the current 5th arrondissement in modern Paris, the college was an elite center of humanist learning, with the renowned classicist Marc-Antoine Muret (1526–1585) just one among its many esteemed teachers. Pasquier gives a brief eyewitness account of the event. The courtyard of the college was so filled with students that the doors could not be closed and "all the balconies were lined with ("tapissees") a great number of persons of honor."[2] Pasquier's description of this enclosed theatrical space momentarily turns the spotlight on the spectators. The metaphor he uses reminds us of literal tapestries—elaborate textile objects used by French aristocrats to keep their homes warm, draw attention to their wealth and status, and serve as conversation pieces among guests regarding mythological and historical scenarios. The viewers of this play, in their isolation from the outside, also felt socially and personally elevated by the dramatic action on the stage. Pasquier, who was sitting upstairs among the "persons of honor" next to the Hellenist Adrianus Turnebus (1512–1565), was fully conscious that viewing this play was equal to participating in a remarkable social event, one that conferred honor onto him as if he were a personage in a tapestry. While the enjoyment of art in Renaissance France always confirmed the privileged status of those who had access to it (that is, educated or wealthy men), this particular play also promoted the agency of its author, Étienne Jodelle (1532–1573), and two poets who played parts within it, Remy Belleau and Jean de la Péruse. These were members of the group of erudite artists that gathered around the Hellenist Jean Dorat (1508–1588) and called themselves the *Pléiade*, after the group of ancient Alexandrian poets and the star cluster of the same name. The performance at the Collège de Boncourt, as described by Pasquier, was the second one, the first having taken place a few weeks earlier in front of the royal court at the Hôtel de Reims (the archbishopric seat of the Lorraine family) with King Henri II and members of his court present. The occasion for the play was the victory of the French army at Metz, a free imperial city. (François Rabelais spent some time there in exile between 1545 and 1547). Metz was ruled by the Protestant Schmalkaldic League and granted to Henri II by the Treaty of Chambord, which was accorded between Henri II and Prince Maurice of Saxony in January 1552. An imperial siege followed in the fall and, one unforgivingly cold winter, the city was successfully defended by the French army led by François de Lorraine II, Duke of Guise (1519–1563).[3] The play does not directly honor the Duke of Guise in its commemoration of the French victory (although he did become a national hero after the siege), but it does celebrate the last ruler of the Ptolemaic dynasty, after whose death Egypt became a province of the Roman Empire. The double performance of *Cléopâtre captive* is telling: The play serves two agendas that, if not antithetical, certainly differ from one another. On the one hand, it aims to project the image of a powerful French monarchy as a defeater of empires—and, on the other, it aims to celebrate the power of artists and foreigners, or artists *as* foreigners. The play turns its attention to Egypt, with whose Mamluk rulers France maintained trade relations throughout the late Middle Ages and that, as a result of the French crown's diplomacy at the Sublime Porte in the sixteenth century, also became the destination of French explorers who traveled on political missions. *Cléopâtre captive* was not just the first classical tragedy in France, as it was praised to be by Jodelle's friend and posthumous editor, Charles de la Mothe; it was also the first Orientalist one. As such, the play does not only represent an imaginary Orient, but it also orients the viewers toward this Orient in the phenomenological sense proposed by Sara Ahmed—that is, as a point of *orientation* for desire. The captive Cleopatra becomes an object toward which French male artists, who operate in a clientele relation with the ruling elite, orient themselves—and, in doing so, these subjects become extended and are made able to do things: "It is the fact that what I am oriented toward is 'not me' that allows me to do this or to do that."[4] In this chapter, I argue that, as a text and a performance, *Cléopâtre captive* continues to tie agency to the humoral body and its actions through ritualized mourning, while also tying an ambiguous animality to race. I use this double schema to carve out an interpretation for what it means to extend one's self and agency by means of strangers in sixteenth-century French theater. I focus on mourning as the most important occult practice, presenting it as both alchemy and magic that use the natural body and give Cleopatra (and, through her, the poet himself) a dangerous, animal, snake-like body and agency in her death. Cleopatra is also whitened as a result of the theatrical performance and serves as a contrast to the dark skin color that is associated with the Orient and North Africa. *Cléopâtre captive* and *Médée*—a second Orientalist play written by Jodelle's friend and fellow Pléiade poet, de la Péruse, who died prematurely soon after *Médée* debuted in 1553—focus on the serpentine powers of two Oriental women who use magic and humoral alchemy to assert their agency and freedom. By elevating the Orient to a power derived from the animality of the *physis*, from pagan animal gods, magic, and the humoral female body, Orientalist theater also places the East, nature, women, non-Europeans, non-Christians, people of color, and unfree people in the place of the invisible and mute, such that they are revealed only to privileged viewers (like Pasquier) in their theaters of the self thanks to French poets and artists. These plays make slavery and unfree persons into a spectacle circulating among viewers—and, with the help of objects (maybe also persons), allow audiences to consider that they have "captured" such racialized bodies. An examination of *Cléopâtre captive* and *Médée* thus allows me to explore the conditions under which unfree people and racialized foreigners were made visible in sixteenth-century theater and court ceremonies.

Humoral Alchemy and Male Becomings

Jodelle's play takes place after Octavian has defeated Antony and Cleopatra's joint fleet at Actium (31 BCE), at the point where the Egyptian queen has become the Roman Octavian's prisoner of war and he has plans to take her with him to Rome as his "trophy." Jodelle based the play on the "Life of Antony," written ca. 75 CE by Plutarch, a Greek author who lived in the empire established by Octavian.[5] Plutarch tells Antony's story as a cautionary tale about a great leader who lost an empire to a younger and less powerful male rival because of his many rash decisions, including those that he made prompted by his passion for Cleopatra. He narrates the power of Cleopatra's sexual charms in separating him from both his wife and his Roman allies, as well as her ill advice to Antony about fighting Octavian at sea, her betrayal of him by sending her own fleet away in the heat of the naval battle, her feigning to commit suicide, her hiding in a "monument" where she lifts up the dying Antony through a high window, her contrite behavior, her negotiations with Octavian and his two men, Proculeus and Cornelius Dolabella, her mourning of Antony, and her mysterious death. Jodelle draws upon these narrative elements in Plutarch, but he also modifies the story a great deal. Instead of focusing on Antony's deeds, the playwright changes Cleopatra's actions in the last days leading up to her death, intensifying her mourning and adding references to Greek and Egyptian religion and magic. While, for Plutarch, Cleopatra is a willing accessory to and enabler of Antony's bad decisions that lead to his demise, Jodelle sets up a rivalry between Octavian ("Octavien"), who desires to possess the vanquished Cleopatra ("Cleopatre") and regards her as his trophy, and the vanquished queen herself, who foils this desire by bringing about her own death by means of her passions and her own body. Rather than using snake poison to commit suicide, Cleopatra, in her defiance, *becomes* snakelike. Unlike in Plutarch, Cleopatra's power in Jodelle's play does not stem from her erotic appeal but rather from her humoral body, her performance of mourning, and her rebellious desire for freedom. It is in her death, which occurs mysteriously in her royal chamber, that Cleopatra acquires her final agency to thwart Octavian's power. Plutarch's historical account thus becomes a play in which the queen (as the physical substitute for the artist, the poet, in the play) is brought to (a stage in) France, where her feminine body (gendered through acts of mourning and crying that also weaken and whiten her) and her power to resist Octavian are acted out by men to mostly male audiences. Finally, Cleopatra's monument (or pyramid) becomes the enclosed space of the body with small openings for spirits, as well as the theater space in which self and other are tied in a solipsistic bind.

The play goes as follows. Act 1 opens in the aftermath of the battle of Actium with a monologue by the dead Antony's "shadow," who describes Cleopatra as a dangerous seductress. Antony relates that he has been seduced by Cleopatra, who used "fascination," a specific form of magic described by Marsilo Ficino,[6] to cause him to abandon his wife, his children, and the Empire. Antony predicts that, by the end of the day, Cleopatra will die because he had appeared to her in a dream and bid her to pour libations on his sepulcher and then bring about her own death. In Act 2, Octavian converses with two advisors, Proculeus ("Proculée") and Agrippa ("Agrippe"). Octavian declares his ambition to extend his rule over the entire globe and become one of the gods. To this end, he intends to take the captive Cleopatra to Rome. Proculeus warns him that this may be difficult, since he had succeeded in secretly entering Cleopatra's palace to spy on her and had found her defiant. Agrippa advises Octavian to have Cleopatra closely watched ("watch her closely, sound her out, visit her, spy on her, and work her") and reminds him of her dangerous political power and her many allies, but Octavian swears to "wipe out" Cleopatra's "desire to kill herself" ("son desire de la mort effacer").[7] In Act 3, Cleopatra continues to plead her case as a "feeble woman" who has lost everything and will find her vindication in "pale death":

> Pale death ("palle mort") will restore my right,
> And soon Pluto will open his residence to me.[8]

At the end of Act 4, the mourning Cleopatra departs from the scene—"With sadness, she departs to see the burial vault ("des sepulchres le clos")"—to perform Antony's funeral.[9] Cleopatra's last verses are a long complaint addressed to Antony in which she vows that, even though she is being held captive, she will "reverse" Octavian's "triumph" over both of them by preventing him from "embellishing" his triumph with their bodies.[10] She also claims that she will confer honor on Egypt by ensuring that her remains will be laid down together with Antony's in a sepulcher that "one day, Egypt will honor."[11] In Act 5, Proculeus, arriving on the scene after her death, is unable to discern the cause. In anticipation of the rules of classical tragedy, Proculeus narrates that he came to calm Cleopatra down but found the guards in front of her chamber first knocking at her door, and then breaking into her locked chamber—where he saw, to his great terror, Cleopatra's dead body "in her royal clothes" accompanied by one dead and one dying servant. Proculeus is stunned by "the concealed courage" of the three women and the power of the "female rage" capable of contravening imperial power like "giant snakes" ("géantes serpetines").[12] Proculeus closes the play in despair about his inability to report to Octavian the cause of her death, to which Cleopatra's pale dead body "without a mark" offers no clue, and he is left speculating that it was "perhaps by the bite of some asp." He is, of course, wrong.

Cleopatra's lamentation and tears constitute a powerful excess of passions that is capable, among other things, of bringing about her death. She leads her women-in-waiting bewailing her own impending death:

> Let us go, dear sisters: let us weaken ourselves ("nous afoiblir")
> Through wails, cries, and tears ("de pleurs, de cris, de larmes") so that through these
> Violent passions ("en ses alarmes") death, so close to us, become less harsh for us,
> Since we will have already half-opened our body for spirits to escape.[13]

The clue to Jodelle's convoluted, perplexing plot is Cleopatra's crying, which literally renders her body porous, recalling the designation of women as leaky vessels in medieval and early modern physiological descriptions. This performance of mourning amounts to a kind of alchemy as, through her tears, her vital spirits leave the humoral body, and she undergoes a significant change in which she weakens, becomes pallid, and eventually dies. Jodelle thus makes Cleopatra change charms, transitioning from sexual seduction, invocations, and potions to an alchemy of tears that renders her ghoulish. Her mourning transgresses the symbolic limitations that were placed on women's voices; Christian humanist culture and French society preferred decorous modes of expressing sorrow and harbored a strong bias against "excessive" grieving that was considered irrational, un-Christian, destructive of feminine beauty, and disruptive of public order.[14] Among the material substances gold, blood, ink, and milk, which are analyzed by Rebecca Zorach as figures of material plenitude and excess in French Renaissance art, three—gold, milk, and blood—appear in Jodelle's play, only to be replaced by tears.[15] As Cleopatra goes from being portrayed as a seductress (in Antony's account), to a mother (worrying about her sons), to a pallid mourner (of Antony), and, finally, to dying from excessive crying, she gradually loses her blood, milk, and color.[16] This ritual of mourning, though excessive, still domesticates Cleopatra in a number of ways. She acts out of obedience to the ghost of Antony; her death is governed by the telos of his will. In her mourning, Cleopatra goes from being erotic and hot to weak, cold, and pale—that is, more White, Christian, and French. This excess of passions and tears is an agency in itself, which is transferred to the poets who played roles in the play, Belleau and de la Péruse.

By way of Jodelle's poetic and dramaturgical invention, the play presents the spectacle of a captive Oriental woman who liberates herself by literally crying herself to death—while also fashioning the strange, exotic, and unfree female body into a symbolic object of desire for educated male viewers, the royal court, and its aristocratic members.[17] The humoral alchemy that Cleopatra practices is viewed by the French poets as a magical art practiced on matter. This prepares her to be "brought" to France through the equally powerful art of poetry, and to be embodied there by a French poet. The chorus speaking at the end of the play claims that time has not only brought Cleopatra's fame to France but that it "will preserve" Cleopatra as well:

> Your Cleopatra, dead in this manner,
> Will not perish for the world.
> Time, which is already carrying her glory
> From the Sun's vermilion entry
> To the place where he goes to sleep,
> Opposite from my country,
> Will preserve her ("la garantira"),

For she preferred being carried in this way,
And die here,
Rather than dying in Rome,
Having more than human courage
Having a heart more than human ("un ceur'plus que d'homme").[18]

Jodelle enlists the cosmic movement of *physis*, the rationality of which he sees embodied by the movement of the Sun (figured as the mythological god Phoebus) from East to West. The chorus speaks from the Orient as "here," and refers to the West, and France, as the place "[o]pposite from my country." Using theater, Jodelle moves a dead queen to France to have her come alive (and die) on stage.[19] Even (or especially) in her death, she is the embodiment of the more-than-divine power of the cosmos, which is now intertwined with the power of the poet. Jodelle conceives of the play as a quasi-magic performance of bringing the queen to France through the power of poetry rather than that of acting, which was believed to entail yielding one's autonomy and a mere subjection of the actor's body to another's passions. The play was not performed after the sixteenth century, probably because of the arcane occult theories about the power of art that were presented through over-complicated braided phrases, which would have proved too difficult for readers to interpret.[20]

In *Cléopâtre captive*, Jodelle engages in his own mythologization of political power by staging—and extending to the East—the obscure medieval concept of *translatio imperii*, according to which history is a linear succession of empire. The play is framed by a message to Henri II, in which Jodelle flatters the king by suggesting that Octavian's fate will be shared by his "successors"—that is, Emperor Charles V (1500–1558):

> ... you will measure/contemplate ("sonderas") Octavian's
> arrogant pride, audacity, and the daily worries ("L'orgeuil, l'audace, &
>   le journel souci") pressed on him by his trophy.[21]

The poet then quickly adds that the French king's audacity will nonetheless outdo Octavian's ("Et plus qu'à luy le tien egaleras"), as "the gods" have already promised the world to Henri, compelling Octavian's "successors" (including Charles V) to cede to Henri's power.[22] The inconstancy of the Sun's circular movement, which is now moving west in a representation of the contingency of the political realm, is counterbalanced in this image by the "gods." Here, Jodelle evokes Stoic cosmology and its rational gods, which he aligns with the Sun's westerly motion—but he also evokes the polytheistic religion of Egypt and the animals that early Christian theologians considered the idols of the Egyptians.

Cléopâtre captive orientates audiences toward Egypt, an ancient and distant culture that Europeans perceived to be a source of esoteric knowledge and power. The play was performed during a moment of veritable Egyptomania that was sparked, in part, by the circulation of the pseudo-Egyptian Hellenistic *Hermetica*, a collection of writings in philosophy and magic that was popular throughout the Middle Ages and attributed to Hermes Trismegistos, a figure associated with the Greek god Hermes and the Egyptian god Thoth. Also contributing to the European fascination for Egypt at the time was the Greek translation of Horapollon's fifth-century *Hieroglyphica*, a compendium of interpretations of hieroglyphs, whose sole manuscript was discovered in 1419 on the Greek island of Andros and subsequently taken to Florence. The latter was the work of an Alexandrian writer containing fragmentary explanations of Egyptian religious myths and hieroglyphs, or "mythograms."[23] The manuscript became very popular in the small circle of Florentine humanists; Pietro Valla translated it into Greek, and Piero Valeriano produced a richly illustrated Latin translation in 1556. The Egyptomania among European humanists and courtiers brought with it a turn to the pre-Roman, pre-Hellenistic "pagan" culture of Egypt. While Plutarch includes few references to Egyptian religion (he mentions Antony's fondness of Bacchus and Cleopatra's project of building monuments near the temple of Iris), Jodelle adds elements to his play that show Cleopatra to be well versed in the sacred arts of Egypt and attributes her ability to subvert the power of her conqueror, the Roman Octavian, as well as that of Roman imperialism itself, to these arts. The play celebrates the power of the irrational magic of the humoral body, performance, and art. According to Yvan Loskoutoff, the playwright evokes several different known kinds of magic throughout the play. These include necromancy (which the poet himself practices by conjuring Antony's ghost in the play), sciamancy (Cleopatra's act of divination with Antony's shadow), fascination (Cleopatra's magic influence over Antony), oneiromancy (practiced by Antony, who appears to Cleopatra in her dream), magic spells, potions, and onomatomancy (the repeated invocation of Antony's name, which Cleopatra uses to bring herself closer to the world of the dead and to hasten her own death).[24] However, Jodelle's portrayal of Cleopatra's sacred arts is not only based on Renaissance treatises on magic written by the likes of Giovanni Pico della Mirandola and Cornelius Agrippa von Nettesheim, as Loskoutoff suggests. The playwright also makes references to the animal gods of Egypt, which are abundantly depicted in the bestiary of Valeriano's illustrated *Hieroglyphica*. For example, it is narrated in the play that Cleopatra dressed in white as the goddess Isis to seduce Antony. Jodelle takes pains to magnify the presence of Isis and Egyptian religion in his play. Egyptian religion was suppressed by Roman and Byzantine proselytizers, but their testimonies of the destruction of religious images nevertheless provided some description of the Egyptian gods. The testimony of Severus, the sixth-century miaphysite theologian and patriarch of Antioch who spent part of his life in Egypt, describes the destruction of the temple of Isis:

> When he [Paralios] saw the multitude of idols and noticed the altar covered with blood, he cried out in Egyptian: "There is only one God," meaning that the error of polytheism had to be extirpated. First, he handed us the idol of Kronos that was completely filled with blood, then all the other idols of demons, and an assorted collection of idols of all kinds, including dogs, cats, monkeys, crocodiles and reptiles; because during that time the Egyptians also worshiped these animals. Furthermore, he handed us the rebel dragon. Its idol was made of wood, and it seems to me that those who worshipped this serpent, or rather that the latter wanting to be worshipped in this way, recalled the rebellion of the first creatures, which happened through the wood (tree), on the advice of the serpent.[25]

In Jodelle's play, Proculeus calls Cleopatra (in addition to her two women in attendance, who die with her) "serpentine giants," rebel snakes, or dragons. Antony describes Cleopatra as "a deadly snake / who encircling me and deceiving my ravished heart / poured into my heart the venom of my life."[26] This reference is missing from Plutarch, but it recalls the first mythogram described in the *Hieroglyphica*: *ouraios* ("cobra" in Greek, also the sacred serpent of ancient Egypt), which is named in Valeriano's *Hieroglyphica* as *aeon* ("eternity" in Latin) or *basilicus* ("serpent" and "lizard" in Greek), and is drawn as a serpent biting its own tail. While Plutarch mentions the temple of Isis, he does not describe the mythograms or the depictions of Egyptian gods. Jodelle wrote his play before Valeriano published his illustrated *Hieroglyphica*. Yet he still evokes the powers of the snake (see Figure 9).

In the play, Octavian's desire to become a god is thus hampered by the gods that hold power over the material elements of the cosmos, with some help from Cleopatra. Jodelle conjures the Egyptian magic of the serpent god via Cleopatra, who is herself a rebel serpent. Thus, the playwright reminds the king of a surplus power to be gained from a mysterious realm of vitality that is embodied by the cosmos in its materiality—as well as by the dying Cleopatra onstage, for her demise, and that of Egypt alongside her, is linked with this power that is now, supposedly, at work in the French theater. Cleopatra's excessive passions reflect this cosmic power that "imprints" worries onto Octavian. Cleopatra's serpent-like quality, which terrorizes Proculeus, also symbolizes her earthy, cosmic, more-than-human power. It is uncertain exactly how much of

Pierii Val. Basiliscus.

phici dedit Ægyptijs sacerdotibus, ut si hominem à calumniatoribus malè acceptum, & mortiferis delationibus afflictatum significare uellent, Basiliscum apponerent: non enim alia ratione calumniatores homines conficiunt, quàm faciat Basiliscus: clàm siquidem illi principum auribus insusurrãt, nullo palàm morsu infixo, quò diluendi ansa præripiatur: atque ita plericp falso delati, extrema quæque pertulere. Sed ne talem ac tantam Basilisco uim inesse quispiam admiretur, Thebiorum natio pestifera adeò fuit, ut uel solus oris eorũ halitus exceptus, interimendi uim habuerit, illorumcp præsentiã nõ animalibus tantùm, uerumetiam satis noxiam fuisse: de quibus hæc & alia secundo Symposiorum Didymus.

IN ea tamen religione Basiliscus habitus apud Ægyptios, ut ex auro dedicaretur. Caput autem illi accipitrinũ faciebant, oculosque eo artificio cõcinnabant, ut & claudi & aperiri possent. Hunc simulatcp oculis adapertis proferebant, uniuersa Ægyptus lætitia atcp hilaritate perfundebatur, perinde ac si deorum oculi eos aspicerent, opemcp præsentẽ omnibus pollicerentur: in luce igitur & in propatulo omnes esse, & risui & iocis atcp conuiuijs dare operam. Quòd si clausis eum oculis extulissent, ibi tum omnia mœrore luctucp confundi, auersos & iratos esse deos existimari, abdere se omnes in tenebras, & obscura penetralia, miserabilicp deploratione pro se quencp niti, ut deorum indignationem quacuncp possent ratione mitigarent. Non fuit horũ ignarus Philon: & Epies quidam diuinorũ interpres apud Ægyptios nominatissimus, rem memoriæ prodidit. Figura autem hæc ita habetur in Bembæa tabula. Vt ueró hæc magis innotescant, Iouem Ægyptij, autore Plutarcho, spiritũ esse dicunt: spiritus nulli animaliũ uehementior quàm Basilisco, ideocp nulli magis diuinitatis symbolum quadrat.

OCVLI DIVVM.

SPIRITVS.

POrrò anguis apud eos hieroglyphicum est spiritus illius qui per uniuersam mundi molem difflatur. Anaxagoras quocp quatuor elementis constitutis, que per anguem significari statim initio diximus, rectorẽ adiungit, siue spiritũ, siue Deum, siue mentẽ, ut Probus interpretatur, per quem hæc quatuor regantur: quod Virgilius etiam nullius ignarus disciplinæ affirmat dicens:

Principio cœlum ac terras camposque liquentes,
Lucentemque globum Lunæ, Titaniaque astra
Spiritus intus alit, totamque infusa per artus
Mens agitat molem, & magno se corpore miscet.

Quem enim Anaxagoras νοῦν, is spiritum & mentem dixit. M. Tullius Platonis sententiam, quæ in libro de anima est, secutus, principió terram ait sitã in media mundi parte, circunfusam esse hac animabili spirabilicp natura, cui nomen aër.

ÆOLIPILÆ.

NOn imperitè igitur qui Æolipilas cauant, solent illis in cõuexo draconẽ superinducere, ex cuius ore circa medium sito spiritalis illa fistula promineat, quæ uentum proflet. Sunt ueró pilæ huiusmodi æreæ, cauæcp, in quas per angustissimum

this esoteric message of the play was understood by its elite audiences, but their enthusiasm for the performance can probably be attributed to the fact that some of them dabbled in esoterica and, as discussed, Egypt was a source of great fascination in France in the year 1553.

Cléopâtre captive was performed the same year that Pierre Belon's *Observations* was published. Jodelle places the action in Alexandria and adds at least two pieces of realia: "the burial vault" ("des sepulchres le clos"), a vague term evoking perhaps a pyramid, and, anachronistically, a scimitar. The play orients the gaze of French readers and audiences toward the culture of Egypt that was being explored by French agents. In August through October 1547, Belon embarked on a trip from Alexandria to Cairo with François de Fumel, a Catholic baron (whose fate was later to be massacred by his Protestant vassals), in the service of the newly crowned King Henri II. Belon describes how, accompanied by a group of "valiant, sober, and modest" Turkish soldiers, the two Frenchmen explored the pyramids of Giza, entered the largest pyramid with the help of local guides, and proceeded through the narrow passages one by one, "slithering like serpents"[27] and holding wax candles, until they found a chamber with an uncovered black marble casket.[28] Belon's description, which is among the first to be written in French about the ruins of ancient Egypt,[29] is dominated by the idea of Egypt's exceptionality. He often lapses into the perspective of seeing contemporary Egypt through the lens of its ancient history and bygone excellence in the arts and technologies. He is fascinated by and takes pleasure in describing the vestiges of the former civilization; for example, chicken-hatching incubators and clothes that its modern inhabitants still wear.[30] In Belon's description, Egypt outdoes ancient Greek and Roman civilizations with its inventions and riches, which are still materially present in the land. Moreover, it is in Egypt that he believes to discern the true order of world history, the view of which he considers having been corrupted by Greek and Latin authors. Belon attributes outsize power to the antiquities of Egypt because of their durability and vitality, even in ruins. Having measured the largest pyramid, he assures his readers that it far surpasses any antiquities left behind by the Romans. He climbs atop it to describe the view. He relates that, unlike the Greek and Roman custom of incinerating the dead, Egyptians embalmed their dead using a type of tar ("catran," from the Arabic *qatrān*) and "nitre" (here perhaps referring to natron, a mixture of salt and baking soda) and placed them in a place that was "sterile," in the sun-drenched desert.[31] He also describes the two smaller pyramids, writing that even the smallest one is larger than any pyramids built by the ancient Romans and better preserved.[32] The Egyptians, he states, built their civilization using the power of the sun, heat, and minerals. In the arid climate mixed with fertile valleys, the notions of death and rebirth seem intertwined with these cosmic material powers that produce powerful drugs and with the art of the people.

In describing the Sphinx of Giza to the left of the great pyramid simply as a "stone atop of a rectangular base," Belon distances himself from earlier descriptions of the statue by Ethiopians, Egyptians, and Romans. He also rejects the authenticity of copies of the Sphinx found at the Capitolium and the pope's collection in the Garden of Belvedere, as well as the bronze ones commissioned by Francis I based on Roman antiquities, calling all of them mere "fables" because they depict the mythical creature differently from the one in Giza.[33] After having made a *tabula rasa* of existing collections, he lends his own in-person observations of the one real Sphinx, describing it in simple terms as a "sculpted face" ("une grande face entaillé") with its nose, eyes, mouth, forehead, and chin well preserved—and emphasizing that, like the pyramids, it is larger than anything the Romans ever erected.[34] Belon evokes the efforts of Francis I to cast a colossal figure of Hercules (the construction of which was interrupted by the king's death) and those of Nero in commissioning an enormous marble sun in Rhodes, both of which failed to produce a monument of the same enormous size. He mistakenly cites Pliny's Latin description of the Sphinx as "Est autem saxi naturali eaborata & lubrica,"—that is, made of natural stone and slippery. Pliny actually says, "Est autem saxo naturali elaborate; rubrica facies monstri colitur,"[35] or the face of the "monster" is painted red as an embellishment. Belon thus omits red ("rubica") from his citation of Pliny's description. This misquote may have been occasioned by a lapse of memory (Belon was notoriously inaccurate in citing ancient authors), and it may also have been because, during the centuries separating him from Pliny, the painting had simply been effaced by the elements. Belon's Sphinx is thus a drab stone with a face carved on it turned toward Cairo ("qui regarde vers le Caire"[36]), thereby serving as a means of orientation toward an important trading port and French consular site in the Ottoman Empire. Its loss of color, similar to that of Cleopatra in the play, renders it a fitting image of cosmic animality as described in, for example, Stoic cosmology or animate minerality, and less evocative of the colors used in ancient Egyptian art.

Belon rejects the achievements of the late French king and the Roman emperor in favor of the art of Egyptians that, as he explains, was not only possessed by pharaohs and their court but also by common people. He notes that many Egyptians, rich and poor alike, built edifices to commemorate their dead (obelisks, sphinxes, pyramids, and, in the case of the poor, "some modest stone constructions").[37] Belon describes Egypt as an extraordinary meeting place of physical forces and religious or esoteric art, both of which are capable of resisting demise and engendering new life even out of death. When it comes to the drug "mummy," the medical efficacy of which was debated in the sixteenth century, Belon sides with those who believe in its power, provided that it is not falsified (by comparison, André Thevet was a skeptic and Ambroisé Paré thought it was junk).[38] For Belon, mummification and embalming, both of which, he notes, came about from Zoroastrian teachings that condemn the destruction of bodies by the elements, strike him not as a means of preserving the material remains of the body but rather as a means of producing a powerful drug.[39] Here, too, the power of drugs goes back to Egyptian art and civilizational achievement. In Belon's description, however, these ruins do not refer to a vertical social system of symbolic, patrilineal, or dynastic values whose continuity helps maintain social order but to a much larger physical world. Significantly, their power does not stem from the status of the persons who have died.[40] When Belon sees ruins, he does not only see the deterioration of an ancient culture. He also sees the continued workings of *physis*, making drugs and producing plants and animals, which continue to have agency even after the demise of the people. Aside from archiving human art, the pyramids, although made up of lifeless stones, are a space for animals to roam and for plants to grow. Belon notes that even in the desert of Giza, the bats, lizards, and flies, as well as the plant *Tithymalus platiphyllos* (broad-leaved spurge), thrive. These animal and botanical manifestations of a particularly sun-drenched, dry, mineral *physis* show that the world keeps growing and expanding, just as "seeds" (Latin "semina") are thought in a Stoic cosmology to unfold into the physical universe.[41] Belon sees Egyptian culture through its singular technologies that bring decay to a halt by way of its monuments and techniques of mummification—and yet these techniques are not seen so much as proofs of the immortality of the emperors, but rather as coeval with the quasi-vegetal growth of *physis* that contains the promise of renewal in Belon's present. In *Cléopâtre captive*, Cleopatra's cosmic, serpent-like animality, her excessive passion, works as a creative force that ensures her power to resist Octavian. It is also this material force that can be appropriated by the French (male) artists who wield power over her symbolic afterlife by rendering her the exotic symbol of their artistic agency.

A second Orientalist play, *Médée*, was also performed in 1553, probably in some haste, as it was still unfinished at the time of the first performance.[42] Medea ("Médée") is the princess from Colchis on the Black Sea who subverts the will of her father, Aeëtes, and steals the Golden Fleece for Jason, leader of the Argonauts. She then marries him and lives with him and their two sons in Corinth until Jason repudiates her to marry Glauce ("Glauque"), the daughter of Creon, king of Corinth. Medea revels in evoking the autonomous world of "furies," populated with "hideous manes" and "serpents," which represents a separate arena of justice from that of Corinth and "the gods of marriage," to whose separate justice she appeals in her "just quarrel."[43] "Those who dare a lot inspire the fear of fortune" ("Ceus qui osent beaucoup font crains de la Fortune"),[44] declares Medea in Act 1. Her loyal female servant ("Nourrice") laments, in response, that after having lost so much, including her good life at her father's court, her brother (whom she murdered to help Jason obtain the Golden Fleece), and now Jason, too, Medea wants to give up more, courting unwisely the upheavals of her fortune, including the loss of her children's lives, solely to exact revenge for Jason's wrongs. This lesson in prudency as political wisdom is lost on Medea, who is, as Usher insightfully suggests, "an avatar of fortune, except that, of course, she is worse."[45]

This play elaborates on one of the many images offered by Jodelle in *Cléopâtre captive*, the performances of which preceded those of *Médée*. The chorus in *Cléopâtre captive* addresses Medea—"Why, Medea, did you lose your Jason?"—to represent passing Oriental glory, portraying the ephemerality of empires through the image of the passing of love. Jodelle's abrupt expression of compassion for Medea appears on at least one more occasion, notably in his dedication to a publication written by a friend, where he asserts: "Someone who wants to vomit his jealousy against the work of my friend, would be similar to Jason, villainously rejecting Medea, who had no other goal than his pleasure."[46] This apology for the friend and fellow author, who is betrayed by the ill will of the very readers whose "pleasure" he aims to serve, is formulated as an apology for Medea, who is also betrayed by the husband for whose interests she labored. The obligations of the author (artist) to his readers, those of the wife to her husband, and those of a servant to his or her master, are confounded here in the scenario of the loyal servant betrayed by those who benefit from such loyalty. The play ennobles Medea's labors, rendering her a "pitiful" spectacle worthy of the audience's sympathy,[47] while Jason is characterized as an oath breaker. There is something remarkable in the fact that an author presents his "service" to readers as analogous to Medea's service to her husband.[48] It is ultimately owing to Medea's ability to guard her agency, even after being abandoned by Jason, that she is chosen as an object of sympathy for (male) poets. Medea is the maker and breaker of Jason's power, and her acts make it clear that no state or prince can hold power without the magic she wields. This quality renders her the extension of the artist while also rendering her tamable only by the symbolic means wielded by the artist, poetry, and performance.

In *Médée*, the heroine's revenge takes place despite Creon's anticipation that Medea may harm his city and his prudent attempt to preempt the catastrophe by banishing her. She succeeds in sending her own sons as envoys to Jason's new wife, along with the fatal gift: a crown that Glauce cannot resist, which sets her on fire and causes the royal palace to burn to ashes. Medea then murders her sons in front of Jason, casts her curse on him and, finally, flies off in a winged chariot in an ambitious *coup de théâtre* of which, unfortunately, no mention is made in known accounts of the performance. Although de la Péruse relies heavily on Seneca's play *Medea*, he, unlike Seneca, gives Medea the final speech. Medea's gift to Glauce, the golden crown, is a gift of a very specific kind. Medea claims it once belonged to Phoebus, her grandfather:

> Arrange it for me that I may give
> A rich crown to your new spouse
> Which used to adorn the Sun's golden head
> Before he gave it to his beloved son, my father—
> I do this so that she may forever remember me
> And regard our poor sons as if they were hers.[49]

Phoebus gave this crown to his son (Medea's father), but, instead of letting it be passed on to the next male descendant (her brother), Medea seized it and took it out of the line of patrilineal ascent as her own form of serpentine revolt. The chorus suggests that Glauce places too much trust in this magnificent gift and advises that "wise distrust" is necessary to discern the "poisonous snake ("Le serpent de venin taché")/hiding under the flowery green" of Medea's present.[50]

Médée is to be read folded into Jodelle's *Cléopâtre captive*, with the two plays referencing and commenting on one another as they also represent different swerves of the animal agency of *physis*. Both plays present the intertwining of politics and love, each of which is defined by the uncertainty of desire, a Lucretian theme that Jessie Hock identifies in the poetry of the Pléiade.[51] Hock points out that these poets rely on Lucretius's depiction of nature as a stabilized realm within the contingent movements of atoms, and that they extend its functions to poetry and art as tools that can serve the stability of the political realm by promoting marriage (as the basis of dynastic political regimes) and by creating the symbols of monarchical power, including jewels and crowns. This conservativism of Lucretian poetics is counteracted by the framing of poetry's seductive erotic power over the readers.[52] Cleopatra and Medea figure both stability and turbulence in politics. Medea's stealing of the crown from her grandfather is to be seen as different from simple treachery or theft. Her figure is akin to that of Prometheus, the son of a Titan who molds living people from clay by stealing fire from the gods (and who took a heavy punishment for it). Prometheus, as the figure of the artist-artisan creating humankind and technology, was the subject of a poem by Belleau.[53] Exquisite crowns, like the one Medea steals from her father, served important symbolic functions in sixteenth-century geopolitics; they played a prominent role, for example, in the rivalry between Suleiman I, Charles V, and Francis I.[54] De la Péruse's compassion (or pity) for Medea is a tactical sideways move away from the straight lines of imperialist historiography, an acknowledgement of the turbulence caused by competing among empires, and a plea for a new equilibrium in which an important place is held by artisans and artists, commoners, and servants of the powerful. The play represents Medea's archaic notion of justice as analogous to the moral value of the loyalty of wives, servants, and artists. Jodelle and de la Péruse envision their poetry as a useful tool for creating the symbolic glue that holds together political regimes, and they praise the transgressive yet conservative powers of art. *Médée* concludes with the spectacular display of Medea's power at the moment in which it *destroys* family and state. The chorus's commonsense advice in *Médée* is that one should mistrust gifts from foreigners. Yet this wisdom harbors the irony that such dangerous presents are coveted and maybe even necessary for maintaining one's power.[55] These heroines are mediations of the power of artists and the servants of the powerful—those who bring that which is foreign to France. They also stray into a more direct political domain, which is exemplified by the fantasy of the Orient as a medium of sorts, if not a tool, for the ascending power of the French monarchy with the intermediary of artists. Cleopatra, who is of "royal race,"[56] corresponds to European ideas of nobility and becomes whitened through her mourning—all the while remaining an enigma, a ghoul, and a strange spectacle, both diminished and eminently visible. Cleopatra, like the Sphinx in Belon's description, becomes the place from which the Western male gaze can be oriented toward the fiction of Egypt and the Orient.

Both *Cléopâtre captive* and *Médée* evoke the serpent as the ontology of the hidden and mute other whose concealed power represents a danger. This looming power is revealed and tamed thanks to the output of artists and poets who not only play these *dramatis personae* but also claim literally to enact their freedom and reveal their agency on stage. The idea of freedom as a transmutation in death is obsessively explored by poets in the mid-century. In Act 4, Erasme describes this freedom acquired through death to Cleopatra:

> Erasme. Oh death, sweet death ("Ha mort, ô douce mort"), the sole redemption
> For these spirits oppressed in a strange/foreign prison ("estrange prison").
> Why do you suffer ("souffrir") this violation of your privileges?
> . . .
> Why do you wish to tolerate that this captive crew,
> Which will not be given the gift of freedom ("le don de liberté")
> Until the spirit is separated by your dart.[57]

These lines are echoed in a poem in which Pierre de Ronsard (1524–1585) commemorates the "the ceremony of the goat," the Bacchic reveling that is re-enacted by Jodelle's friends to celebrate the success of *Cléopâtre captive* in April 1553. In Ronsard's poem, the ceremony is presented as a wine-induced vision in which the poet sees the familiar forest of Arcueil, where the ceremony was conducted just south of Paris, populated by frenzied maenads with snakes in their hair, satyrs, Silenus, and other companions of Bacchus, along with the god himself. Ronsard praises Bacchus as the god of heroic freedom that chooses death over subjugation to a tyrant:

> Freedom ("liberté"), who would rather sacrifice herself
> And die ("s'offrir à la mort") than suffer ("souffrir") a Tyrant's will,
> Is in your debt . . .[58]

Besides their repetition on the level of allegorized notions ("liberté," "mort," "souffrir"), both Jodelle's play and Ronsard's poem associate freedom with ritual, offerings, sacrifice, and death, in which rebirth to a symbolic order of existence is possible. The autonomy of the artists forms the counterpoint to the animality of captive, snake-like Oriental women.

The Color of Cleopatra:
Race in Orientalist Poetry and Theater

A paleness haunts the theatrical representations of Oriental characters in 1550s France and marks their appropriation at the hand of the artists and creators of elite French culture. Cleopatra's anemic dead body directly contrasts with the dark color of the Alexandrian inhabitants evoked in the play. At the end of Act 1, the chorus of Alexandrian women names the Orient as the past beneficiary of the Sun's attention:

> We see at this very hour
> This land gilded ("Ce pays coloré")
> By the supreme flame
> Of the God with the golden chariot.
> And it seems that the face of this inconstant God
> Makes of the city
> The honor of the Orient (. . .)[59]

These lines link the Orient, and especially Alexandria—the city founded by Alexander the Great and in which Cleopatra, his descendant, reigned—to the Sun, personified as Phoebus. Phoebus turns his face toward the city with an inconstant admiration, as a fickle lover would to a beloved. The chorus attributes the demise of Cleopatra's empire to this inconstancy of (male) desire and positions her defeat and captivity by Octavian as a direct result of this. These events render Cleopatra the object of the audience's sympathy, as solicited by the chorus. Although Phoebus-Sun turns his face toward the Orient in the morning, "regard[ing] himself in her," and lavishes his praises on her, "this inconstant God" also abandons "her" during its daily course. The attraction of the Sun to the Orient engenders its "glory"

> That draws sweetly,
> Through its vivid rays,
> The human mind to her.[60]

It also, however, engenders the source of instability as an inconstant passion. Images of natural, amorous, and political inconstancy multiply in the text through countless images such as the decline of Troy, the rose that blooms for a single day ("rose journalière") and that is soon to be "ravished" by the Sun's rays, and the Caucasian magician Medea, whose "arts," "poison," or "savage beast . . . could not save her from her death." The Orient, "[t]his honorable land, /this fortunate country . . . finds her fortune ("Son heur importuné") / Short-lived."[61] Yet this admission of the finitude of all things, which is consistent with the view shared by Stoic and Epicurean philosophers in antiquity that the cosmos has a beginning and an end, also comes with a movement from east to west. In this configuration, the East is defined as the object of desire and as the place darkened by this erotic desire, while the West is defined as the place toward which the Sun newly moves, and the place from which one looks *at* the East. The Orient is described as "pays coloré," where "coloré" means both the golden hue of the Sun's rays and the darker skin color of the inhabitants, signaling its past glory and its present abandonment. This image deviates from the basic prejudices of Renaissance climate theories at much the same time as it presupposes them. These theories maintained that there exists a correlation between the climate of a place and the nature of its inhabitants, and this view was often disseminated through both medical discourses on the human body and travelers' accounts in European vernacular languages. The skin of the inhabitants of Africa, for example, was thought to be dark because of the heat of the sun.[62] By whitening Cleopatra, Jodelle also changes Cleopatra's temperament, which was presented by Plutarch as inconstant, treacherous, and sexualized. Jodelle thus follows this conflation of climate and temperament, which, according to Sara Miglietti, was routinely executed and consolidated by the end of the sixteenth century.[63] Although the play communicates its ideas by way of idealizing the queen, it also connects dark skin with male desire (as its object), thereby contributing to the hypersexualization of people of color. The theme of abandonment also directly ties in with the idea of excessive passion in the abandoned beloved, characterized by mourning (in Cleopatra), or rage (in Medea), which renders them both powerful yet unstable, dangerous, and animal beings. In Jodelle's play, Cleopatra's cold and pale color, her anemic body without milk, bereft of the queenly luster of golden ornaments, contrasts with the dark color of North Africans. Cleopatra, whose place of living, Alexandria, is inhabited by people of dark skin, is pale in death and her symbolic rebirth, at which point she remains seductive yet is no longer sexualized. This makes her both more acceptable for the moral standards of sixteenth-century France and more White.[64] In order for Cleopatra to appear on French stage, she is to become paler and thus reflect the geopolitical movement of the Sun toward the West. And this movement, the westward direction of empire—embodied by Cleopatra and acted out and mastered by male poets in France—offers an impetus for recognizing a community united by the white, or pale, color of Cleopatra's body that has been long used in medieval and early modern representations as the color of European skin.[65]

Orientalism, the fascination with a declining Orient in the play, is structured similarly to fantasies that informed the French crown's own politics of diplomacy in the Ottoman Empire. Diplomats and spin doctors often formulated this politics in terms of "taming" the Ottoman other, which was admired for having immense power and resources, while also being described as governed by an unbridled appetite or "greed" that needed to be brought into accord with the moral ideals of Christianity. Agrippa's advice to Octavian, to keep a close watch on Cleopatra's every move, mimics the extreme care taken by the French crown to spy on and gather information from its mighty ally. This was not only done in the interests of obtaining concrete information on the policies of the Sublime Porte, but also to make the entire Ottoman Empire the object of countless "singular" observations in a project that testifies to the infinite suspicion and the stunning ambition of influence that were directed toward the Ottoman Empire. This ambition came about in the aftermath of a failed attempt by the young Francis I (1515–1547) to acquire the title of "Holy Roman Emperor." The king sent ambassadors to Frankfurt to solicit the support of the constituents there by promising that, if elected, he would wage war against the "Turk" and deliver Christianity from this "menace."[66] Instead, the Spanish Charles V was elected to this lofty title, which had a legal and ideological basis in medieval universalism. But the somewhat antiquated ideal of the universal emperor blended into a new form of globalism that arose in Europe and spread around the world in the age of European colonial expansion in Africa, India, and the Americas. After the debacle of Pavia (1525), Francis I brought about a veritable reorientation in politics by allying with the Ottoman Empire to counter

Charles V's growing global power. This shift brought imperialistic dreams that were channeled through the Ottoman Empire, its military resources, and its influence in the territories under its control. Since one of the attributes of the Holy Roman Emperor was to be the protector of Christianity and a crusader against the "infidels," this diplomatic move represented a turn that was completely unprecedented. In imaginary scenarios of *translatio imperii*, the Ottoman Empire replaced the Holy Roman Empire (with which French kings engaged in a traditional rivalry, competing for the title of the emperor) as the power soon to surrender its empire to France.

In projecting a French rule that is seen to be prefigured through the demise of the Orient, *Cléopâtre captive* anticipates two *mascarades* (choreographed theater-style dancing performed by masked actors) and several allegories that Jodelle staged five years later, on January 8, 1558, at the Hôtel de Ville in Paris, on commission from the city of Paris to celebrate the French victory over the imperials in Calais. Just as the preface to *Cléopâtre captive* designates the king as the privileged viewer of the piece, so, too, were the emblems that decorated the hall and archways during these performances strategically placed so that they would be best visible to the king as he passed to and from his seat. For example, the hall was decorated with intertwined crescents of ivy hanging from the frieze with the inscription "iunguntur" ("They are joined"). The crescent moon was Henri II's *impresa*, signifying, according to contemporary interpretations, his impending universal rule,[67] and Jodelle deliberately conflated this motif with the Ottoman imperial symbol of the crescent moon. As he explains in the *Recueil des inscriptions*, which he published after the event, this conflation was to represent the alliance that gave the French monarchy greater military power (see Figure 10).[68] Jodelle's message to Henri was that he should not be afraid that "a great lion lying in ambush" (the Ottoman Empire) would take advantage of the fact that "the brave rooster" (France) is fighting with "the eagle" (the Holy Roman Empire), for the Ottomans wish for the French to hold the reigns of the Empire and are aware that their fate is to be eventually conquered by France. Of the two *mascarades* that follow, the one entitled "Les Argonauts"[69] features fourteen characters and a model of the ship Argo (carried in on the shoulders of sailors to symbolize the support of the citizens of Paris), with talking rocks that respond to Orpheus in Argo's crew. In the allegory of Antony and Cleopatra, Henri II appears as "our Ceasar,"[70] and in that of Jason and Medea, he is "fatal Jason" to "those who wear around their neck the 'Fleece'" (members of the Spanish Order of the Golden Fleece, established in 1429).[71] But, here, Jodelle continues to advocate for himself and for the others who serve the king; Henri should also not behave like Jason who betrayed Medea. As in de la Péruse's play, the message in the *mascarade* is one of moral

DE PAVLO IOVIO. 25

demeurãt dans les flammes ne se consume point: auec le mot Italien, qui disoit, NVTRISCO ESTINGVO: estant propre qualité d'iceluy animal, de disperser de son corps vne humeur si froide sur les brases, qu'il ne craint point la force du feu: ains plustost le tempere & estaint. Et fut bien vray qu'iceluy heroique & treshumain Roy ne fut iamais sans amour, s'estant monstré tresardent à congnoistre les hommes vertueux, & de courage indomptable contre la fortune (comme la Salamandre au feu) en tout cas & euenement de guerre. Et ceste inuētion fut forgee de son tresnoble esprit.

DONEC TOTVM IMPLEAT ORBEN

Encor ne cede à la susdicte celle, qu'à present porte son filz & successeur, le magnanime Roy Héry: lequel perseuere à porter la deuise, qu'il fit desia quand estoit Dauphin: qui est le Croissant, auec ce mot braue & plein de graue

d

and political autonomy. Henri should follow Jason's example and conquer the Fleece through virtuous actions, without resorting to "horrible poisons, vile murders, and terrible treachery." This formulation implies that all these acts now redound not to Medea, but to Jason in these representations of fantastic imperial conquest, which contain anxieties about royal betrayal of servants.[72] Quite aside from their imagery of a future French victory over the Ottomans, these performances are noteworthy because of their spectacular failures in terms of staging.[73] In an apology, Jodelle describes a series of debacles: the poor technical realization of his designs ("they brought me bell towers instead of rocks"[74]), the incompetence of the actors who failed to learn their lines, and the two rocks and a great ship with a long mast that were brought into the already crowded *grande halle* and only added to the disorder.[75] Jodelle's self-defense is not a mere rhetorical trick. As Zorach explains, the elite culture of sixteenth-century France was invested in art that was both beautiful and difficult, which resulted in practices that are hard to understand or even remain completely lost to later generations. As we have seen, Jodelle's *Cléopâtre captive* not only enacted symbolic mastery over the Egyptian queen but also imbued her with an esoteric, pagan, animal animacy that was available only to the elite members of society who had access to the Renaissance cult of Egypt. Zorach surmises that, in this later instance, Jodelle's pageantry baffled even his contemporaries and the bourgeois of Paris who commissioned it.[76] Such an artistic failure, exacerbated by the pressures of time and the dearth of material support that the artist describes, reveals that, in sixteenth-century French society, it was the poet—much more so than the prince and head of state, to whose vulnerability tragedy was supposed to call attention for the purpose of moral instruction—who found himself exposed to the contingencies of his own work.[77] Court theater was an occasion for the ostentatious display of material wealth, and its financing, which was apparently the responsibility of Jodelle, came to a veritable fortune for the financially strained poet.[78]

A likely source for Jodelle's *mascarades* of 1558 is the *Promptuaire des medalles* (Lyon, 1553) by Guillaume Rouillé, which presents Antony and Cleopatra as an illustrious couple (see Figure 11). Some of the famous couples to whom Jodelle compares Antony and Cleopatra, including the contemporary power couple Mary Stuart and Philip II of Spain, and Alexander the Great and the Amazon queen Thalestris, also appear in Rouillé's book. In the pageant, Jodelle seizes on exactly the same detail that Rouillé singles out from Plutarch's "Life of Antony": Cleopatra's richly decorated barge, with a golden mast and silver sails and cords, where she sat under a golden tent impersonating the goddess Venus.[79] Jodelle's *Recueil des inscriptions* follows much the same pattern of mixing moral and political allegories that can be discerned in Rouillé's

170　　LA PREMIERE PARTIE DV

M. ANTOINE Conful, pourchaceant les meurdriers de Cefar, aufquels le Senat fauorifoit, troubloit Romme & faifoit des méchancetez: dont fut par le Senat declaré ennemi. Panfa & Hircius vont côtre luy, auec Augufte, ieune de 18. ans: il eft vaincu, & apointe auec Augufte, qui luy laiffe l'Afie, & le païs dict le Pont. il delaiffe la fœur d'Augufte, prend Cleopatre à femme, qui luy fait fils & fille, à la premiere groffeffe, lefquels il nomme le Soleil & la Lune. il vainq les Perfes. puis Cleopatre, par vne conuoitife de femme, defirant aufsi regner à Romme, l'incite à la guerre ciuile: vaincu fus mer, par Augufte, s'enfuit en Egypte, & fe tue. Augufte fe fait feigneur d'Egypte. Voyez Sueto. en la vie d'Augufte. & Appian.

CLEOPATRE Royne d'Aegypte, n'eftoit point tât belle, comme douce, & de bône grace: mais ce qu'elle auoit de beauté, eftant aydé de fes vertus & graces, faifoit efmerueiller tout le môde. elle parloit prôptement à toutes fortes de nations, en leur lãgage, vfant de fa langue côme d'vn inftrumêt de plufieurs cordes: & n'vfoit gueres de truchement. elle vint vers Marc Antoine auec vne pompe incroyabe, en l'an du monde 3 9 2 3. auãt la nati. de Ief. 3 9. ans, fus le fleuue Cydnus: le derriere du nauire eftoit d'or, les voiles d'efcarlate: les auirons ou rames d'argent, eftoyêt demenez au fon des inftrumens de mufique. elle comme vne Royne, en eftat de Venus, eftoit afsife en fa tente doree, ayant autour d'elle de beaux petis enfans comme de Cupidons: les belles filles habillees comme Nereides & Graces, manioyêt le gouuernail, & les cordages: les damoifelles braues rempliffoyent l'air de parfuns tout le long du riuage. Voyez Pluta. en la vie de M. Antoine, apres la mort duquel elle fe feit mourir par vn afpic, pour ne venir entre les mains d'Augufte.

Figure 11

numismatic descriptions, while also aggrandizing the artist as the privileged manipulator of semiophores upon which the powerful rely.[80] In this way, Jodelle moves a little further away from the celebration of the cosmic agency of nature, to instead making a moral claim that was also used by coin collectors to mitigate the desire of possession and the commodification of material things like coins and statues. Collectors of coins steered clear of the grand claims of agency that informed the writings of agents and authors of the Pléiade. Cleopatra and Medea also lingered on in numismatic collections, where their significance transformed into something more modest. Rouillé's *Promptuaire des medalles* presents a global array of famous people from antiquity to the mid-sixteenth century. It makes Cleopatra's charms accessible to the educated classes.[81] Jodelle's image of Alexandria as the land "gilded" by the Sun's rays appears in the performance of the play that took place the same year as the publication of Belon's *Observations*, in which the author describes modern Egypt as a place where shepherds, tending their herd, sift through the sandy soil looking for the gold and silver medals with which their land is littered.[82] Guillaume Postel, who collected Hebrew coins, similarly claims that coins were found every day by ditch-diggers in Jerusalem, while the fact that they were buried deep in the rubble indicates their antiquity.[83] For scholars like Belon and Postel, Levantine soil did not simply hide rich metals that conferred status and power on the wealthy elite; it also contained, buried deep within it, knowledge and information about the history of empires and the ways people lived. Coins allowed people to handle these tokens of royal and princely power. Eventually, those who became connoisseurs developed a special interest in imperial emblems and founded numismatics based on a moral claim, spelled out clearly by Antoine Le Pois in his *Discours sur les medalles* (1579), that the value of coins does not have to do with the metals used in minting them, but rather with their antiquity and, additionally, their educational value. Le Pois also underscores the time it takes to study the coins, to take them "into one's hands again and again," such that the learning gained from it at the cost of the antiquarian's effort and time becomes a significant part of its value. Collecting thus distinguishes itself from the extreme care taken by the prince in availing himself of the spy's eyes and feet and directing his affairs in faraway courts. Instead, it transforms itself into a quieter agency, asserted from a moral vantage point from which geographically and historically distant places and persons can be observed. For Le Pois, Antony and Cleopatra are emblems of "arrogance." He criticizes more concretely their use of the diadem—that is, the emblem of Caesar that Antony gave Cleopatra—and speculates that the "turban" worn by Oriental monarchs derives from the diadem, thus suggesting that an Oriental excess is revealed in the turban. Le Pois publishes a picture of a coin depicting Cleopatra with the inscription "Queen Cleopatra, Servant of the All" ("Basilises

Cleoptras Ossan Soteras"), which he translates as "guardian" of everything (see Figure 12). Le Pois's Cleopatra suffers from a "marvelous arrogance" and "usurps" that which belongs to god, the guardianship of the universe. Cleopatra becomes the opposite of the slow reflection that defines the European collector and antiquarian who has no regard for material riches—he who, instead of the

Figure 12

"All," concerns himself with material things that are minute and relatively valueless. She not only figures the arrogance of empires but also the Oriental person allegedly incapable of such quiet appreciation of history. Paré offers a concrete description of this obsession with the simultaneous ephemerality of art *and* the power of its materiality when he relates that "I saw in Thevet's cabinet of curiosities a small white marble idol, inlaid with green, which he tells me to have brought from over there, having found it near a mummified body."[84] These spoils seem smallish even to these erudite men; they are not exactly the spoils of armies. Nor are they monuments erected by victors or lavish works commissioned by the powerful. They remind us of the Latin origin of spoils, the dead skin shed by molting lizards and snakes; they, too, are the crumbled, dry shells or skins left behind by civilizations long gone. The antiquarianism that emerges in this way is prompted by both a desire to capture things and by an awareness of the vulnerability that pertains to both material artifacts and people—thereby evoking a sense of *vanitas*, the instability of the political realm, and the acute sense that things are falling apart (including empires), yet creating the conditions for European individuals to make modest moral gains out of the spectacular fall of distant civilizations.

Invisible People on the Stage

Cleopatra acts upon her freedom in captivity in a manner that both corresponds to and contrasts with another enactment of the freedom of the other, which came down to us through the account of Pierre Bourdeille, better known as seigneur of Brantôme. During the parleying after the 1552 Spanish siege of Metz, Brantôme recounts, the Duke of Guise refused to turn over the "Moorish or Turkish slave" of a Spanish general, citing "the privilege of France from time immemorial . . . that the least barbarian or foreigner, having put only his foot on French soil, is immediately free and removed from slavery or captivity."[85] This event represents one of the first evocations of the "free soil principle," which, as Gillian Weiss shows, helped the French monarchy and French religious orders in their efforts to liberate enslaved persons and thereby gain greater control over the population of France and solidify its representation as free, Christian, and White.[86] More specifically, as Weiss argues, around 1550, "liberating slaves from North Africa changed from an expression of Christian charity to a method of state building and, eventually, a rationale for imperial expansion."[87] While imperialism may not have emerged in France with quite so sudden an onset, appearing instead as a simmering fantasy that coincided with several policies and laws promulgated by the French crown, Jodelle's play nevertheless serves as proof of the intensification in thinking about the liberation of captive persons in the mid-sixteenth century. Brantôme's account equates slavery with barbarism, and the free soil principle is evoked to signal the presence of civilization in France. The vague depiction of the slave as "Moorish or Turkish" could refer to a vast ethnic and geographic pool comprising Muslim Turks, Muslim North Africans, and Black Africans. The free soil principle did not abolish all forms of slavery in France; galley slaves, at the very least, were exempt. Moreover, the principle did not prevent French legal scholars and the monarchy from continuing to think that it was legal to keep people captive under certain conditions. Pasquier may have been contemplating the rational origins of slavery while he was watching the play, as he later justifies it in his *Recherches de la France* (1560): "When a man has been made a prisoner of war, it was found more expedient to keep him (alive) ("le conserver") than to kill him."[88] Pasquier argues that, while all persons are originally born free, the desire to grow one's power through the use of weapons leads to legally established forms of servitude such as the use of serfs for military purposes of war, and he goes on to claim that prisoners of war must be put to profitable ("pour ne rendre cette prise infructueuse") uses. The legal scholar also revives a murky and limited legal tradition originating in 1315 that involved the liberation of serfs, for a fee, to argue that the ban of slavery on the soil is a peculiarity of French law (although he also grants that, in some provinces of France, the bondage of tithe-paying serfs to the land still existed at his time under varying conditions).[89] The legal fiction of the free soil principle was thus derived from limited fourteenth-century precedents and went hand in hand with the French state's respect of monopolies and agreements with the Ottomans—both of which were violated, however, by privateering French merchants and ship owners. The Norman Jean Argo (1480–1551) from Dieppe often plundered Spanish and Portuguese vessels, traded in West Africa, and, though we do not know how many slaves he sold, we do know that he possessed art depicting slaves from Africa and that he was favored by Francis I (even if he eventually ran afoul of the royal administration for failure to pay taxes).[90] Sue Peabody cites the case of a Norman slave merchant who was arrested for attempting to sell a cargo of slaves in Bordeaux in 1571. In this case, the slaves were freed.[91] These cases suggest that the liberation of slaves became part of the French monarchy's policies that strove to enforce monopolies, to please the Sublime Porte, *and* to create French subjects by way of ransoming or negotiating the release of enslaved Christians. It became one of the routine duties of the French ambassadors and consuls in the Ottoman Empire to keep track of, and negotiate the liberation of, French and Christian subjects.[92] Freedom was viewed as a privilege of certain people. Slavery was often publicly rejected, but unfree people (and I use "unfree" here to designate both the enslaved and people who were not legally enslaved but who were tied by obligations of service, conversion, Christening, or coercion to masters) certainly existed in sixteenth-century France.

The free soil principle was repeatedly invoked to elevate France as the land of freedom over and above empires that relied on slavery, such as the Spanish and the Ottoman Empires. *Cléopâtre captive* and *Médée* represent a minor deviation, a "swerve," from this emerging state-ideology, from the "ties between saving slaves and making Frenchmen."[93] They brought exotic, captive *dramatis personae* to elite French audiences at a time when it was fashionable to include actual captured or coerced foreigners in court ceremonies and theater. However, unfree foreigners only rarely gain acknowledgement in the documents and papers extant in archives.[94] This effacement of women, non-Christians, and people of color by French artists and authors is especially stark because symbolic representations of unfree people in contrast to freedom appeared most visibly in the public realm of theater and ceremony, as did that of people of color in contrast to Whiteness, and disenfranchised women and slaves in contrast to agency. There are no records to show whether slaves or captured but baptized foreign servants were involved in the performances of *Médée* or *Cléopâtre captive*. However, Catherine de Médicis's surviving register of expenses for the year 1556 reveals that Oriental objects were used as props, and three "Moorish slaves" played mute roles wearing turbans of white, gray, and green taffeta in the staging of the play *Sophonisbe*, a play commissioned by Catherine de Médicis and staged in Blois in 1556. Scévole de Sainte-Marthe reports that it was performed "with all the props and almost all the pomp of ancient theater."[95] The play was staged in the open air, in front of a building completely covered in white cloth. A "Turkish hat" was also worn by one of the characters.[96] Like *Cléopâtre captive*, *Sophonisbe* also featured a North African (Punic) heroine who defied the military might of the Roman Empire by committing suicide at the urging of her fiancé, Massinissa, King of the Massilians (Numidians).

In contemporary feminist and postcolonialist readings, Medea is often seen as the outsider, as the minority woman, or woman of color.[97] *Cléopâtre captive* evokes skin color in conjunction with captivity (imprisonment) and slavery (of prisoners of wars, condoned by Pasquier); indeed, the words *captif* (from Latin *captivus*) and *esclave* (from Latin *sclavus* and the Byzantine Greek *sklabos*, meaning Slav) were synonymous in sixteenth-century French.[98] Cleopatra's physical presence on the stage—rendered by proxy of male artists, of course—corresponded to the Valois court's interest in captured Ottoman subjects, who were seen as "free" or "freed" rather than as slaves or coerced subjects.[99] Brantôme does not tell us about the fate of the "Moor" whom the Duke of

Guise liberated from the Spanish captain, but subjects thus liberated often remained tied to aristocratic courts by coercion or necessity. They served elite courts in diplomacy and were participants in court life, including ceremonies. The Marseille pharmacist Honorat Valbelle mentions in his journal that two women—one of whom was the servant or slave ("esclavonne") of Jean Emerich, a citizen of Marseille—were whipped for attempting to steal wheat in the cold winter of 1527. As Valbelle's editor and translator Roger Duchêne indicates, the word could signal the status of a domestic slave or it could equally refer to her ethnic origin as a Southern Slav.[100] Many stories that may involve trade or coercion contain important lacunae. While the free soil principle was used on occasion to differentiate the French kingdom from Spain or the Ottoman Empire, which degrees and modes of unfreedom were recognized in sixteenth-century France? Jodelle's claim that Cleopatra "will not die" because "time will preserve her" resembles Pasquier's fiction of justifying slavery in the past by way of the rational decision to "preserve" or "keep [the captured person] alive" as a slave. The degrees between galley slavery, serfdom, domestic slavery, coerced service, and symbolic or hidden modes of enslavement remain unnamed in documents that (barely) mention those who may have been affected by it. Valbelle also reports that, in 1532, the son of the king of Tlemcen (belonging to Moroccan ruling dynasty) was baptized in Marseille with the Baron of Saint-Blancard and Anne Cépède as the baptismal parents, after which he was given the name "Bertrand."[101] The agent Jean de Véga, who embarked on a mission to meet the Sublime Porte in the Mediterranean in 1537, reveals the presence of a man wearing a long (Turkish-style) mustache, beard, a Turkish hat, and boots under French-style clothing in Saint-Blancard's crew, which was sailing toward Tunis.[102] François Escalopier, Charles IX's envoy to the Transylvanian court of Stephen Báthory who stayed in the Ottoman Empire, relates that one other member of his group, a certain "du Tillet," who was "black like an African" and spoke Spanish well, was captured on a trip to Jerusalem and Damascus upon being taken for a Spanish spy. He and his translator spent four months in prison until the French ambassador attested that they were French and freed them.[103] These stories testify to a French version of the phenomenon termed by Imtiaz Habib as "the missing (black) subject" in English archives (a similar case could be made for missing unfree women and non-Christians as well). Habib argues that telling the stories of people of color requires a projective historiography, for their experiences and stories were largely "unseeable and unnameable" in Europe.[104] Since these people were often, if not always, coerced or captured, these stories of unfreedom were similarly invisible.[105]

This analysis of *Cléopâtre captive* and its broader cultural context reveals that people of color and unfree people, enslaved or otherwise, were at the extreme poles of cosmopolitan culture in sixteenth-century France: They were rendered invisible, without agency. The word *captif* has the same roots in French as *chétif*, meaning "feeble," "miserable," "humble," or simply "bad." Rather than compassion or understanding, "pity" is the emotion that Jodelle and de la Péruse consider it appropriate to feel toward the captive or slighted Oriental woman (notably, the same emotion that Grandgousier feels toward the Canarrians). Medea calls upon the furies to watch the "pitiful spectacle" of her "just quarrel." The word *captive* in the play's title is a pejorative term much like *chétive*, and only the symbolic transformation of Cleopatra through her mourning and the alchemy of her tears, made possible onstage through the intermediary of Jodelle's art, is what renders her visible in her power. Slaves and enslavement, too, abound as poetic images or demonstrations of sovereignty in French poetry, theater, and historical chronicles that assist in constructions of metaphysical freedom and the spectacle of royal power alike. Slavery was viewed as "spiritually inflicted," yet it was tied beyond eschatology to passions in war and love, with conversion and redemption as its desired endpoint.[106] From the mid-sixteenth century onward, *esclaver* appears in French as a neologism to signify internal obligation: a metaphorical slavery of the will, as, for example, when one is dominated by passion. Ronsard makes the first recorded use of the verb in "Ode to Vulcan," published in the *Mélanges* of 1555, where the poet has Bacchus declare to Vulcan:

> I have no worries of the Great Turk,
> Nor does the gold of the Great Sudan,
> Enslave my life ("n'esclave point ma vie").
> I have no jealousy of kings,
> But care solely about
> Cleverly applying perfume
> To my beard,
> And worry that a garland of flowers
> Adorn my head.[107]

Here, (Ronsard as) Bacchus declares his disinterest in both power and gold as the material means of wars and, by extension, of empire. Yet Ronsard's nonchalant Oriental god of conjuring ceremonies not only provides expandable limits of agency but also has a geopolitical history of its own. Ronsard looks to the East and Africa to extend his imaginary self through poetry, and, although Bacchus declares himself no slave to gold, he allows Ronsard to contemplate slavery's metaphorical modalities. Bacchus's internal freedom consists of standing outside the affairs of politics and outside the making of wealth and power, such that a person's freedom is mirrored in the unfreedom of others. *Cléopâtre captive* creates an intimate link between freedom, performance, and the body, just as the insouciant Ronsard does with sophistication in hair care, grooming, and simple adornments.

The grandiose yet violent passions of Medea are rendered in a spectacular fashion in a series of dramatic images created by René Boyvin, an Angevin engraver associated with the so-called school of Fontainebleau. Boyvin's engravings, after designs by Leonard Thiery, were published in his *Livre de la conquette de la toison d'or* about ten years after the first performance (see Figure 13).[108] Boyvin's images include Medea welcoming the chariot drawn by dragons with the image of the Sun in the background. Medea can be seen as the priestess of such a hedonic devotion to destructive desire and as the spectacle of libertine freedom through the *deus ex machina* of violent passions.[109] These ritualized spectacles of liberation—spectacular, exotic, monstrous, or pitiable—reminded French men that they, too, were servants and political subjects to those in higher ranks, at much the same time as they allowed them to present symbolic representations of their own freedom and acquire agency by defining others. However,

Figure 13

these very French libertine, existential, and mystical notions of freedom excluded the non-French, non-White, female, and non-Christian subjects whose freedom (and unfreedom) was not an issue, for whom these libertine acts of freedom did not bring visibility or greater status, and whose status came solely from living and serving entirely within domestic, royal and aristocratic, or Christian social institutions. It is no wonder that humanists and servants, agents of the monarchy at home or in foreign lands, emphasized and strove to raise the value of their own work. They did this by finding others—geographically distant people like Cleopatra and Medea—whose art and ingenuity they used as models to show the value of their service.

4
Nicolas de Nicolay's Empire of Ink

A drawing prepared by Antoine Caron (1521–1599) ca. 1562 depicts the exchange of presents between Pope Clement VII and Francis I of France. The image offers an idealized portrait of the Valois court three decades earlier,[1] simultaneously recalling the history of its alliance with the Ottoman Empire and the justification of this alliance as beneficial for Christian Europe (see Figure 14). This drawing also calls attention to the ambivalent status of those employed by the courts to manage dangerous or exotic animals—and, by extension, those who did the legwork in managing contacts with foreigners. The drawing commemorates the marriage ceremony between Francis I's son, Henri d'Anjou (later Henri II, King of France), and the pope's niece, Caterina de' Medici (later queen, then queen mother Catherine de Médicis), which took place in Marseille on October 28, 1533. Among other things, Francis I gave the pope a lion and a tapestry, the latter of which reproduced the scene of the Last Supper in the famous painting by Leonardo da Vinci.[2] However, instead of the biblical scene depicted in Leonardo's painting, Caron depicts a courtly dinner scene in the tapestry-in-the-drawing, with Christ sitting at the table, a small child in his lap, and several courtiers sitting with him at the table. The woman to his right is possibly Catherine de Médicis, Caron's patron.[3] Francis I stands in the foreground to the left next to Clement VII and points with his left hand at the tapestry held up by two women. Also in the foreground is a large, muscular lion being led off by a handler to the right, toward the pope's nephew (and Catherine's second cousin), Ippolito de' Medici (1511–1535), who is wearing a cardinal's cloak. Francis I's right hand, held horizontally in front of the pope, points outside the frame toward the viewer. This outstretched hand is an orientating gesture, linking this scene from the past with the future, the viewer's

Figure 14

present, forming a straight (hence rational) line connecting the two temporalities. There is a sharp contrast between the bucolic banquet scene depicted in the tapestry, in which men, women, and children mingle and food is being served, and the political scene in the foreground, with its solemnly and elegantly dressed statesmen. The proliferation of fruit and plants amid the female bodies represents an excess of matter that frames the somber political scene in which the future of Christian Europe is being determined. Francis I's right hand points toward an imagined spiritual community of Christians to be found ahead, in times to come (which must also signal the irony of its failure to viewers in the 1560s), but it also directs the gaze toward the lion. The lion was originally a present from Hayreddin Pasha (also called "Barbarossa" in Europe) when the newly minted Pasha sent forth an envoy to Francis I in July 1533, a mere three months before the events referenced in Caron's drawing. As an exotic animal from North Africa, it is a reminder of the French–Ottoman alliance, which aided the French in negotiating the intervention of Ottoman galleys against Spanish territories. The animal's body stands for the power and vigor associated with the military might of the Ottomans, including the material resources of war. But the scene also visualizes the repeated claims made by the French monarchy through its propagandists that the alliance helped to maintain peace in European Christianity by protecting it from the incursions of the Ottomans. The lion is supposedly also the tamed might of the Ottomans, depicting a raw force transformed into courageous power. Caron's drawing thus visually reproduces the Christian-Platonist rationale given by the French court to justify its strategic decision of allying itself with the Suni Muslim Sublime Porte.

Caron was known for hiding satirical portraits of his own society behind elegant courtly, exotic scenes. Here too, the prominent placement of the lion and its handler calls upon the viewer to question the official propaganda. The viewer must also consider the historical distance between the past moment depicted by the artist and the present of the drawing, which was made after the peace treaty of Cateau-Cambrésis with Spain concluded in 1559 and the death not only of Francis I but, more recently, of King Henri II, who was killed in a jousting accident shortly after the conclusion of the treaty. The drawing captures the ambivalent cosmopolitanism of the Valois court that insisted on including the Ottomans in its calculations yet was intent on reducing them to the spectacle of a domesticated exotic other through symbolic means. The doubling of the animal body with the muscular, almost naked body of the animal handler, both of which are represented with strong, elongated limbs, is the center of Caron's commentary on the scene.[4] The handler's nudity signifies a lower social class and, potentially, foreignness and animality, both of which are ambivalent qualities in sixteenth-century France. The handler is an outsider in a world of neo-Platonic Christianity and elite, (White) cosmopolitan male politics that surrounds itself with images of women and nature, including wild animals, to mark its status—and yet he manages his own symbolic self-representation by keeping the lion tamed and makes his own claim thus to symbolic power and agency. His ethnicity is less visible than his class, but one or both set him apart. His nakedness is overdetermined. In *Renaissance Clothing and the Materials of Memory*, Ann Rosalind Jones and Peter Stallybrass discuss the significance of livery worn by servants of aristocrats, which could signal both high and low status.[5] Here, the unclothed muscles of the lion handler—distinguished by his *not* wearing livery or clothing marked with the insignia of the aristocrat he is serving—functions in a similar way. He is set apart from the wealthy group dressed in luxurious textiles, and his bare muscular body signals his natural force, unshackled from the connotations of subordination that came to be associated with livery by the sixteenth century.

Nevertheless, his unclothed state remains ambivalent, as nakedness also retained connotations of the *too* natural, the untamed, and the uncivilized. The handler is poised ambiguously as both the carrier of the symbolic empire over nature and a marginal figure, obscured as he is amid the elite male viewers and the ornamental artifacts (and women) depicted in the scene. His bare skin, unmarked by color, adds to this ambiguity.

As elite French culture became more cosmopolitan in the mid-sixteenth century, so, too, did race increasingly emerge as the discernable property of others. This cosmopolitanism was extended to broader audiences with aspirations to status by way of theater (as we saw in the previous chapter) and, even more so, by way of travel books made available for purchase by a well-to-do international clientele. The image of the nude, muscular handler indicates the symbolic ambivalence that tied race and class to claims of status that proceeded by way of naturalizing moral and physical qualities. This ambivalence about the bodies of others, bodies seen as natural and often depicted as gesturing, informs the most popular book about the Ottoman Empire in the sixteenth century, Nicolas de Nicolay's *Les Quatre premiers livres des navigations et pérégrinations* (first printed in 1567). Although *Navigations et pérégrinations* is usually described as a costume book and provides the reader/viewer with a catalog of eastern Mediterranean ethnicities and social ranks through depictions of codified clothing and a few props,[6] the body (both covered and uncovered), skin, and textile play privileged roles in his textual descriptions and images. We see this, for example, in his recollection of a young Hungarian slave girl at the market who is undressed and sold amidst the clutter of the Bazaar. So, too, do we see it in his descriptions of the drooping breasts of the women on the island of Chios,[7] the naked skin of dancing, reading, and self-cutting dervishes, skin that has been cauterized and lacerated, body hair, feathers, and clothing, all of which contribute to the ornamental dimensions of the book. Nude bodies of foreign, non-Western European, and non-French people, women, mythological persons, and even saints adorned the interiors of aristocratic homes, circulating more broadly among collectors in cheap print formats in sixteenth-century France and Europe. The Council of Trent's decree regulating pious images and banning nudity and lascivious content (Lat. "lascivia") in 1563 did not affect aristocratic tastes. Nor did it affect those who imitated them.[8] Nicolay's many images offer illicit pleasures to audiences that aspire to genteel status, shifting quickly from sparking erotic desire to kindling a sense of compassion or moral outrage. The combination of erotic or material pleasures with zealous moralizing is key to the success of the book. Nicolay establishes a parallel between the French crown's unilateral claims to cosmopolitan civilized desires as a means of justifying its use of the material world of the Ottoman Empire and the access accorded to male readers and art buyers to the pleasures contained in the book.

The book was published by Guillaume Rouillé, a business-minded printer-entrepreneur from Lyon who learned the trade in Venice and specialized in printing illustrated books in several European languages. Rouillé catered to bourgeois desires for material things, all the while maintaining close contacts with Venetian printers and booksellers.[9] The book Rouillé printed for Nicolay was itself the product of two visual-minded authors: a spy of the Valois who had been appointed the role of royal cartographer by the time the book was published (that is, Nicolay himself) and the artist "Lyon Davent" (Léon Davent),[10] who was known to have made engravings of Fontainebleau's interior for Francesco Primaticcio as well as reproductive etchings based on designs by Giulio Romano, Francesco Parmigianino, Primaticcio, and Luca Penni.[11] Davent repeatedly produced images depicting people in ancient or exotic costumes and erotic scenes.[12] Nicolay (1517–1583) was an agent of the French crown in the 1540s and 1550s and was working on maps of France commissioned by Catherine de Médicis in the year 1567 when *Navigations et pérégrinations* was published. The collaboration between printer, author, and artist resulted in textual descriptions and visual images that racialized Ottoman subjects based on aesthetic qualities like harmony and disharmony, and that rendered skin color readable across class and language boundaries in Europe.

So far, the handful of critics that have devoted critical attention to this book have largely focused on its representations of the Ottoman other, which they have sought to explain through the vicissitudes of *realpolitik*. The time that elapsed between Nicolay's mission and the publication of the book was indeed marked by a myriad of political changes. After the Treaty of Cateau-Cambrésis (1559), the French crown was reluctant to send a resident ambassador to the Sublime Porte, leaving the task of the ambassador instead to two secretaries between 1559 and 1566: first François Dolu, then François Petremol, sieur of Norroy, neither of whom had sufficient experience to deal with the affairs of France at the Porte. The cooling of French enthusiasm for the alliance is demonstrated by the fact that in 1565 Charles IX decided to meet Ottoman envoys secretly while publicly entertaining a Spanish delegation in Bayonne. However, in the same year, consular outposts were established in the Ottoman Empire.[13] In the 1560s, efforts to liberate French subjects captured in the eastern Mediterranean intensified.[14] In the mid-1560s, Protestant and Catholic factions radicalized in France.[15] The editors of the book, Marie-Christine Gomez-Géraud and Stéphane Yérasimos, attribute the harsh anti-Ottoman tone in the book to the slowing of diplomatic relations and the coming to a halt of military cooperation between the French and the Ottomans after 1559.[16] Marcus Keller attributes the relentless vilification of the Ottomans to the French civil wars. He argues that, for Nicolay, the Ottoman Empire became an exotic screen onto which the author could project the religious schisms, moral decline, and crises of authority that he perceived to be threatening France while also promoting the ideal of a French nation united by the Catholic faith and common culture.[17] In what follows, I build on these two readings but also show that, by setting his colonial perspective apart from the ambassador's diplomatic one, Nicolay continues to graft idealized ideas of French agency onto an imperialist narrative. He then projects internal colonies onto the Ottoman Empire and its fringes in an act of symbolic mastery. Nicolay's perspective can only be understood as an amalgam of agendas: factional (Catholic) politics; the fiction of the outsize role of himself as the crown's agent; the use of the able, well-born body and well-informed mind to claim noble status and moral agency; and the aesthetic possibilities of imitating the aristocratic culture of consumption, all of which Nicolay consolidates against the backdrop of images of servile people and slaves, wild men, uncontrolled abundance, and brown and Black skin, which enter into and define the economy of visual pleasures in the book. These tensions created a paradoxical state of affairs in which all things Ottoman carried out multiple functions: They served as inverted mirrors of national values, became a source of imitative desire for readers and agents aspiring to genteel status, and became bodies upon which notions of future domination could be projected. Nobility or the status of being well-born as a fantasy object of desire in *Navigations et pérégrinations* rests on a contrast with those described as conquerable, whose bodies are symbolized by the female servant and the enslaved body: dark skin, boundless passions, and a penchant for moral vices that distort the body and threaten its unity. Just as in Caron's image of the handler, the agent, who manages the symbolic control of others, remains ambiguous, and his visibility is secured by the view of those over whom he claims symbolic mastery.

The Cosmopolitan Agent, the Ambassador, and the Deli

In the Preface, Nicolay echoes the cosmopolitan ideology that emanated from the French court; that is, its claim to make all differences and antagonisms disappear under French rule in a Platonic ideal of unity and peace, which often remained blind to the political or cultural differences that formed the basis of the emerging culture of diplomacy:

> ... with the help of these pilgrimages and communications ("pérégrinations et communications") all nations of the world grow gentle and

familiar with one another ("s'apprivoisent et familiarisent les unes aux autres"), mutually correct each other's barbarous vices, teach each other the true religion, virtues, and moral, civil, and political righteousness, communicate with each other and distribute among each other, through mutual commerce and the equitable and gracious exchange of their goods, metals, wood, drugs, fruits, plants, animals, linen and textile, silk, hides, manufactured goods, and other merchandises and commodities, compensating thus for the lack of one thing or the abundance of another in their own land, in such a fashion that the whole earth with all its goods can be seen as common property, common to everyone and to each and every man no matter from which country, language, or nation he is, with the help of mutual visitation knowledge and communicative alliance ("connaissance et communicative alliance"), destroying the arrogance of the Greeks and Romans who called other men and other nations more barbarous than their own[.][18]

This blatantly imperialist, totalizing use of universalism is the hallmark of what James der Derian has called an "anti-diplomatic" attitude to diplomacy.[19] Within the visions of writers such as François Sagon, François Rabelais, and Guillaume Postel, gentleness and civilized conduct were associated with the possibility of a utopian community whose boundaries remained open to at least some "Turks" (Grandgousier's alliance with Alpharbal, Postel's bonds with "simple Turks," and Pierre Belon's working relationships with various inhabitants of the Ottoman Empire all function here as a case in point). Nicolay, on the other hand, a loyal Catholic, renders this idea almost exclusive—with indeed very few notable exceptions—to a restricted notion of Frenchness and Europeanness. He outlines here a "mutual exchange" ("mutuel commerce"[20]) as a disinterested form of exchange that is distinguished from interest-driven mercantile exchanges. This rhetoric of reciprocity, and the example of exchanges of material goods such as luxury artifacts, natural resources, and antiquities that Nicolay recounts, imply an emerging ideology of a civilizing colonial mission that is premised upon France offering nonmaterial (superior or equal) "goods" in exchange for the material resources that are available in the Ottoman Empire. The "goods" that Nicolay names as being offered by France pertain to the protection of "true religion" (Catholicism)—but this would, in later, seventeenth-century contexts, come to be complemented by claims about the superiority of French-made luxury goods, culture, and civilization.[21] While, as we have seen in previous chapters, other authors created visions of an empire to come that were based on Christian heterodoxy, mysticism, and pagan and occult notions of the divine (whose visions nonetheless remained unachieved, utopian totalities), Nicolay's universalist cosmopolitanism rests on the idea that French Catholicism is the sole source of moral principles and rationality to transcend individual interest—which, presumably, it falls upon the French to teach to the Ottomans and the world. In the Preface, Nicolay defines the human as colonizer, dubiously promoting Adam, the biblical first man, to the status of being seigneur of the Earth: "The name [Adam] signifies terrestrial or of the Earth, not only because the material of his body was earth but because the Earth was given as property ("pour propre possession corporelle") and home ("habitable demeurance") to this earthly monarch of animals, while the heaven was reserved for the Lord God and the good spirits born in him and returning to him."[22] Thus stating that to be human is to have lordship over the Earth, Nicolay makes those he distinguishes with the privilege of being cosmopolitan ("cosmopolite, c'est-à-dire citoyen du monde"[23]) the rightful colonizers of the entire Earth. Nicolay's celebration of human diversity through the famous citation of Terence's dictum, "I am a man, I consider nothing that is human alien to me," has a perverse ring given how restrictive Nicolay's notion of the human turns out to be.[24] And yet, claiming mobility and cosmopolitanism as values serves him not just as a means of presenting some as less than human, but also as a means of associating his own agency with that of exotic foreign actors who become his doubles.

Nicolay presents his *Navigations et pérégrinations* as the "fruits" of travels that all "good and noble spirits" ("tout bon et noble esprit") "well formed" and "educated" by nature ("de nature bien informé") are "naturally inclined to," for the "sublime spirit" "elevate[s] and set[s] in motion their massive bodies, carrying them toward various foreign and distant places." Noble spirits are well-informed by nature, in possession of information appropriate for the spy. Nicolay completes this bombastic claim with a simile from military technology— their spirit moves their bodies like "fire imparts a sudden movement to the heavy and inert artillery bullet."[25] Travel, mobility in space outside one's native region and kingdom, he claims, is a special mark and privilege of those who are both excellent in body and mind and are capable of gathering information from nature—that is, possessing natural nobility that manifests itself through mobility and ruse. The Aristotelian image of form imprinted on matter, according to which mere matter is something dangerous that must be contained, acquires military undertones through this image of animating fire. The word "fruit" refers to both the generativity of nature and the results of the labors of the agent himself, with the descriptions and images in the book being the products of both. Thus, people, artificial things, products of nature, and objects of art are to be judged analogously as products of nature and as "fruits" brought to France by the agent through description. Ultimately, these descriptions render visible differences that exist, he affirms, not only in the physical makeup of the body but also in the spirit. The images of the "noble spirit" moving the agent's body and the "fire" moving the "inert" bullet mix references to Stoic reason informing nature and the cosmic order (often designated as fire) with references to gunpowder and firearms, whose use in the fifteenth and sixteenth centuries transformed warfare and rendered fortifications necessary—along with spies, like Nicolay, to scope out enemy fortifications. With this image of the book as a cornucopia of wholesome and sweet "fruits," the author claims to transform the "inert" matter of the physical, material world—a category in which he includes the near totality of the Ottoman Empire, reduced to material objects and bodies—into a more refined and pleasing spiritual fare.

Fictions of agency relying on the cosmic material animacy of the *physis* did not prevent agents from facing constant material challenges. We might look, by way of example, at Pierre Gilles (d. ca. 1555), a humanist scholar of Byzantium who was a contemporary of Nicolay. Gilles's modern editor, Jean-Pierre Grélois, estimates that it was a lack of money and a willingness to serve the monarchy (revealed through his activity as a propagandist for the court in previous decades) that earned him the assignment to gather information, books, and objects in the Levant, rather than his knowledge of Byzantine history. Gilles was one of the scholars, along with Postel, Belon, and Nicolay, who traveled in the Ottoman Empire in the mid-sixteenth century. He left for the Levant in 1544 and accompanied the French ambassador Gabriel de Luels d'Aramon (d. ca. 1553) to Persia with the Ottoman army led by Sultan Suleiman I in 1548, which he describes in a letter to a friend. His patron, the cardinal and diplomat Georges d'Armagnac (1501–1585), reported to Henri II Gilles's achievement of obtaining several precious manuscripts ("en a arresté un grand nombre") but also noted that, because the moneys the previous king ordered to be paid to him were not delivered, the servant could not send them to France.[26] Gilles struggled with loss in many ways, including losing his notes while being held captive by pirates and dealing with the rivalry of fellow humanists. Jean Chesneau documents one bitter argument Gilles had with Postel over old Hebrew and Greek manuscripts in November 1549 while both scholars were residing in Jerusalem. In addition, Belon was accused of plagiarizing some of Gilles's work.[27] Calling attention to the special power of the Ottoman Empire and its richness in natural resources by reducing it to an overflowing material plentitude was a way for both Gilles and Nicolay to give importance to their own activities in the eyes of their readers. In his topography, Gilles describes Constantinople (he never uses the term "Istanbul") as a city inside an almost boundless sylvan space, even though deforestation affected the area just as it affected European forests. He also describes it as having the shape of a "mouth" and a "horn of plenty."[28] This image is repeated by Nicolay's metaphor of the "fruits" of the Ottoman Empire, which he purports to bring to the readers and to the king. Notably, the "Turkish cook" is depicted in one of the book's images as in the act of handing the fruits to the viewers, seeming to offer them out of a horn-shaped dish (see Figure 15). This image reduces the fruits to objects of consumption in such a way that the French appetite and, by extension, the readers' appetite in this international production, mimics yet also domesticates the Ottoman appetite. Unlike in Rabelais's story about medlars and giants, fruits here are given a symbolic, rather than material, reality; they are both ornaments and metaphors of nature's plenty that can be turned into material resources and riches. If Rabelais and Belon entertain nature as both the universal realm in which their agencies unfold and a realm in which a particularly French cosmopolitanism is made susceptible and indeed subject to constant contestation, then Nicolay's authoritative symbolic gestures deny all possibility of contestation by calling it out as tantamount to moral deprivation and political disintegration.

Creating the fiction of a natural nobility and mobility, both of which are supposed to transcend inert matter, serves Nicolay to develop a persona that rivals that of the French ambassador d'Aramon. *Navigations et pérégrinations* presents this persona to invert the usual hierarchy and order of narration—that is, to allow Nicolay, the agent and spy, the one tasked with extra diplomatic and clandestine affairs, to come to the fore and outshine the ambassador, the official representative of the French court at the Sublime Porte. Nicolay's perspective is defined by a recognition, albeit unspoken, of his own precarious position—and by his response to this, which is not so much to represent the interests of his master, the king, as the ambassador is tasked with doing, but to usurp the king's authority. Nicolay accompanied d'Aramon on his second mission to the Ottoman Empire (1551–1553). A French nobleman who had been banished from France in 1540 for committing violence against peasants on his lands, d'Aramon entered into the service of Francis I after first serving Guillaume Pellicier (ca. 1490–1568), the French ambassador to Venice. D'Aramon was seeking to establish his status in the international space of diplomacy through his work as the king's ambassador, and this is rendered especially apparent in the zeal with which he approached the Franco–Ottoman negotiations.[29] His ambitious career as ambassador is revealed by the fact that, while in Venice, probably in 1541–1542, he sat for his portrait by Titian (1490–1576), an artist who was celebrated for his dramatic tableaux of biblical and historical scenes and renowned as a portrait maker of the rich and famous. In the portrait, d'Aramon is depicted in a confident pose holding a bunch of arrows.

Figure 15

These arrows are likely similar to the metaphorical ones evoked by Blaise de Monluc in his defense of Francis I's alliance with the Sublime Porte, which was made to the Venetians after the Ottoman navy's aid in the siege of Nice. According to Jean de Monluc, who wrote the memoirs of his brother Blaise de Monluc (French ambassador in Venice from 1542), Blaise said that Francis I "may make arrows of all wood" against his enemy,[30] with the "wood" being here an allusion to the Ottomans. The portrait presents d'Aramon holding the arrows (or the Ottomans, as Francis I's "arrows") in his clenched fist (see Figure 16). The ambassador's open face, lively eyes, straight upper body, and resolute grip around the arrows, combined with his brocade overcoat, white shirt, and the chain of a knightly order, St. Michel (proffered by Francis I), are all displays of the power and dignity of the French monarch—as well as the excellence of the man, d'Aramon, who represents his interests.

D'Aramon's first mission (1546–1551) was both ambitious and costly. In the winter of 1547, he began his tenure as Francis's I's resident ambassador and presented the sultan with an expensive clock made in Lyon.[31] He joined Suleiman I on his campaign against Persia the next summer, carrying with him the *lys de France* on his banners and clothing, giving advice to the sultan on the attack of the fortress of Van, and purchasing an elephant, which it befell to Gilles to anatomize. His first mission was documented by his secretary, Jean Chesneau, from whom we know that the ambassador gave many presents to various members of the Ottoman court. Chesneau reveals his own understanding of the value the Ottomans placed on gift giving,[32] as well as the power of gifts more generally to create human bonds, by tersely remarking "we were welcome because we gave."[33] D'Aramon's embassy was focused on efforts to push the Ottomans to attack Spain—for example, by giving them news about the Spanish conquest of Mahdia in Tunisia.[34] At a time when the Ottoman army was engaged in Persia, and the Sublime Porte was seeking and concluding peace with the Habsburgs in 1547 (a treaty in which the Ottomans gave the emperor three months to hand back Mahdia), it was the job of the ambassador to break up this peace. In January 1551, d'Aramon departed from Constantinople to return to France, possibly to persuade Henri II to join a military campaign with the Ottomans.[35] He recommended to King Henri II a joint campaign to capture Sicily and Puglia. In his report dated April 7, 1551, d'Aramon urges the king to make a decisive sign of his commitment to send his galleys to partake in a campaign "to show the Grand Seigneur that you include him in your plans by giving him some presents, so he sees that you desire to keep his friendship and do away with the suspicion that those who wish to harm you want him to have."[36] The ambassador presents himself as an experienced observer of the ambitions or "passions" of the Ottoman elite, who not only represents the French king at the Ottoman court but also represents the Ottomans *to* the French

Figure 16

king as reliable negotiating partners—while, at the same time, warning the king that too much temporizing on the part of the French would give the Ottomans the wrong message.

In May 1551, Henri II sent d'Aramon back in great haste with a promise to keep his fleet ready to be deployed in the Provence. This decision was made by the French court in agreement with d'Aramon's reports, which translated the distant possibility of military cooperation between the Ottoman and the French navies into an imminent certainty.[37] The Ottoman fleet departed from Constantinople at the end of June 1551, heading to Malta and Tripoli to revenge Charles V and his corsairs, the Knights of St. John, for the imperial capture of Mahdia. D'Aramon left Marseille on July 5, 1551. He had no news of the Ottoman fleet except for rumors that the Ottomans were headed to Sicily and Puglia. D'Aramon's first diplomatic stop was at Hasan Pasha's court in Algiers. The Ottoman fleet did not attack Puglia or Sicily—but, after some small raids, it proceeded to Malta and then to Tripoli. D'Aramon, who had hoped the fleet would attack southern Italy, gave chase and reached them near Tripoli in early August 1551. Because d'Aramon could not dissuade Sinan Pasha, the Ottoman grand admiral, from attacking Tripoli, he tried to persuade Henri II that an Ottoman capture and subsequent transformation of Tripoli into a "nest of corsairs" would also be advantageous for France.[38] D'Aramon's work was hampered by the low interest of both the Ottomans and the French in committing resources to a joint venture.[39] Despite his efforts, the Ottoman fleet and the French military forces did not join. Instead, the Ottomans waited for the French ships in vain at Naples when they arrived on July 15, 1552, " . . . so that, your Majesty, I had never been as tormented as then, even when dealing with such people, whose nature is known to be suspicious, capable of losing trust because of the smallest problem."[40] By June 1553, Henri II had confided in d'Aramon and the Baron de la Garde that he was sending his forces to northern France instead of sending galleys to assist in an Ottoman naval attack in Italy (Naples and Siena), which he had earlier requested, "to exploit something that seems to me more aligned with my interests."[41] Henri II also excused himself for not being able to send money to his diplomats, alleging that the Venetians were blocking the way,[42] and let his ambassadors know that he was planning a joint attack on Corsica but that he did not wish the galleys of the naval commander Turgut Reis (1485–1565) to winter in France.[43] Thus, after this perceived failure of cooperation, the king signaled his lack of trust in the Ottomans "because they are friends of time and money only," accusing them of pursuing their material interest and strategical advantage to justify his own similar actions.[44] Despite the ambassador's efforts and confidence in his skills, he failed to anticipate the plans of either the Ottomans or his court in time to realize the cooperation.

Nicolay's self-presentation in *Navigations et pérégrinations* offers an antidiplomatic narrative that usurps the monarch's moralizing perspective and sets the agent apart from the ambassador, to the detriment of the latter. There is little doubt that Nicolay was a spy.[45] Before embarking on his mission in the company of d'Aramon, Nicolay's first encounter with the Ottomans was probably during the siege of Nice in 1543.[46] A few years later, in 1546, he gained the trust of Henry Dudley, Henry VIII's ambassador to Francis I, whom he followed to England, and from whom he was able to gain precious information about the plans of the English fleet in Scotland, along with a valuable manuscript and portolan chart. This information contributed to the successful French siege of the Scottish fortress of Saint Andrews.[47] In 1551, he joined d'Aramon and stayed with him until July 22, 1552, at which point the ambassador left with the Ottoman fleet for Naples, and Nicolay for France. By the time of d'Aramon's mission, Nicolay was a cagey servant of the king who was seasoned in previous battles and spy missions, although he reveals little about this in his narrative. When he compares himself to Ulysses, it is the soldier and spy that he sees in the Greek hero: "He who took Troy, and then, while erring,/Saw the cities and customs of many peoples."[48] Francis I's famous *Galérie d'Ulysse* by Primaticcio in Fontainebleau is no longer extant, but it indicates the importance of Ulysses as a figure for the idealization of the soldier-adventurer of the court. One of the frescos was independently reworked by the artist in ca. 1560 and is now preserved in the Toledo Museum of Art in Toledo, Ohio. It depicts Ulysses after he has returned to Ithaca, reclining in bed with his wife, Penelope, and they are recounting their adventures to one another in this intimate setting. Here, knowledge is represented as sensitive and sensual, even erotic (see Figure 17).[49] Ulysses embodies the overlapping of political and private pleasures: the presence of sexual desire in politics and that of acts of domination in sexual

Figure 17

relations. To him, libidinal pleasures, political interests, and strategic opportunities all blend. Much like Ulysses in the painting, Nicolay mixes erotic and political desires for dominance, narrating them in a storytelling mode to generate more desire in the audience such that the readers of the book take on the role of Penelope, becoming beneficiaries of intimate, sensual knowledge (with François Rabelais's seasoned fictional traveler Panurge, the teller of his bawdy adventures to his master Pantagruel, acting as a predecessor and role model). Nicolay's book reveals that sexual allurement continued to play a role in the construction of post-Tridentine French masculinity as a means of both affirming its animal (transgressive) nature and marking out a private space of privilege and homosociality: one that implied a network of shared gazes, with unique access to political and erotic knowledge.[50] Nicolay gives his readers access to intimate, voyeuristic scenes of knowledge adjacent to the scenes of practical information he most likely described in greater detail to his patrons.

In the Preface, Nicolay poetically describes having left "the dolphin's gut" (i.e., the Dauphiné region of southeast France) at the age of five in 1542 and going through the "mouth of the lion" (i.e., the city of Lyon) before beginning his voyages.[51] These fanciful allusions to marine and terrestrial animals add the feel of a chivalric adventure to the author's truncated biography (from which his secret missions have been excluded), suggesting that his experiences took him through a visceral and intimate relation to animal bodies—and that he, the agent and author, was tested by these very close encounters with wild and dangerous bodies on land and sea. These animal encounters prefigure those he had with racialized people in his descriptions of the Ottoman Empire. While other travelers to the Ottoman Empire (for example, Belon and Postel) acknowledge that their movements were governed by local customs and laws, prohibitions and privileges that were accorded to French subjects, Nicolay rewrites the space in which he moves as if it were entirely lawless. Presenting himself as the hero of adventures of chivalric proportions, the agent thus inscribes himself into the "lawless space" of romance that is distinct from the regulated space of the diplomat, returning to chivalric notions of self and other formed in battle while also attacking conventional notions of nobility.[52] Emphasizing his own mobility allows Nicolay to invent a new identity for himself and to appropriate a space—one that is being contested by empires and emerging absolutist states—for the purposes of deploying his own agency. *Navigations et pérégrinations* is a representation, however indirect and contorted, of Nicolay's role in the mission. Book 1 is the most instructive in this regard and contains several allusions to information-gathering about areas under Ottoman control and about Malta, its fortifications, water supplies, ports, and geography. Nicolay was not present in the Ottoman Empire to fight in a specific battle (in fact, he left the mission before negotiations about the naval campaign had even been concluded), but rather to serve the goals that remained external to the mission. His was an arcane, cunning kind of prudence that was increasingly recognized as essential to the functioning of the state. In the Preface to his book, Nicolay rehashes neo-Platonic clichés about the primacy of the eye over hearing and the spirit over matter to claim that there is a new professional class of agents who "prefer to expose themselves to dangers . . . in order to see with their own eyes, more reliable than hearing, the marvels that the sovereign architect has placed into his excellent work of the world." These agents, he proclaims, have served the monarchy better than the erudite humanists who stay at home and study books "like a turtle in its house, which they would take to be prison, or like the proverbial lame cobbler in his house . . . like the idle man who is a useless weight on the earth" ("l'homme oiseux et inutile charge de terre").[53] In this way, Nicolay shifts the prestige of knowing away from bookish humanist erudition and toward the collection of information that is useful for the state.[54]

Nicolay chronicles d'Aramon's mission without revealing much, if anything, of the actual negotiations. However, while describing the mission's specific stops in Algiers, Malta, Tripoli, and Edirne, Nicolay depicts d'Aramon's performance of gift-giving to Sinan Pasha in the following way:

> And as soon as he performed the obligation of sending a present both to the Pasha and to others who were in his service—for, since time immemorial, everyone who wants to negotiate with these barbarians must follow this custom—he was led to the pavilion that had been prepared for him.[55]

Nicolay praises d'Aramon for his sophisticated mastery of Ottoman customs. And yet, instead of recognizing the custom of exchanging gifts as the mark of civilization in Ottoman culture and a basis for protocols of exchange and negotiation, he describes the Ottomans as "barbarians," a pejorative term whose meaning ranged in the sixteenth century from "non-Christian" to "cruel" and "violent." The term goes back to an ancient Greek stereotype in which barbarians were defined by what they lacked and by what the Greeks possessed: notably, the implementation of laws, written records, cities, institutions like marriage, and the use of clothes. Analyzing the impact of Aristotle's distinction between natural slaves and natural despots, Justin E. H. Smith argues that such a delineation relies on an implicit separation between people who are purported to be more like animals and people who are purported to be more rational. In this way, the concept of the slave in Aristotle's thought maps onto the ancient Greek categories of barbarians (non-Greeks), who are seen as the counterparts to those who are civilized (Greeks).[56] Nicolay, too, used the alleged barbarism of the Ottoman other, if not to justify enslavement, at least to justify the European desire for conquest and dominance. He employs many scales of value and disparagement, competence and incompetence, virtue and vice, usefulness and useless inertia—for as we have seen, he disparages humanists for their useless sedentary learning—but gravest of all is the barbarity of those who are governed by their passions, as he often suggests is the case for the servants of the Sublime Porte and the officers of Islam.

Nicolay describes the ritual civilities exchanged between the Ottomans and the French in Algiers in such a way that the material richness of the things offered by the Ottomans inevitably reveals their moral corruption. He describes how the French ambassador marched into Algiers on a horse that had been sent to him as a gift by the "king of Algiers" (as Nicolay called the governor, Hasan Pasha) and was led into the magnificent palace, whose luxurious waterworks, mosaics, and columns Nicolay does not fail to describe, to be greeted and waited on by an ornately dressed court.[57] However, Nicolay (like Henri II) measures the Ottomans by the ethical yardstick of disinterested exchange, which allows him to subject them to vilification while also morally idealizing the French.[58] Nicolay describes the French mission's actions as generous and friendly: "We stayed one week in a liberal and friendly manner, conversing with each other with great familiarity."[59] He describes the court of Hasan Pasha, meanwhile, as the opposite, for, "out of greed," they expected monetary compensation for the abundant plates of food that they provided.[60]

The accounts of d'Aramon and Nicolay overlap in describing the failure of Hasan Pasha's Algerian corsair subjects to respect either the rights of the French ambassador or those granted by the Sublime Porte to the French subjects. They converge, too, in narrating the corsairs' act of raiding the two French galleys.[61] Nicolay also relates that he was captured by the corsairs on his way back from the Pasha's court to the French ship, chained to the corsairs' galley, and held hostage until the French restituted the Christian slaves who fled from the *fustes* (small galleys) of the corsairs onto the French galleys. Nicolay demonstrates (to the reader) his own resourcefulness:

> the whole time showing a confident expression, I made to them so many protestations and reproaches about the wrongs and injuries that they were doing to our ambassador and his people, whose master (who was also our master) was great and powerful enough to revenge himself that they agreed to let me go.[62]

When he and his servant are about to be overpowered and taken captive, Nicolay communicates through his body language and his words to persuade the corsairs to let him go. His agency hinges on the representation of the French monarch, whom he describes as "great and powerful" and capable of revenge. He usurps the diplomatic powers of representation, especially of representing the monarch, and thus the Algerian corsairs are threatened with revenge and retaliation by the French king.

Having missed the Ottoman fleet, d'Aramon was forced to accept the lukewarm hospitality of the corsairs of Malta (the Knights of St. John), many of whom sided with Spain and looked at the Ottoman-allied French with hostility. Tight-lipped as ever, Nicolay describes this sojourn as *aguillade*, a Sabir word for a stop to replenish the fresh water supplies. The French spent only one day on the island, since Juan de Homedes y Coscón, grand master of the order, asked d'Aramon to sail to Tripoli and prevent the Ottoman fleet from besieging the fortress held by the French section of the order.[63] In Nicolay's description, the French were entertained during the dinner with stories of the cruelties of Sinan Pasha's fleet, which had recently looted the island of Gozo, located in the Maltese archipelago and the east coast of Sicily. The knights' recantation of Ottoman cruelties relies on the perception that Christians are tied by blood in Christ and by place through the Holy Land, the nominal goal of the knights' military activities. Robert Bartlett calls the formation of a cohesive European identity through faith, figured despite linguistic, ethnic, and geographic differences, "the 'ethnicization' of Christianity."[64] And, in Malta, at the table of the knights—all of whom came from different nations—the French were invited into a community of Christian "blood brothers" viewed as a quasi-ethnicity and made to feel at home through stories of the Ottomans' spilling of Christian blood that evoked the language of race and blood to reaffirm this sense of community.[65] Nicolay's narrative repeats these old fictions of crusader identity. However, there were political tensions within this community.[66] Legally, the knights operated under the protection of various European authorities, including the pope, the Spanish king, and other European princes. Both Francis I and Henri II sought alliances with the order, many members of which were French—including the commander of French knights, Nicolas Durand de Villegagnon, who just two years later, in 1555, would lead the first French colony in Brazil. Nicolay was more than a little influenced by the crusader's perspective adopted by the French knights about the French king's Ottoman allies. And, despite the complexity of the geopolitical situation, he weaves their perspective into his relentless narrative about the "barbarity" of the Ottomans, even as he remains equally unsympathetic to the pro-Spanish de Homedes, Villegagnon's rival.[67]

As Nicolay continues to narrate the events of the siege at Tripoli, he inscribes his own actions and gestures into the events. According to his letters, d'Aramon hoped to persuade Sinan Pasha to partake in a joint campaign against the

Tunisian coastal city Mahdia but failed to do so even after he finally caught up with him in Tripoli.[68] Afterward, de Homedes publicly blamed the chief of the French garrison, Gaspar de Vallier, for parleying with the Ottomans (which was forbidden by papal law), and Villegagnon, who was present at the defense of Tripoli, defended de Vallier in a pamphlet printed in multiple languages to reach readers in Europe.[69] As a result, Nicolay's narrative places as much blame as possible on the Ottomans, whose friendly reception of the French, promises, and gifts—including Sinan Pasha's requests that the French stay—Nicolay describes as many traps rather than as tools of negotiation between allies.[70] According to d'Aramon, "immediately" after the fortress was surrendered, the Ottomans asked him to transport the two hundred knights to Malta under the knights' wishes.[71] Nicolay's account, however, is more complicated. He reports that two of Sinan's officers, Dragut (Turgut Reis) and Salih Reis, falsely promised to liberate all the soldiers and their possessions to prevent the knights from changing their minds and refusing to surrender. Nicolay, moreover, reports that Sinan Pasha also agreed to the plan and sent an envoy "carrying false and mendacious words" to the knights.[72] Sinan Pasha's messenger was "the most cunning one that he had the pleasure to choose" and had been given orders to offer himself as a hostage and spy on the knights.[73] Nicolay describes de Vallier being received in the Ottoman camp with a different offer, according to which the knights were free to go after paying for the expenses of the Ottoman fleet. He reports that de Vallier was subsequently put in chains, while his companion was sent back to carry the new terms to the knights. After having established the deceptiveness of the Ottomans, Nicolay goes on to describe d'Aramon's efforts to mediate, starting with the successful liberation of two hundred of the "oldest and least useful" members of the garrison, along with Vallier and other knights. While Nicolay's narrative overlaps with that of d'Aramon on the basic facts, fifteen years after the events, he focuses on instances of Ottoman animosity and even minor insults aimed at the French mission.[74] In Nicolay's story, the lavish celebration of Ottoman victory, to which the French are invited and at which they are offered their own pavilion, is overshadowed by the Ottomans' double-crossing of the knights. He describes the gifts of the "barbarians" as deceptive. Nicolay emphasizes this as he tells of Sinan Pasha gifting d'Aramon a dress of gold cloth and then immediately follows it up with the gruesome story of a captured knight—an old French cannoneer—whom the Ottomans, despite d'Aramon's generous gifts, retained, maimed, buried in an upright posture, and executed by shooting arrows at him. The spilled blood of the cannoneer does not only signal his martyrdom and Christian brotherhood in blood, however. Because he is reportedly from the same Dauphiné region as Nicolay and de Vallier, it also effectively transfers French blood from a specific region to North African soil.⁷⁵ Nicolay was mapping French soil when *Navigations et pérégrinations* was published, and he extended this mapping through the symbolic transformation of North African soil into French soil via the shedding of blood. Ultimately, d'Aramon rationalizes the events to Henri II by resorting to an argument that accorded with the politics of diplomacy of the French court to promote its influence in the Mediterranean, saying that, while the Ottoman attack on and capture of Tripoli hurt the king's reputation, the Ottomans were now in a better position for attacks on both Sicily and Naples, which served French interests as allies of the Ottomans in potential future campaigns.⁷⁶ In a very different tone, Nicolay insists on the irrationality of diplomacy with the Ottomans, "the most barbarous, greedy, and cruel people in the whole world, who (also) have the least amount of truthfulness and loyalty."⁷⁷ The episode of negotiating in Tripoli, and the all-too-much trust of the knights in the "feigned and mendacious words" of the Ottomans, show that the tactical and mobile agency of the spy in service of an arcane *raison d'état* has superseded the old-fashioned knight's representative power as conferred upon him by the ancient and medieval legal construct of the *ius gentium*.⁷⁸

While Nicolay presents the Ottoman Empire as a lawless world of greed, deceit, and villainy that calls for his hidden, cunning agency, he nonetheless exhibits a reliance upon precisely the people he vilifies: renegades, people with flexible identities whom he approaches for information, and people on the margins of Ottoman society whom he describes as having cunning intelligence. As the translator of Pedro de Medina, Nicolay presumably understood Spanish, and his familiarity with the Mediterranean *lingua franca* gave him an advantage in the multiethnic world of the Mediterranean by allowing him to communicate with Christian converts to Islam, whose multilingual, flexible culture made them ideal interlocutors, on occasion, informants.⁷⁹ These linguistic skills attest to his ability to act in contexts outside or on the margins of the diplomatic mission. In the Preface, Nicolay touts language—"oratory and spoken language in various languages" ("l'oraison et parole communicative en diverses langues")⁸⁰—as a great connecting force among different ethnicities and cultures. This is likely a thinly veiled allusion to his own skills, showcased as they are through references to his mastery of the Mediterranean *lingua franca* and gestural language.⁸¹ For example, after several days of besieging the fortress at Tripoli and after the Turkish army had suffered some great losses, Nicolay is asked to inspect the trenches of Salih Reis. Murat Aga, described as a Ragusan eunuch, tries to enlist Nicolay's expertise in military engineering by asking him "several things that pertained to the siege and the strength of a fortification." Nicolay, however, resorts to the clever trick of answering each question by saying the opposite of "what I knew by reason of war and experience."⁸² He narrates that the Aga promptly saw through his trick, an acknowledgment of which he revealed with a smile, a tacit gesture that establishes a sense of understanding between them. This smile creates a moment of bonding between these two "frenemies," making them brothers in ruse and secrecy, and showcases the endless capacity of the agent for clever and flexible problem-solving. Michel de Certeau defines the secret as an inter-subjective game, "a play between actors." The secret is thus socially performed—and, for Nicolay, this performance involves non-French actors, who become his accomplices in secrets.⁸³

The author describes himself as able to enter into successful exchanges with strangers of multiple worldviews and identities by crossing political, religious, and cultural boundaries. The persons with whom he engages, whether converts, renegades, or other cunning tricksters, all serve him in constructing a totalizing perspective—all the while celebrating the plasticity of agency in his own actions, in congruity with his strange use of the citation of Terence about the infinite possibilities of being human. In Algiers, it is a Spanish renegade that shows Nicolay how to acquire a view from above by taking him to a hill overlooking the city. This knowledge allowed the French agent to observe a fortification, a water tower to supply the city with fresh water, and a windmill, thereby collecting information that would be indispensable in a siege.⁸⁴ During the siege of Tripoli, he reports having gained insight into the knights' situation through another Spanish convert to Islam, from whom he learned that they had successfully captured a Turkish soldier.⁸⁵ While d'Aramon enters into negotiations with Sinan Pasha, Nicolay is guided by a "Moorish inhabitant of the land" as he inspects the Bazaar⁸⁶ and tours the ruins and antiquities of the city, including a marble arch with the allegorical winged figure of Victory on a chariot pulled by griffons. The figure is a symbol of both mobility and conquest that eludes the French on this mission but is, nevertheless, reclaimed by Nicolay as a representation of his own agency.⁸⁷ It is by showcasing his ability to enter into exchanges with people who are on the social fringes—renegades, poor women, and former servants at the Sublime Porte⁸⁸—rather than with those at the center, that Nicolay can present an image of himself "hover[ing] over the fray of cultural difference and international conflict" and to render his perspective authoritative.⁸⁹ In the fourth book, which is devoted to a general discussion of ethnic groups and peoples in and around the Ottoman Empire, the author mentions accompanying d'Aramon to Edirne and encountering a *deli*, a light cavalry soldier hired for raiding the frontiers, "who followed us to our quarters, where, while we gave him something to eat and drink, I drew a sketch of him and his strange habit (see Figure 18)."⁹⁰ The delis, literally meaning "crazy" or "daredevil," usually of Bosnian origin and recent converts to Islam,

Delli de nation
Parthique qui signifie
fol hardy ou enfant perdu

Figure 18

were best known for wearing bizarre and frightening outfits replete with plumes and furs. The deli is both an outlandish figure and a person with a flexible identity. Nicolay describes his conversation with him in the following manner: "I asked him why he dressed so strangely and adorned himself with such large feathers. He responded that it was to show himself more furious and frightening to his enemies."[91] This response makes the deli less strange by inscribing him into the logics of warfare, stratagem, and dissimulation, affording him an interiority of cunning and heroic virtue much like Ulysses or Nicolay. He is framed, too, as "well born" ("gentil"), meaning also "civilized," "stylish," and "genteel," as is evidenced when Nicolay reports that the deli allegedly "feigns" to follow Islam while considering himself Christian—and of Parthian origin, no less:

> ... Nonetheless I was curious, and I questioned him with the intermediary of a dragoman to see which nation he belonged to and what religion he professed. To which he wisely responded that he was of the Serbian nation, but his grandfather was of Parthia, a people that used to be of great renown and esteemed the fiercest of all in the Orient. And, as for his religion, while he dissimulated to live with the Turks according to their law, he was by birth, in his heart and will, Christian and to prove it to me, he recited in vulgar Greek and Serbian the Holy Father, the Angelic Greeting, and the Symbol of the Apostles.[92]

Nicolay finds the flexible religious identity of the deli palatable only because it is presented as a ruse. The deli's body is adorned with animal plumes and his actions are shaped by courage and transgression, which allows him to become the double of the self to which Nicolay aspires, all the while remaining decidedly non-French, foreign, exotic, and thus worthy of being depicted. This encounter shows not only that the deli is perceived as having the manners and appearance of a well-born person at much the same time as he is exoticized or rendered wild in sixteenth-century France, but also that, in Nicolay's text, genteel identities are no longer tied to the traditional *moeurs* of the aristocracy. Instead, they have everything to do with an exoticized notion of nobility, which leans on the symbolic power of non-French persons to elevate, give clout to, and render visible the agent's own self.[93]

Low-Hanging Fruits

The extravagantly dressed deli who draws the agent's gaze reveals an economy of the gaze in which remarkable, outlandish, or exotic bodies gain special visibility and value. The deli is the agent's exotic double, which confers visibility onto him and draws attention to his own desired qualities, such as courage, which connotes nobility. At the same time, the deli confirms that the agent is among untamed people, acting as a marker for war, hostility, and simply strangeness and savagery. The fact that the agent appropriates some of the signs of heroism from the deli does not make him any less exotic. The episode of the brief exchange between the agent and the deli thus serves as a link to an economy of the gaze that informs the illustrations of this costume book, serving the purpose of sparking delight while also training the eyes of those armchair travelers, Nicolay's readers, for whom French/European identity is defined as cosmopolitan and as *not*-Ottoman, unassociated with the parts of Europe and North Africa controlled by the Ottoman Empire. The printing press and the publishing houses worked for moneyed buyers of illustrated books, with the circulation of images of things from places without (or without abundance of) printing presses functioning as a strong marker of what came to be Western Europe or just Europe. One could summarize the visual logic of Nicolay's images thus: the bodies upon which Ottoman influence and conquest are deployed are also those that are conquered by appetite, greed, or excessive desire—and it is these bodies that become the terrain of the book's visual mastery. On the one hand, *Navigations et pérégrinations* enacts visual power by offering readers a view of bodies as either subdued or in need of being subdued and governed, and on the other, as a vantage point for the pleasures that await readers during their own viewing and handling of the book object. Nicolay takes the images that he sketches and then describes them in the text using spying methods and makes them visible from within the private spaces of viewers, who are then free to engage in imitative rivalry with the Ottomans from a safe distance. In the Preface, Nicolay establishes genteel status and mobility as natural and spiritual qualities that give shape to the inert body. This claim necessitates a complex interplay between the outside and the inside, in which the agent is defined through the body—the "well-formed" outer body that is mobile, malleable, and can imitate strangers to ensure the mobility of the self—while the inner element remains selfsame, thanks to a superior and active moral agency that animates it. The aesthetics of Nicolay's costume book commodify the desire for luxury, foreign items and "refined things" and bring the materiality of foreign cultures within reach of readers who wish to consume luxury articles associated with aristocratic taste. However, those who become the object of the readers' gaze in the book are often defined through manipulations and distortions of their bodies, which reveal mechanical or unchecked passions.

 As Rebecca Zorach shows, the Fontainebleau aesthetics created under the sponsorship of Francis I and Henri II strongly privileged the natural over the artificial, such that art had to be seen as a continuation of the natural abundance and "artificial" was rendered a negative, pejorative term. Art, however, was also always ambivalent: "In France, making artifice was associated with foreignness (in particular Italianness), with the excesses of fashion (as fashioning), with the superfluity of decoration."[94] Zorach shows that there was a strong desire in Renaissance France to collect these ambivalent objects of abundance. This demand increased not only in the art of the so-called school of Fontainebleau but also in the cheap reproductive prints available to larger audiences, whose popularity confirmed the ambivalent, often eroticized desire for the artificial or overly material foreign.[95] In *Navigations et pérégrinations*, this aesthetic ambiguity is compounded by the ambiguity of the same feelings toward the Ottomans. If artists in France had to work with the strong bias against art and artifice, then Nicolay exploits the space of ambivalence that already exists in visual art—in which art itself is always morally suspect as well as desirable—by shifting this same logic onto his depictions of the Ottoman Empire itself. In his illustrations, just as in his descriptions, there is a desire to go beyond the surface: to reveal the costumes as covers (that can be removed), the penetrability of skin, and the presence of moral vices (sodomy, drunkenness, greed, etc.). Meanwhile, another force directs the gaze to the surface, the skin, the textiles, and the lacerations—all of which function as ornament upon which the reader's/viewer's gaze is permitted to linger with pleasure.

Nicolay draws attention to the visual power of his book by underscoring the power of images to strike the "spirit." He explains that images produce a sensual effect on the eye, affecting it with "grace and delectation," and that this effect also reaches the "spirit" and produces refined delight. He thus claims that reading the book and beholding its images is an ennobling kind of pleasure.[96] This pleasure derives from not only variety but also the visual procedures and sensual material delights the book offers while sublimating them into the realm of the spirit. Recalling Rabelais's medlars, the book presents metaphorical "fruits" that avoid the risks inherent to the biblical forbidden fruit. Instead, they take the form of natural bodies offered to the eyes for consumption, where the various shells and teguments, from the human skin to artful surfaces (especially textiles), promise the readers access to refined pleasures that can be enjoyed in the privacy of their own space, away from dangers. As with Pantagruel's race, readers can enjoy these images and feel ennobled by the pleasures they offer. Nicolay's descriptions, which create desires for exotic and expensive products, including textiles,[97] are doubled by Davent's copperplate etchings that turn the body into ornament and art, cauterizing or otherwise altering the skin via clothing, jewelry, and pose. In many images, there also exists a clear analogy between artistic and anatomical depictions—and it is often the depicted subjects that invite the anatomical gaze, from the dervish wielding the knife to the woman lifting the hem of her dress to reveal more layers of clothing underneath. In these images, the body does not open entirely to show the internal organs, as in the anatomical theater, but it nevertheless subjects itself to the curious gaze of the viewer by yielding up extra visual layers. Zorach reminds us that, in the context of sixteenth-century art, "[p]rints are a model of promiscuity because of their abundance."[98] The image of the "dervish," then, perversely reproduces the act of cutting and etching by opening the body in layers, producing an image that is a pleasure to the beholder while also implying the presence of a deeper agency, foreign and immoral, animating the body from within.

This series of images takes on a specific political significance in the context of Nicolay's commentary and the ordering or deployment of the images, in which unfreedom and religious heterodoxy come to be associated with one another. For example, Book 3 presents a series of persons of increasing villainy, beginning with the *acemi oğlanlar* ("children of the tribute")—that is, the Christian boys "gathered" for Ottoman service—and chronicling their ascent through the ranks to janissaries, *boluk başi*, *solak* ("left-handed archer") and *peyk* ("running footman"), who were slaves of the Sultan, or *kuls*, and who represent moral degradation in various forms of vice according to Nicolay's bizarre moralizing account. These officers of the Sublime Porte are followed by portraits of wrestlers, drunkards, and dervishes to instill a mixture of apprehension and curiosity in the readers. All four groups of dervishes that Nicolay describes, which form the basis of my analysis here, are directly copied from the Italian Giovanni Antonio Menavino's *Trattato de' costumi et vita de' Turchi* (1548) and showcase the appeal of the strange and frightening exterior.[99] However, unlike in the case of the deli, whose fierce and exotic appearance is described as concealing a noble and Christian spirit, these figures denote moral vices, including sodomy, drunkenness, and hypocrisy (that is, according to an interpretation that Nicolay adds to Menavino's descriptions, after having eliminated the original author's sympathetic explanations). And since moral depravity, drunkenness, and sodomy are also the vices that Nicolay attributes to renegade Christians who convert to Islam, the representations of dervishes amount to nothing more than a wholesale condemnation of Islam.[100] Other travelers who write about dervishes try to understand them by comparing them to religious groups with which they are familiar. Menavino sees dervishes as comparable to mystics of an unspecified cult of love in Italy; Guillaume Postel acknowledges their holiness while also considering some of them "fools" (while, in a rare moment of humbleness, admitting his limited comprehension of them);[101] and Belon notes their similarity to Gaulish druids, except he feels compelled to add that they appear less authentic and more hypocritical in their devotions.¹⁰² The illustrations in Nicolay's book leave the reader's gaze free to travel across the exposed skin of these men, roaming over their bodies-made-ornament draped in lion's or leopard's hides, with their long hair, dreadlocks, musical instruments, books, lacerations, knives, hatchets, and deer (see Figures 19 and 20). They join other instances of "the wild man" archetype, such as

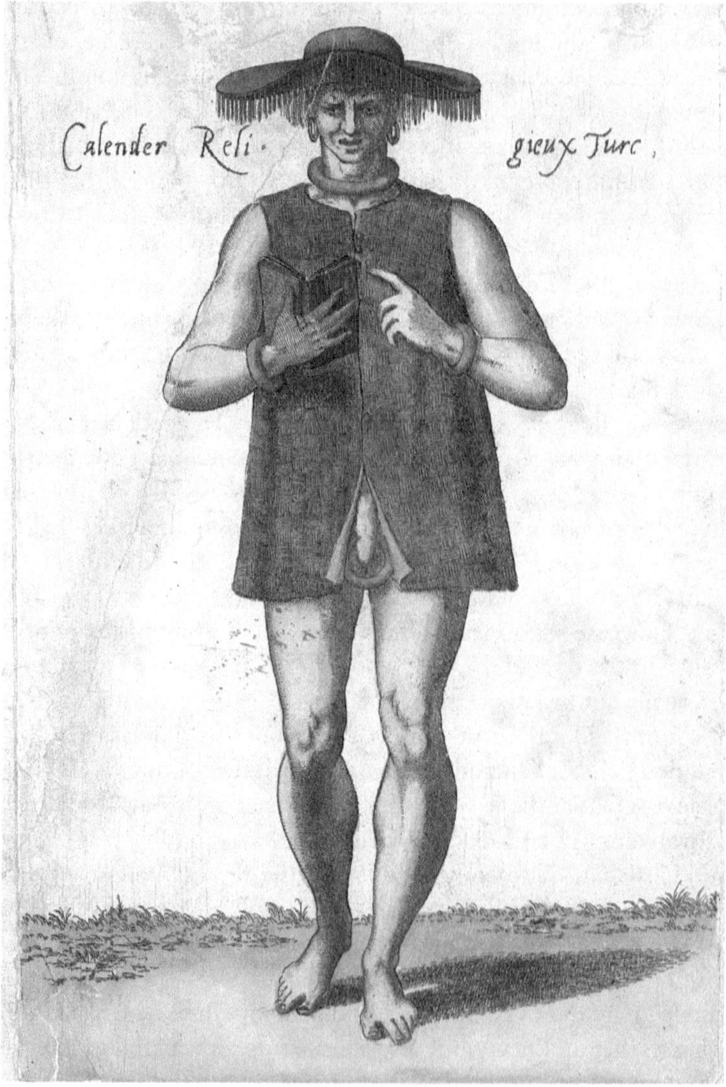

Figure 19

Figure 20

Diogenes, Pan, and Priapus (see Figure 21), all of whom were itinerant masculine bodies that fascinated European men at the time. The hide, the lacerations, the hatchet, and the hand cutting the arm (vertically, in the exact manner labeled by Belon in his 1553 *Observations* as hypocritical) supposedly stand in for the abject animality, or the "bestial life," of the person.[103] However, the cuts

DISCOVRS SVR LES
PRIAPVS.

Le second medaillõ.

Figure 21

covering the surface of the body also evoke the medium of engraving, the very medium of representation, which suggests that the image makes its own medium visible through decoration and the dervish's hand gesture of cutting. Nicolay's pejorative presentation of these religious men as being governed by violent and dangerous passions can also be likened to French Catholic depictions of Protestants in the 1560s and beyond as being driven by monstrous and unnatural passions. Nicolay's vilification of the dervishes possibly reflects his own view of French Protestants, whom he considers to be governed by an unstable and menacing flux of humors.[104]

The book's images apply the serial logic of prints, including erotic prints, to Ottoman subjects, such that these subjects—"the drunkards," the "Algerian slave girl," the "Turkish lady," and so on—came to be depicted as stereotypes and circulated as part of an economy of collectibles. While in Tripoli, Nicolay visited a slave market containing enslaved peoples taken from Malta and Sicily. Being stripped of their clothes ("les faire dépouiller tout nus, et les faire cheminer") is the sad fate to which the "Turks" and "Moors" subject the "poor Christian slaves at the market."[105] In particular, he describes having seen a Hungarian girl "thirteen or fourteen years of age, of middling beauty" ("médiocrement belle"), being undressed, examined, and sold to an old Turkish merchant."[106] With the degree of beauty (moderate, according to Nicolay) of this girl serving as an indicator of her value, Nicolay, too, is enabled to appraise the girl as a disembodied eye. But there is more happening here than an imaginary rivalry waged on the basis of possession and looking with the old Turkish merchant. The viewing of this enslaved girl, whose body is inspected for "defects of nature," carries with it geopolitical ambitions and imperial fantasies. The slave buyer's perspective, his search for the perfect, healthy, able body, overlaps with an older tradition of White slavery practiced by Venetians in the Middle Ages and by Ottomans starting in the fifteenth century. Nell Irvin Painter estimates that the sale of one type of slave, "the luxury slaves, those valued for sex and gendered as female," defined the aesthetic standards, beginning in the early modern period, that gradually came to be consolidated into the racist norm of beauty defined as white (or lighter) skin and ugliness as black (or darker) skin.[107] Nicolay is not alone in passing judgment on the beauty of women in the Ottoman Empire. In Chapter 3, we saw that, by popularizing Cleopatra, Jodelle's *Cléopâtre captive* takes a stand in the false debate around the respective beauty of women of different ethnicities and skin colors, according to which the lighter skin color of Egyptians and Turks caused European observers to consider them as more beautiful—or simply as closer to Europeans, which amounted to the same thing—than their darker-skinned counterparts. Belon, for example, compares the coal-hued blackness of Ethiopian women to the "beautiful" Turkish women, which implies that a lighter skin color is more beautiful and confirms the solidification of racialized ideas of beauty in early modern Europe: "For, even the Ethiopian women, who are darker than a charcoal seller ("qu'un charbonnier"), cover their face with a mask, just as the most beautiful Turkish women do."[108] These aesthetic discussions, as Painter shows, will go on to influence the eighteenth-century philosopher Immanuel Kant, among many others, and lead to a false racial theory that gave us the category of "Caucasians." They happened in the sixteenth century (and thus well before François Bernier's 1684 article on the four races of the world[109]), when the memory of the medieval slave trade by the Venetians and the Ottomans was still part of the collective consciousness. Indeed, it was given new life by the interest of French travelers in fantasized rivalries with Ottoman slave traders, who saw in it a way of elevating their own status by way of making aesthetically articulated racial judgments.

The fact that Nicolay feels confident enough to judge the Hungarian slave girl's beauty suggests that he has at least a vague awareness of this history of luxury slave trade. By placing himself as the judge of beauty, Nicolay also arrogates the perspective of Venetian and Ottoman slave traders and slave buyers. Eastern Europe and the Balkans, as the border zone between the Spanish/Hapsburg and Ottoman Empires, appeared in French politics as a zone of rivalry with these empires. Before Europe was divided into civilized "West" and backward "East," and before Western Europeans' sense of difference from and superiority over Eastern Europeans was etched into their minds (a sense that Larry Wolff charts in the political imagination of the Enlightenment), French ambitions were predicated on a distinction between empires and conquerable lands.[110] The Ottoman Empire and the study, however superficial, of Ottoman history and political agency was a lesson that enabled French agents and those serving the ruling elite to begin viewing parts of Europe, North Africa, and Eurasia as colonizable spaces—a logic that, in mythical scenarios peddled to the court and the ruling elite, also extended to the Ottoman Empire itself as the colonizer of European, North African, and Eurasian territories. Instead of "Eastern" Europa, this was a notion of Europe invaded by and controlled by the Ottomans, not unlike the Ovidian legend of the rape of Europa by Jupiter in the shape of a bull. "Europe," in this sense, is symbolized by the slave girl, and Europe emerges as the violated inner colony. Meanwhile, France appears in Nicolay's presentation as a universal, cosmopolitan power, as *not-Europa* (i.e., passive or helpless object of conquest): Modeled upon expansionist empires of trade and wealth production, it emerges according to its own self-presentation as both imitating the wealth production and, simultaneously, correcting and mitigating the military force of the Ottoman conqueror. Put otherwise, in this imaginary scene of geopolitical dominance, Nicolay aligns the French (and, by association, the elite Europeans who are the readers of his book) with the very Ottomans whose violent and lustful desire he claims to sublimate. In Book 3 of *Navigations et pérégrinations*, in which Nicolay presents a panorama of sorts of the different ethnic groups living in the Ottoman Empire ("sujets et tributaries"), he begins with a portrait of the ancient Persian Empire—a choice that seems random, and that can be justified solely by the fact that Nicolay saw Persians at the Sublime Porte. Persia receives a favorable description in Nicolay's (heavily plagiarized) account, which is not unrelated to the fact that Persians are "mortal enemies" of Turks.[111] Others, such as Arabs (solely represented by the image of the Moorish slave), Jews, and Orthodox Greeks (whose religious difference from Roman Catholicism he blames for the decay of Greece[112]), are described in harshly pejorative terms as evil, treacherous people. Nicolay's othering was directed most at those who fit into the order of Ottoman society, served its institutions, and were willing to cooperate with the Ottomans. He exempts the Armenians and the Karamians (those living on the south-central Anatolian coast of the Mediterranean, whom he describes as artisans making beautiful artifacts) and the Ragusans (who carried messages between Venice and Constantinople, including for the French ambassador), as well as the southern Slavic deli. In Book 4 especially, Nicolay relies heavily on descriptions of ancient peoples of the region that he plagiarized from classical sources and very little on his observations and experiences, which usually appear as moments of appreciation in a digest of bookish histories and moralizing put-downs. In Nicolay's *Navigations et pérégrinations*, just as in Belon's *Observations*, Thevet's *Cosmographie de Levant*, and Postel's *De la Republique des Turcs*, there emerge groups of people that are seen as treacherous or to be conquered, including Jews, Greeks, and other Eastern Christians, Christian Slavs from Eastern Europe, Arabs, Roma and Sinti, and Moors—all of whom constitute the subjects and tributaries of the Ottoman Empire and whom, by way of imitative rivalry, French agents view as conquerable, colonizable subjects. French agents routinely denigrated Eastern Christians. Among them, the semi-nomadic Roma or Sinti receive a universal gesture of exclusion. Belon notes groups camping near the Nile between El Matareya (then outside Cairo) and Cairo and that in "many villages," they are "just as foreign ("étrangers") in these lands as they are in ours."[113] He also notes, however, that they are Christian, speak many languages, and that the men work as smiths, while the women are given permission to sell their bodies. Belon considers them to be people from the Balkans, Wallachia (which became an Ottoman vassal principality), and Bulgaria (subjugated in the early fifteenth century).[114] Roma and Sinti were already doubly colonized in early modern Europe. Both were controlled by the Ottoman

Empire, where they lived after the Ottoman conquest of the Balkans and were considered universally foreign by the French.[115] They were subject to regulation and exclusion from European societies—or they were tolerated only on the margins, similar to Jews,[116] Greeks,[117] Slavs of the Balkans, and Eastern Europeans, all of whom were forced to develop multiple identities, serving and making a living within the Ottoman Empire while also identifying with their own culture, and sometimes developing syncretic beliefs and flexible worldviews as a result. From the point of view of the agents of the French crown, these people were generally seen to be servile and colonizable. In some cases, they were seen as potential allies, such as when they showed personal aspirations for advancement or colonial ambitions. The extreme interest of Nicolay and other agents in the beauty of women and the various ethnic groups that can be classified in terms of their degree of servility shows that their position was anti-diplomatic and imperial, a perspective that we have seen directly expressed in Nicolay's imaginary and belated rivalry with d'Aramon.

Nicolay's description of the forceful stripping of the Hungarian slave girl serves the purpose of engendering both pity and erotic desire in his readers because the triangulation of desire—in which the author is watching the Turkish merchant examining and eventually buying the girl—draws the reader into a homosocial competition with the old Turkish man. Nicolay planned to write a book devoted to the topic, promising to describe "the pain, calamity, and miserable servitude" of Christian slaves in a projected second volume. Such a book would have contributed to the growing desire to "buy back" ("racheter") the European and French Christians captured and sold into slavery in the Ottoman Empire. However, the actual politics of *rachat* was selective, acted out by ambassadors in specific instances and under French Catholic orders, and served to reinforce the limits of French identity that remained tied to the idea that certain subjects—eastern Christians, Protestants, or Greek Orthodox people in particular—were less free. Pity is thus a feeling that implies the exclusion of some alongside the possibility of becoming aware of a commonality with others, as is anticipated by Grandgousier's gesture of generously shedding tears over the Canarrians. However, Nicolay's agenda has shifted away from inciting a feeling of commonality with North Africans, whom he depicts as valiant if somewhat untamed allies, to a projection of French and European community in Christianity.

Giving access to women's bodies is a political gesture, as is evinced by the explanations that Nicolay provides for two images: "grand Turkish lady" and another "noble Turkish woman" ("Gentille-Femme") from the Harem. Nicolay's first title offers a vague designation for the high-ranking women from the Harem, who bore official titles, including *Valida* (the sultan's mother) or *Haseki* (the sultan's favorite) at the Ottoman court. At the time of Nicolay's travel during Sultan Suleiman I's reign, the favorite was Haseki Hürrem Sultan (also called "the mother of princes," ca. 1502–1558), better known as "Roxelana" in the West in reference to her legendary Ruthenian and Christian origin. She was captured by Crimean Tatars during a slave raid and eventually taken to Istanbul, where she became Suleiman I's favorite concubine around 1521. The sultan freed and married her in 1536 in an unprecedented gesture, breaking with the Ottoman tradition of polygynous dynasty in which a sultan kept a concubine as his favorite until she bore him a son, at which point he would move on to a new concubine. But Nicolay only names her according to an empty function, "grand Turkish lady." This erases the actual person who possessed active agency in the drama of Ottoman succession and who fashioned her own social image.[118] Instead, Nicolay's depiction suggests that the image is of any high-ranking woman at the sultan's court—and that, furthermore, it is her clothes that provide her rank. Nicolay explains that he obtained the costumes from a "eunuch" in the Saray and clad two "public women" ("femmes publiques," a pejorative term meaning women engaged in sex work) in them, who then stood for the drawings to be made. With this act of representing the *kuls*, or palace slaves, who had their own slaves and a great deal of status, with the metonymic designation of "public women," Nicolay creates images that tie, once again, the capturing and trade of Eastern European women to the erotics of male desire. The commodification of women levels the differences among different ranks and social groups described in the book (including the Hungarian slave girl, the high-ranking women in the sultan's household, the "public women" from the city, and the "Moorish" slave girls whom Nicolay describes as wearing bracelets with cheap, inexpensive stones, and who were allegedly willing to take off their skirts for a few coins) in a metonymic extension of the many bodies available for purchase in Nicolay's book.[119]

The promise of voyeuristic pleasures presented in *Navigations et pérégrinations* is not unique, for it is also exemplified by an eroticized depiction of Ottoman women in a sixteenth-century print found in a collection of drawings held at the Bibliothèque nationale in Paris. The drawing depicts a love triangle with a stereotypical old husband who is blind to his wife's cheating, and a second female figure actively flirting with the wife, which allows the viewer to master the visual field by means of taking the perspective of the female lover (see Figure 22). This print attests to the appeal of the theme of lesbian desire (popularized by the costume book of Luigi Bassano, which contained etchings of Fontainebleau artist Jean Mignon's prints) beyond aristocratic viewers and collectors. The title, "A Turkish Woman Making Love," refers to the woman dressed in a simple white kaftan signaling, with her eye, to the other woman,

Figure 22

whose ornate, expensive clothes designate her as the wife of the similarly dressed rich and old husband. The cuckolded husband was a stereotype in the French and European cultures—and, once again, the advanced age and apparent wealth of the husband invite the challenger to supplant his authority. As was common within Renaissance art, same-sex relations are represented here with two female figures depicted frontally and thus made available to the gaze of male viewers.[120] This viewer momentarily replaces the agency held by the "Turkish woman" in the title. The female lover thus becomes the stand-in for the gaze of the (male) viewer. The print orients the viewer's gaze toward a sexualized image of Ottoman women with the purpose of replacing masculine Ottoman authority with the desiring French and European male gaze. The Turkish woman's simple clothes suggest a lower social status or cross-dressing, implying her mobility and prudently masked interior autonomy; her desire, which she shows only through signs, assuages a crucial element of the European fantasy of extending one's agency by desiring material things in the East. The Ottoman woman in the print is recognized as crossing limits, as did the agents themselves—but, this time, the transgression is offered to any viewer able to purchase the print. By way of contrast, Sara Ahmed defines the queer phenomenology of the "'contact zone' of lesbian desire as opening up lines of connection between bodies that are drawn to each other in the repetition of this tendency to deviate from the straight line" and by the fantasy of finding others who are "like me."[121] To expose the love triangle in the image to the male viewer's gaze is to reestablish the straight line from the viewer to the frontal scene in the image, while establishing the "like me" outside of the picture in the community of male subjects, repeatedly viewing this and similar images through the possession of cheaply printed images. In the case of agents, the fleeting moments of transcultural connections both transgress and refer to how the norms of their own (French) society shape their identities.

The illustrations in *Navigations et pérégrinations* were sometimes hand colored in versions prepared for patrons and wealthy buyers, of which a handful of copies have been preserved. One such copy of the first edition is held at the municipal library in Moulins, whose binding bears the insignia of King Charles IX. This copy was illustrated in vivid colors that underscore the richness of material and color in the costumes and the different shades of skin color from black through brown to white.[122] Colored images mark the contrast between the elegant Turkish lady, whose light skin is just barely visible from under sleeves and veils, and her darker-skinned servant, whose face and hands are exposed and directly visible. Both high-ranking Ottoman ladies are depicted as fair-skinned. The darker skin of the Algerian slave girl and one of the two wrestlers (the other one is light-skinned, for contrast) exposes dark skin tones to the wealthy viewer who could afford both the colored book and the privilege of viewing brown or Black bodies, along with the costumes and other luxury goods, and bodies, as ornaments (see Figure 23). By characterizing at least some Muslims as Black Africans or dark-skinned North Africans, the artist

Figure 23

who hand-colored the illustrations exaggerates their otherness. This coloring intensifies the economy of exposure and becoming-ornament, as well as the proto-imperialist politics of the visual pleasures to which privileged readers of the book have access. *Navigations et pérégrinations* not only offers a panorama of the Ottoman Empire but also trains the eye of the reader to see another part of Europe and the world beyond it as colonizable.

5
Distancology and Universalizing French Masculinity

In Turkey especially many go about naked for the sake of their religion.
—MICHEL DE MONTAIGNE

What the animal disarms in advance, even in its cruelty (outside the range of human barbarity), is our duplicity. The human subject is divided, exilic.
—ANNE DUFOURMANTELLE, *THE POWER OF GENTLENESS*

In *L'Anti-christ* (first printed in 1597), in which the author summarizes arguments of prominent Jesuits against Protestant adversaries of the papacy, the Catholic polemicist and jurist Florimond de Raemond publishes an anecdote about François de Noailles (1519–1585), bishop of Aix and French ambassador to the Sublime Porte. Raemond claims to have heard the tale at a dinner party from the bishop himself:

> On the appointed day, dressed in a brocade dress worked with gold threads ("une robe de drap d'or frisé sur frise"), he went to the Saray in the company of eighteen French gentlemen. This number had been much debated before, for the bashas only wanted to admit eight of them. The gentlemen wore cramoisy satin dolmans and purple velour jackets with gold passements. At the Palace, while they were being offered a festive meal, Selim observed them through his jalousie. After the meal, they arranged themselves to enter and make the reverence. At the gate of the Divan, where the Grand Seigneur was, two *kapıcıs*, doormen, wanted to grab the Ambassador in their usual way by the

end of his sleeve, to escort him like a tied prisoner to the feet of their master, as they do, by custom, with everyone who wants to salute him, since the assassination of one of their emperors. But this fearless great seigneur pushed them away and ordered that they be told, with the intermediary of translator, that the dignity of a French bishop did not tolerate being led like a *forçat* (galley slave). He fought in such a way that he got the better of them and, free, walked up to Selim's seat, whom he saluted without bending any further down than was necessary to kiss the hand and the robe, in the name of the king. . . . There was never an ambassador who represented with so much resolve the honor and greatness of his master as he.[1]

Raemond cites this incident as a small digression in his discussion of the customary nature of ceremonies of honor, the historically and culturally variable character of such "external gestures" involving the "submission of the body" rather than expressions of the spirit. The larger context for this discussion is the goal of justifying the elaborate ceremonies of reception at the papal court and the institution of the papacy. Thus, Raemond emphasizes that the ambassador's body must change according to the cultural milieu in which it is positioned to remain loyal to the spirit of the mission. The Ottomans are no exception here; their customs (and those of the Chinese mentioned in another passage) are just as much to be respected as any other custom. "May one live in Rome in the Roman manner, and in Constantinople in the Turkish manner," declares Raemond,[2] who also demands that the Jesuit envoy sent to Elizabeth's court greet her by kneeling before her, and that the Puritan envoys kiss the pope's slipper. This conception of the body (including gestures and clothing) as changeable and indifferent, *adiaphora*, is the result of the Roman-Christian tradition of cosmopolitanism adopted by the French crown to justify and conduct an alliance with the Sublime Porte. The Catholic polemicist is thus exercising the newfangled ideas of cultural relativism, which also offers Catholics a tool to respond to Protestant critiques of papal ceremonies. Raemond declares the body capable of almost unlimited transformations without "polluting or contaminating the soul." After this categorical assertion of the universal reign of custom, however, Raemond reveals that Noailles did *not* respect Ottoman ceremonial etiquette. His abrupt disregard of custom and the risk and courage it is supposed to entail, as well as his passionate performance, are interpreted as proof of the purity of his Catholic self ("la dignité d'un Evesque français") and his loyal representation of the dignity of the prince ("l'honneur et la grandeur de son maistre").

In this final chapter, I begin by unfolding the exemplarity of Noailles's diplomatic antics at the Sublime Porte and trace from there the conviction of

French men of this generation that the passions, the material body, and the animality of the body represent a potential for agency and a natural kind of nobility so long as it is in good hands. Notably, the essayist Michel de Montaigne (1533–1592), an occasional agent, follows the agents who travel to the Ottoman Empire in defining his self through an agency that is intimately tied to the natural—animal—body. By showing his fascination with the literature of travel and embassy, I show that Montaigne's persona in the *Essays* is based on testing and risks—whether they come from the outside elements or the inside, in the form of passions and desires or illness—and these risks become the very extension of the self, which only becomes "mixed" and "universal" in the process. In this chapter, I contest the apolitical notion of text and subjectivity, whose fiction Montaigne constructs for himself in the form of a universal self. Under pressures of service, this self is revealed to be defined by its relation to another.

The Supple Body and French Masculinity

Noailles comes down to us as an exemplary negotiator on behalf of the Valois monarchy, especially in the Ottoman Empire, where he served as resident ambassador to King Charles IX from 1571 to 1575. Like most *robins* serving as ambassadors, he was a moderate Catholic, loyal to the king, whose political career started under the patronage of Cardinal Châtillon. A substantial part of his extant letters and papers was published in the nineteenth century, in the third volume of Ernest Charrière's four-volume edition of the correspondence of sixteenth-century French ambassadors and envoys sent to the Ottoman Empire. Charrière celebrates Noailles for setting France on the course of a grandiose international politics by negotiating a peace treaty between Venice and the Sublime Porte in the aftermath of the battle of Lepanto, for working on liberating enslaved French subjects in Algiers,[3] and for obtaining Ottoman support for the crowning of the Duke of Anjou (later Henri III) as king of Poland. According to this nineteenth-century historian, Noailles was a great spirit, perhaps the greatest among all sixteenth-century French ambassadors. Charrière even compares Noailles's verve to that of Montaigne, noting that, while Montaigne philosophized about history, personal experience, and passages borrowed from ancient authors, Noailles excelled in "applying the art of observation to Man and character, which he use[d] specifically to render the traits of a particular society and to paint the *tableau* of politics in the period."[4] Charrière sees in Noailles a personage situated right at the center of political happenings at the Sublime Porte, one who can develop an internal point of view at a remove from Ottoman and international society that is comparable to

Montaigne's famous metaphor of the *arrière-boutique* (back of a shop), a private mental space. Charrière's comparison suggests that a private space of reflection was developed in Noailles's writing in response to the pressures of service—and this is likely the case for Montaigne too. Montaigne imitated Noailles and those others who were sending back observations about the Ottoman Empire to develop his own space of reflection, which later led to the fiction of the *sui genesis* of the *honnête homme* (the gentleman) from a private practice of reading and writing.[5] Pierre Villey, Montaigne's editor who remarkably read the *Essays* in *braille*, assumed that the book presented a portrait of the author's inner, immaterial psychological development and posited that Montaigne's evolving but unique spirit could become knowable through reading it. This "mimetic model," Warren Boutcher argues, was called into question by the semiotic approaches that became prevalent in the 1960s—but only partially, because they still relied on Villey's work and core assumptions that there existed an apolitical space of linguistic play in the text.[6] Charrière's description of Noailles as a kind of Montaigne in Constantinople—the educated moralist, the detached observer of others, capable of looking through the artifice and vanity of Ottoman high society—is steeped in this idealized perception of Montaigne writing from his tower.

Raemond's anecdote does not only reflect the continuing anxiety of French men about losing their freedom under the double pressure exerted by the Ottoman court combined with their own. It also, paradoxically, sets out to reassure male readers that the malleability of the body, the many acts the body was required to perform in service of a master (or two), does not contaminate the spirit. A lesser-known anecdote by Pierre Lescalopier, a French jurist who served on a minor mission, relates some sharp comments made by Mehmet Pasha that call into question the court's reliance on spies in the Ottoman Empire:

> Mehmet told us through his translator that he was surprised by the curiosity of the French, who, without any specific business, just to pass the time, which he considers unhealthy, travel to such faraway lands. Turks go on pilgrimage rather than visiting foreign lands. The ambassador [François Noailles] responded that we travel over the entire world out of the love we feel for our king so we can serve him at any place where he sends us.[7]

Lescalopier was sent to Transylvania in 1574 by Noailles to conduct negotiations (ultimately unsuccessful) concerning a marriage between Stephen Báthory, the Voivode of Transylvania, and Renée de Rieux, Catherine de Médicis's lady-in-waiting. Mehmet's noncomprehension of the common practice among French monarchs of dispatching agents to the Ottoman Empire and the lands under its control in Eastern Europe and North Africa, despite the differences between Ottoman laws and institutions and French practices, is probably feigned and ironic. With the term "curiosity," Lescalopier, quoting Mehmet, deploys a code word for practices of sending spies. The word denoted extreme carefulness ("souci, préoccupation exagérée"), and, as I show in Chapter 3, Jodelle, for instance, describes the "daily worry" of Octavian in his 1553 play *Cléopâtre captive* in much the same sense. Lescalopier is likely using the word to translate Mehmet's ironic comment on the "unhealthy" care taken by the French monarchy to observe and spy on its ally or the "unhealthy" effects this curiosity had on agents themselves. Without speculating on what Mehmet Pasha meant by "unhealthy" (if he indeed made such a comment), we can segue into what Lescalopier may understand as the mixed agency of the agent, subject to the obligation of loyalty to the monarch and striving for his personal well-being and personal autonomy. Agents were in possession of agency because of their unwavering loyalty to the king and the court—their "love," as Noailles puts it in the anecdote—even as they also sought out agency through more lateral means by way of transgressing norms and through others, both animal and foreign. Philippe Desan observes, "Rather than membership in the high nobility, royal agents were required to have negotiating abilities, a proximity and indefectible loyalty to the king's person—and not to the state or to France—a talent for psychological analysis, and an adequate knowledge of the political culture of the country of residence."[8] This unflinching loyalty is perhaps the sole virtue François Rabelais's Panurge can claim for himself, making him a comic and sometimes downright nasty character. It is also an uneasy part of the trope of curiosity as the orientation of the self toward the world and toward others—a marker of the open, cosmopolitan attitude—for the agent's curiosity is always defined by the "curiosity" of his master. As part of the lip service paid by the loyal servant, there existed a remarkable readiness to celebrate a French empire even before it came into existence. This celebration was not disinterested, however, because it also allowed personal agencies to be grafted upon the imagined imperial powers of the monarch. The orientations of this self that claims agency over the world are spelled out, for example, by the poet Pierre Ronsard, in a poem prefixed to the first edition (and all subsequent sixteenth-century editions) of Nicolas de Nicolay's *Les Navigations et Pérégrinations* (1567). The poet praises the author and spy for describing these Oriental regions:

> So well that from now on, without leaving France,
> The French will have perfect knowledge
> Of these faraway peoples, whom the Great King Charles,
> Will one day subjugate and rule over ("leur donner sa Loy").[9]

The French king will subjugate faraway people "one day" in the uncertain future, but the French and international readers of Nicolay's book can already indulge in the mental attitude of exercising their freedom and autonomy by observing and delighting in the parade of passions in the book.

Lescalopier was interested in the Ottoman perspective and in Ottoman institutions and laws, which he describes in detail in his memoir (to this day unpublished in French) as fair and applying equally to everyone. He admires, for example, caravansaries, or Ottoman lodgings providing basic accommodations for travelers with different backgrounds and their animals. Within such spaces, people of different ethnicities and religious faiths could sleep next to one another, satisfying their basic needs for shelter, bed, and food. Everyone had to follow the same rules—travelers were locked up together for the night— in exchange for receiving the same provisions, safety, and minimal comforts. In Lescalopier's admiring description of an Ottoman caravansary, one can also detect an implicit distrust of luxuries and a preference for simplicity measured according to the natural needs of the body. The Ottoman Empire was better suited for people who desired to go about their business, for it recognized the basic natural needs of the body and resolved conflicts through direct arbitration by the law. Lescalopier's account of Noailles's house in Constantinople, in which he describes clean, whitewashed, and bare rooms that were always furnished with a good fire, says a lot about his perception of the ambassador. The simplicity of the ambassador's household renders it not unlike the bare comforts offered by caravansaries, shaped by the needs of the human travelers and their horses, and provides a counterpart to the privileges and lifestyle of the French aristocracy, along with the requirements of luxury when they and their retinue traveled. France was in the middle of a brutal civil war led by opposing elite families and, after the Massacre of Saint Bartholomew's Day that occurred barely two years before in 1572, the idea of reconciliation between Catholic and Protestant factions, the court, and the Malcontents (a group of rebellious nobility of both Catholic and Protestant faiths) was a very distant hope. For this Frenchman, the orderly microcosm of the caravansary was a desirable counterpart to the France torn apart by the private interests of the elite and the different religious convictions of the population at large. He projects Mehmet's perspective in his journal to express his disappointment with the effects of the war on France and perhaps also with the lack of laws allowing for the peaceful coexistence of various people. Such instances of French agents candidly criticizing the French institutions for being too weak to curtail privileges were not frequent in the period. Agents typically strove to obtain privileges individually by transgressing boundaries and often endeavored toward a sense of community. Raemond's discussion of customs reveals a degree of awareness that the requirement for subjects to perform certain acts was consequential and that there was a felt need for the preservation of a private space—*forum internum*, or an unsullied spirit—as well as perhaps an anxiety that the latter was not always possible. Historian Alin Fumurescu argues that the French type of individualism espoused by Rabelais, Montaigne, and others was rooted in the medieval distinction between *forum internum* and *forum externum*: the former being the realm of conscience and authenticity, and the latter that of social roles and offices. Part of this conception of the individual—in contrast with the English political model of direct representation of individual wills or with the Ottoman model of laws that regulated the peaceful coexistence of different social groups, was that the idea of a community, stemming from a Christian notion of *universitas* and a political notion of the common good, that served as a rational model. Fumurescu argues that this political identity could make the French very individualistic in their *forum internum*, forming the basis for French libertinism and also for religious faith, freedom of conscience in the reformed and Gallican traditions—and that it could make them correspondingly conformist in the *forum externum*, until a compelling political reason for resistance occurred.[10] The French political model of individualism is thus constitutive of its own flipside: this need for a sense of belonging within a community, which is never conceived as a loose collection of individuals defined by private interest alone. It is because of this desire for community that Rabelais, Pierre Belon, Guillaume Postel, and other agents tie the fictions of their agency to visions of communities to come—much too often, sliding into visions of *empires* to come. The imperial fantasies of agents stem not just from the simple need to serve and pander to the crown but also from their eagerness to project themselves into universalizing moral perspectives. Thus, imagining community and commonality with others was tied to the self at the level of the *forum internum*, which was never "individualistic" in the liberal sense but instead gave rise to fantasies of communities in the free imagination of the *forum internum*. However, these fictions of community that pertained to the *forum internum*, or fictions of community as imagined by a subject according to his own concept of agency and alliance with other actors, were often brought into alignment with (although not a part of) the demands of authorities or the pressures of the public role they played. Thus, the neat separation presumed by Fumurescu was, at best, a product of work and performance; in fact, these subjectivities are always mixed, always elsewhere and exilic in this sense, withdrawing in public performances and aware of their debt of loyalty in private moments. In *Fictions of Embassy*, Timothy Hampton shows that the high value Montaigne puts on the private self, alongside his eccentric personality, forgetfulness, and blunt speaking, contributes to constructing a persona constantly up for private examination, and that would be at a distance from the dangerous moral and linguistic conundrums that diplomats had to manage—especially when their mission exposed them to risks to their own person. No doubt, Noailles's eccentric performance at the Sublime Porte also represents a provocative attempt to gain distance from the pressures of French or Ottoman authorities while paradoxically demonstrating his service to the crown.[11] But Montaigne's universal persona ("la condition universelle de l'homme"), which formed a similar escape route (without having to give up his loyalty to the realm), and the fact that he wrote for "friends" while leaving the category open to future readers, counting on their willingness to take him as authentic, raises the question: What kind of community does Montaigne imagine, to which his readers can still relate? And what or whom does it exclude?

Getting Used to Pressure

The word "custom" in sixteenth-century political discourse was used as a synonym for political institutions and the power of the princes they supported. For this reason, the demand for a flexible body that could perform different acts was made not only for cultural reasons but also because of political pressures applied by a concrete master; as we saw through Étienne de la Boétie's account in the Introduction, suppleness of body and mind was a requirement for each courtier. The ability to mold the body to customary ceremonies thus implies the double demand of a cosmopolitan career and an unwavering loyalty to one's master and state, with the "spirit" remaining immutable throughout. Raemond's position dovetails with other views validating the laws and customs of states; for example, Étienne Pasquier's acceptance of slavery as a historical and legal fact that he considers justified in Roman society (as discussed in Chapter 3) and Montaigne's repeated criticism of the "tyranny" of custom, in which he recognizes its arbitrary origin and the irrationality of its laws along with the necessity to respect and care for it. Montaigne did not convert to Protestantism but instead maintained the old religion because he believed that the institutions of France were tied to Catholicism. This respect for institutions translates into service and loyalty to masters and patrons as well. Through his protector, Germain Gaston de Foix, Montaigne was tied to both the Catholic family of his patron and the Protestant king of Navarre (because he was Foix's seigneur) and the king (because he was Navarre's cousin). He kissed the pope's slipper when in Rome, attended Lent sermons and exorcisms, and went on a pilgrimage to Our Lady of Loreto—but he also, according to his travel journal, debated with a Protestant theologian at Aisne, dined with reformed theologians Thomas Platter and François Hotman in Basel, attended Lutheran baptisms and a circumcision, and visited the Patriarch of Antioch in Italy. Spanish and

English ambassadors reporting on Montaigne's mission in Paris, where he represented Henri, king of Navarre, thought that he was working on converting the king to Catholicism with the help of Navarre's mistress, the Catholic Countess de Guiche.[12] Montaigne remained loyal to the monarch and other members of the establishment while embracing cultural relativism and cosmopolitanism. Desan explains the genesis of the *Essays*, admittedly with some speculation, as the consequence of the author's failed ambitions to be named ambassador to the Holy See in the early 1580s, a career for which, Desan surmises, Montaigne consciously prepared himself by reading moral philosophy and travel reports about all parts of the world. Desan suggests that it was this failure that prompted Montaigne to turn to his own life through the famous self-portraiture that "universalizes" his person. However, as attractive as Desan's narrative of professional failure and subsequent pivoting to a new career in Montaigne's life might be, it is unnecessary to explain the turn to a universalized self, which was readily available in writings by agents. As we have seen, agents used references to the agency of the body indexed to nature and the cosmos to fashion their own agencies, and Montaigne often embraces these fictions of agency. Apart from his post at the parliament of Bordeaux and his function as mayor of Bordeaux, Montaigne provided services for the crown, which included mediating between moderate Catholic and Protestant factions.[13] He was also a wartime informant during the 1580s, the third decade of France's civil wars, and there likely were more that have not come down to us. These circumstances prompt us to think more about his universal self "painted" in the *Essays*, the desire to see his self as other—famously, "the cannibal," and less famously but analogously, the dervish—and the pressures of providing service for patrons and the crown, to which he owed loyalty.

During his tenure as mayor of Bordeaux (1581–1585) and afterward, Montaigne regularly informed Jacques Goyon de Matignon (1525–1598), then lieutenant-general of the king and, from 1584, governor of Guyenne, of the comings and goings of both the Catholic Leaguers and the king of Navarre and his men. Throughout the 1580s, this loyal royalist and informant wrote many short missives to Matignon. The anecdote of the young woman holding a calf in her arms serves as a commentary on Montaigne's complicated view of custom and political institutions and the pressures of these institutions on his own agency, which shape and, at the same time, threaten it:

> The power of habit was very well understood, it seems to me, by the man who first forged that tale of a village woman who had grown used to cuddling a calf and carrying it about from the time it was born: she grew so accustomed to doing so that she was able to carry it when a

fully grown bull. For, in truth, Habit is a violent and treacherous schoolteacher ("une violente et traistresse maistresse d'escole").[14]

This tale showcases the ability of the peasant to cross interspecific lines as she builds and maintains an intimate relationship with the newborn calf, caring for it continuously as it grows into a bull. Is it important that this is a woman and that the burden is an animal: She extends her gentle care to an infant animal, which very gradually transforms into a crushing burden, at which point the woman continues to treat it with the same gentleness she applied to the farm animal at its birth. The farm animal, whose name ("un veau") was also an insulting term for human stupidity, is figured here as inert weight, a heavy mass of meat and muscle—but also as a living being, a vulnerable newborn animal, and the object of the woman's affective care—and it continues to be this object of care even later on. The tale also reveals the plasticity of the human that makes habit possible in the first place. This is embodied not only in the image of the woman holding the growing animal but also in the potential of subservience implied by this plasticity, which Montaigne calls "the tyranny of custom." The woman caressing the calf (and bull) is the figure of violence *and* gentleness in nonreciprocal response to violence. This is because, as Anne Dufourmantelle reminds us, violence cannot be cognizant of gentleness, only gentleness to violence.[15] Is Montaigne discovering in this woman the power of gentleness with which he hoped to treat the violence of political rivalry and religious wars, the weight of the institutions of the monarchy that he so unflinchingly served? In Montaigne's use, the woman's gentleness becomes a figure of subtle resistance to subvert or manage the crushing power of oppression, to attend to the vulnerable animal that she discerns in the dead weight pressing down upon her. The story narrativizes the unfolding of a potentiality in the body and its gestures while incorporating a folding-upon of matter to make it more resistant. The woman in this image represents both this potentiality of the body—its agency in pushing back gently without doing harm—and its fragility. Will she be crushed? While Raemond is concerned with the supple cosmopolitan body and its unwavering spirit, Montaigne reworks the relation to institutions as a careful balancing act, a constant and dynamic oscillation between the care for and the resistance to the crushing power of institutions. This dynamic attitude informs and shapes subjectivity rather than implying that one can act in multiple ways while maintaining a singular spirit. Dufourmantelle describes gentleness as an animal in its disturbing connection to violence. The woman has an intimate connection to the animal and is herself the image of animality: as gentleness, as "an intelligence, one that carries life, that saves and enhances it." It is "an intimate connection to animality, to the mineral, the vegetal, the stellar."[16]

What of the gendering and classism of the image? For the peasant woman's passive resistance renders her increasingly immobilized by the weight of the adult animal. She is still holding it and able to practice her caring, but the weight threatens to crush her agency as it is exerted through this same care. The challenge of carving out a space for freedom and resistance when one is weighed down by the tyranny of custom—particularly within the institutional or legal sedimentation that props up political systems such as the French monarchy and elite society—is one that Montaigne himself takes on in the *Essays*, a book in which the author involves himself in creating that space where one gains agency from supporting, both actively and passively, the inert weight of custom, from pushing back without contesting its power. Custom is made possible by plasticity in that, as both Raemond and Montaigne proclaim, it is randomly different in different parts of the world. The violent and treacherous arbitrariness of its authority is denoted through the metaphor of the schoolmistress, whose irrational authority conjured up by Montaigne (who was educated without one, in a free learning environment). Institutions have no rational justification (for example, in divine will), for they are heavy sediments—but this only means that one must treat them with gentle care, and Montaigne and Noailles were both invested with responsibilities to ensure the strength and stability of the monarchy. Yet Montaigne figures this care, the gentleness vis-à-vis the weight of power, just as he figures the violent, irrational authority of custom: gendered as feminine. Is there a blindness here to his subjectivity being formed under the pressures of the very regime it was called to serve? How does he figure his male subjectivity, which is defined by a heightened awareness of the need to care for and respect customs insofar as they guarantee the unity of the state? Is the private self, the one that has sheltered itself from direct risk, gendered as masculine? Reading Montaigne's *Journal de voyage*, the account of his travels in Europe in 1580 and 1581, Louisa Mackenzie suggests that, on occasion, Montaigne adopts femininity to shape his itinerant self. She underscores that these performative gestures do not, however, prevent him from creating a masculine self and that they lead to the appropriation and effacement of femininity.[17] Here, too, masculinity is defined by the necessity of remaining blind to one's own vulnerability by imagining oneself as female, passive, on the cusp of being overpowered.

Noailles was dispatched to Constantinople on May 24, 1571, with a hefty to-do list. In his letters, Noailles deliberately contrasts himself to his recent predecessors: Guillaume de Grandchamp, who was sent in 1566 to explain that the monarchy did not support the pro-Spain Henri, Duke of Guise's participation in Philip II's campaign against the Ottomans, and Charles du Bourg, who was sent in 1569 to renew the capitulations that had expired after

Suleiman I's death in 1566, and to settle the French crown's debts with the Jewish Ottoman merchant Joseph Nasi. Both men were unsuccessful and discredited themselves, and Noailles references this in a letter to Catherine de Médicis: "May it please God, Madame, at least that the memory of both these men be buried in this theater where they have made themselves into public scandals to the detriment of Your Majesty's reputation!"[18] Noailles uses the metaphor of the theater to denote the poor performance of the ambassadors who preceded him, depicting them as bad actors who followed either their own passions or those of other actors averse to the interests of France. Acting and theater here take on a negative value, as they do in the writings of Étienne de la Boétie, Joachim du Bellay, and, as we shall see in this chapter, Michel de Montaigne. It was better to have unflinching spirit, but this spirit manifested itself through the ability to sway the world around one. Underscoring Noailles's ability to gain epistolary leverage at a time of deepening financial and political crisis for the monarchy,[19] Matthieu Gellard shows that the bishop's letters abound in manifestations of political loyalty, as is demonstrated by his dramatic plea in a letter addressed to the French king on July 31, 1572: "I am among barbarians here without any civil conversation."[20] This statement is to be understood as a description of his own distance (his "exile") from the court, recognized as the sole source of patronage and love, and an emphasis on his own precarious position were France to abandon the alliance. This kind of centripetal rhetoric of political loyalty, always referencing the center, forms the counterpart to the actual focus of his letters—that is, the Sublime Porte, the events and persons of which he was predominantly engaged in describing. Noailles's depiction of the vicissitudes of Ottoman "greed" serve as a foil to this self-representation in relation to the political center of the French kingdom. Gellard notes that, although Noailles's letters abound in pejorative statements about the Turks, they do not specifically refer to their cruelty or their religion but rather to how difficult it is to negotiate with them.[21] Indeed, Noailles reveals a great deal of ideological flexibility. He shows himself to be open to negotiating with the Ottomans even as he describes them almost invariably as creatures of greed.

In a long *mémoire* (diplomatic report) that Noailles composed during the early months of his mission to persuade the king to maintain the alliance (in jeopardy at the time, because of the Ottoman defeat at Lepanto and a fiasco in which the merchandise of French merchants was seized in the ports of Alexandria), the ambassador calls the king's attention to the political theater in Constantinople. This arena would have been less apparent to a French court that was all-too preoccupied with the political rebellion against the Holy Roman Empire in Flanders:

> While the farce will be played over there [in Flanders], it must not stop here, for we are poised to win the game ("car la partie est forte"). It is true that I have come to know these people as full of both good and evil, that is, of all sorts of riches and voluptuousness, and it seems that we would please them if we allowed them to have fun ("de les en laisser joyr") for a few years, but I do not think they esteem their reputation so much that they would not gladly retire [their forces] now, given their loss in naval battle."[22]

Ottoman "voluptuousness" (which here does not signify strong sexual libido but rather political ambition) is so unbridled that it alone provides certitude in a contingent field of international political action. While the Turks would like to retire from fighting at that particular moment in time (because they lost at sea at the battle of Lepanto), they (maintains the ambassador) still love riches, glory, and reputation. They thus need to be pushed to keep following this trajectory, to enter more wars, and it is for this that Noailles advocates. Ottoman vices, Noailles seems to say, can be made into French virtues if used right—not unlike Rabelais's fictional character, Grandgousier, domesticating the Canarrians by redirecting their appetite. The ambassador extends his agency—that is, of being able to turn Ottoman passions into actions compatible with French ambitions—far beyond this context, even as far as the Massacre of St. Bartholomew's Day, which contributed to the prolongation of his mission. The seventeenth-century libertine Gabriel Naudé named the massacre of Protestant leaders during the night of August 24, 1572, and the alliance with the Ottoman Empire as the two successful coup d'états of the Valois kings in the sixteenth century in his treatise *Considérations politiques sur les coups d'état*.[23] The crown's own mechanisms of self-preservation undoubtedly weighed heavily upon Noailles. The news of this event reached him in Ragusa in November 1572 after he had, characteristically, on his own decision, already departed from Constantinople. When he was sent back to Constantinople to protect the crown's interests at the Sublime Porte, Noailles wrote back, explaining his fears that the Ottomans may interpret the massacre as a sign that the French were turning away from the alliance and favoring Spain and the pope. Without commenting on the massacres or attributing responsibility to the French court, Noailles points out the bad timing of both his mission and, especially, his return: "Please remember that you originally sent me to Turkey, as you are resending me now, in a strange season" ("par une estrange saison").[24] The expression "in a strange season" signifies that, in moments of crisis, the time such events take place operates outside of the temporal norm. Here, the timing itself is a reference to the unpredictability of the court's motives toward the ambassador. But this signaling to the court is only momentary. In a letter dispatched a few weeks after the successful signing of the peace treaty between Venice and the Sublime Porte on March 3, 1573, as Noailles was negotiating, with "vehemence and ardor," the Ottoman support for the Duke of Anjou's candidacy to the Polish throne,[25] he reinterprets the question of timing by writing to the king that the massacre put pressure on both the Venetians—who were afraid of losing the support of the French—and the Ottomans, who also felt the threat of losing the alliance of the French. This pressure is what brought about the Ottoman–Venetian peace[26] and, on top of the bargain, also disposed the Ottomans favorably toward Anjou's candidacy. Noailles's bravado in claiming to work upon the unpredictable passions of non-French actors, including the Ottomans and the Venetians, who make up the political theater in which everything can change in the "blink of an eye" ("quasi en un clain d'oeil"),[27] allows him to restage the drama in a heroic fashion and claim agency for himself.

Noailles's letters reveal the careful creation of his ambassadorial persona for the court, in which his agency depends on the projection of greed upon the Ottomans. A more personal account of Noailles's second mission to the Sublime Porte by Philippe du Fresne-Canaye (1551–1610), the young scion of a Huguenot family and, later, a diplomat for the French king Henri IV (former king of Navarre, 1553–1610), exists in the account of his trip to Istanbul in 1573. Fresne-Canaye's descriptions also revolve around the ceremonies of reception at Selim II's court. He describes the ceremony of kissing the sultan's robe and, after having admired the rooms and the sultan's magnificent dress and making three reverences "à la française," his efforts to display French courtly protocols of civility were put to an abrupt end by those who control protocol at the Ottoman court:

> When I came close to the emperor, those leading me kneeled and I, humbly, kneeled too and kissed the hem of his clothes. Then suddenly lifted by them, I returned backwards, walking like the crawfish of Treviso ("à la façon des écrevisses de Trévise,"), so fast that I did not have the chance to take in the room and the Great Turk as I would have liked to. However, I do remember that he did not turn his face to us but with cloudy eyes ("avec l'oeil trouble"), which appeared evil and frightening, he turned his head toward the fireplace, appearing not to notice those who came humbly to appear in front of him. All around this hall, countless numbers of mutes ("muets") were hidden, who are the most loyal and tried executors of the atrocious commands of this tyrant. And the most favorite of all is

the one who, upon the sultan's order, strangled with an arch cord his son Mustafa.[28]

The rituals of submission that Fresne-Canaye observed and was also subjected to at the Sublime Porte give the curious young man the impression of being reduced to one of the small crustaceans he may have seen at markets or on dinner tables in Venice. His description echoes the common anxiety of French agents vis-à-vis Ottoman institutions and authorities.[29] The moment he is seized by hands that prevent him from viewing the court from the distance of an observer, the young aristocrat grows an imaginary crustacean shell. The animal's image and movement somewhat alleviate the awkwardness of the young traveler's position, where he is forced to crawl backward out of the sultan's presence, unable to see, let alone observe. This leads to a mental movement back in time, to the memory of the execution of Prince Mustafa by Selim's father, Sultan Suleiman I, in 1553. This story of Mustafa as an example of a victim of Turkish despotism reverberated through the multiple accounts and dramatizations of Mustafa's murder in diplomatic reports, rumors, and pamphlets that circulated around Europe. The mutes also figure, notably, in a French play, Gabriel Bounin's *La Soltane*, which was printed in 1561 with a preface praising Catherine de Médicis and her politics of reconciliation not long after the repression of the "Conjuration of Amboise," when a group of lesser Protestant noblemen tried to assert their control by kidnapping the young king Francis II.[30] In the play, which has a German pamphlet as its source, Mustafa has a friend, "the Sophy," who prudently counsels him not to appear at his father's summons. The Sophy in the play represents the Sufis, a mystical religious movement founded by Rumi that was recognized and commented upon (under the name "Sophies") by contemporary commentators like Nicolas de Nicolay.[31] Bounin shares the Stoic cosmopolitan outlook that we have seen voiced by Postel and Nicolay, according to which there is a universal morality, and he shows that good or bad action in the Ottoman Empire is compatible with good or bad action in France and elsewhere. Sufis figure as Islamic representatives of Christian French values, especially those espoused by the royalist moderates, or the *politiques*, whose views Bounin championed. Bounin identifies Mustafa with the unjustly persecuted religious minority. "Moustapha" is also upheld in the play as the model of a ruler—one that tragically fails in the Ottoman Empire but is still to come in France under the tutelage of Catherine de Médicis. Given these intertextual precedents and the French tendency to view Ottoman society through an allegorical lens provided by their own, it is possible that Fresne-Canaye does the same and views Mustafa—loyal, and unjustly persecuted—as his double. This allows him to voice his own loyalty to a persecuted community (indirectly, through the figure of Mustafa) but also to evade talking about the massacres and representing his vulnerability vis-à-vis the French state. Fresne-Canaye's father converted to Catholicism and thereby saved his social status and wealth. But his uncle was among the Protestants executed in Toulouse in 1568, while another uncle had to leave France for Germany. As a member of a Protestant family, it is hard to believe that the young aristocrat did not feel implicated in the violence of sovereign power after the Massacre of Saint Bartholomew's Day and that he did not feel that his loyalty as a servant of the court was in tension with the persecution faced by members of his family. He notes that he joined the French embassy in Constantinople without his father's knowledge or permission, but this profession of filial disobedience masks the fact that it would have been imprudent for him to return directly to Paris from Venice because of the massacres.[32] In the Ottoman Empire, the twenty-two-year-old Frenchman and future diplomat immerses himself in the politically influential social world of the Ottoman capital by not only exploring the Byzantine monuments already familiar to him from the books of Nicolay and Pierre Gilles but also by enjoying the hospitality of the Ottoman elite, including Sokollu Mehmed Pasha, Selim's grand vizier and powerful son-in-law (*damad*). The agent (here in training) is no longer like the migrant bird or cosmopolitan mollusk that changes shells, transgresses boundaries, and moves forward. Instead, he is a crustacean whose movements are oriented backward, away from the current political crisis in France and into a state of muteness, which allows him to gain momentary independence from royal policies in France and paternal authority alike. The cosmopolitan, mobile person also conceals the vulnerability of being a Huguenot and his inability to name his belonging to that group. The phenomenology of the body, walking backward while looking down, shapes Fresne-Canaye's relation not only to the Ottomans but also to his cosmopolitan self as a future diplomat of Henri IV, which entails both self-knowledge and self-effacement.

Montaigne: The Gentle Gesturing Animal

Like the village woman holding the calf, Montaigne develops his own agency in relation to the tyrannical forces of institutions (and masters that rely on them), which allow him to gently preserve and mold his agency to them. Alison Calhoun shows that Montaigne's notion of testing the body and its natural abilities takes on specific qualities that deviate from the traditional account of a noble line, including a diversion by way of illness and vulnerability to pain and death. In her reading, Montaigne turns the ability to suffer pain as a result of illness into the quality that separates nobility from the common sort of people.

This is because Montaigne associates the pain of the stone, excruciating and menacing, with death—but he *also* considers the management of this pain, the successful avoidance of suffering, to be a test that is ennobling in itself, thereby advancing the notion of noble living constituted otherwise than through heredity or knightly heroism.[33] While, in "On Physiognomy," Montaigne admits, "Not only in men but in the animals serving me I consider beauty to be only two fingers away from goodness" ("Non seulement aux hommes qui me servent, mais aux bestes aussi, je la [beauty] considere à deux doits pres de la bonté"),[34] he also suggests that "beauty" and "ugliness" oversimplify the characteristics from which moral virtues and vices can be inferred. Montaigne thus claims to provide a more subtle physiognomic principle by praising "graces" shaped by natural simplicity ("la nayfveté et la simplicité")[35] and credits his own physiognomy, his direct and sincere gestures, "my countenance and my frank behavior" ("mon visage et ma franchise").[36] On occasion, this helps him to find common ground even in the most difficult situations; for example, when facing a home invasion in his castle from his Protestant neighbors during the civil wars or, on a second occasion, when he is attacked by bandits in the forest:

> On another occasion, trusting to some truce or other which had just been proclaimed between our forces, I was on the road travelling through some particularly ticklish terrain ("par pays estrangement chatouilleux"). As soon as wind of me got about, three or four groups of horsemen set out from different places to trap me. After three days one of them made contact with me and I was charged by fifteen or twenty masked gentlemen followed by a wave of mounted bowmen. There I was, captured; having surrendered I was dragged off into the thick of some neighboring forest ("dans l'espais d'une forest voisine"), deprived of my horse and luggage, my coffers ransacked, my strongbox seized. Horses and equipment were divided between their new owners. We haggled for some time in that thicket ("dans ce halier") over my ransom, which they had pitched so high that it was obvious they knew little about me. A great quarrel started between them over whether they would let me live. They were indeed several threatening circumstances which showed what a dangerous situation I was in:
>
> *Tunc animis opus, Aenea, tunc pectore firma.* ("Now, Aenas, you need all your courage and firm mind.")
>
> I continued to hold out for the terms of my surrender: that I should give up to them only what they had won by despoiling me (which was not to be despised), with no promise of further ransom. We were there for two or three hours when they set me on a nag unlikely to want to

bolt away and committed me, individually, to be brought along under the guard of some fifteen or twenty men armed with harquebuses, while my men dispersed among other such soldiers, each with orders to escort us as prisoners along different routes. I had already covered the distance of some two or three harquebus shots,

> *Jam prece Pollucis, jam Castoris implorata*, ("Having by then prayed to Pollux and implored Castor.")

When, all of a sudden, a most unexpected change came upon them. I saw their leader ride over to me, using the most gentle words ("avec parolles plus douces") and putting himself to the trouble of searching among his troops for my scattered belongings, which, insofar as he could find them, he returned to me, not excluding my strong-box. In the end they gave me my best present, my freedom ("ma liberté"): the rest hardly affected me at the time.

The true course of so novel a volte-face, of such second thoughts which derived from no apparent impulse, of so miraculous a reversal of intent, at such a time and in the course of such an operation which was fully thought through and deliberated upon and which custom had made lawful (for from the outset I openly admitted ("je leur confessay ouvertement le party duquel j'estois") which side I was on and the road I was taking), I certainly do not really know even now. The most prominent man among them took off his mask and informed me of his name ("se demasqua et me fit cognoistre son nom"), he then told me several times that I owed my liberation to my countenance as well as to my freedom and firmness of speech ("je devoy cette delivrance à mon visage, liberté et fermeté de mes paroles") which made me unworthy of such misfortune ("me rendoyent indigne d'une telle mesadventure"); and he asked me to promise if necessary to return him the compliment.[37]

Montaigne, like other Frenchmen, was obsessed with the face ("visage" or "mine") having a special and civilizing effect on others, especially in real or imagined situations of conflict. Because Montaigne also recounts this event of robbery in a letter to Matignon, the maréchal of France[38] after 1579, we can compare his elaborate narrativization in the essay with his terse, informative account in that letter. In what is the last extant letter we have by Montaigne, written in 1588 (the same year he published this account in the *Essays*) to Matignon, the lieutenant-general of the king, he names the place of attack near the forest of Villebois, his attacker, Lignou (a Huguenot bandit), and one of his companions, Thorigny (the son of Matignon). He also reveals that he was freed on orders of the Prince of Condé, but he informs his patron that he lost most of his belongings, including his money, his strongbox, and most of his papers. In his essay, Montaigne presents himself as an avatar of Aeneas, getting the better of his adversary in a lawless situation thanks only to "courage" and a "firm mind." He thus remains silent about important facts and even embellishes the story—creating a fiction of his agency through an account of the efficacy of his gestures and comportment—while hiding not only facts that were supposed to remain secret (Thorigny's and Ligou's names), but also the actual political chain of command that ultimately ensured his liberation. The essayist Montaigne thus construes a fiction in which some form of reciprocity comes about between men thanks to his own positive, noble, corporeal subjectivity—that is, thanks solely to his gestures and actions, and unrelated to his place in a hierarchical social order.

Montaigne's identifications with animal, vegetal, and human others, which require traversing cultural, linguistic, religious, historical, social, and species boundaries, all depend on the assumption that the body is expressive and agential in and of itself. Montaigne's belief that we can communicate with others through our bodies by mute gestures forms an essential part of his argument that we can bridge the gap between us (i.e., European male human beings who were trained to view themselves as exceptionally rational) and animals as well as culturally and geographically differentiated others. The essayist's insistence on the continuity between human and animal subjectivity is one of the most analyzed aspects of his writing and thought. Montaigne feels the pain and fear of the hunted animal. He toys with the possibility of his cat playing with him as he plays with her. He considers the intelligence, social organization, and language of animals. He even advocates for respecting plants.[39] These transgressions, even if they occur through the affective avenues opened up through acts of reading and writing, are the essayist's ways of exploring the potentialities of his subjectivity through corporeal, gestural relations to others. Yet this expressiveness that characterizes the body is denied to those gender, race, and class-specific others who, as we shall see, lack moderation—while others are condemned by Montaigne to express something the essayist himself wants them to express. Instead of "difference," Montaigne tends to use the word "distance," suggesting a profound relation to space—geographic and ontological, familiar and unfamiliar, but also moral and hierarchical—that underlies his preoccupations with differences of status and race. Montaigne could be described playfully as a distancologist: one that is preoccupied with identifying and measuring the distance to be traversed between people and between people and things, who uses his fanciful phenomenological sense of the space separating self and other to enable him to feel close to or distant from others. Of these boundaries, he considers those existing between human beings to be the most difficult to cross. In his essay "On the Inequality There Is between Us," Montaigne states that "there is more distance between one man and another than between men and animals" ("il y a plus de distance de tel à tel homme qu'il n'y a de tel homme à telle beste").[40] This affirmation of human closeness to animals, and of distance from other human beings, resists the easy celebrations of human diversity witnessed in Nicolay, who invokes Terence to claim that nothing human is alien to him, only then to exclude some from the category of the human. But how exactly did Montaigne measure the distance between himself and other people, and how did gender, race, and class become a factor in this measuring process? Montaigne's statement, no doubt intended as a provocation, echoes Cynic moral philosophy according to which the reduction of a human to animal needs is a tool for revealing moral differences among people. Montaigne cites the example of noble animals like horses, hounds, and hunting birds, whose bodies—that is, the body parts that ensure fast movement, rather than their harnesses, collars, leash, and bells—are inspected thoroughly before purchase. According to this logic, the natural body harbors intrinsic qualities that can be discerned through physiognomy by the act of looking. This fundamentally animal body can be tested to reveal "proper qualities" ("ses propres qualitez") like mobility, speed, and performance.[41] Moreover, this natural functioning of the body is one that can be described and depicted. Throughout the essay, Montaigne argues that it is natural qualities rather than acquired and external ones, including wealth, clothing, and other markers of social status, that matter in judging and testing people. Does this embracing of the Cynic and naturalist way of defining the human by the yardstick of the animal provide a way to resist the weight of institutions? While "race" was thought of as the justification for social hierarchies and positions by bloodlines and birth, Montaigne thinks that testing, rather than pedigree, determines corporeal agency. The essayist accords value to the natural virtues that are discernible in the body to an outside observer to bring down those of high social status and especially to challenge the social expectation to obey or respect social superiors like princes and kings. Montaigne offers an ironic portrait of the insouciance of the country squire whose court is "lying far from the court—Britanny, say" and whose self and nobility are rooted in a vaguely defined cousinship with the king that relies on old documents held in the archives of his own *château* ("quelque vieux cousinage que son secretaire tient en registre").[42] Montaigne rejects definition by pedigree (understandably, since his own nobility went back two generations) and the myopic perspective of the anecdotal Breton nobleman, who does not even realize his distance from the court. Instead, the essayist turns to testing himself to find proofs of nobility that are outside the registers and bloodlines. He aspires to freedoms that are not myopic but cosmopolitan, even as he steadily idealizes his own agency. And cosmopolitanism does not so much chart one's bloodline to the king but includes awareness of one's precise distance from the monarch (and other masters) and the will to move closer or farther—as the situation and one's need for privacy dictates—from their interests.

While Montaigne valorizes the ability to see and communicate at a distance, finding ways to reduce one's distance from others, prejudices about social groups nonetheless slip into his writing—ones that assert the existence of moral differences and hierarchies of natural bodies, affects, and even pleasures, including those he levies against the "mob," actors, and women. Montaigne has two groups in mind. On the one hand, there are those who stand the test of nobility, similar to animals used in breeding and sale (or gift exchange). On the other hand, there are those whom he describes as having an unnatural relation to nature, the "mob" who are too much under the sway of passions—"the mass of men nowadays, senseless, base, servile, unstable, continually bobbing about in a storm of conflicting passions" ("continuellement flotante en l'orage des passions diverses qui la poussent et repoussent")[43]—and who are thrust into situations where they forfeit agency to passions, illness, or too much pleasure. Montaigne names the examples of choir boys who do not enjoy the music, courtiers who do not enjoy the ceremonies, and actors who do not enjoy the farces they perform because they have no "thirst" for the pleasures they so often consume and, presumably, have too much sway over them.[44] In these examples, we catch a glimpse into Montaigne's fear of the capacity of passions to sway people, similar to his friend Étienne de la Boétie's desire for freedom from tyranny.

Cosmopolitan, Stoic, and Epicurean-inspired notions of the natural body extend the excellence of physical and intellectual traits and their transmissibility beyond heredity to persons outside the world of European aristocracy, but they also allow Montaigne to view himself through others by abstracting from their cultural, historical situation and their concrete personal views. Just as the "traveler" narratives were wont to do, Montaigne's examples of persons from other cultures show these selves as subject to phenomenological reductions through which they are made to fit seamlessly into the perceptions of the self—Montaigne's self—and its world. "A 'gentleman is a man of parts,' said Montaigne ("Un 'honnête homme, c'est un homme mêlé,' disait Montaigne"). Identity is a private story, dependent on relative ability to interiorize or reject instilled norms. Socially, a person constantly deals with a galaxy of individuals, each of whom has multiple identities."[45] There are two ways of reading Montaigne in this citation by Serge Gruzinski: either by emphasizing "the gentleman," rising above the fray, which places us in "the school of Montaigne," or by emphasizing "the mix," in which case we end up having to consider Montaigne an exception to the Western, including French, hegemonic identity. I am trying to avoid the dualist logic of both readings here by examining the concrete pressures and political forces, norms, and conversations that shaped Montaigne's self. In "On Vanity," Montaigne professes his fascination with cosmopolitanism and his ability to subordinate ("postposant") his national ties to the more universal ones he enjoys by way of his example of a Pole: "I reckon all men my fellow-citizens, embracing a Pole as I do a Frenchman, placing a national bond after ("postposant") the common universal one."[46] Montaigne does not tell us if this perceived closeness was because the Valois harbored an interest in Poland (and, reciprocally, the Valois featured in Poland's imperial ambitions).[47] It seems that Montaigne placed national ties after universal or cosmopolitan ones, but this order of priority did not prevent him from harmonizing his cosmopolitan sentiments with his loyalty to the king and his patrons. In "On the Custom of Wearing Clothes," Montaigne questions the rationale of wearing clothing to protect the human body from the cold and other environmental aggressors, arguing that clothes are not necessary for this purpose, for the human skin is similar to animal and vegetal skins, husks, and shells. When it comes to the human body's ability to withstand cold, Montaigne estimates it to be on par with animal and plant bodies. In a provocative gesture concerning contemporary customs, beliefs, and even scientific consensus, he argues that the skin is people's best defense: "just as plants, trees, animals, and all living things are naturally equipped with adequate protection ("naturellement equippé de suffisante couverture") from the rigour of the weather."[48] If, by nature, human beings can defend themselves against the weather no less than plants and animals, then clothing is something simply "borrowed" by custom and serves goals other than the protection and defense of the body.[49] In defining the human skin as a sufficient protective layer in and of itself—and thereby opposing humoral medicine that considered the skin to be porous and dangerously open, needing to be covered and protected with clothing—Montaigne arguably moves the human body closer to animal and even vegetal bodies and, in a Cynic fashion, indexes it to universal natural needs, from which he excludes clothes. The nude human body is presented as universal, not unlike the depictions of animality, skin, and "simple" clothes in the accounts of Belon and Postel, as we saw in Chapter 2. Montaigne thus not only promotes the human skin to the status of a protective layer but also emphasizes that the self's contours are defined by the skin insofar as it is the sensorial boundary that must withstand tests coming from the physical world. This articulation of the powers of the bare human body straddles the differences between, on the one hand, an early modern notion of "nature" as all-powerful, surrounding all things human and nonhuman, living and nonliving, and comprising political relations, generation, growth, and sexuality—and, on the other hand, a kind of biopower that modern political subjects can acquire according to the historical paradigm initiated by Michel Foucault, which ushers in modern biological and racial categories. The skin provides important contours for human subjectivity defined as animal and corporeal, transgressive and cosmopolitan, because the skin is the very place of testing, a constant barrier between inside and outside, a site of transgression where the self comes into contact with the outside and is made under its pressures. The skin is also a place of sensation (for example, cold) that directly connects the self to the material world, making it a dynamic product of this barrier's permeable-yet-resistant nature. Montaigne's images highlight the thin and bare qualities of the human skin and emphasize the risk involved in being a self. Some of Montaigne's final examples show precisely what it means to live with this sense of risk. He recounts the loss of the freezing Roman army against the Carthaginians because the latter's soldiers were protected by the fires Hannibal had lighted for them. He also references the misfortunes of the Greek army in the mountains of Armenia. Even fruit trees, he maintains, can benefit from being buried to prevent exposure to frost. Such risks can be managed by developing "a thicker skin" ("une peau plus espoisse"), which correlates with a greater inner ability to endure various temperatures and conditions and a more excellent character.[50] In this essay, Montaigne also argues that a person's excellence stems from the care one takes of the body, in this case, by exposing it to cold, but in others by protecting it, yet in others by using clothing consciously to style the self. For clothing, rejected as a mark of status and a necessary protection, is freed as a consciously chosen representation of the self, its noble qualities, as agents' self-styling in Ottoman clothing and Montaigne's preference for black color evinces. Much like eating for Rabelais and haircare for Ronsard, the care of the body through everyday practices such as wearing the simple, old-fashioned attire the essayist's father was used to wearing, eating certain foods, taking the cure at baths, and purgation is for Montaigne an important concern of the gentleman, and part of the fiction of agency. The essayist sets these reflections on the importance of the skin, not clothing, in developing one's character against a global array of examples of those who go about naked, ranging from aristocratic women in France, Turkish holy men, a French beggar, and Roman soldiers, to kings and princes present and past (the Duke of Florence; King Masinissa; Emperor Severus; the ancient Persian army; King Agesilaus; Julius Caesar; Hannibal; Native Americans; and Stephen Báthory, the Voivode, then Prince of Transylvania and successor to Henri de Valois to the Polish throne).

Montaigne's examples also revolve around contemporary persons who were allies of the French court in a broad sense, including the Duke of Florence, the Tupinamba of Brazil, and King Báthory, as well as historical persons often idealized as models of French kings, such as the Carthaginian Hannibal, defeater of the Roman Republic.

Montaigne moves from the more distant lands of the New World to the closer regions of the Eastern Mediterranean (rendered quasi-familiar by the many books on the Ottoman Empire, far more of which circulated in sixteenth-century France than those about the so-called New World) and gives the example of dervishes in Turkey who "go around naked, out of devotion."[51] Montaigne could have gotten the idea about the pious and virile nudity of itinerant Turkish holy men from Postel's *De la Republique des Turcs* (1560), which acknowledges their holiness most readily among the contemporary French accounts (see my discussion in Chapter 4). The naked dervish makes up just one small part of Montaigne's many examples that prove the unclothed human body is universally able to withstand the test of weather—but it is nonetheless an important example because the dervish's nudity serves as a link to a much more famous figure in the *Essays*. This figure is the cannibal, whose nude body stands in for social and personal virtues and that Montaigne promotes to a kind of nobility of its own, which he sees as absent in war-torn France. In Montaigne's account, the dervish's nudity shows that he can withstand the test (presumably by exposing the body to external circumstances like hot, cold, and social judgment) and thereby proves his single-minded and exemplary devotion. Montaigne's point is not to promote public nudity but to argue, once more, that embodied acts alone—including what one wears or does not wear—can reveal a person's excellence. This rehabilitation of "dervishes" (whom Montaigne no doubt only knew from books) is even more remarkable. They are cited as examples of devotion to the point of shedding all regard for particular practices and beliefs.[52] Devotion was the virtue of the pious and also that of the servant. In an undated letter, Montaigne responds to Matignon's command that Montaigne come to him by evoking his single-minded devotion to his master: " . . . regarding the order that you were pleased to give me, to come and find you, I beseech you very humbly to believe that I do nothing more willingly. And I will never give myself over so much to solitude nor will I withdraw from public affairs so much that I do not reserve a singular devotion to your service and a desire to be wherever you are."[53] The educated gentleman then had to balance his ability to live through his affection for others and his openness to faraway customs with his devotion of service. At the same time, as with Caron's drawing analyzed in the previous chapter, the dervish's nudity, the naked human body, is ambivalent. It implies both increased status, even nobility—as is exemplified by French ladies wearing décolleté, which associates nudity with the artistic, transgressive tastes of the elite[54]—and uncivilized, wild, and threatening characteristics. In the final years of his reign before he was assassinated in 1589, Henri III's strategy was to join the League to dominate and dissolve it (as he had already done in 1576), but to no avail. Henri famously also adopted an exclusively Catholic policy and engaged in penitential rituals such as marching in Paris in a simple cloak, flagellating himself with other penitents. The king's failure was also a failure of masculine agency—one requiring strong public manifestations of devotion to Catholicism, the pillar of the crown. In Montaigne's projection, the dervish achieves what Henri III attempted to do: communicating his steadfast piety ("devotion") through his embodied practice, shedding conventional markers of status while elevating himself in the eyes of others. And yet the devotion of dervishes is also one that requires no words, no confession of faith. These figures exemplify the expressiveness of the walking body, evincing mostly banal gestures. As such, they become the figure of Montaigne's self-portrait: blunt but also mute about many things and depoliticized.

Dervishes are thus not so much exemplary for their scandalous actions as for performing their devotion through simple acts—without preaching—like walking around wearing little clothing. The dervish, like the cannibal (whose figure I can only evoke here), walks around naked in a banal, universalized, depoliticized gesture of the moral values that the king failed to perform. Montaigne's dervish, like his masculinity, is itinerant only within boundaries set by Montaigne himself. In "On Friendship," Montaigne's most-cited essay, the essayist praises the freedom and equality that only exists between men (as enacted through the voluntary bonds of social equality, never in marriage) but refrains from endorsing male homosexual bonds, designating such ties as Greek excess ("cet'autre licence grecque").[55] Too much freedom is not good, but how much is too much—and when does it become servitude to passions?[56] The supposed monstrosity of immoderation prompts Montaigne, in the essay "On Moderation," to resort to a strong metaphor and state that immoderation "enslaves ("esclave") our natural freedom."[57] Immoderation is thus unnatural, monstrous, similar to slavery and, by synecdoche, to slaves. "Even when an immoderate zeal for the good does not offend me, it still stuns me and makes it difficult for me to give it a Christian name" ("m'estonne et me met en peine de la baptiser").[58] For Montaigne, balance, or moderation, represents an inner value that tames or "christens" excess. That which is "Christian" is moderate, devoid of excess and strangeness; it does not stun, like Nicolay's sensationalist images of Muslim characters in the previous chapter. Montaigne aligns moderation with Christian ways of life. In the same way, he genders moderation as masculine.[59] When he discusses immoderation in philosophy and in sex, he reminds husbands not to fall into excess when enjoying the pleasures of sex with their wives because their pleasures may be immoderate, even if women offer their "parts" to be mastered (or raped) ("garçonner"[60]). In both literary examples, freedom is considered something internal, as in Stoic philosophy or Christianity, but not something that is granted by legal or other social institutions. In a society that afforded very few legal protections to women,[61] Montaigne, like other Frenchmen of his generation, is concerned with men's inner self-control. That is because he claims autonomous agency to be rooted in the body, in affective ties to social peers and superiors, and in the ability to manage passions, rather than in some abstract notion of legal personhood. Men benefited from this definition of agency as something that is (allegedly) natural, involving mobility and natural skills, rather than being socially determined through the perception and judgment of others.[62] However, if Muslims are given credit for imposing moderation on the desire of husbands, Persian kings are given only ambiguous credit for sending their wives away and calling in "other women whom they were not bound to respect."[63] The obligation of moderation is limited by class; women are protected because they have husbands, and Persian prostitutes appear as the appropriate object of sexual desire, enslaving the kings' will only at times when such enslavement is deemed suitable. In other examples, women appeal to the reason of moderation only by citing a (male) reason, as in the case of the woman who repudiates her husband for his sexual excesses, whose very example is taken from sermons by the Church Fathers.[64] In all this, women are never able to say "no" on their own, by their own desire. While Persian Shahs are recognized for their moderation in indulging in the excesses of sexual desire only with women who are deemed socially appropriate, it is Christian reason alone that effectively reigns in sexual appetite. Thus, women are either slaves to the passions of men in a way that is acceptable (for example, for certain women in Persian culture, according to Montaigne) or they are subject to the critique of immoderation, which always represents a male, Christian reason. Women represent this immoderation either through their lesser capacity for moderation or by contaminating men's self-control.[65] While Montaigne became famous for his views affirming cultural relativity and sensitivity about the conditions of women, prisoners, animals, and even plants, he was also the author who considered the institution of Christianity sacred and, seemingly paradoxically, as we see here, affirmed the importance of a (male) Christian perspective. Cosmopolitanism is also best in moderation.

By using the image of baptism, of giving something a Christian—that is, familiar—name to mean moderate or tame, Montaigne calls attention to the practice of giving French (or Christian) names to non-Christian foreigners (after baptizing them). Montaigne's treatment of women as having a voice and visibility only insofar as they voice male Christian reason—as well as giving Christian names to non-Christians—is echoed in the diplomatic discussions of two Turkish women (or girls, as they are consistently called in diplomatic texts that do not specify their age), daughters of an Istanbul woman, Humā Hatun, who were captured while on a pilgrimage to Mecca by Francis of Lorraine, brother of the Duke of Guise and grand prior of the Knight of St. John. They were sent to France and entered the court in 1557, where they either converted or were converted to Christianity and served Catherine de Médicis. Susan A. Skilliter has pieced together their story insofar as it is readable to us through diplomatic archives—which is to say, remaining largely unseeable and unnamable—and she guesses that the women lived as members of Catherine de Médicis's female courtiers, or "the flying squadron," who, among other things, spied on her behalf. Skilliter shows that the archives of French–Ottoman diplomacy yield repeated but not always clear references to these women (and to a brother on a few occasions). More consistently, the archives report the persistent demands made by their mother for the return of her daughters, which reach the point of disturbing diplomatic contacts. Letters by French diplomats in Constantinople and a letter by Sultan Murad III (1574–1595), who intervened in the French court in 1581, give us very few details about the actual lives they led, and one of them is simply no longer mentioned after ca. 1560. The one formerly known as "Faty" was christened "Catherine," after the queen, and was often referred to as "la Turque." The other was christened "Marguerite," after the king's sister (following the common practice of naming people of color, servants, and slaves by the first name of their master or mistress), and was also called "la More."[66] The French court refused to return them on the pretext that they had converted to Christianity,[67] married, and no longer wished to return. In 1564, the French ambassador in Constantinople, François Petremol, who was trying to free over a hundred French slaves in the Ottoman Empire,[68] claims to have offered to arrange a trip for the girls' father or a man acting on their behalf to the French court to resolve the issue.[69] As late as 1581, Murad mentions that Humā Hatun continued to petition the Porte to intervene and free her daughters and that during the previous reign of Sultan Selim, three prisoners in the Imperial Arsenal had been set free in exchange, but to no avail.[70] Murad warns that holding "the girl" [sic] at the French court violates the agreement between the French court and the Sublime Porte. The court's repeated efforts to make the case for the legality of keeping the girl (or girls) by referencing conversion and marriage, and their social status, allow it to speak for them. The purported "will" of these young women is manifested through conversion and marriage, service and social rank, all institutional rationalities, while the mother appears in the diplomatic correspondence as, at best, a nuisance. One French ambassador complains that the mother "cries by petitions" ("crie ordinairement par roccaz") that she sends to high officials of the Sublime Porte, where she risks troubling diplomatic relations; the mother's voice is described as an annoying disturbance ("importunité").[71] Letters issued by the French court handle conversion and marriage as synecdochical with the will of young women, as replacements for those voices easily dismissed as excessive.

While recognizing their mixed agency made Noailles and Montaigne, among other agents of the court, careful to enact their devotion to the institutions (by which they also meant influential persons like the king and patrons), they were equally able to characterize others as servile. These authors' eccentric, anti-institutional performances of internal freedom allow them to acquire agency by gently managing the weight of institutions (what Montaigne calls "moderation")—the very same institutions that silence and disparage the voice of the Turkish mother as a disturbing "nuisance." From Panurge to Montaigne, French literature abounds in fictions of masculine agencies that hide their political support systems and rely on the agency of material nature and the body, which they also treat as ambivalent. The French gentleman's carefully cultivated cosmopolitan autonomy derives from the stunning excesses of others, which, as Noailles demonstrates by way of his actions in Constantinople, they constantly manipulate to their own ends.

Coda:
Race and Self-Discovery

Jean Palerne's travel account of a trip to the Ottoman Empire in the years 1582 and 1583 offers a glimpse into the immediate afterlife of the fictions of the agent that we have charted on the pages of this book. Palerne's story was printed posthumously under the title *Pérégrinations* in 1606. In the account, the author often signals his familiarity with Nicolay's *Navigations et pérégrinations* (1567) and Belon's *Observations* (1553) by repeating or copying these earlier texts; indeed, his very title reproduces that of Nicolay. Palerne orients himself by the same experiences and things as these agents and authors, copies their itineraries by visiting the same sites and reenacting some of the situations, and echoes their belief in the freedom and mobility of Frenchmen. This book proves that French men have become like pigeons, carrying messages and symbolic representations concerning their own and others' embodied subjectivities on the other side of the Mediterranean. Palerne was a French Catholic who undertook his trip to the Ottoman Empire after having taken leave from his career as the secretary to Hercule-Francis, the Duke of Alençon, who also went by the name of "le Monsieur" and was the brother to two kings, Charles IX and Henri III, of France. In 1575 and 1576, Monsieur was the chief of the Malcontents and led a faction of rebellious nobility made up of both Catholics and Protestants. He was also a longtime suitor of Elizabeth I of England and, in the last years of his life, titular sovereign of the Netherlands.[1] For all these titles, Monsieur comes down to us as a relatively marginal or marginalized figure of the Valois dynasty whose power, at some points, he actively tried to limit. In *Pérégrinations*, Palerne, whose literary ambitions and devotion to the Catholic faction are evinced by his poetry and travel writing, attempts to recreate the mastery of representation achieved in Belon's and Nicolay's books about the Ottoman

Empire and its habitants—but he often fails. Palerne is a gentleman traveler with resources who undertakes the trip with another gentleman from Melun, the two being perhaps the first Frenchmen to travel in the Ottoman Empire just for pleasure. As the title page announces, Palerne discusses a bit of everything. This includes "several singularities and antiquities," as he states, from Egypt, the desert lands of Arabia, the Holy Land, Anatolia, Syria, and Greece, as well as the customs of Arabs and Turks; he even adds a small dictionary of useful words and expressions in six foreign languages spoken in these lands. Reading through these pages, it is striking just how much Palerne sees the Ottoman Empire through his own readings; not through the Bible, as pilgrims hoped to, nor through classical authors, as humanists tried to, but through the writings of the other Frenchmen who preceded him there in the previous decades. If there is one discernible arc here, it is that humanist exemplarity gives way to a French sense of the self that orientates itself toward the world by way of experiencing the Ottoman Empire.

Palerne repeats Nicolay's observation that poor and young North African women remove their clothing for a small amount of money in his description of Egyptian girls, whose "private parts" are uncovered when they run and which they show "willingly" for a piece of bread.[2] Like Belon, Palerne too throws bread to children while traveling by boat on the Nile.[3] These repetitions suggest that Palerne's activities in the Empire were strongly influenced by his readings; in fact, he is a one-man example of the impact that agents' books on the Ottoman Empire had on their male readers' sense of orientation in the world. He approaches the Ottoman Empire as a source of pleasure (despite the risks of travel, which in his case included two shipwrecks, the second of which claimed the life of his traveling companion) and his belief that, as a Frenchman with means, he was entitled to these pleasures. The author makes the accidents and fortuitous events that befall travelers, small mementos gathered at ancient ruins, and chance encounters with locals into the organizing theme of the narrative. He travels during the embassy of Jacques de Germigny (1579–1585), shortly after the French ambassador was able to renew the capitulations in 1580 following a period of disfavor by the grand vizier Semsi Ahmet Pasha. In the same year, the French crown turned down the invitation sent by Sultan Amurat III via an envoy to France to attend the circumcision ceremony of his son, Prince Mehmed, in Constantinople in 1582. The French did not send a special representative, despite the overture made by the Sublime Porte—but Palerne was there, by a singular devotion to his own freedom to travel, and he describes attending the splendid festivities in Constantinople.

Palerne's book also allows for moments in which the author is not in control of the representation of the space and welcomes interruptions by others. One such example is Palerne's description of the great pyramid of Giza. Palerne climbs inside two of its chambers, traversing its ascending and descending passages, and reports that he and other visitors took away a piece of the empty garnet sarcophagus found in the pharaoh's chamber.[4] Palerne is more willing than Belon to believe in representations and hearsay about the Sphinx and shies away from mounting it because of the revenge the statue reputedly took on visitors. However, he still claims the fragment of stone and reports that "each of us shot a bullet from our arquebus at it, for our pleasure."[5] His bravado in firing at the somber Sphinx, immobile, half buried in the sand, and yet still perceived as having agency that the travelers felt compelled to rival, may bespeak a failed possession and mastery—but it makes for a successful adventure nonetheless.

In another anecdote, Palerne recounts his experience of involuntarily offending a stallholder in Egypt:

> One day, we found ourselves in Khān al-Khalīlī (a commercial quarter in Cairo) to look at the Bazaar and the market, and it so happened that without giving it any thought, we leaned against the stall of a merchant, to whom we turned our backs, and we amused ourselves by looking at the square in front of us. But right away, we heard the merchant's cries attacking us with pretty insults, calling us *kalb* and *kalb 'ibn*, that is, "dogs" and "sons of bitches." (Which I do not find strange given that the English too, and the Spaniards, even though they are Christians, call us this way: the English say "French dogs" and the Spaniards "perro.") Our Moor kept on insulting us, calling us now *marfūs* ("wretch"), now *'arsa* ("pimp"), and he picked up a stick pretending to want to beat us, having found us without translators and officers to protect us, so we decided to move on because it is forbidden to defend ourselves. For if a "Frank," as they call us, has hit a Muslim (*Mahometiste*) in front of a witness, his punishment is death: and for this reason this country makes wimps out of people if they stay there. We asked [others] why the merchant attacked us thus, and they said that they consider it an insult and a cause for anger if someone turns them his back, which they interpret as if the person disrespected them since he shows them his backside.[6]

Palerne quickly justifies the stallholder's insults, remembering that citizens of Christian nations insult Frenchmen with words similar to the slurs used by the Egyptian merchant. His account even gives a voice to the Egyptian stallholder, albeit only by reporting his disparaging language. His acceptance of the differences in customs and rules is mixed with a concern for his mobility.[7] In a description of the baths, he notes the presence of female prostitutes and dancers (he is not entirely sure which) and acts of sodomy but cuts himself short with a sententious "it's better to quit talking in this odious way despised by god and people" to announce that Christian morality is the sole limit to a French gentleman's freedom to travel and enjoy himself in the Middle East.[8]

Traveling without sufficient water in the desert, he and his companion run into an oasis and a group of "Arabs" with tents and camels who demand payment in exchange for their water. The Frenchmen have their translator tell them that water belongs to everyone and that the sultan allows everyone to travel in his land and make use of the necessary commodities.[9] He does not hesitate to evoke Ottoman law and the authority of the sultan, at least in his own telling, which promotes the Ottoman ruler into the sovereign protector of the rights of cosmopolitan travelers like Palerne to mobility and natural resources. The Bedouins' territorialism is here called backward and rebellious, while French cosmopolitanism is upheld in the name of the sultan. Another astonishing anecdote illustrates Palerne's strong pride in his French identity, which can tolerate conversion to Islam but not the loss of autonomy. He relates that, while he and his fellow travelers were in Damascus, two "dervishes" sat down in their midst, and the Frenchmen, thinking that they would not understand them, began to berate the men and Islam. The dervishes, however, responded in French, warning them to be careful about what they say in front of strangers. Palerne closes the anecdote (which reveals his parochial naivete) with the reasoning that these French-speaking dervishes were probably captured and enslaved Frenchmen who learned some Turkish and decided to convert and become dervishes to have the most freedom possible. A Frenchman forced to live in the Ottoman Empire *would* become an itinerant dervish, because to be French is to value physical and spiritual freedom! Montaigne would have probably approved. Because Palerne lacks the terms to describe such flexible identities, these dervishes, diametrically opposed to French and Christian morality in Nicolay's depiction, are made into the very examples of French cultural chauvinism.

In Cairo, Palerne's gaze moves through the city's rich gardens and markets, and he repeatedly stops to regard the city's Black African population, called "Ethiopians" (from the ancient name "Ethiopia" given to the little-known parts of the African continent south of North Africa in ancient cartography). Palerne wonders about the water carriers he sees transporting small mirrors in Cairo and notes that they "like to see themselves even though they are black."[10] Water carriers, menial laborers without compensation, were Blacks and often slaves in Cairo in the sixteenth century, as this was also the case in Lisbon. In early modern Europe, mirrors were expensive, luxury objects and were often associated with vanity and extravagance (as is the case in de la Péruse's *Médée*, in which Glauce admires herself wearing Medea's crown in the mirror—to no good end, as we saw in Chapter 3), and this offhand comment suggests that Palerne also considers seeing one's face in a mirror to be the exclusive privilege of those who have white or lighter skin. In early modern Europe, dark skin had associations with low social status (peasants were often described as dark-skinned in medieval and early modern Europe), and in countries like Portugal where many Blacks lived, dark skin became a marker of low status, often of slavery.[11] The water carriers looking at their reflections in the mirror thus put into question European assumptions about beauty and status. However, they are remarkable to Palerne as another rebellion against the norm. These interruptions to commonly held preconceptions are thus quickly resolved by Palerne, who is inclined to see his subjectivity in the embellishing mirror of those he encounters: the Egyptian stallholder's liberal use of insults, the "French" dervishes' autonomy, even the watercarriers' (allegedly) transgressive use of mirrors. Toni Morrison argues that the obsession with Blacks in classical American novels stems from the need to assuage the anxieties of the self felt by European colonizers of America and their descendants: their low status in the Old World, their ability to make a clean slate of their former selves, and the fear of freedom. "The fascination of an Africanist persona is reflexive; an extraordinary meditation on the self; a powerful exploration of the fears and desires that reside in the writerly conscious."[12] This self-recognition in the mirror of the Black gaze represents an early modern instance of Cord J. Whitaker's metaphorical logic of inversion or "shimmering" at work, forming the metaphorical basis for Morrison's "reflexive" fascination with Blackness, in which the other is also me.[13] Thus, racism is not just the division of people into dominant and subordinate groups contrived along geopolitical, cultural, and religious lines, producing maps with unequal zones. One can only wonder what "fears and desires" Palerne compensated for by recognizing himself in the mirror of other subjectivities. The meeting of French dervishes, free Ottomans, and Black water carriers incites reflective moments in the author, similar to the way in which "black people ignite critical moments of discovery or change or emphasis in literature not written by them," according to Toni Morrison.[14] Palerne also observes enslaved people at the market in Cairo (Palerne calls them Christian slaves) and, noting that he saw about four hundred, "most of them black," he informs his readers that they were snatched at the border of Ethiopia.[15] Palerne also notes that many Black slaves have tattoos on their faces, without attempting to describe or interpret them. The fact that he cannot assign any significance to these tattoos, which works as a silent admission of the foreignness of their culture while also depriving them of their individuality, also points to a curiosity about markings and adornments available for the European self.[16] *Pérégrinations* is noteworthy because it welcomes these *failures* to enact representational control over the other, which leads to moments of self-discovery. In a world where he does not understand much, Palerne looks for new ways of styling his own self. In the manuscript copy of his poems, Palerne fashions his own signature, DEPALERNE, with the drawing of a turban on top of the letters. He leaves the "cloth" of the turban signified by the white space on the paper inside the contours that he draws in black ink, complete with the red-top, or the *mücevveze*, the marker of a sophisticated, stylish Ottoman culture.[17] Since Ottoman law did not allow Palerne to wear such a turban, it is unlikely that he ever did. However, he may have known it from depictions of Ottoman persons in print or coins, or from having seen persons (European or foreign) wearing Ottoman clothing in courtly ceremonies. Considered "arrogant" by the numismatist Antoine Le Pois, the turban here becomes an extension of the author's self into the fiction of distant, foreign symbols of identity. This symbol of Turkish identity is the one that Palerne adopts: It is not only white but also recognized as a marker of status in the Ottoman Empire. The long habit worn indistinctively by many may have been a tool of cosmopolitan identity. But Palerne chooses a sartorial symbol that distinguishes him from all those in the Mediterranean who did not have the right to wear it—and curiously, makes it the symbol of French freedom and extra-social nobility.

Agents without Empire shows that spying done by Frenchmen in the Ottoman Empire changed French culture. The practice of spying extended to the aim of achieving control over the material world, including but not limited to the humoral bodies or "passions" of the Ottoman ally, according to the interests of the French crown. Far from being an isolated practice, spying permeated French culture in large part because those who spied also worked as knowledge producers, propagandists, and artists; it changed what it meant to be cultured and elite, and it created new avenues of race- and gender-specific consumption for men that affected literature, politics, prints, clothing, personal hygiene, and leisure. The fantasies of creating embodied agencies that disregarded authoritative institutions allowed agents to claim certain privileges and, in the same gesture, exclude others from these privileges and allowed for mentalities that anticipated those of settler colonialism. While agents did not become settlers and begin new lives or start with a clean slate as in the New World, they were able to put on new clothes and change their subjectivities; they were able to act as if they were animals, or as minor, pluralistic, or marginalized identities in the space of the Ottoman Empire, with which they learned to operate in "shifting terrain."[18] Culture, including literature, is about giving one the flexibility to change, and this flexibility is baked into sixteenth-century French culture as a privilege of the few (despite being hard-earned, and often in dangerous circumstances). In the long term, the aesthetics of images brought to France by spies and agents in the sixteenth century allowed consumers of literature, art, and fashion to move without hindrance from the Old World to new colonies in the Caribbean and elsewhere in the New World. Parlerne's travel account shows that racialized notions of masculine, White, French agency were learned ideas. Frenchmen in these contexts carry their own racializing prejudices; they view the world from their perceived cosmopolitan bodies, with the trained "inner eyes" provided by the accounts of agents sent to the Ottoman Empire that make possible a fluid and unhindered movement in the world. This fluidity is only broken up through the specificity and incongruity of the particular visions they provide.

Acknowledgments

Over the course of my work on this project, I have accumulated many debts of gratitude. I thank the Early Modern Studies Institute at USC and the Huntington Library for their joint fellowship in the spring of 2012 for allowing me to begin my research. I am grateful to curator Catherine Hess for showing me the ropes of curatorial work in the space of the small exhibit "French Travelers to the East" at the Huntington Art Collections from April 21 to July 24, 2012. My colleagues at USC have also been a source of both support and intellectual inspiration. I especially want to thank Gian-Maria Annovi, Olivia Harrison, Edwin Hill, Rebecca Lemon, Natania Meeker, Lydie Moudileno, Panivong Norindr, Béatrice Mousli, and Margaret (Tita) Rosenthal. Rebecca Zorach, Todd W. Reeser, and Phillip J. Usher have read and commented on the entire manuscript; their suggestions and insights have considerably enriched it. Over many years, I have had the very great pleasure of talking with a large number of colleagues, mentors, and friends, including Talal Asad, Nada Ayad, Jane Bennett, Dominique Brancher, Tom Conley, Gérard Defaux, Marcel Detienne, Pauline Goul, Timothy Hampton, Indravati Félicité, Peter Frei, Katherine Ibbet, Ellen McClure, Isabelle Nathan, Jane O. Newman, Diego Pirillo, Nathan Perl-Rosenthal, Ian Smith, Caroline Trotot, Ellen R. Welch, and Toby Wikström. These conversations have all left a mark on these pages. I owe them for their generous suggestions and simply for the conversations that helped me along the way. I also apologize to those of you whom I forgot to mention. I am very grateful to my friends and colleagues who taught me about Istanbul and its Ottoman past, including Kim Fortuny, Ismail Hakkı Eren, and Antony Greenwood and ARIT, for hosting me for a month and giving me access to their wonderful library in Istanbul. The Dornsife College at USC has generously provided financial support on several occasions.

I thank Tom Lay at Fordham University Press for having faith in the project. My immense gratitude goes to Daisy Reid, who edited the entire manuscript with expert care. A small section of Chapter 4 was published under the title "The Ambassador, the Spy, and the Deli: Self-Representation and Anti-Diplomacy in Nicolas de Nicolay's *Navigations*" (*Modern Language Notes* 131, no. 4 [September]: 1012–1022). The idea about "Pan" came while writing a presentation for the symposium "Politics of the Obscene / Politiques de l'obscène," organized by Peter Frei and Nelly Labère at UC, Irvine, on February 27, 2019.

Most of this book was written during the COVID-19 global pandemic, and the support provided by family and friends, my dear animal companions, and cafés was inestimable. I thank my family in Hungary, Newton, Mass., and Los Angeles, especially Alice Flather and Félix Flather Szabari, for not just putting up with my being busy all the time but also encouraging me with their love and humor, as well as Amanda Smith, Anikó Imre, and Julia Sushytska for the walks and the conversations.

Notes

Preface

1. Henceforth, I will use the term "race" in quotation marks whenever I refer to its use in sixteenth-century texts.

2. I borrow Wes Williams's formulation here. Williams criticizes the heroic narratives of new historicist readings of early modern travel literature for "still project[ing] a grid of reading along axes inherited from the nineteenth-century Orientalists." Williams, *Pilgrimage and Narrative in the French Renaissance: "The Undiscovered Country"* (Oxford: Clarendon Press, 1999), 6.

3. Studies of representations of the Ottoman Empire, or "Turks" according to positivist literary historical methodologies form extensions of a colonial project of gathering and processing knowledge. A classic study that represents this methodology is Clarence Dana Rouillard, *The Turk in French Thought, History, and Literature (1520–1660)* (Paris: Boivin & cie, 1941).

4. Studies that present nuanced analyses of this dominant masculinity in the French Renaissance include: Kathleen P. Long, ed., *High Anxiety: Masculinity in Crisis in Early Modern France* (Philadelphia: Penn State University Press, 2002); David P. LaGuardia, *Intertextual Masculinity in French Renaissance Literature: Rabelais, Brantôme, and the Cent nouvelles nouvelles* (London: Routledge, 2009); and Todd W. Reeser, *Moderating Masculinity in Early Modern Culture* (Chapel Hill: University of North Carolina Press, 2006). On the heteronormativity of Renaissance masculinity, see Reeser, *Setting Plato Straight: Translating Ancient Sexuality in the Renaissance* (Chicago: University of Chicago Press, 2016).

5. Ahmed's queer phenomenological account relies on Maurice Merleau-Ponty's concept that being-body, the experience of the self in and as body, conditions the ability to look at the world, at something or someone else, such that what one looks *at* defines what one *is*. Ahmed principally asks what it is like to look at the world

as a migrant body in the postcolonial world, or as a female, lesbian, queer body. Sara Ahmed, *Queer Phenomenology: Orientations, Objects, Others* (Durham, N.C.: Duke University Press, 2006), 9–10.

6. David Damroch, "World Literature in a Postcanonical, Hypercanonical Age," in *Comparative Literature in an Age of Globalization*, ed. Haun Saussy (Baltimore: Johns Hopkins University Press, 2006), 43–53.

7. This race blindness in sixteenth-century literary studies is a learned one, for, as my analysis shows, sixteenth-century texts contain codes that pertain to race. In English literary studies, I consider exemplary the work of Ian Smith, who has pointed to layers of readers' responses that mask codes that were readable as racial and, specifically, anti-Black in Shakespeare and other English Renaissance texts. Besides numerous articles by the author, see Ian Smith, *Race and Rhetoric in the Renaissance: Barbarian Errors* (New York: Palgrave Macmillan, 2009).

Introduction: French Agents in the Ottoman Empire

1. François Rabelais, *Les cinq livres*, ed. Jean Céard, Gérard Defaux, and Michel Simonin (Paris: Livre de Poche, 1994), 299–307. This edition reproduces the 1534 edition of *Pantagruel* (François Juste, Lyon) with the variants from the first edition by Claude Nourry ca. 1531–1532.

2. According to Genesis 9:20–27, Noah cursed Ham's son Canaan after Ham saw his father naked. David M. Goldenberg traces the double misattribution of the curse and black skin to Ham back to late antiquity: first to Arabic culture in the seventh century, after the Islamic conquest of Africa, due to the association of Blacks with the slave class, then to the Christian West in the fifteenth century with the European slave trade in Africa. In Renaissance humanist culture, Noah's three sons, Japeth, Sem, and Ham, were seen as descendants of Europeans, Semitic people, and Africans respectively. In his two-volume "Who Is Who" of world history, a digest of famous people from biblical antiquity to the mid-sixteenth century (excluding the New World), Guillaume Rouillé, a contemporary of Rabelais, reproduces this genealogy (albeit without mentioning skin color). David M. Goldenberg, *The Curse of Ham: Race and Slavery in Early Judaism, Christianity, and Islam* (Princeton, N.J.: Princeton University Press, 2009), 170–175; Guillaume Rouillé, *La première partie du promptuaire des medailles de plus renommees personnes qui ont esté depuis le commencement du monde* (Lyon: Guillaume Rouillé, 1553), 7.

3. Rabelais, *Les cinq livres*, 301.

4. Jouanna's multivolume study examines the French idea of race, the notion that natural qualities were transmitted by blood, in its capacity to mark social distinctions and assign people places in society. The author argues that tensions and conflicts between old and new nobility in the sixteenth and seventeenth centuries placed an ever-greater weight on race defined as bloodline and on notions of social status determined by birth. Arlette Jouanna, *L'idée de race en France au XVIe siècle (1498–1614)*, 3 vols. (Lille: Atelier reproduction des thèses, 1976; published as a

book under the title *Ordre social. Mythes et hierarchies dans la France du XVI*ᵉ *siècle* [Paris: Hachette, 1977]); see also André Devyver, *Le Sang épuré. Les préjugés de race chez les gentilhommes français de l'ancien régime (1520–1720)* (Éditions de l'Université de Bruxelles, 1973).

5. Rabelais's colleague in Lyon, the physician Symphorien Champier, noted the separation between nobility and royal power: "The King can grant nobility, but he cannot make gentlemen." Symphorien Champier, *Le fondement et origine des tiltres de noblesse* (Paris: D. Janot, 1544), np; translation mine here and elsewhere in the book unless otherwise noted.

6. On this older concept of "race," which Pierre H. Boulle distinguishes from biological concept of race that emerged in the eighteenth century, see his *Race et esclavage dans la France de l'Ancien Régime* (Paris: Perrin, 2007), 63–64, 66.

7. For example, the genealogy of Pantagruel has been read as a tale about the distinctive moral and spiritual responsibility of the giant prince to bring about reconciliation in the aftermath of fratricide. Edwin Duval, *The Design of Rabelais's Pantagruel* (New Haven, Conn.: Yale University Press, 1991), 22.

8. Dominique Brancher notes that Rabelais's novels become increasingly decentralized in "Dégeler Rabelais," in *Christian Prigent: trou(v)er sa langue*, ed. B. Gorillot and F. Thumerel (Paris: Hermann éditeurs, 2017), 227–244.

9. Rabelais, *Les cinq livres*, 301.

10. Jeffrey Jerome Cohen warns us that the monstrosity of the "other" bodies suggests anxieties displaced onto these bodies that "tend[ed] to be cultural, political, racial, economic, sexual." Jeffrey Jerome Cohen, "Monster Culture (Seven Theses)," in *Monster Theory: Reading Culture*, ed. Jeffrey Jerome Cohen (Minneapolis: University of Minnesota Press, 1996), 3–25, 4–7.

11. See Aristotle, Book IIII, in *The Nicomachean Ethics*, trans. H. Rackham, Loeb Classical Library 73 (Cambridge, Mass.: Harvard University Press), 117–153.

12. Aristotle, *Nicomachean Ethics*, 153.

13. Giovanni Pico della Mirandola, *Oration on the Dignity of Man: A New Translation and Commentary*, ed. Francesco Borghesi, Michael Papio, and Massimo Riva (Cambridge: Cambridge University Press, 2016).

14. Heng's concept of race, rooted in medieval cultural studies, is also detached from the Western world and functions globally and across various historical periods. Geraldine Heng, *The Invention of Race in the European Middle Ages* (Cambridge: Cambridge University Press, 2018), 3, 31–33. Before Heng, Peter Erickson argued for the valid use of the concept of race in the sixteenth and seventeenth centuries. Using the example of Shakespeare's *Othello*, Erickson argues for the centrality of Blackness (rather than ethnicity or other categories of difference) to the notion of race. See Erickson, "The Moment of Race in Renaissance Studies," *Shakespeare Studies* 26 (1998): 27–36. Erickson, in turn, leans on feminist studies on race in early modern England, including Kim E. Hall, *Things of Darkness: Economies of Race and Gender in Early Modern England* (Ithaca, N.Y.: Cornell University Press, 1996).

15. Cord J. Whitaker presents an alternative concept of race by defining Blackness as a metaphor or "shimmering" in Western Christianity and Western culture that is also transhistorical, embracing medieval and contemporary racism, and that allows for the view of the racializing regime of modernity as an irrational, rhetorical construct. I will come back to Whitaker's shimmering in later chapters of the book, especially in the coda. Cord J. Whitaker, *Black Metaphors: How Racism Emerged from Medieval Race-Thinking* (Philadelphia: University of Pennsylvania Press, 2019), 20.

16. Heng, *Invention of Race*, 3. Cf. Justin E. H. Smith, who, following the methodology of philosophical anthropology, inspired by Michel Foucault's archeology, extends the paradigm of biopolitical regimes backwards into the sixteenth and seventeenth centuries. Crucial texts that constitute this modern colonial notion of race are François Bernier's "The New Division of the Earth" (1684) and the infamous *Code noir* (first promulgated in 1685). The modern notion of race served economies of the plantation and the social function of reproducing Whiteness and preventing miscegenation, in sharp contrast with ancient and medieval/early modern practices of slavery. E. H. Smith argues that it was the slow emergence of naturalism, which at times was used to combat Catholic dogma and theological universalism, that enabled the naturalization and realism of race. His historically specific analysis is intimately tied to early modern globalization, Western discovery of the world, and "ethnoprospecting," the mapping of human diversity. Justin E. H. Smith, *Nature, Human Nature, and Human Difference: Race in Early Modern Philosophy* (Princeton, N.J.: Princeton University Press, 2015), 2–10.

17. Heng, *Invention of Race*, 5.

18. Studies on the long pedigree of Whiteness include Richard Dyer's *White*, a cultural analysis that ties the modern representation of Whiteness in the Western world to the earlier Christian notion of existence "in the body but not of the body," fictions of universalism, and the associations with light. See also Nell Irvin Painter's *The History of White People*, a long view of intellectual history that draws out the randomness of a category of skin color while tracing the notion of "White people" back as far as Greek perceptions of Scythians in antiquity and early modern European fascination with Circassians—that is, Caucasians—as both the people best fit for slavery and those having the most beautiful women, along with eighteenth-century racial "science" that originated in Germany. Richard Dyer, *White: Twentieth Anniversary Edition*, with a new introductory essay "Looking into the Light: Whiteness, Racism and Regimes of Representation" by Maxime Cervulle (London: Routledge, 2017); Nell Irvin Painter, *The History of White People* (New York: W. W. Norton, 2011).

19. Heng calls the Saracen an "ingenious lie" because Saracens were reputed to take the name of Sara disingenuously in order to disguise their descendance from Hagar. Heng, *Invention of Race*, 111, 112.

20. St. Bernard, the Cistercian Abbot of Clairvaux who popularized the newly minted order of Templars, holy warriors, during the Second Crusade, called

Muslims *malefactors*, agents of evil in the world, in his *De Laude Novae Militiae* ("In Praise of the New Knighthood"). Not all medieval theologians agreed with Bernard that Muslims were to be extirpated, but they believed in a spiritual crusade. This ethos was defended notably by Peter the Venerable, the initiator of the Toledo translation project involving a Latin translation of the Quran in 1141–1143. Heng, *Invention of Race*, 115–116, cites Tomaz Mastnak, *Crusading Peace: Christendom, the Muslim World and Western Political Order* (Berkeley, Calif.: University of California Press, 2001), 125, n. 262.

21. Sylvia Wynter, "Unsettling the Coloniality of Being/Power/Truth/Freedom: Towards the Human, After Man, Its Overrepresentation—An Argument," *CR: The New Centennial Review* 3, no. 3 (September 2003): 257–337.

22. Foucault has described a moralist ascetic tradition beginning in Greek antiquity that privileges sexuality as the domain of the self. Michel Foucault, *The History of Sexuality, vol 2: The Use of Pleasure*, trans. Robert Hurley (New York: Vintage, 1990), 97.

23. Wynter, "Coloniality of Being," 288.

24. Wynter, 289.

25. Along with the Portuguese, the Ottomans and the Spanish made claims to universal rule through exploration and trade, supported by arms and sailing technology. In *The Ottoman Age of Exploration*, Giancarlo Casala draws a parallel between the 1494 Treaty of Tordesillas and the 1517 Ottoman conquest of Cairo. In the former, Pope Alexander VI quite brazenly divided up the world between the crowns of Portugal and Spain, while, in 1517, the Ottomans claimed supreme authority over all Muslims of the Indian Ocean by claiming the title of the Caliph and Protector of the Holy Cities. Casala presents a critique of the Eurocentric narrative of encounter studies by juxtaposing them with an Ottoman perspective. Giancarlo Casala, *The Ottoman Age of Exploration* (New York: Oxford University Press, 2010), 7.

26. For example, see Leslie P. Peirce, *A Spectrum of Unfreedom: Captives and Slaves in the Ottoman Empire* (Budapest-New York: Central European University Press, 2021).

27. In the seventeenth century, the French developed centralized policies of cultural and religious assimilation in "New France" by encouraging French settlers to marry indigenous women or "savagesses" as exemplified in Jean-Baptiste Corbert's instructions to Intendant Talon. However, the French state preferred settlers to marry French women, who were sent to the colonies as "filles du roi" with larger dowries than the intermarriage of settlers with native women could offer. Guillaume Aubert traces the gradual restrictions imposed on interracial marriages in French colonies up to and beyond 1685, the year the *Code noir* was issued, which permits the marriage of single (White) Frenchmen and Black slave women in the colonies, but not "concubinage," sexual relations between slave women and married Frenchmen. Interracial marriages were further limited through discourse that attributed hypersexuality to Black women. Colonial administration systematically established

links between the corruption of "blood" and the corruption of social order and increasingly policed intermarriages and the liberation of slaves. "'The Blood of France': Race and Purity of Blood in the French Atlantic World," *The William and Mary Quarterly* Third Series, vol. 61, no. 3 (July 2004): 439–478, 452–455.

28. Wynter, "Coloniality of Being," 269. Justin E. H. Smith discusses the political uses of this boundary in the New World in the debate between Bartolomé de las Casas and Juan Ginés de Sepúlveda. More broadly, Smith analyzes the naturalization of the metaphysical gap between body and soul in the sixteenth and seventeenth centuries and its use to justify slavery. Smith, *Human Difference*, 74–75.

29. De Lamar Jensen, "The Ottoman Turks in Sixteenth-Century French Diplomacy," *Sixteenth Century Journal* 16, no. 4 (Winter 1985): 451–470, 461.

30. This is not to say that there was no growing interest in France in vying with Venetian merchants. Yet, for example, Michel de Codignac's advice (ambassador to the Porte from 1553–1556) to Henri II to steal the spice trade from the Venetians by maintaining royal galleys and leasing them to merchants found no interest at the cash-stripped court. Ernest Charrière, *Négotiations de la France dans le Levant*, 4 vols. (Paris: Imprimerie nationale, 1848–1860), 2:315.

31. Géraud Poumarède, "Justifier l'injustifiable: l'aliance turque au miroir de la chrétienté," *Revue d'histoire diplomatique* 111 (1997), 216–246.

32. In addition, Louis XII received a capitulation from Mamluk Sultan Qansuh al-Guri in 1512. French merchants received protection for up to three months in a year. After the Ottoman capture of Cairo in 1517, Selim I extended these rights to French merchants in a *berat*. French subjects enjoyed many privileges even before the first state-level agreement, including freedom of traffic, salvage from shipwreck, internal French lawsuits through the French consulate, release of French slaves, and friendly salutation on the high seas of French and Ottoman ships. Alexander H. De Groot, *The Historical Development of the Capitulatory Regime in the Ottoman Middle East from the Fifteenth to the Nineteenth Centuries. Oriente Moderno.* Nuova serie, Anno 22 (83), Nr. 3, *The Ottoman Capitulations: Text and Context* (2003): 575–604, 578.

33. De Lamar Jensen, "Ottoman Turks," 453–454.

34. For the text of the first *ahidnâme*, see Ignace de Testa, *Recueil des traités de la Porte Ottomane, avec les puissances étrangères, depuis le premier traité conclu, en 1536, entre Suléyman I et François I, jusqu'à nos jours*, 11 vols. (Paris: Amyot, Muzard & Leroux, 1864–1911), 1: 15–21.

35. De Lamar Jensen, " Ottoman Turks," 456.

36. J. Ursu, *La Politique orientale de François I, 1515–1547* (Paris: Honoré Champion, 1908), 27–40.

37. Ursu, *La Politique orientale de François I*, 31.

38. Arthur Nussbaum, *A Concise History of the Law of the Nations*. Revised Edition (New York: Macmillian, 1961), 64.

39. Ernest Charrière, *Négotiations de la France dans le Levant*, 1:259.

40. Paul Veyne, "Humanitas: Romans and Non-Romans," in *The Romans*, ed. Andrea Giardina, trans. Lydia G. Cochrane (Chicago: University of Chicago Press, 1993), 342–369, 343.

41. In antiquity, Stoics adopted Cynic cosmopolitanism through Zeno of Citium (ca. 334–262 BCE), who had direct ties to Diogenes through his teacher Crates of Thebes (ca. 365–285 BCE), believed to be Diogenes's teacher. Zeno promoted citizenship in a universal cosmopolis, an idea taken up by Roman Stoics, especially Cicero and Marcus Aurelius.

42. Veyne, "Humanitas," 347.

43. See James Der Derian, *On Diplomacy: A Genealogy of Western Estrangement* (Oxford: Basil Blackwell, 1987), 98.

44. Historian Dan el-Padilla Peralta points to the exclusivist model that held sway even within Roman cosmopolitanism and that repeatedly led to the expulsion of specific groups like Bacchants (186 BCE), philosophers (161 and 154 BCE), Chaldeans and Jews (139 BCE), and the perceived "too many foreigners" at different times during the Roman republic. Dan el-Padilla Peralta, "Barbarians Inside the Gate," Part I *Eidolon* (November 9, 2015).

45. The medieval Crusades led to increased contacts between Muslims and Christians and more nuanced ideas about Islam in Christian Europe starting in the twelfth century, but the idea of Islam as heresy remained rooted in Europe throughout the Middle Ages. Heng, *Invention of Race*, 126; John V. Tolan, *Saracens: Islam in the Medieval European Imagination* (New York: Columbia University Press, 2002), 294.

46. Heng, *Invention of Race*, 124. This argument is developed by Joshua Prawer in *The Crusaders' Kingdom: European Colonialism in the Middle Ages* (Essex, Vermont: Phoenix, 2001).

47. Tellingly, in Monbart's text the term "slave" is metaphorically applied to those outsiders and non-Europeans taken to France, like Zeïr, the protagonist, to denote the contempt of the court and these outsiders' economic dependence on the elite, to whom they owed loyalty. Joséphine de Monbart, *Lettres tahitiennes*. Modern Humanities Research Association Critical Texts, vol. 36 (Cambridge: The Modern Humanities Research Association, 2012), 67, 76.

48. See Jean Vigne and Olivier Halévy's lecture ("Présentation du colloque") on the year 1553 as a political and artistic turning point presented at the conference "Paris, 1553: audaces et innovations poétiques. Colloque international organisé avec le concours de la Bibliothèque nationale de France" (April 3–4, 2008). Audio recording accessed at www.bnf.fr.

49. Talal Asad, *Formations of the Secular: Christianity, Islam, Modernity* (Stanford, Calif.: Stanford University Press, 2003), 192.

50. As Weiss shows, the influence of the Valois court, along with that of Catholic orders, in the liberation of Christians slaves in the Ottoman Empire made possible the control of religion in its territory. Gillian Lee Weiss, *Captives and Corsairs: France and Slavery in the Early Modern Mediterranean* (Stanford, Calif.: Stanford University Press, 2011), 2.

51. For the last point, achieved by Henri IV, see Weiss, *Captives and Corsairs*, 13.

52. Hampton shows that the ambassador's autonomy from structures and ever-shifting strategies of power slowly emerges in the fifteenth and sixteenth centuries, taking the form of a fragile body of legal and literary fiction that focuses on the self of the ambassador. Hampton makes an important point about the precariousness and ambiguity of the institution of diplomacy, which not only extends the operation of the modern state but also limits sovereign power and forms part of the liberal political tradition. In his analysis, it falls to literature to support these fictions of the institution and, also, to reflect on these instabilities. Timothy Hampton, *Fictions of the Embassy: Literature and Diplomacy in Early Modern* Europe (Ithaca, N.Y.: Cornell University Press, 2013).

53. On the diplomatic career of exiled Italian Protestants including Alberico and Scipione Gentili in European diplomacy, see Diego Pirillo's *The Refugee-Diplomat: Venice, England, and the Reformation* (Ithaca, N.Y.: Cornell University Press, 2018).

54. Étienne de La Boétie, *Le discours de la servitude volontaire* (Paris: Payot, 1976), 155.

55. The ascetic tradition was defined by the freedom that comes from controlling the passions: "This individual freedom should not, however, be understood as the independence of a free will. Its polar opposite was not a natural determinism, nor was it the will of an all-powerful agency: it was an enslavement—the enslavement of the self by oneself. To be free in relation to pleasures was to be free of their authority; it was not to be their slave." Foucault, *History of Sexuality*, 79.

56. Joachim du Bellay, *Les Regrets suivis des Antiquités de Rome et du Songe*. Edited by François Roudaut (Paris: Livre de poche, 2002), 29.

57. In medieval French, the word "esclave" could be used to refer to several things, including: Eastern Slavs, enslaved persons, exotic objects or persons, things from far away, and a person inspiring fear (i.e., pirate). It was also used to denote the coarse pilgrim's cape and the relationship of the lover to the beloved. Anna Kłosowska, "The Etymology of 'Slave,'" in *Disturbing Times: Medieval Pasts, Reimagined Futures*, ed. Catherine E. Karkov, Anna Kłosowska, Vincent W. J. van Gerven Oei (Santa Barbara, Calif.: Punctum Books, 2020), 151–217, esp. 156.

58. On the antithesis of freedom and the various forms of "feigning" of the courtier, see du Bellay, *Les Regrets*, 12, 39, 48; on Jean du Bellay, see *Les Regrets*, 49.

59. See Sonnet 60 in du Bellay, *Les Regrets*, 108.

60. "Connaître les humeurs, connaître qui demande." Du Bellay, *Les Regrets*, 85.

61. Robert Mandrou, *La France au XVIIe et XVIIIe siècles* (Paris: Presses Universitaires de France, 1967), 148.

62. François Sagon, *Apologye en defense pour le Roy, fondée sur texte d'evangile, contre ses ennemys & calumniateurs* (Paris: Denys Janot, 1544).

63. Katherine Ibbet shows that this model fails to include French Protestants, and the Edict of Nantes is revoked in 1685 without troubling the rhetoric of

compassion. Katherine Ibbett, *Compassions Edge: Fellow-Feeling and its Limits in Early Modern France* (Philadelphia: University of Pennsylvania Press, 2018), 159–195.

64. On Postel's contribution to the study of the Samaritan, see, among other sources, James G. Fraser, "The Inauguration of Semitic Epigraphy and Paleography as Scientific Disciplines," in *Perspectives on Language and Text: Essays and Poems in Honor of Francis I. Andersen's Sixtieth Birthday*, ed. Edgar W. Conrad and Edward G. Newing (University Park, Penn.: Eisenbrauns, 1987), 19–33, 24–33. Sagon may have been familiar with Postel's description of Samaritan language in his *Linguarum duodecim characteribus* published in 1538.

65. Frequently attributed to Ottoman prophecies, this belief was often cited in laudatory texts about the Valois monarchy. See Michael J. Heath, "Foolish or Fearsome Franks? The Supposed Ottoman View of European Christians in the Sixteenth Century," in *Conceptions of Europe in Renaissance France: Essays in Honour of Keith Cameron*, ed. David Cowling, Faux Titre, 281 (Amsterdam: Rodopi, 2006), 153–176.

66. Jessica L. Wolfe, "The Cosmopolitanism of the Adages: The Classical and Christian Legacies of Erasmus' Hermeneutics of Accommodation," in *Cosmopolitanism and the Middle Ages*, ed. John M. Ganim, Shayne Aaron Legassie (New York: Palgrave Macmillan, 2013), 207–230, 212–213 and passim.

67. Augustine calls their "doglike" immodesty incompatible with Christian virtue. Augustine, *The City of God Against the Pagans* (Cambridge: Cambridge University Press, 1998), 619.

68. *Collected Works of Erasmus: Spiritualia*, Volume 66, ed. Jophn W. O'Malley (Toronto, ON: University of Toronto Press, 1988), 93.

69. The adjective "cosmopolitan" and the abstract noun "cosmopolitanism" were coined much later, in the eighteenth century. Another source of the notion is Plutarch, who attributes to Socrates the saying (not attested elsewhere) "that he was no Athenian or Greek, but a "Cosmian" (as one might say "Rhodian" or "Corinthian"), because he did not shut himself up within Sunium and Taenarus and the Ceraunian mountains." Diogenes Laertius, *Lives of Eminent Philosophers*, vol. 2, trans. R. D. Hicks, Loeb Classical Library 185 (Cambridge, Mass.: Harvard University Press, 1959), 63; Plutarch, "On Exile," in *Moralia*, vol. VI, trans. Phillip H. de Lacy and Benedict Einarson, Loeb Classical Library 405 (Cambridge, Mass.: Harvard University Press, 1959), 526.

70. Serge Gruzinski, *The Mestizo Mind: The Intellectual Dynamics of Colonization and Globalization*, trans. Deke Dusinberre (New York: Routledge, 2013), 11; *La pensée métisse* (Paris: Pluriel, 2012), 23.

71. Chiara Thumiger, "Holism, Parts, Holes," in *Holism in Ancient Medicine and Its Reception* (Leiden: Brill, 2021), 25–46, 32–33.

Brooke Holmes moreover argues that the Western notion of the body originated in the simplification of living systems "to a handful of core elements with ostensibly predictable patterns of behavior subject to manipulation—including bile, phlegm, water, blood—allowing for medical or philosophical control and the setting of boundaries around the body, and the practice of this control became the privilege and duty of free, male bodies in ancient Greece." Brooke Holmes, "The Body of Western Embodiment Classical Antiquity and the Early History of a Problem," in *Embodiment: A History*, ed. Justin E. H. Smith (New York: Oxford University Press, 2017), 18–50, 35.

72. Plato, *Timaeus, Critias, Cleitophon, Menexenus, Epistles*, trans. R. G. Bury, Loeb Classical Library 234 (Cambridge, Mass.: Harvard University Press, 1929), 35A.

73. In *Accidental Agents*, Martin Crowley considers theories of distributed agency that attribute ontological equality to all human and nonhuman beings (notably, the philosophies of Bruno Latour, Jane Bennett, Bernard Stiegler, and Catherine Malabou) and anthropocentric political philosophies of social and political change that demand (ant)agonistic action (notably, the thought of Chantal Mouffe, Olivier Marchant, Rafaele Marchetti, and Alain Badiou). Crowley plots the ways in which a dialogue between the two theories can contribute to both agency and ontological egalitarianism within the context of contemporary ecological movements. Martin Crowley, *Accidental Agents: Ecological Politics Beyond the Human* (New York: Columbia University Press, 2022), 5.

74. Lois McNay, "Agency," in *Oxford Handbook of Feminist Theory*, ed. Lisa Disch and Mary Hawkesworth (New York: Oxford University Press, 2016), 39–57, 53.

75. See Mel Y. Chen's *Animacies: Biopolitics, Racial Mattering, and Queer Affect*, "Perverse Modernities," ed. Jack Halberstam and Lisa Lowe (Durham, N.C.: Duke University Press, 2012), in which the author rereads Aristotelian matter as inherently animate. Also, Donna Haraway, *Cyborg Manifesto: Science, Technology, and Socialist-Feminism in the Late Twentieth Century* (Minneapolis: University of Minnesota Press, 2016 [originally published in 1985]), 28.

76. Recent studies have described the agency of matter in early modern French perceptions of nature and the physical world from an ecocritical viewpoint: notably, Phillip John Usher, *Exterranean: Extraction in the Humanist Anthropocene* (New York: Fordham University Press, 2019), and the essays in *Early Modern Ecologies: Beyond English Ecocriticism*, ed. Pauline Goul and Phillip John Usher (Amsterdam: Amsterdam University Press, 2021).

77. Examples include the male sperm, which imprints form on the shapeless embryo in Aristotelian natural history, and without which women conceive shapeless masses. Rebecca Zorach, *Blood, Milk, Ink, Gold Abundance and Excess in the French Renaissance* (Chicago: University of Chicago Press, 2005), 136.

78. Malabou notes the etymology of "plastic" in Greek *plassein* (to open, to mold), but also the evolution of its meanings to include, for example, the plastic versions of money, wood, and the sense of explosiveness. Catherine Malabou, *Plasticity at the Dusk of Writing: Dialectic, Destruction, and Deconstruction*, trans. Carolyn Shread (New York: Columbia University Press, 2010), 66, 67.

79. Iman Jackson reads the blackening of humanity as hierarchizing plasticity, depriving it of "epistemological, economic, or symbolic capital," in which animality

Chapter 1: Big Appetite and Rabelais's Multiracial Empires

1. Davis begins *The Gift in Sixteenth-Century France* with an analysis of this episode to show that a gift economy of the kind analyzed by structuralist anthropologists existed in early modern France. This gift economy, Davis argues, was not beyond self-interest but constituted a precapitalist social and economic structure. Natalie Zemon Davis, *The Gift in Sixteenth-Century France* (Madison: University of Wisconsin Press, 2000), 3–4.

2. François Rabelais, *Les cinq livres*, ed. Jean Céard, Gérard Defaux, and Michel Simonin, La Pochotèque (Paris: Le livre de poche, 1994), 244.

3. Rabelais, *The Complete Works of François Rabelais*, trans. Donald M. Frame (Berkeley: University of California Press, 1999), 112. I have slightly modified Frame's translation; Rabelais, *Oeuvres complètes*, ed. Mireille Huchon and François Moreau (Paris: Gallimard, 1994), 133.

4. Timothy Hampton explains the logic of exemplarity within the early modern humanists' understanding of history as a "reservoir of models for present action" that can be repeated. Within this reservoir, antiquity received a priority that was "ontological as well as historical." However, later humanists, Erasmus and Budé especially, labored to reconcile the exemplarity of ancient texts with Christian Scriptures and the life and actions of Christ. Timothy Hampton, *Writing from History: The Rhetoric of Exemplarity in Renaissance Literature* (Ithaca, N.Y.: Cornell University Press, 1990), 9.

5. In his analysis of Rabelais's indebtedness to Guillaume Budé, Claude la Charité shows that Rabelais shifts Christian exemplarity from reading the Scriptures to acts of the body, inspired by Budé's critique of the Stoic notion of *apathea*, the dispassionate attitude of the sage vis-à-vis fortune, in his *De contemptu rerum fortuitarum* (1520). While Budé recommends the reading of the Scriptures and prayer to manage passions, Rabelais replaces prayer and biblical study with the acts of the body, especially those that bring joy ("gaieté"), in his strategy for coping with the adversities of fortune. With this, Rabelais initiates an attitude that La Charité interprets as a version of the Epicurean embrace of voluptuous pleasure. Claude La Charité, "Rabelais et le *De contemptu rerum fortuitarum* (1520) de Budé," *Revue d'histoire littéraire de France* 108, no. 3 (July–September 2008): 515–527.

6. Rabelais, *Complete Works*, 112–113, modified; Rabelais, *Oeuvres complètes*, 133.

7. See Grotius's idea of a natural voluntarism that does not depend on a law. According to this principle, human beings were animals first ontologically, focused on

self-preservation, but they were morally predisposed to transcend narrow animal self-interest. See Johan Olsthoorn, "Grotius and Pufendorf," in *Cambridge Companion to Natural Law Ethics*, ed. Tom Angier (Cambridge: Cambridge University Press, 2019), 51–70, 55–56.

8. Rabelais, *Complete Works*, 113.

9. Chapters 12–16, *Quart livre* (12–16); Guy Demerson, Rabelais (Paris: Fayard, 1991), 236–237.

10. Rabelais, *Complete Works*, 113; Rabelais, *Oeuvres complètes*, 134.

11. Grandgousier's crying evokes two other episodes of important tears in Rabelais's novels: the child Gargantua's spontaneous reaction to his new preceptor Eudemon's ceremonious greeting by erupting in tears and "crying like a cow" in *Gargantua*, and Pantagruel's tears recalling the death of Christ in the *Tiers livre*. Tears are indicators of an emotion that is both spontaneous (Gargantua rejects the rules that his preceptor tries to impose on him) and of divine inspiration in the Christian tradition.

12. Rabelais, *Complete Works*, 113; Rabelais, *Oeuvres complètes*, 134.

13. For a long time, Roland Antonioli's *Rabelais et la médecine*, *Études rabelaisiennes* 12 (Geneva: Droz, 1976) was the sole study on Rabelais's medical practice. Recently, there has been a revival of the study of Rabelais in the context of his studies and practice of medicine, notably, in Emmanuel Naya's *Rabelais, une anthropologie humaniste des passions* (Paris: PUF, 1998). On humors, see also Alison Williams, "Sick Humour, Healthy Laughter: The Use of Medicine in Rabelais's Jokes," *The Modern Language Review* 101, no. 3 (July 2006): 671–681.

14. Emmanuelle Lacore-Martin, "'Encores me frissonne et tremble le coeur dedans sa capsule': Rabelais's Anatomy of Emotion and the Soul," *Renaissance and Reformation/Renaissance et Réforme* 39, no. 3 (Summer/ÉTÉ 2016): 33–58, 58.

15. Lacore-Martin, "'Encores me frisonne . . . ,'" 56.

16. Lacore-Martin, 41.

17. Rabelais, *Les cinq livres*, 39.

18. These fictional "pigmies" are also described by André Thevet in *Cosmographie de Levant* (Lyon: Jean de Tournes, 1544), 145–146.

19. Rabelais's story of the origins of "little men" regurgitates tropes of transcultural humoral racism of antique and medieval sources. The tenth-century Arabic polymath from Bagdad Al-Mas'udi attributes to Galen the description of sub-Saharan Africans as having ten properties, some of which mark their humoral inferiority: curly hair, thin eyebrows, splayed nostrils, thick lips, sharp teeth, smelly skin, black skin, long feet and hands, large genitals, and excessive petulance. In Vivian Nutton, "Epidemic Disease in a Humoral Environment: From *Airs, Waters, and Places* to the Renaissance," in *Holism in Ancient Medicine and Its Reception* (Leiden: Brill, 2021), 357–376, 366.

20. Imtiaz Habib, *Black Lives in the English Archives, 1500–1677: Imprints of the Invisible* (London: Routledge, 2008), 24.

21. Habib, *Black Lives in the English Archives*, 25.

22. Albrecht Dürer, *Les quatre livres d'Albert Durer, Peinctre et Geometrien Tres excellent, De la Proportion des parties & pourtraicts des corps humains, Traduicts par Loys Meigret* (Paris: Charles Perier, 1557), 85.

23. This pan-Mediterranean historical hypothesis of slave trade in the Middle Ages is synthetized in Catherine Coquery-Vidrovitch, *Les routes de l'esclavage. Histoire des traites africaines, VIe–XXe siècle* (Paris: Albin Michel, 2021), 84–102.

24. Coquery-Vidrovitch, *Les routes de l'esclavage*, 87.

25. This capacity for mimicry could be seen as both an entertaining and preposterous pretense. In the sixteenth century, and before 1700, Europeans were not familiar with hominoid great apes but only with smaller monkeys like Egyptian baboons, tailed monkeys, and so-called Barbary apes. Erasmus uses the metaphor of aping for Ciceronians in the sense of preposterous pretense in his polemic against them, in which he claims that only Christian imitations of Cicero are authentic. Giovanni Boccaccio rehabilitated aping somewhat by noting that all poetry is imitation of nature. H. W. Janson, *Apes and Ape Lore in the Middle Ages and Renaissance* (London: The Warburg Institute, 1952), 15, 290–293, 331–332, 335–336.

26. Civets are described as nocturnal animals capable of being domesticated according to the French naturalist Pierre Belon, who spots them in Alexandria. Pierre Belon, *Voyage au Levant (1553). Les Observations de Pierre Belon du Mans*, ed. and intr. Alexandra Merle (Paris: Chandaigne, 2001), 267–268.

27. Geraldine Heng, *The Invention of Race in the European Middle Ages* (Cambridge: Cambridge University Press, 2018), 222.

28. Rabelais, *Complete Works*, 163; Rabelais, *Oeuvres complètes*, 246.

29. Rabelais, *Complete Works*, 163; Rabelais, *Oeuvres complètes*, 246.

30. Michelle Miller notes that Pantagruel gives Panurge his livery, and thus Panurge becomes a member of his household. She argues that their relationship is defined by love and constraint, engaging Panurge as both part of Pantagruel's retinue and his servant, and that their relationship shows how service and friendship were precisely being rethought by Christian humanist writers. In this sense, Panurge's nobility does not simply refer to status and birth but also good humor and loyalty. François Rigolot also examines the redefinition of the master's role as "condescendence" (a word that, unlike today, had a positive significance in Christian humanism) and shows ethical subjectivity to consist in the charitable stooping toward people of more lowly status, which is being practiced by Pantagruel toward Panurge. Michelle Miller, "Constrained Friendship: Rabelais and the Status of Friendship in Evangelical Humanism," *Renaissance and Reformation / Renaissance et Réforme* 33, no. 1 (Winter 2010): 31–54; François Rigolot, "Tolérance et condescendence dans la littérature francaise du XVIe siècle," *Bibliothèque d'humanisme et Renaissance* 62, no.1 (2001): 25–44.

31. Subsequent editions of Rabelais's work in the sixteenth century were abundant, despite Rabelais's works being placed on the Index of Prohibited Books in 1564, but

these editions tended to be heavily altered Protestant editions. By the seventeenth century, Rabelais was no longer deemed suitable for general readers and his works were rarely reprinted, yet they were appreciated for their cruel wit by a small number of *Libertins*. Stephen Rawles and Michael Andrew Screech, *New Rabelais Bibliography* (Geneva: Droz, 1987).

32. Extending Gérard Defaux's observation that Panurge is a "queer" (as in "strange," "odd," and "counterfeit") character, Freccero argues that Panurge is also queer in the sense added to the English word in the late nineteenth century of sexual deviance, and in the late twentieth century of questioning sexual and familial norms. Carla Freccero, "Queer Rabelais?," in *Approaches to Teaching the Works of François Rabelais*, ed. Floyd Gray and Todd W. Reeser (New York: MLA, 2011), 182–191, 184.

33. In her classic study *Between Men*, first published in 1985, Sedgwick renders the category of homosociality more dynamic by pointing to the mostly invisible ties between homosociality, or male bonding, and homosexuality. Eve Kosofsky Sedgwick, *Between Men: English Literature and Male Homosocial Desire*, Thirteenth Anniversary Edition (New York: Columbia University Press, 2015).

34. Michael Randall, *The Gargantuan Polity: On the Individual and the Community in the French Renaissance* (Toronto: University of Toronto Press, 2008), 173.

35. François Rigolot, "Rabelais, Misogyny, and Christian Charity: Biblical Intertextuality and the Renaissance Crisis of Exemplarity," *PMLA* 109, no. 2 (March 1994): 225–237.

36. Rabelais, *Complete Works*, 112–113; Rabelais, *Oeuvres complètes*, 133.

37. Rabelais, *Oeuvres complètes*, 133.

38. In his journal, the pharmacist Valbelle does not say when or under what circumstances the animals arrived, but only notes the date on which they departed for the king's court (August 12) and that one camel and one ostrich died on the way. Honorat de Valbelle, *Histoire journalière d'Honorat de Valbelle (1498–1539). Journal d'un bourgeois de Marseille au temps de Louis XII et François I*, ed. V. L. Bourilly, Lucien Gaillard, and Charles Rostaing (Aix-en-Provence: J. Laffitte, 1985), 219.

39. The Castilian Rincón left the service of Charles V to serve Francis I after the *Comunidades* in 1521 and was sent by the French king on missions to Poland and Hungary and on two missions to the Ottoman Empire. In 1528, he negotiated a treaty between the Voivode of Transylvania and the French court, just before the Voivode became the vassal of Suleiman I (the Ottoman siege of Buda occurred shortly thereafter with the participation of French soldiers). Rincón was pro-Ottoman and established good contacts with Ibrahim Pasha at the Sublime Porte. Rincón's 1541 assassination by agents of Charles V provoked a war and a long debate concerning the immunity of ambassadors. Rincón received a pension from the French king in 1541 and appears in the royal registers as the king's former ambassador in the Levant. In diplomatic correspondence, Rincón is repeatedly praised as a competent negotiator; for example, by Guillaume Pellicier, Francis I's

ambassador in Rome, who credits him with obtaining the Hungarian crown for the young son of John Sigismund Zápolya from Suleiman I. Victor-Louis Bourrilly, "Les diplomates de François Ier. Antonio Rincón et la politique orientale de François I (1522–1541)," *Revue historique*, 113, no. 2 (1913): 268–308; Bourrilly, "La première ambassade d'Antonio Rincón en Orient (1522–1523)," *Revue d'histoire modern et contemporaine* 2, no. 1 (1900): 23–44; Michèle Escamilla (with María José Bertomeu Masiá), "Antonio Rincón: Transfuge, espion, ambassadeur et *casus belli* à temps de Charles Quint," in *Ambassadeurs, apprentis espions et maîtres comploteurs* (Sorbonne, Paris: PUPS, 2010), 87–171; and J. Ursu, *La Politique orientale de François I, 1515–1547* (Paris:. Honoré Champion, 1908), 134.

40. Charles V mentions in a letter from January 1535 to his ambassador at the French court that a commercial treaty with the Ottoman Empire was proclaimed in France at the time of the arrival of an Ottoman envoy. Ernest Charrière, *Négotiations de la France dans le Levant*, 4 vols. (Paris: Imprimerie nationale, 1848–1860), 1:252n.

41. The single extant copy of the first printed version ("A") of *Gargantua* is missing its frontispiece, which has sparked a debate between literary historians Gérard Defaux and Michael Andrew Screech. Defaux argues that the book appeared before October 1534, based on a reference to "placards" (polemical printed sheets). Screech, however, uses the references to Tunis and Barbarossa in Chapter 10 of *Gargantua* to date the book in the early months of 1535. See Screech, "Some Reflexions on the Problem of Dating *Gargantua*, 'A' and 'B,'" *Études rabelaisiennes* 11 (1974): 9–56; Screech, "Some Further Reflections on the Dating of *Gargantua* (A) and (B) and on the Possible Meaning of Some of the Episodes," *Études rabelaisiennes* 13 (1976): 79–111"; Gérard Defaux, "Rabelais et les cloches de Notre Dame," *Études rabelaisiennes* 9 (1971): 1–28.

42. Captain Polin was the perpetrator of the massacre of Waldensians in Cabrières and Mérindol in 1545. Brantôme alleges that the sultan ordered Barbarossa to obey Polin "in everything." Seigneur de Brantôme, *Oeuvres complètes de Pierre de Bourdeille, Seigneur de Brantôme*, 11 vols. (Paris: Jules Renouard, 1868), 4:142.

43. Ernest Charrière, ed., *Négotiations de la France dans le Levant*, 1:340–347.

44. While these later court ballets elevated French-style diplomacy within a projected international European community, the Ottomans were represented as a marginal, exotic nation that threatened the unity of Europe—a symbolic mastery whose ambivalent beginning point can be discerned in Rabelais's tale. Ellen R. Welch, *A Theater of Diplomacy: International Relations and the Performing Arts in Early Modern France* (Philadelphia: University of Pennsylvania Press, 2017), 89.

45. Richard Cooper shows that the experiences, observations, and objects collected by Rabelais during his four trips to Rome were not simply ornamental to his *oeuvre* but also constitutive of a vision of the world that reappears in his fiction. Cooper, *Rabelais et l'Italie*, *Études rabelaisiennes* 24 (1991).

46. Rabelais, *Oeuvres complètes*, 989.

47. Rabelais, 989.

48. It has been suggested that Rabelais edited and published a now lost book entitled *Stratagemata* in 1539, in which, according to eyewitness accounts, he reproduced the du Bellay brothers' (Guillaume and Jean) writings with introductions written by him. See John Lewis, "From *Gargantua* to the *Tiers livre*: Rabelais's Quiet Years?," *The Modern Language Review* 107 (July 2012): 729–755.

49. Loris Petris, "Entre implication et distanciation: Pouvoir et écriture dans la correspondance du Cardinal du Bellay," *Seizième siècle* 6 (2010): 165–184, 172.

50. The official occasion for this trip was du Bellay's elevation to cardinal, but he was also to negotiate the place of the general council that Pope Paul III intended to summon for the following year. For Jean du Bellay's instructions issued by Francis I, see "Memoire des principaulx poinctz et propoz que le cardinal du Bellay aura a tenir de la part du Roy a nostre Sainct-Pere," dated June 24, 1535. Du Bellay, *Correspondance du Cardinal Jean du Bellay*, ed. Rémy Scheurer, 2 vols. (Paris: Klincksieck, 1973), 2:2–9.

51. Rabelais, *Oeuvres complètes*, 1002.

52. Rabelais, 1003.

53. Rabelais, 1003; translation mine here and elsewhere in the book unless otherwise noted.

54. Cooper, *Rabelais en Italie*, 134, n67.

55. Rabelais, *Oeuvres complètes*, 1009.

56. Demonet suggests that Rabelais may have avoided prosecution for his unorthodox views by taking refuge in one of the two former monasteries (Castelas or Porquerolles) on the island, which had been abandoned because of frequent attacks by pirates. The island was turned into a refuge for those outside the law by Francis I, who promised them amnesty for living there and defending the islands in 1531. Marie-Luce Demonet, "Rabelais et l'utopie de l'ermitage," in *VII Jornadas sobre el pensamiento utópico. Religión en Utopía* (Madrid, November 2010), ed. Iveta Nakládalová (Berlin: Akademia Verlag, 2013), 71–96.

57. Pantagruel's erudite and curious servant, Epistemon, confirms the sighting of extraordinary and unnatural signs "five or six days" before the death of Guillaume du Bellay. Rabelais, *Les cinq livres*, 1029–1031, 1033.

58. On the melancholy constitutive of Renaissance texts, see Carla Freccero, "Early Modern Psychoanalytics: Montaigne and the Melancholic Subject of Humanism," *Qui parle* (Winter 1999): 89–114, 108.

59. Martin du Bellay, *Les Mémoires de Messire Martin du Bellay, Seigneur de Langey*, Book VI (Jacques Chouet, 1594), 383.

60. Du Bellay, *Les Mémoires de Martin du Bellay*, Book VI, 383–384; Ursu, *La Politique orientale de François I*, 133.

61. Joan Scott points out that women "have been invisible as historical subjects," even though "they have participated in the great and small events of human history." For Scott, this seemingly antithetic nature of gender to the real business of politics is what makes gender, beyond the concept for social relations based on the difference between sexes, a "primary way of signifying relationships of power." Joan

W. Scott, "Gender: A Useful Category of Historical Analysis," *The American Historical Review* 91, no. 5 (December 1986): 1053–1075, 1067, 1074.

62. Timothy Hampton, "'Turkish Dogs': Rabelais, Erasmus, and the Rhetoric of Alterity," *Representations* 41 (1993): 58–82, 62; Hampton reworked and republished the article as a chapter in his *Literature and Nation in the Sixteenth Century: Inventing Renaissance France* (Ithaca, N.Y.: Cornell University Press, 2000), 35–65. Frédéric Tinguely analyzes Erasmus's metaphorical references to "Turks" in "*L'alter sensus* des turqueries de Panurge," *Études rabelaisiennes* 42 (2003): 57–73.

63. Erasmus openly promoted cosmopolitan virtues as striving for peace in his 1517 pamphlet "The Complaint of Peace," in which he makes Peace speak directly to appeal to European elites' better selves, their rational ability to understand the benefits of peace and friendship and the horrors of war. In the 1529 "War Against the Turks," in the direct aftermath of the Ottoman siege of Vienna, Erasmus criticizes those who denigrate Turks as "dogs" or "barbarians" to justify waging war against them, but he condones a war of defense to save Christianity so long as it is fueled by true Christian sentiments. Erasmus also spiritualizes combat by redirecting attention to the internal combat against one's own sins, which he calls one's inner "Turk."

64. Hampton, "Turkish Dogs," 59.

65. Hampton, 73.

66. "At its most demonic—one might almost say ludic, or ludicrous—Saracens appear monstrous by being fused with animals, so that in the *Chanson de Roland* (*Song of Roland*) they have spiny bristles like a boar, or skin hard as iron, or they bark like dogs." Heng, *Invention of Race*, 118.

67. On the racial construction of Muslims as "dogs," with frequent distortions of the name Muhammad as *Maounde* in English and the dog as a metaphor of spiritual evil and the promise of redemption, see Cord J. Whitaker, *Black Metaphors: How Racism Emerged from Medieval Race-Thinking* (Philadelphia: University of Pennsylvania Press, 2019), 36–40.

68. Pascale Barthe, *French Encounters with the Ottomans, 1510–1560* (London: Routledge, 2016), 83.

69. Rabelais, *Oeuvres complètes*, 263.

70. Barthe, *French Encounters*, 86.

71. Barthe, 84–86.

72. Barthe reads Chapter 5 of *Pantagruel*, which references the burning of people at the stake for religious unorthodoxy similarly to "salt herrings" in Toulouse. Barthe, *French Encounters*, 87.

73. Historian Pierre Vidal-Naquet reminds us that eating and appetite were considered to be both natural and cultural in ancient Greek culture, and what people ate revealed not just human nature but also the means of production. Odysseus travels outside the Greek world, defined by bread, into lands inhabited by "gods, the dead, cannibals, or Lotus-eaters." Pierre, Vidal-Naquet, *Le chasseur noir*; published in English under *Black Hunter: Forms of Thought and Forms of Society*

in the Greek World, trans. Andrew Szegedy-Maszak (Baltimore: Johns Hopkins University Press, 1986), 2.

74. I thank Edith Adams for calling my attention to the outsize significance of this naming act.

75. The function of Christians' sometimes self-instigated martyrdom is a symptom of racial tensions in contact zones, even when acculturation between different (notably, Muslim and Christian) populations occurs. It serves to "etch clearer and more determinate identity boundaries"; Heng, *Invention of Race*, 113.

76. Rabelais, *Les cinq livres*, 391.

77. Rabelais, 393.

78. Rabelais, 391.

79. Michel Foucault, *The Courage of Truth: The Government of Self and Others II*, "Michel Foucault: Lectures at the Collège de France," Book 8, trans. Graham Burchell (New York: Picador, reprint, 2012), 195–196.

80. Foucault takes the association with Friedrich Nietzsche's existentialist philosophy from Paul Tillich's 1953 book *Der Mut Zum Sein* (Stuttgart: Steingrüben, 1953); Tillich, *The Courage to Be* (Yale University Press, 2000). Foucault, *Courage of Truth*, 178.

81. Foucault, *Courage of Truth*, 262–263.

82. Foucault, 264.

83. Foucault, 239.

84. Foucault, 242.

85. Foucault, 201.

86. Foucault, 208.

87. In *Plant Theory*, Jeffrey T. Nealon challenges precisely this animal self of modern (and late modern) subjectivity by opposing it to the atelic being of plants. Nealon argues that Foucault's interest in Cynic animality places him right inside the genesis of the liberal subject of capitalism, defined in its transgressive and existential configuration, and shows that Foucault's focus on animality is an indication of the hegemonic nature of this modern subjectivity whose ethical implications continue into late capitalism. Jeffrey T. Nealon, *Plant Theory: Biopower and Vegetable Life* (Stanford, Calif.: Stanford University Press, 2015), 9–10, 109–110, and passim.

88. Rebecca Zorach, *Blood, Milk, Ink, Gold: Abundance and Excess in the French Renaissance* (Chicago: University of Chicago Press, 2005), 134.

89. His gait, we are told, is that of a "scrawny cat" ("un cat maigre"). Rabelais, *Les cinq livres*, 387.

90. Gérard Defaux, *Pantagruel et les sophistes. Contribution à l'histoire de l'humanisme chrétien au XVIe siècle*. International Archives of the History of Ideas Archives/internationales d'histoire des idées, Book 63 (New York: Springer, 1973).

91. Vinciane Despret, *Our Emotional Makeup: Ethnopsychology and Selfhood*, trans. Marjolijn de Jager (New York: Other Press, 2004), 150–151.

92. For Aristotle's notion of natural slavery, see Aristotle, *Politics*, section 1254b, trans. H. Rackham, Loeb Classical Library 264 (Cambridge, Mass.: Harvard University Press, 1932), 16–21.

93. Barthe, *French Encounters*, 81.

94. Belon was aware of the use of homing pigeons for carrying messages, and he notes their existence in France, where they were not used for this purpose. He opines that the French draw "greater profit" from them than people in Asia by breeding them for food. See also the chapter "Le coulombier" in Charles Estienne and Jean Libault, *L'agriculture et la maison rustique* (Paris: Jacques Dupuys, 1583), 51b–53a.

95. Goul's ecological reading shows that stories of Diogenes washing cabbage circulated in Hellenist philosophy and points to a specifically Renaissance iteration of Diogenes in Rabelais, which is neither the noble moralist above the crowd nor the disillusioned and indifferent observer of the world's troubles but "a critical, marginal character, who produces reverse, futile movements." Pauline Goul, "Pointless Ecology of Renaissance Cynicism," *The Comparatist* 43 (October 2019): 159–172, esp. 166.

96. Rabelais, *Les cinq livres*, 393.

97. For this episode of Panurge in Pantagruel's mouth, see Chapter 22, *Pantagruel*, in Rabelais, *Oeuvres complètes*, 330–333.

2. Bird-Man 2, Female Androgyne, and Other Speculative Transformations

1. Phillip John Usher, "Walking East in the Renaissance," in *French Global: A New Approach to Literary History*, ed. Christie McDonald and Susan Rubin Suleiman (New York: Columbia University Press, 2010), 193–206, 204.

2. For a discussion of the rejection of curiosity by Castella and other pilgrims, see Jane Grogan, *Beyond Greece and Roman: Reading the Ancient Near East in Early Modern Europe* (New York: Oxford University Press, 2020), 170–171.

3. Pierre Belon, *L'histoire de la nature des oyseaux, avec leurs descriptions, & naifs portraicts retirez du naturel*, illus. Pierre Gaudet (Paris: Guillaume Cavellat, 1555), 190.

4. Belon, *L'histoire de la nature des oyseaux*, 189.

5. Belon, 189.

6. Belon, 189; translation mine here and elsewhere in the book unless otherwise noted.

7. Jessie Hock, too, notes the recurrence of the analogy "between political leadership and the control of nature" in analyzing Remy Belleau's *Les pierres* and suggests that it is the control of nature that renders art and natural history similar to statecraft. Jessie Hock, *The Erotics of Materialism: Lucretius and Early Modern Poetics* (Philadelphia: University of Pennsylvania Press, 2021), 70.

8. It was recognized in late medieval hunting and husbandry manuals alike that both farm animals and hunting animals stood to benefit from kindness in training. Hannele Klemettilä, *Animals and Hunters in the Late Middle Ages* (New York: Routledge, 2015), 128.

9. The history of equitation and human–horse relationships in sixteenth- and seventeenth-century Europe reveals the dualism of seeing the horse as a partner in possession of another intelligence and will and seeing it as a fearful, passionate animal in need of control. See Pia F. Cuneo, "Just a Bit of Control: The Historical

Significance of Sixteenth- and Seventeenth-Century German Bit-Books," and Elisabeth LeGuin, "Man and Horse in Harmony," in *The Culture of the Horse: Status, Discipline, and Identity in the Early Modern World*, ed. Karen Raber and Treva J. Tucker (New York: Palgrave Macmillan, 2005), 141–173, 175–196.

10. Thanks to the patronage of René du Bellay, Belon studied at the University of Wittenberg and later at the University of Paris, traveled in the Swiss cantons and in the Ottoman Empire, and published his very popular work, *Observations* (1553), alongside several other books on ornithology, ichnology, and conifer trees. He came from the village of Cérans-Fouilletourt in the Sarthe region, was self-taught, moved often, worked as pharmacist's assistant, pharmacist, and gardener before his formal studies, and never became a licensed doctor.

11. Exotic animals were handled by special experts, many (although not all) of whom came from foreign lands and possessed special skills. On the Italian context, see Sarah Cockram, "Interspecies Understanding: Exotic Animals and Their Handlers at the Italian Renaissance Court," *Renaissance Studies* 31, no. 2, Special Issue: The Animal in Renaissance Italy (April 2017): 277–296.

12. Ilana Zinguer, "Narration et témoignage dans les *Observations* . . . de Pierre Belon (1553)," *Nouvelle Revue du seizième siècle* 5 (1987): 30.

13. Alexandra Merle, Introduction to *Voyage au Levant* (1553), ed. Alexandra Merle (Paris: Chadeigne, 2001), 30. In maintaining this view, Belon was in disagreement with other travelers, including the observer André Thevet, who claimed in his *Les singularités de la France antarctique* that nature is moved by divine intention that cannot and should not be scrutinized. The rift separating these two views emerged in thirteenth-century Europe, following the influx of Aristotelian texts with Arabic commentaries in translation into Europe, and was represented by the theological faculty of the Sorbonne, on the one hand, and any body of knowledge that challenged it (including natural theology and medicine based on anatomy), on the other. See Kellie Robertson, *Nature Speaks: Medieval Literature and Aristotelian Philosophy* (Philadelphia: University of Pennsylvania Press, 2017), 3–8.

14. In *Plants and Empire*, Londa Schiebinger argues that explorations of the New World caused an epistemological shift away from the authority of ancient sources, notably Diascorides, Pliny the Elder, and Galen. Belon, while eager to correct these sources, still considered them authoritative. Smith, following Schiebinger, shows that nature is degraded in modernity into "mere rationality," of which some people can be seen as excrescence, and that European explorers and natural scientists encountering native knowledges in the New World distinguish between know-how or skill that indigenous people possess "naturally" and proper knowledge based on reason. Londa Schiebinger, *Plants and Empire: Colonial Bioprospecting in the Atlantic World* (Cambridge, Mass.: Harvard University Press, 2007), 75–76; Justin E. H. Smith, *Nature, Human Nature, and Human Difference: Race in Early Modern Philosophy* (Princeton, N.J.: Princeton University Press), 81–82.

15. Rafael Nájera, "Scholastic Philosophers on the Role of the Body in Knowledge," in *Embodiment: A History*, ed. Justin E. H. Smith (New York: Oxford University Press, 2017), 143–169.

16. Thomist theology does imply that each being in nature is unfree, for free will is accorded to human beings only.

17. Belon, *L'histoire de la nature des oyseaux*, aiii.

18. On the meaning of "absolute" power in medieval and early modern France, see Arlette Jouanna, *Le pouvoir absolu. Naissance de l'imaginaire politique de la royauté* (Paris: Gallimard, 2013).

19. See Grevase Markham, *Cauelarice, or The English horseman containing all the arte of horse-manship, as much as necessary for any man to vnderstand . . .* (London: Edward White, 1607), Book VII, Ch. 1, "Of the composition of horses . . . ," np; cited in LeGuin, "Man and Horse in Harmony," 187–188. On horses and music, see LeGuin, "Man and Horse in Harmony," 188–194.

20. Belon, *Voyage au Levant*, 87–88.

21. Gianna Pomata, "Observation Rising: Birth of an Epistemic Genre, 1500–1650," in *Histories of Scientific Observation*, ed. Lorraine Daston and Elizabeth Lunbeck (Chicago: University of Chicago Press, 2011), 45–80.

22. Belon, *Voyage au Levant*, 60.

23. Tom Conley remarks that in the Middle Ages, when bird migration was unknown, birds were seen as the mysterious automata that disappeared in the fall and reappeared every spring to build nests. Their skills were considered as allegorical lessons for human beings; for example, the swallow was praised for its nest-building, which can "teach human beings a good number of things about domestic space." Tom Conley, *An Errant Eye: Poetry and Topography in Early Modern France* (Minneapolis: University of Minnesota Press, 2010), 188.

24. He also contradicts Aristotle, who claims that turtle doves do not migrate, by conceding that it may be true for some parts of Greece but not in France. Belon, *L'histoire de la nature des oyseaux*, 309.

25. Belon, *Voyage au Levant*, 262.

26. Belon, *L'histoire de la nature des oyseaux*, 40.

27. Conley, *Errant Eye*, 182.

28. Gilles Deleuze, *Cinema 1: The Movement Image*, trans. Hugh Tomlinson and Barbara Habberjam (Minneapolis: University of Minnesota Press, 1986), 20.

29. Frédéric Tinguely, *L'écriture du Levant à la Renaissance. Enquête sur les voyageurs français dans l'empire de Soliman le Magnifique* (Geneva: Droz, 2000), 155–169.

30. Belon, *Voyage au Levant*, 280.

31. Sara Ahmed, *Queer Phenomenology: Orientations, Objects, Others* (Durham, N.C.: Duke University Press, 2006), 1–2.

32. Belon, *Voyage au Levant*, 280–281.

33. Belon, 283.

34. Belon, 59–60.

35. Bruno Latour, *The Pasteurization of France*, trans. Alan Sheridan and John Law (Cambridge, Mass.: Harvard University Press, 1988), 194; cited by Martin Crowley in *Accidental Agents: Ecological Politics Beyond the Human* (New York: Columbia University Press, 2022), 59.

36. Margócsy identifies a bronze murex that depicts a snail with large spikes in the Kunsthistorisches Museum in Vienna and attributes it to the popularity of Belon's description. Dániel Margócsy, "The Camel's Head: Representing Unseen Animals in Sixteenth-Century Europe," *Netherlands Yearbook of Art History* 61 (January 2011): 63–85, esp. 69–70.

37. Belon, *Voyage au Levant*, 120.

38. Marcel Détienne and Jean-Pierre Vernant, *Cunning Intelligence in Greek Culture and Society*, trans. Janet Lloyd (Sussex: Harverster Press, 1978), 12.

39. De Certeau distinguishes between the "art of the weak," which is deployed on the territory of the other by delimiting and controlling its own space, law, and norms, and "strategy," pursued by centralized and "strong" powers. "The space of tactics is the space of the other." Michel de Certeau, "'Making Do': Uses and Tactics," in *The Practice of Everyday Life*, trans. Steven F. Rendall (Berkeley: University of California Press, 2011), 29–42, 37.

40. Belon, *Voyage au Levant*, 250.

41. Belon, 249–250.

42. Belon, 250.

43. Scholars who have considered this possibility cannot fully cast it away. Jean-Marie Constant refers to Belon as a spy without entering into details in his lecture, "Responsibilités politiques et rapports de force à la cour d'Henri II," at the conference "Paris, 1553. Audaces et innovations poétiques. Colloque international organisé avec le concours de la Bibliothèque nationale de France" (April 3–4, 2008). Audio recording accessed at www.bnf.fr.

Christine Isom-Verhaaren notes that Belon's secrecy, the fact that he never speaks of his mission, may be an indication that he was a spy. Alexandra Merle rejects this view but acknowledges that Belon mentions and describes several strategic sites like forts, the positions of the Ottoman army, cities, ports, and infrastructure, of which he was a keen observer. Isom-Verhaaren, *Allies with the Infidel: The Ottoman and French Alliance in the Sixteenth Century* (London: I. B. Tauris, 2013), 170; Belon, *Voyage au Levant*, 33.

44. Jacques Rollet, Introduction to *Des histoires orientales et principalement des Turkes ou Turchikes et Schitiques ou Tartaresques et aultres qui en sont descendues, oeuvre pour la tierce fois augmenté. Et divisé en trois parties avec l'indice des choses les plus memorables y et continues par Guillaume Postel cosmopolite deux fois de là retourné et veritablement informé*, by Guillaume Postel, ed. Jacques Rollet (Istanbul: Isis, 1999 [Facsimile edition of book printed in Paris, by Guillaume Caveillat, in 1575.]), ix–xxxiii, esp. xxiv.

45. François Rabelais, *Oeuvres complètes*, ed. Mireille Huchon (Paris: Gallimard, 1994), 373.

46. Cultural historical explanations for the appearance of this triangular flap, which was made of the same cloth as the breeches, laced to it, and then heavily padded and boned to form an aggressive protrusion, include: protecting the genitals from the swords, pouches, and instruments carried by men; covering (rather than displaying) the penis; decorum; and acting as a container (similar to pockets). See Grace Q. Vicary, "Visual Art as Social Data: The Renaissance Codpiece," *Cultural Anthropology* 4, no. 1 (February 1989): 3–25. Vicary ultimately links the codpiece's popularity to the appearance of syphilis.

47. Rabelais, *Oeuvres complètes*, 373.

48. Matthew Elliot studies the Ottoman dress codes for foreigners in the Ottoman Empire before the *Tanzimat* (the period of reforms) in the nineteenth century. Laws before the eighteenth century forbade non-Muslims, *franks* as well as *zimmis*, "from riding horses in the presence of Muslims, striking back when hit, and wearing white turbans outside their travels." Matthew Elliot, "Dress Codes in the Ottoman Empire: The Case of the Franks," in *Ottoman Costumes: From Textile to Identity*, ed. Suraiya Faroqhi and Christophe K. Neumann (Istanbul: Eren, 2004), 103–124, esp. 112–113 and 119.

49. Belon, *Voyage au Levant*, 107.

50. On the Ottoman sartorial rules "regarded . . . as sanctioned by religion," see Suraiya Faroqhi, "Introduction, or Why and How One Might Want to Study Ottoman Clothes," in *Ottoman Costumes: From Textile to Identity*, ed. Suraiya Faroqhi and Christoph K. Neumann (Istanbul: Eren, 2004), 22. For Belon's description of sartorial rules, before 1553, see *Voyage au Levant*, 467. Select sixteenth-century ordinances during the rules of Selim II (1566–1574) and Murad III (1574–1595) regulating the clothing of non-Muslims have been published in Ahmed Refik, *Ononcu asr-ı Hicrīde Istanbul Hayatı* (1495–1591) (Istanbul: Enderun Kitabevi, 1988), 71–73, 77–78.

51. Belon, *Voyage au Levant*, 183.

52. Belon, 185.

53. Leslie Peirce, A *Spectrum of Unfreedom: Captives and Slaves in the Ottoman Empire* (Budapest-New York: Central European University Press, 2021), 13–14.

54. Honorat Valbelle describes the departure of the Baron of Saint-Blancard on August 15, 1537, and the separate departure of the Duke of Somma and the Prince of Melfi (with whom Borderie traveled) on two armed galleys on September 7. He notes that the destination of the ships was unknown because "these days everything is different and things are so secret that no one knows anything, and only the end will reveal it to us." Honorat de Valbelle, *Histoire journalière d'Honorat de Valbelle (1498–1539). Journal d'un bourgeois de Marseille au temps de Louis XII et François Ier*, ed. V. L. Bourilly, Lucien Gaillard, and Charles Rostaing (Aix-en-Provence, Marseille: J. Laffitte, 1985), 306–307, 318.

55. Tinguely shows that the poem creates an "erotic topography" in which the description of places and things (for example, the extraction of mastic) anticipates erotic seduction and the reunion with the beloved. Frédéric Tinguely, "Éros

géographe. Bertrand de la Borderie et le *Discours du voyage de Constantinoble,*" in *La Génération Marot. Poètes français et néo-latins* (1515–1550), Actes du Colloque International de Baltimore (December 5–7, 1996), ed. Gérard Defaux (Paris: Champion, 1997), 471–486.

56. The vegetal abstraction of interconnected branches maps a quasi-infinite space that is similar to Conley's insular spaces, a figure of ordered chaos. *The Self-Made Map: Cartographic Writing in Early Modern France* (Minneapolis: University of Minnesota Press, 2010), 167–169; on the "nest" and insularity, see Conley, "A Space-Event: The 'Apologie' in the *Essays* of 1595," *Montaigne Studies* 8 (October 1995): 113–115.

57. Bertrand de la Borderie, *Le Discours du voyage de Constantinoble* (1542), ed. Christian Barataud and Danielle Trudeau (Paris: Champion, 2003), 62.

58. The poem justifies the French presence in the region, in accordance with the official justification, by alleging to assume the role of the mediator and claiming that this alliance can prevent the Ottoman Turks from attacking Hungary and the rest of Christian Europe. Borderie, *Le Discours du voyage de Constantinoble,* 71.

59. Borderie, *Le Discours du voyage de Constantinoble,* 135–136.

60. The single most important piece of clothing in sixteenth-century France is the breeches ("haut de chausses"), tight fitting, short hose that replaced for men the long garments worn in the Middle Ages (while long habits continued to be worn by clerics and men "of the robe"). It was worn with a short jacket, which revealed the shape of the buttocks and the legs, and with a "codpiece" (*braguette*). Rachel H. Kemper, *Costume* (New York: Newsweek Books, 1977), 81.

61. Rabelais, *Oeuvres complètes,* 407.

62. Plutarch, *Lives.* Vol. IX, trans. Bernadotte Perrin, Loeb Classical Library 101 (Cambridge, Mass.: Harvard University Press, 1920), 146.

63. For a cultural history of the skin, see Steven Connor, *The Book of Skin* (Ithaca, N.Y.: Cornell University Press, 2004), and Georges Vigarello, *Concepts of Cleanliness: Changing Attitudes in France since the Middle Ages,* trans. Jean Birrell (Cambridge: Cambridge University Press, 1988). On medical history, see Mieneke Te Hennepe, "Of the Fisherman's Net and Skin Pores: Reframing Conceptions of the Skin in Medicine 1572–1714," in *Blood, Sweat, and Tears: The Changing Concepts of Physiology from Antiquity into Early Modern Europe,* ed. Manfred Horstmanshoff, Helen King, Claus Zittel (Leiden: Brill, 2012), 523–548.

64. I omit here the discussion of the baths by Nicolas de Nicolay, whose *Navigations et pérégrinations* I discuss in Chapter 4. On the figure of the veiled Turkish woman going to the hammam in the travel literature of the sixteenth century as a limit to the travelers' power to seize everything through sight and description, see Frédéric Tinguely's insightful and detailed analysis in *L'écriture du Levant à la Renaissance,* 155–188.

65. Elsewhere, Belon does note the Islamic injunction of ablutions: "Mohammed gave them forgiveness of their sins if they wash often their private parts." Belon, *Voyage au Levant,* 475.

66. Guillaume Postel, *De la Republique des Turcs: & là ou l'occasion s'offrera, des moeurs & loy de tous Muhamedistes par Guillaume Postel cosmopolite* (Poitiers: Enguibert de Marnef, 1560), 29.

67. It was augmented and republished under the title *Des histoires orientales* in 1575 in Paris, by Jérôme de Marnef.

68. See Rollet, Introduction, xix.

69. On the possible influence of Arabic heterodoxy in Postel's thought, see William Bouwsma, *Concordia mundi: The Career and Thought of Guillaume Postel, 1510–1581*, Harvard Historical Monographs (Cambridge, Mass.: Harvard University Press, 1957), 165.

70. Jean-Pierre Brach, "Illicit Christianity: Guillaume Postel, Kabbalah, and a 'Transgender' Messiah," *Téma* XXVII 1 (2019): 3, 4–5.

71. Bouwsma, *Concordia mundi*, 173. This kind of pejorative portrayal of Islam by way of citing distorted versions of the hadiths was different from those in the *chanson de geste*, romances, and liturgical plays, where Muslims were derided as pagan idolaters. The Western parodies of the hadiths used knowledge to caricature Islam and often originated in Mozarabic or Iberian Christian authors. John Victor Tolan, *Saracens: Islam in the Medieval European Imagination* (New York: Columbia University Press, 2002), 152.

72. See Carla Freccero's analysis, following the essayist Michel de Montaigne and Jesuit historian Michel de Certeau 1925–1986, of the cannibalism of melancholic male subjectivity, which consists in incorporating the lost object of desire, in Freccero, "Early Modern Psychoanalytics: Montaigne and the Melancholic Subject of Humanism," *Qui parle* (Winter 1999): 89–114.

73. Postel, *De la Republique*, 17–18. On their prevalence in French and Italian accounts of the Ottoman Empire, see Carla Zechner, "The çengî: Descriptions of Professional Female Performers in French and Italian Accounts of Travel to the Middle East, 1550–1650," *L' Esprit Créateur* 60, no. 1 (Spring 2020): 148–158.

74. Postel, *De la Republique*, 19.

75. The authors argue that the figure of the beloved, the passive object of active male sexual desire, was common to the patriarchal early modern cultures in East and West—but in Islamic cultures, including the Ottoman Empire, it was more frequently a young boy: "Anyone who can be penetrated and dominated can be the object of sexual desire." They describe the *köçek* and the *çengî* as young male and female performers dressed similarly, of whom the "girl-boy were more available to younger men without households of their own." Walter G. Andrews and Mehmet Kalpaklı, *The Age of Beloveds: Love and the Beloved in Early-Modern Ottoman and European Culture and Society* (Durham, N.C.: Duke University Press, 2005), 178.

76. Brach, "Illicit Christianity," 9.

77. "Hermaphrodite" was the early modern classificatory term, now rejected in favor of the terms "nonbinary," "intersex" and "transgender," among others, to denote sexually fluid and hybrid physical bodies. Medical interpretations and

alchemical notions of early modern hermaphrodites, along with the figure of the hermaphrodite in lyrical poetry and satire, are discussed by Kathleen P. Long in *Hermaphrodites in Renaissance Europe* (New York: Routledge, 2016). Theological, legal, medical, and alchemical discussions of various nonbinary bodies and their interpretation with respect to defining self and other in medieval Europe are analyzed by Leah DeVun in *The Shape of Sex: Nonbinary Gender from Genesis to Renaissance* (New York: Columbia University Press, 2021).

78. Postel follows the *Zohar* in his *Le Thrésor des Prophéties de l'Univers*, where he translates YHWE as "he-she" (The Hague: Nijhoff, 1969). It is Bomberg who is believed to have sent him back to the Levant to look for manuscripts. Postel declares this and adds that Bomberg paid the cost of his trip in *De Phoenicum literis . . . commentatiuncula* (Paris: Martinus Juvenis, 1552). Postel also took the four metaphysical entities—Father, Mother, Son, Daughter—as a conformation of the dual nature of the divine. Brach, "Illicit Christianity," 10.

79. Brach, "Illicit Christianity," 11.

80. On the mystical tradition and Postel's discovery of it, see Mark Sameth, *The Name: The History of the Dual-Gendered Hebrew Name for God* (Eugene, Oreg.: Wipf and Stock, 2020), 115.

81. Anne Dufourmantelle, *Power of Gentleness: Meditations on the Risk of Living*, trans. Katherine Payne and Vincent Sallé, with Foreword by Catherine Malabou (New York: Fordham University Press, 2018), 34–35.

82. Brach, "Illicit Christianity," 12.

83. Postel, *De la Republique*, 23–24.

84. In the Preface to the *République des Turcs*, Postel addresses the dauphin, the future Charles IX, and presents his vision of a universal empire ruled by the French king after he conquers the Ottoman Empire (a project he later touts, unsuccessfully, to the Spanish ruler Ferdinand). Postel, "Au roy dauphin," in *De la Republique*, np.

85. Postel, *De la Republique*, 70–71.

86. Postel, 72.

87. Postel, 13–14.

88. Postel, 72.

89. Postel, 27.

90. Postel, 72.

91. Rollet, Introduction, xxvii.

92. Carla Freccero, "Queer Rabelais?," in *Approaches to Teaching the Works of François Rabelais*, ed. Floyd Gray and Todd W. Reeser (New York: MLA, 2011), 182–191, esp. 184.

93. On utopian thought, see the Weimar-era Marxist philosopher Ernst Bloch's *The Spirit of Utopia*, trans. Anthony A. Nassar (Stanford, Calif.: Stanford University Press, 2000), originally published in German under the title *Geist der Utopie* in 1918. For more recent rethinking of Bloch's project, along with the queerness of

hope, see José Esteban Muñoz, *Cruising Utopia: The Then and There of Queer Futurity* (Sexual Cultures, 50) (New York: New York University Press, 2019).

3. Snake Women of the East: Staging Freedom and Invisible Unfreedoms

1. Étienne Pasquier, *Les Oeuvres d'Étienne Pasquier* (Amsterdam: Les libraires associéz, 1723), 1:706. This description is cited in Michel Dassonville, ed. (1550–1561), *La tragédie à l'époque d'Henri II et de Charles IX*, vol. 1 (Florence-Paris, Olschki-PUF, 1986), 59.

2. Pasquier, *Les Oeuvres d'Étienne Pasquier*, 704; translation mine here and elsewhere in the book unless otherwise noted.

3. The surgeon Ambroise Paré was present and wrote an account describing the cold and other challenges facing the French army. Paré, "Le voyage d'Ambroise Paré à Metz—1552," *L'Austrasie* 2 (1906–1907): 231–238 and 369–375, esp. 236, 373.

4. Sara Ahmed, *Queer Phenomenology: Orientations, Objects, Others* (Durham, N.C.: Duke University Press, 2006), 115.

5. Plutarch, *Roman Lives: A Selection of Eight Roman Lives*, trans. Robin Waterfield, with Introduction and notes by Philip A. Stadter, Oxford World's Classics (New York: Oxford University Press, 1999), 360–430.

6. Marsilio Ficino says in his commentary on Plato's Symposium that vulgar love, which is not merely spiritual but "infected by the blood," is a kind of fascination (*fascinatio* or enchantment) born when "the eye, wide open and fixed upon someone, shoots the darts of its own rays into the eyes of the bystander, and along with those darts, which are the vehicles of the spirits, aims that sanguine vapor which we call spirit [. . .]. Hence the poisoned dart pierces through the eyes, and since it is shot from the heart of the shooter, it seeks again the heart of the man being shot, as its proper home; it wounds the heart, but in the heart's hard back wall it is blunted and turns back into blood. This foreign blood, being somewhat foreign to the nature of the wounded man, infects his blood. The infected blood becomes sick. Hence follows a double bewitchment." Marsilio Ficino, *Commentary on Plato's Symposium of Love by Marsilio Ficino*, trans. with Introduction and notes by Sears Jayne (Dallas: Spring Publications, 1985), 160.

7. Étienne Jodelle, *Les Oeuvres & meslanges poetiques d'Estienne Jodelle, sieur du Lymodin* (Paris: Nicolas Chesneau, 1574), 234a.

8. Jodelle, *Les Oeuvres & meslanges poetiques d'Estienne Jodelle*, 239a.

9. Jodelle, 246a.

10. Jodelle, 147a.

11. Jodelle, 247a.

12. Jodelle, 249b.

13. Jodelle, 246a.

14. Kate van Orden shows that lamenting, a quintessentially feminine activity, was often composed and even recited or sung by men in lyric poetry that assigned

erotic longing to men and mourning to women. See Orden, "Female *Complaintes*: Laments of Venus, Queens, and City Women in Late Sixteenth-Century France," *Renaissance Quarterly* 54, no. 3 (Autumn 2001): 801–845.

15. Rebecca Zorach, *Blood, Milk, Ink, Gold: Abundance and Excess in the French Renaissance* (Chicago: University of Chicago Press, 2005).

16. Asking for Octavian's compassion for her two sons, she points to her desiccated breast and torn shirt. Jodelle, *Les Oeuvres & meslanges poetiques d'Estienne Jodelle*, 239b.

17. This symbolic transformation of the material body is described in Guy Rosolato, *Essais sur le symbolique* (Paris: Gallimard, 1969), 70; cited by Zorach, *Blood, Milk, Ink, Gold*, 69–70.

18. Jodelle, *Les Oeuvres & meslanges poetiques d'Estienne Jodelle*, 234.

19. By bringing Cleopatra to the French stage, Jodelle also partakes in the rivalry over Cleopatra as a figure in sculpture in France and Italy, which came about through the misidentification of a Hellenistic statue of a reclining female nude acquired by Pope Julius II. Leonard Barkan notes that the identification provided the statue with political significance that was useful for the imperial propaganda of Popes Julius II and Leo X, who identified themselves with Julius Caesar (conquerors of Egypt) and Octavian Caesar (defeater of Cleopatra). Barkan also points out that du Bellay, in *Antiquitez de Rome* (1558), acknowledges the impossibility of the acquisition of antiquities like this one for the French king other than through bringing them to life with the help of poetic description. In 1553 (the year when du Bellay moved to Rome), Jodelle is more ambitious than du Bellay. Leonard Barkan, *Unearthing the Past: Archeology and Aesthetics in the Making of Renaissance Culture* (New Haven, Conn.: Yale University Press, 1999), 235.

20. Emanuel Buron notes that Jodelle was a skilled poet of "écriture rapportée," consisting of braiding together several distinct phrases. This type of poetry is not so much organized around figures of speech as around figures of thought; it is as intellectual as it is bewildering. Emanuel Buron, ed., with Introduction to *Les Amours, Contr'amours, Contre la riere-Venus*, by Étienne Jodelle (Publications de l'Université de Saint-Étienne, 2003), 27–28.

21. Jodelle, *Les Oeuvres & meslanges poetiques d'Estienne Jodelle*, 223v–224a.

22. Jodelle, 224a.

23. "Horapollon" was possibly the fifth-century Alexandrian writer Flavius Horapollon, who became the object of attacks by proselytizing Christian Romans and who, eventually, converted to Christianity. I cite here Pedro Germano Leal's article, in which he contests the hypothesis that the *Hieroglyphica* transmits corrupt, allegorized accounts of correct, ideogrammatic use of Egyptian pictograms, by placing the work in its historical context in Byzantine Egypt and reassessing the function of hieroglyphs as "mythograms" (using André Leroi-Gourhan's term); see Pedro Germano Leal, "Reassessing Horapollon: A Contemporary View of the Hieroglyphica," *Emblematica* 24 (2014): 37–75, 51.

24. Yvan Loskoutoff, "Magie et tragédie. La *Cléopâtre captive* d'Étienne Jodelle," *Bibliothèque d'Humanisme et Renaissance* 53, no. 1 (1991): 65–80.

25. Zacharias Scholasticus. *Vie de Sévère d'Antioch, par Zacharie le scholastique*, ed. Marc-Antoine Kugener, 2 vols. (Paris: Patrologia Orientalis, 1907), 2:29; cited and translated by Leal, "Reassessing Horapollon," 68.

26. Jodelle, *Les Oeuvres & meslanges poetiques d'Estienne Jodelle*, 225a.

27. Pierre Belon, *Voyage au Levant* (1553), ed. and intr. by Alexandra Merle (Paris: Chadeigne, 2001), 313.

28. Belon, *Voyage au Levant*, 313.

29. Another account was provided by André Thevet, which is much less detailed and relies heavily on citations of classical authors on the topic. Thevet merely remarks that he has seen a sarcophagus, "[a] large marble stone, cut in the shape of a sepulcher." André Thevet was in Egypt just the year before the play was performed—probably, according to Frank Lestringant's careful reconstruction of his itinerary, in the winter, from November 1551 to March 23, 1552, when he left for Mount Sinai. Thevet was likely on a mission sent by the Valois court. He admits that he had to stay there, maybe for administrative or diplomatic reasons that he does not specify. *Cosmographie de Levant* was published in 1554. André Thevet, *Cosmographie de Levant*, ed. Frank Lestringant (Geneva: Droz, 1985), 154.

30. Belon, *Voyage au Levant*, 287.

31. Belon, 310–311.

32. Belon, 315.

33. Belon, 316–317.

34. Belon, 318.

35. Some think, Pliny the Elder says—but Belon forgets to cite it—that the god Horos is inside it. Pliny, *Natural History*, Volume X: Books 36–37, trans. D. E. Eichholz. Loeb Classical Library 419 (Cambridge, Mass.: Harvard University Press, 1962), Book 36, chapter 81; Belon, *Voyage au Levant*, 317.

36. Belon, *Voyage au Levant*, 318.

37. Belon, 315–316.

38. The mummy had a complicated history as a medical drug. Authors in medieval Arabic medicine promoted a substance called *momya* (from Persian *mum* for wax) by which they referred to the bituminous substance reputed as remedy for broken bones and an antidote for poisons. Confusions and shifts in meaning—notably, from bitumen to the resinous exudate that came from the corpses found in Egyptian burial sites, to the material used for embalming, and finally to the mummified corpses of Egyptians themselves—occurred in the erudite circles of medical authors involving Avicenna, Pliny the Elder, and Diascorides, and the *momya* became simply the "mummy." In the heyday of selling, buying, and consuming the mummy, from the fifteenth to the seventeenth centuries, the bodies of the poor buried during the Ptolemaic period became especially coveted merchandise. Karl H. Dannenfeldt, "Egyptian Mumia: The Sixteenth-Century

Experience and Debate," *The Sixteenth Century Journal* 16, no. 2 (Summer 1985): 163–180.

39. Belon affirms that the real mummy has healing powers, but not the fake ones, made of bodies of people who died in the desert. Belon, *Voyage au Levant*, 319–320.

40. This view is to be contrasted with that of Paré, who appreciated another aspect of the mummy: the eternalization of memory. He compared mummified corpses to the *gisants* in French Medieval and early modern funeral ceremonies of kings. Paré imagines ancient Egypt as a society in which dutiful children have their fathers' bodies embalmed and "put them in the most honorable place of their homes." He describes a system of moneylending in ancient Egypt, in which the lender gave his ancestor's mummy as gage for the loaned money, risking, in the event of failing to return the sum borrowed, to forfeit the actual body of his ancestor and, with it, his reputation. Paré, *Discours . . . de la mummie, des venis, de la licorne et de la peste* (Paris: Gabriel Buon, 1582), 3ro.

41. In Stoic thought, the seed is both creative force and the origin of the universe. In Renaissance thought, the notion informed alchemical mineralogy. Although Belon does not mention the notion specifically, his hylozoist description of life springing forth from the mineral desert is likely inspired by this notion. Belon, *Voyage au Levant*, 416. Hiro Hirai, "*Logoi Spermatikoi* and the Concept of Seeds in the Mineralogy and Cosmogony of Paracelsus," *Revue d'histoire des sciences* 61, no. 2 (2008): 245–264.

42. The finished text was published in 1556 after de la Péruse died at the age of twenty-five. Raymond Lebègue, *La tragédie religieuse en France* (Paris: Honoré Champion, 1923), mentions several editions in the sixteenth and seventeenth centuries and two performances (1553 and 1572), 114–115. Pasquier indicated the play was unfinished by remarking that although it "was not too disjointed" ("n'estoit point trop descousuë"), it did not receive the favor it merited. Pasquier, *Les Oeuvres d'Étienne Pasquier*, 704.

43. Dassonville, *La tragédie à l'époque d'Henri II et de Charles IX*, 140.

44. Jean de la Péruse, *Médée, Tragédie et autres diverses poésies, Par J. de la Péruse* (Poitiers: Marnefs & Boutsetz frères, sd), 4.

45. Phillip John Usher, "Prudency and the Inefficacy of Language: Re-Politicizing Jean de la Péruse's Médée (1553)," *Modern Language Notes* 128, no. 4 (September 2013): 868–880.

46. Étienne Jodelle, "Préface," *L'histoire palladienne, traitant des gestes et généreux faitz d'armes et d'amours de plusieurs grandz princes et seigneurs, spécialement de Palladien, filz du roy Milanor d'Angleterre, et de la belle Sélerine, soeur du roy de Portugal. Nouvellement mise en nostre vulgaire françoys, par feu Cl. Colet . . .* (Paris: J. Dallier, 1555), np.

47. Dassonville, *La tragédie à l'époque d'Henri II et de Charles IX*, 140.

48. Michel de Montaigne also refers to his relationship to the reader in terms of service, albeit by disavowing his service to the reader, in his preface "To the Reader"

to the *Essays*: "I have not been concerned to serve you nor my reputation" ("Je n'ay eu nulle consideration de ton service, ny de ma gloire"); Michel de Montaigne, *The Complete Essays*, trans. M. A. Screech (London: Penguin, 2003), lxxiii, and *Les Essais*, ed. Marcel Conche, Verdun-Louis Saulnier, and Pierre Villey (Paris: Presses Universitaires de France 2004), 3.

49. De la Péruse, *Médée, Tragédie et autres diverses poésies*, 32.

50. Dassonville, *La tragédie à l'époque d'Henri II et de Charles IX*, 169.

51. Analyzing the reception of Lucretius's *De rerum natura* in French Renaissance poetry, including Joachim du Bellay's 1558 translation of the first twenty-two lines, Hock argues that Pléiade poets embraced the Lucretian theme that desire shapes love and politics either by engendering *ataraxia*, calm and stability, or by creating turbulence. Jessie Hock, *The Erotics of Materialism: Lucretius and Early Modern Poetics* (Philadelphia: University of Pennsylvania Press, 2021).

52. Hock evokes the last part of Book IV in *De rerum natura* and poet Lisa Robertson's phrase "supple snare" to describe the poetic power of seduction. Hock, *Erotics of Materialism*, 178.

53. Hock emphasizes that, while Belleau's poems on Prometheus "tend toward social stability," his poem "L'amour ambitieux d'Ixion" describes love disrupting social and religious hierarchies. Hock, *Erotics of Materialism*, 65. This chapter was previously published under the title "Waging Loving War: Lucretius and the Poetry of Remy Belleau," *The Romantic Review* 104, no. 3–4 (May 2013): 275–291, esp. 284.

54. A very unique crown was made by Venetian goldsmiths for Suleiman I in 1532, which became legendary as reports and images of the crown traveled in Europe. This crown combined elements of Eastern and Western iconographies of power and was an elaborately decorated four-tier gold tiara combined with a plumed aigrette. Its function was to incorporate elements of the papal tiara and the imperial crown to challenge Charles V's and Clement VII's claims to universal rule. See Gülru Necipoğlu, "Süleyman the Magnificent and the Representation of Power in the Context of Ottoman-Hapsburg-Papal Rivalry," *The Art Bulletin* 71, no. 3 (September 1989): 401–427.

55. Dassonville, *La tragédie à l'époque d'Henri II et de Charles IX*, 168–169.

56. Dassonville, 224v.

57. Dassonville, 245b.

58. Pierre de Ronsard, *Oeuvres complètes*, ed. Jean Céard, Daniel Ménager, and Michel Simonin, 2 vols. (Paris: Gallimard, 1993), 1:568.

59. Jodelle, *Les Oeuvres & meslanges poetiques d'Estienne Jodelle*, 228a.

60. Jodelle, 228a.

61. Jodelle, 230b.

62. In André Thevet's 1558 *Les singularitez de la France antarctique*, the dark skin of many people in Africa is described as an effect of heat. Thevet, *Les singularitez de la France antarctique, autrement nommée Amérique, & de plusieurs terres & isles découvertes de nostre temps: par F. André Thevet, natif d'Angoulesme* (Anvers, Christophle Palantin, 1558), 16vo. By contrast, Guillaume Postel, who adopted the

view of the late-fifteenth- and early-sixteenth-century forger and commentator of allegedly ancient documents, Ioannes Annius of Viterbo, directly attributed the dark skin color of Africans to the curse of Ham, as punishment for unspecified sexual crimes. See David Mark Whitford, *The Curse of Ham in the Early Modern Era: The Bible and the Justifications of Slavery*, St. Andrews Studies in Reformation History (Farnham: Ashgate, 2009), 101–102.

63. Thevet, moreover, also attributes temperamental qualities to dark-skinned Africans, which provides an example for Sara Miglietti's argument that "[b]y the end of the sixteenth century, the geographical model of *klimata* and the meteorological model of five zones were so closely intertwined that one was rarely discussed in isolation of the other, and the two were sometimes used interchangeably." Miglietti references the sixteenth-century Italian medical doctor Federico Bonaventura (1555–1602) but notes that the use of climate to refer to both meteorological and temperamental qualities was made widespread by travel writings. Thevet, *Les singularitez de la France antarctique*, 29^{ro-vo}; Sara Miglietti, "Climate Theory: An Invented Tradition?," in *Spreading Knowledge in a Changing World*, ed. Charles Burnett and Pedro Mantas-España (Córdoba and London: UCO Press and The Warburg Institute, 2019), 205–224, 211–212.

64. Peter Biller, "Black Women in Medieval Scientific Thought," *Micrologus* 13 (2005): 486; cited by Geraldine Heng, *The Invention of Race in the European Middle Ages* (Cambridge: Cambridge University Press, 2018), 181.

65. Madeline Caviness locates the turning point in the second half of the thirteenth century, when Europeans became conscious of their skin tone as "white" using representations made for the court of the French crusader king Louis XI. Heng, *Invention of Race*, 182–183.

66. See royal order of May 12, 1519, Bibliothèque nationale de France, manuscript fr. 5756.

67. "Until it embraces the whole world" ("Donec totum impleat orbem") was the inscription on Henri's impresa. It was interpreted in different ways in emblem books. Paoblo Giovio depicts a single crescent moon and explains that Henri adopted the impresa before his coronation in anticipation of his future royal power. Claude Paradin depicts three intertwined crescent moons and interprets them to represent the "militant Church," its "vicissitudes," and Henri as the protector of the Church. See Paolo Giovio, *Dialogo dell' Imprese militari et amorose* (Lyon: Guillaume Rouillé, 1559), 24; Claude Paradin, *Les Devises héroiques* (Lyon: Jean de Tournes and Guil Gazeau, 1557), 20.

68. Étienne Jodelle, *Le recueil des inscriptions, 1558: A Literary and Iconographical Exegesis*, ed. Victor E. Graham and W. McAllister Johnson (Toronto: University of Toronto Press, 1972), 86.

69. The iconography of the Argonauts (together with Hercules and Ulysses) was used in ducal entries in the fifteenth century in Bourgogne and, subsequently, in Francis I's entry into Paris in 1536. The vessel of the Argonauts, the Argo, was the symbol of both the state and the city of Paris. Antoinette Huon, "Le thème du

Prince dans les entrées parisiennes au XVIᵉ siècle," Les fêtes de la Renaissance I (Paris: CNRS, 1956), 26.

70. Jodelle, *Le recueil des inscriptions*, 97.

71. Jodelle, 108.

72. Jodelle, 110.

73. We know about the debacle because Jodelle felt compelled to write a defense in the form of a short book. Jodelle, 86, 97, 108.

74. The French version ("on m'avoit fait au lieu de rochers des clochers") suggests that Jodelle was playing with rhyming words here.

75. Jodelle, *Le recueil des inscriptions*, 118.

76. Zorach, *Blood, Milk, Ink, Gold*, 48.

77. Jodelle defends himself by blaming the shortness of time (three days) he had to compose and stage the festivities and the fact that he had to employ his friends as "mute actors" and clothe them. Jodelle, *Le recueil des inscriptions*, 118.

78. A record of Jodelle's debt to the bureau de la Ville de Paris shows that he borrowed "great quantities of silk cloth and gold canetille." See Ph. Renouard, "Notes sur le Lymodin et les créanciers d'Étienne Jodelle," *Revue de l'histoire littéraire de la France* (November–December 1922), 484–488.

79. Jodelle, *Le recueil des inscriptions*, 96–97.

80. On "semiophores," see Krzysztof Pomian, Collections and Curiosities: Paris and Venice, 1500–1800, trans. Elizabeth Wiles-Portier (Cambridge, Mass.: Polity Press, 1990), 34.

81. On the *Promptuaire*, see John Cunnally, *Images of the Illustrious: The Numismatic Presence in the Renaissance* (Princeton, N.J.: Princeton University Press, 1999), 99–102.

82. Belon, *Voyage au Levant*, 277, 292.

83. Guillaume Postel, *Linguarum duodecim characteribus introductio* (Paris: Pierre Vidoue, 1538), f. C 3ᵛᵒ.

84. Paré, *Discours . . . de la mummie . . .* , 4ʳᵒ.

85. Seigneur de Brantôme, *Oeuvres complètes de Pierre de Bourdeille, seigneur de Brantôme*, 11 vols., ed. Ludovic Lalanne (Paris: Jules Renouard, 1864–1882), 4:193.

86. See also Sue Peabody, *"There Are No Slaves in France": The Political Culture of Race and Slavery in the Ancien Régime* (New York: Oxford University Press, 1997).

87. Gillian Weiss, *Captives and Corsairs: France and Slavery in the Early Modern Mediterranean* (Stanford, Calif.: Stanford University Press, 2011), 2.

88. Pasquier, *Les Oeuvres d'Étienne Pasquier*, 373.

89. Peabody shows that the original ordonnance by King Louis X applied only to serfs on royal territory, and they, too, had to purchase their freedom. The practice was extended in the next century to other territories. Peabody, *Political Culture*, 28.

90. Jean Michel Massing, "Black African Slaves in Renaissance Spanish Literature," in *Black Africans in Renaissance Europe*, ed. T. F. Earle and K. J. P. Lowe (Cambridge: Cambridge University Press, 2005), 48–69, 48–59.

91. Peabody, *Political Culture*, 12.

92. In 1551, d'Aramon informed Henri II that North African corsairs had captured about two hundred Frenchmen on the coast of Southern France in another violation of the agreement according to which the French king and the Ottoman sultan do not hold each other's subjects captive. *Pièces fugitives pour servir à l'histoire de France*, ed. M. Ménard (Paris: Chaubert, 1749), 1.1: 116.

93. Weiss, *Captives and Corsairs*, 5.

94. The French court was fond of using exotic costumes for its spectacles. From the journal of the diplomat Jean d'Yversen, dated only three years after the performance, we learn that one of his duties was to dispatch from Istanbul to Venice a packet with 84 "Turkish hats" eventually destined for Henri II. Marie-Thérèse de Martel, "La Mission de Jean Yversen à la Porte du Grand Seigneur (mai-juin 1559)," *Revue d'histoire diplomatique* 93 (1983): 5–53, 20.

95. Scévole de Saint-Marthe, *Eloges des hommes illustres. Qui depuis un siècle ont fleury en France dans la profession des lettres.*, trans. G. Colletet (Paris: Sommaville et Courbé, 1644); cited in E. H. Balmas, *Un Poeta des Rinascimento Francese, Étienne Jodelle* (Florence: Olchiski, 1962), 273.

96. Raymond Lebègue found the records of Catherine de Médicis's expenses in the French National Archives. These records provide us with intriguing details about the staging of this play at Blois at her expense. See Lebègue, *Études sur le théâtre François 1. Moyen Âge, Renaissance, Baroque* (Paris: Editions A.-G. Nizet, 1977), 160–165. Mellain de Saint-Gelais remarks that he had to simplify some of the original Italian text, for "it contained many lengthy passages that would have taxed the princesses' memories." P. Leblanc, *Les écrits théoriqes et critiques français des années 1540–1561 sur la tragédie* (Paris: Seuil, 1972), 107.

97. Michèle Longino reads Pierre Corneille's seventeenth-century play *Médée* as a reflection on debates around topics including Turks, "barbarians," and travel to the Ottoman Empire in France in the 1630s. On Corneille's *Médée* and on readings by Constance Caroll, Christa World, and Marie Cardinal of Medea as the outsider, minority woman, or woman of color, see Michèle Longino, *Orientalism and French Classical Drama* (Cambridge: Cambridge University Press, 2002), 29–76, 30–31.

98. Weiss, *Captives and Corsairs*, 10.

99. Zorach reflects on aesthetic means of capturing in the arts. "The femininity, foreignness, animality, monstrosity of architectural ornaments—in short their strangeness—is then on some level intended to represent the conquest of these peoples and principles." Zorach, *Blood, Milk, Ink, Gold*, 155–156.

100. Honorat de Valbelle, *Histoire journalière d'Honorat de Valbelle (1498–1539). Journal d'un bourgeois de Marseille au temps de Louis XII et François Ier*, ed. V. L. Bourilly, Lucien Gaillard, and Charles Rostaing (Aix-en-Provence, Marseille: J. Laffitte, 1985), 177, 522.

101. Valbelle, *Histoire journalière*, 240.

102. Ernest Charrière, ed., *Négotiations de la France dans le Levant*, 4 vols. (Paris: Imprimerie nationale, 1848), 1:341.

103. The original manuscript is held at Montpelier, Bibliothèque de la faculté de Médicine. H. 385. fol. 40–41v, 48v–64. A xerox copy was provided by Ráday Könyvtár, Kézirattár o. 617. Lescalopier's travelogue has been published in Hungarian (only) under the title *Pierre Lescalopier utzása Erdélybe (1574)*, trans. and notes Lajos Tardy and Kálmán Benda, Bibliotheca Historica (Budapest, 1982), 51–2.

104. Imtiaz Habib, *Black Lives in the English Archives, 1500–1677: Imprints of the Invisible* (London: Routledge, 2008), 20, 26.

105. Indeed, the recent *Dictionnaire de gens de couleur dans la France moderne*, in three volumes divided by geographic regions, contains a mere ten entries for the sixteenth century. Érick Noël, ed., *Dictionnaire des gens de couleur dans la France moderne. Paris et son basin* (Geneva: Droz, 2011), 1–2; *Dictionnaire des gens de couleur dans la France moderne. La Bretagne* (Geneva: Droz, 2013), 1–2; *Dictionnaire des gens de couleur dans la France moderne. Le midi* (Geneva: Droz, 2017), 1.

106. Weiss, *Captives and Corsaires*, 10.

107. Ronsard corrected "esclaver" to "maistriser" [sic] in later editions. Ronsard, *Oeuvres complètes*, 1:825.

108. René Boyvin, *Histoire de Jason et de la conquête de la toison d'or* (Paris: Jean de Mauregard, ca. 1563). Boyvin's twenty-six plates were engraved after the originals by the Belgian painter Léonard Thiery. See also Willis Bowen, *Jacques Gohory* (PhD dissertation, Harvard, 1935).

109. Francis Yates identifies Jacques Gohory, who provided the Introduction and commentary, as a Parisian apothecary, alchemist, a friend of Pléiade poets, and an adherent of the spiritual sect the "Family of Love" that taught the separation of god from the physical world, and practiced a sensual and sexual form of libertinism; cited in Zorach, *Blood, Milk, Ink, Gold*, 167–168.

4. Nicolas de Nicolay's Empire of Ink

1. See also *Gifts of the Sultan: The Arts of Giving at the Islamic Courts*, ed. Linda Komaroff, Los Angeles County Museum of Art (New Haven, Conn.: Yale University Press, 2011), 290–291.

2. The tapestry is preserved in the Vatican Pinacoteca. Leonardo da Vinci worked at the French court from 1517 to his death in 1519.

3. Caron's long career is remarkable for the fact that he became successful at a time, after 1559, when patronage for the arts was in crisis. He started out as painter for Francesco Primaticcio (1504–1570) and found the patronage of the Duchesse de Valentinois (better known as Diane de Poitiers) just three weeks before Henri II's death. In 1560, he gained the support of Hicolas Houël, the apothecary who commissioned art for Catherine de Médicis, and started painting the Artemisia cycle on his order to celebrate Catherine de Médicis. It was in this period that he made the drawing, probably as another work depicting Catherine and her family. Caron became famous for organizing court festivities from 1573 onward, including

the reception of the Polish ambassadors at the Valois court in the same year. He was close to the *politiques*, the royalist party composed of moderate Catholics and Protestants. See Jean Ehrman, *Antoine Caron, peintre des fêtes et des massacres* (Paris: Flammarion, 1986), 91–93, fig. 80.

4. The bodies of both the lion and the handler have been elongated by Caron and they are oversize compared to their small heads, which, as Ehrman underscores, leads to the "exaggeration of gestures." Ehrman, *Antoine Caron*, 12.

5. The authors explain that, while originally "livery meant 'all sorts of non-monetary payment'" to servants including food and hay for horses, it came to mean marked clothing in a narrower sense. "On the one hand, such marking could be seen as a privilege, giving protection and security, but from the late fifteenth century marked livery came to be seen by many as an unacceptable form of subordination." Ann Rosalind Jones and Peter Stallybrass, *Renaissance Clothing and the Materials of Memory* (Cambridge: Cambridge University Press, 2000), 17.

6. Chandra Mukerji, "Costume and Character in the Ottoman Empire: Dress as Social Agent in Nicolay's *Navigations*," in *Early Modern Things: Objects and Their Histories, 1500–1800*, ed. Paula Findlen (London: Routledge, 2013), 151–169.

7. Nicolas de Nicolay, *Dans l'Empire de Soliman le Magnifique*, ed. and intr. M.-C. Gomez-Géraud and S. Yérasimos (Paris: Presses du CNRS, 1989), 108. The book was first printed under the title *Les quatre premiers livres des navigations et pérégrinations orientales de N. de Nicolay, . . . Avec les figures au naturel tant d'hommes que de femmes selon la diversité des nations, & de leur port, maintien & habitz* (Lyon: Guillaume Rouillé, 1567). Gomez-Géraud and Yérasimos's edition is based on the (second) 1576 edition by Silvius, printed in French in Antwerp.

8. On the circumstances of the decree, brought about by the urging of the French delegation dispatched by Catherine de Médicis in 1562, see John W. O'Malley, "The Council of Trent (1545–63) and Michelangelo's 'Last Judgment' (1541)," *American Philosophical Society* 156, no. 4 (December 2012): 388–397, 394–395.

9. See Natalie Zemon Davis, "Publisher Guillaume Rouillé: Businessman and Humanist," in *Editing Sixteenth-Century Texts*, ed. Richard J. Schoeck (Toronto: University of Toronto Press, 1966), 72–112.

10. Catherine Grodecki has identified the illustrator of the book with the engraver and etcher best known by his sign "Maître L.D." Grodecki, "Le graveur Lyon Davent, illustrateur de Nicolas de Nicolay," *Bibliothèque d'Humanisme et Renaissance* 36, no. 2 (1974): 347–351. For discussion of Léon [Lyon] Davent's etchings, see Henri Zerner, *The School of Fontainebleau: Etchings and Engravings* (New York: Harry N. Abrams, 1969).

11. The contract between Nicolas de Nicolay and "Lyon Davent" for eighty "Oriental costumes," signed in 1555 and preserved at the Archives nationales in Paris, is reproduced in Catherine Grodecki, "Le graveur Lyon Davent," 351.

12. There is evidence that the sixty-one drawings by Davent published in *Les quatre premiers livres* in 1567 (instead of the original eighty in the contract) were produced in the year after the signing of the contract (one of the plates dates 1556).

Davent's images were intended to illustrate only one of the four books by Nicolay, who, according to the original privilege issued by King Henri II in 1556, planned to write three other books on ceremonies, the origin of the Ottomans, and the government of the "Great Turk."

13. These consular outposts were stuffed with people from Marseille, for Marseille and other port cities had been sending consuls to the Mediterranean since the Middle Ages. Gillian Lee Weiss, *Captives and Corsairs: France and Slavery in the Early Modern Mediterranean* (Stanford, Calif.: Stanford University Press, 2011), 229.

14. During the 1560s, the French ambassador François Petremol was working on the release of over a hundred "French slaves" in Constantinople. See the letter of Petremol to Jean Hurault de Boistaillé, 1562, June 8 and 16 in Ernest Charrière, *Négotiations de la France dans le Levant*, 4 vols. (Paris: Imprimerie nationale, 1848–1860), 2:696. Petremol, Constantinople, July 15 and September 27, 1565; cited in Ernest Watbled, "Aperçu sur les premiers consulats dans le Levant et les états barbaresques," *Revue africaine* 16 (1872): 20–25, 30–31.

15. Denis Crouzet dates the radicalization of Catholic anti-Protestant arguments, presented as accusation of treason, around 1568–1569 and the parallel radicalization of Protestant justifications of resistance around 1567–1570. A third war between the two fractions broke out in 1568. Crouzet, *Les Guerriers de Dieu. La violence au temps des troubles de religion vers 1525–vers 1610*, 2 vols. (Paris: Champ Vallon, 1990), 2:22, 30.

16. Nicolay, *Dans l'Empire de Soliman le Magnifique*, 91.

17. Marcus Keller, "Nicolas de Nicolay's *Navigations et peregrinations* and the Domestic Politics of Travel Writing," *L'Esprit créateur* 48, no. 1 (2008): 18–31.

18. Nicolay, *Dans l'Empire de Soliman le Magnifique*, 46; translation mine here and elsewhere in the book unless otherwise noted.

19. Der Derian's diplomatic theory relies on a particular reading of both Hegelian dialectics and estrangement as the basis of a diplomatic situation in which everyone is presumed to be estranged from the universal and must share it. Diplomacy mediates between estranged parties, while utopian visions of the world that project a universal principle beyond estrangement are "anti-diplomatic." James der Derian, *On Diplomacy: Genealogy of Western Estrangement* (Oxford: Blackwell, 1987), 141–152.

20. Printed in London in 1611, Randle Cotgrave's *Dictionarie of the French and English Tongues* defines "commerce" in such broad terms as "intercourse of traffick, familiaritie, or acquaintance gotten; correspondancie, or intelligence continued, between people, in dealing or trading, together."

21. This rhetoric of French cultural superiority and its pressures on some of the French merchants and mediators in the Ottoman Empire are presented by Michèle Longino in *Orientalism and French Classical Drama* (Cambridge: Cambridge University Press, 2002).

22. Nicolay, *Dans l'Empire de Soliman le Magnifique*, 43.

23. Nicolay, 44.

24. Nicolay, 46.
25. Nicolay, 46.
26. Jean-Pierre Grélois, Introduction to *Itinéraires byzantins*, by Pierre Gilles, ed. and trans. Jean-Pierre Grélois (Paris: Association des amis du Centre d'histoire et civilization de Byzance, 2007), 29–30.
27. On Postel's debate with Gilles during the second trip, see Jean Chesneau, *Le Voyage de Monsieur d'Aramon*, ed. Charles Schefer (Paris: E. Leroux, 1897), 138–139.
28. Pierre Gilles, *The Four Books of the Antiquities of Constantinople*, trans. John Ball (New York: Italica, 1986), xxxviii.
29. Christine Gomez-Géraud and Stéphane Yérosimos detail his untiring efforts to promote the alliance and military cooperation between the Valois court and the Sublime Porte. Nicolay, *Dans l'Empire de Soliman le Magnifique*, 13.
30. Jean de Monluc, *Commentaires, 1521–1576*, ed. Paul Corteault (Paris: Gallimard, 1964), 81–82.
31. Chesneau, *Le Voyage de Monsieur d'Aramon*, 13.
32. Natalie Zemon Davis observes that the French had an understanding that the Ottomans valued gifts and, moreover, saw them as civilized. Davis contrasts these gifts given to the Ottomans with the small trinkets given to the Indigenous peoples of the Americas. Davis, *The Gift in Sixteenth-Century France* (Madison: University of Wisconsin Press, 2000), 138.
33. Charrière, *Négotiations de la France dans le Levant*, 2:16.
34. For example, in September of 1550, d'Aramon tried to compel the Ottomans to act by suggesting that the Spanish were spreading rumors that the Ottoman empire had been weakened after the Spanish capture of Mahdia. Nicolay, *Dans l'Empire de Soliman le Magnifique*, 14; Letter from April 7, 1551, in *Lettres et mémoires d'état*, ed. Guillaume Ribier, 2 vols. (Blois: J. Hotot, 1666), 2:294–295.
35. Gomez-Géraud and Yérosimos note that there is no evidence that Suleiman I sent him back. Nicolay, *Dans l'Empire de Soliman le Magnifique*, 15.
36. Ribier, *Lettres et mémoires d'état*, 2:297.
37. Nicolay, *Dans l'Empire de Soliman le Magnifique*, 17.
38. Ribier, *Lettres et mémoires d'état*, 2:307–308.
39. Braudel says that the Ottomans were more interested in plundering in the 1550s. Fernand Braudel, *La Méditerranée et le monde méditerranéen à l'époque de Philippe II*, 3 vols. (Paris: Armand Colin, 1949), 1:14.
40. Charrièrre, *Négotiations de la France dans le Levant*, 2:213.
41. Charrièrre, 2:262.
42. Chesneau describes bringing d'Aramon's pension for one year to Constantinople and that the ambassador was glad to see him because he had not heard from the court for a long time. As soon as he received the money, he packed up, presented Chesneau to Rustem and left. Charrière, *Négotiations de la France dans le Levant*, 2:280n, 262.
43. Charrière, 2:265fn.
44. Charrière, 2:263fn.

45. On the details of his life, see Robert Barroux, "Nicolaï d'Arfeuille, agent secret, géographe et dessinateur (1517–83)," *Reveue d'histoire diplomatique* 51 (1937): 81–109.

46. Davis, *The Gift in Sixteenth-Century France*, 9.

47. Nicolay lists this accomplishment in his preface to Anne de Joyeuse in Nicolas de Nicolay, *La Navigation du roi d'Écosse Jacques cinquième du nom autour de son royaume et îles Hébrides et Orchades* (Paris: Gilles Beys, 1583).

48. Nicolay, *Dans l'Empire de Soliman le Magnifique*, 51.

49. Giancarlo Fiorenza, "Penelope's Web: Francesco Primaticcio's Epic Revision at Fontainebleau," *Renaissance Quarterly* 59 (2006): 795–827, 804.

50. Naked bodies in Fontainebleau art and in private collections served the function of signaling a sense of belonging to the elite thanks to the shared privilege of looking. Many contemporaries and visitors to Fontainebleau confirm that Francis I enjoyed sharing the sight of the nude statues that he collected in Fontainebleau with foreign guests, ambassadors, and dignitaries. In an anecdote, the ambassador of the Duke of Este reports that Francis viewed a statue of nude Venus with the Duchesse of Estampes in the presence of the ambassador, see Nicole Bensoussan, *Casting a Second Rome: Primaticcio's Bronze Copies and the Fontainebleau Project* (Dissertation, Yale University, 2009), *ProQuest Dissertations and Theses*, 231–232.

51. Nicolay, *Dans l'Empire de Soliman le Magnifique*, 50–51.

52. Timothy Hampton, *Fictions of Embassy: Literature and Diplomacy in Early Modern Europe* (Ithaca, N.Y.: Cornell University Press, 2012), 89.

53. Nicolay, *Dans l'Empire de Soliman le Magnifique*, 47.

54. In the seventeenth century, Gabriel Naudé argued that books, too, if collected and used in the right way—that is, in a new way that is different from the humanist search for wisdom—contributed to the "ruse and stratagem" of the state. The systematic collection of the correspondence of French diplomats (including extant copies from the sixteenth century) begins in the seventeenth century when these documents will become part of the library of the Minister of State Jean-Baptiste Colbert. Gabriel Naudé, *Advis pour dresser une bibliothèque* (Paris: M. Targa, 1627), 10.

55. Nicolay, *Dans l'Empire de Soliman le Magnifique*, 91.

56. Smith traces this Greek political distinction through its early modern revival in the sixteenth and seventeenth centuries in the Americas, where Europeans transported it to classify non-Christians. Justin E. H. Smith, *Nature, Human Nature, and Human Difference: Race in Early Modern Philosophy* (Princeton, N.J.: Princeton University Press, 2015), 74–76.

57. Nicolay, *Dans l'Empire de Soliman le Magnifique*, 60.

58. Nicolay therefore does not simply return to a description of the Turks as enemies of the Christians provided in the popular book by Bartolomej Georgijević, a Croatian who fell into Turkish captivity, a rhetoric that was reversed in travel accounts by Postel and Belon. On this reversal, see Frédéric Tinguely, *L'écriture du Levant à la Renaissance. enquête sur les voyageurs français dans l'empire de Soliman le Magnifique* (Geneva: Droz, 2000), 252.

59. Nicolay, *Dans l'Empire de Soliman le Magnifique*, 61.

60. Nicolay, 61.

61. D'Aramon reports that Hasan Pasha was plagued by financial troubles and rebellious subjects. M. Ménard, ed., *Pièces fugitives pour servir à l'histoire de France* (Paris: Chaubert, 1749), 1.1: 116.

62. Nicolay, *Dans l'Empire de Soliman le Magnifique*, 62.

63. Ribier, *Lettres et mémoires d'état*, 2:304.

64. Robert Bartlett, *The Making of Europe: Conquest, Colonization, and Cultural Change, 950–1350* (Princeton, N.J.: Princeton University Press, 1993), 252; cited in Geraldine Heng, *The Invention of Race in the European Middle Ages* (Cambridge: Cambridge University Press, 2018), 124.

65. Tomaz Mastnak argues that the First Crusade, notorious for the atrocities committed by Christian soldiers in Jerusalem, including mass killings and cannibalism according to eyewitness accounts, sealed the consciousness that Christians are blood brothers under Christ; cited by Heng, *Invention of Race*, 123.

66. Costas M. Constantinou argues that the privateering activities of the knights were made possible by legal justifications provided by European powers, which competed for their services. Constantinou, *States of Political Discourse: Words, Regimes, Seditions* (London: Routledge, 2004), 57–58.

67. Nicolay, *Dans l'Empire de Soliman le Magnifique*, 74.

68. The Pasha claims to have received no orders and explains that the Spanish have promised to surrender Mahdia. The Ottoman-Spanish peace treaty is still intact at this point. He moreover justifies the Ottoman siege of Tripoli arguing that the city was Muslim territory in the past. D'Aramon to Henri II, Charrière, *Négotiations de la France dans le Levant*, 2:158–159.

69. For the French version, see Nicolas Durand de Villegagnon, *Le discours de la guerre de Malte, contenant la perte de Tripolis & d'autres fortresses faulsement imposée aux Français* (Lyon: Jean Temporal, 1553).

70. Nicolay, *Dans l'Empire de Soliman le Magnifique*, 79.

71. Charrière, *Négotiations de la France dans le Levant*, 2:161.

72. Nicolay, *Dans l'Empire de Soliman le Magnifique*, 86.

73. Nicolay, 86.

74. For d'Aramon's report of the accusations to Henri II, see Ribier, *Lettres et mémoires d'état*, 2:161.

75. Nicolay, *Dans l'Empire de Soliman le Magnifique*, 85.

76. Charrière, *Négotiations de la France dans le Levant*, 2:162.

77. Nicolay, *Dans l'Empire de Soliman le Magnifique*, 92.

78. The fallacy of trusting—and not just the Ottomans—is also revealed by Nicolay's story about a Provençal soldier-turned-spy who informed the Ottoman camp about the weak places in the fortification. Nicolay, 84. On the trope of betrayal in an earlier French account of Ottoman-Christian warfare, see Pascale Barthes, "Du Turc au traître: Les chevaliers de Saint-Jean-de-Jérusalem, les

Ottomans et la France de François I dans *L'oppugnation* de Jacques de Bourbon," *French Historical Studies* 30, no. 3 (2007): 427–449.

79. Bartolomé Bennassar and Lucile Bennassar have found archival traces of 172 French converts, about half of them from Province, the other half from Brittany and other parts of the western coast of France. They argue that these converts had flexible and multiple identities and were able to think of themselves as both Muslims and Christians. Ninety-eight of those found in the archives had participated in raids against Christian populations. See *Les chrétens d'Allah. L'histoire extraordinaire des renégats* (Paris: Perrin, 2001), 260, 429, 165–167.

80. Nicolay, *Dans l'Empire de Soliman le Magnifique*, 45.

81. For a more in-depth analysis of the paradoxes in this statement, see Keller, "Politics of Travel Writing," 20.

82. Nicolay, *Dans l'Empire de Soliman le Magnifique*, 84.

83. Michel de Certeau, *La Fable mystique XVIIe siècle* (Paris: Gallimard, 1982), 133, translated into English under the title *The Mystic Fable*, ed. Luce Giard, trans. Michael B. Smith (Chicago: University of Chicago Press, 2015) 2: 97. The integration of the spy into the modern state was seen as a necessary evil that was fundamental to its functioning but external to it. This integration (that was never meant to be seamless) was already on its way in the Renaissance, when European monarchs employed spies disguised as travelers, envoys, and negotiators. See Alain Dewerpe, *Espion, une anthropologie historique du secret d'État contemporain* (Paris: Gallimard, 1994).

84. Nicolay, *Dans l'Empire de Soliman le Magnifique*, 66–67.

85. Nicolay, 81.

86. Nicolay, 83.

87. Nicolay, 89.

88. Barroux makes a relevant but unverified suggestion that Nicolay's many mentions of "public women" indicate that he treated them, too, as sources of information. See Barroux, "Nicolaï d'Arfeuille, agent secret, géographe et dessinateur," 98.

89. Keller, "Politics of Travel Writing," 21–22.

90. Nicolay, *Dans l'Empire de Soliman le Magnifique*, 227.

91. Nicolay, 227.

92. Nicolay, 229.

93. In analyzing Agrippa d'Aubigné's epic poem *Les tragiques*, Hampton notes that the sixteenth-century bourgeoisie was prone to appropriating tropes of heroism. Timothy Hampton, *Writing from History: The Rhetoric of Exemplarity in Renaissance Literature* (Ithaca: Cornell University Press, 2012), 137 and n5.

94. Rebecca Zorach, *Blood, Milk, Ink, Gold: Abundance and Excess in the French Renaissance* (Chicago: University of Chicago Press, 2005), 193.

95. Within this dichotomous world of early modern materiality, "abundance" referred to a fertile, maternal earth. Zorach, *Blood, Milk, Ink, Gold*, 30.

96. The author expresses a preference for pleasure over intellectual insight but qualifies this pleasure as "spiritual." Nicolay, *Dans l'Empire de Soliman le Magnifique*, 52.

97. In Renaissance France, the demand for luxurious clothing exceeded the capacity of the French textile industry, which produced mostly plain cloth for everyday wear. In the second half of the sixteenth century, an industry making luxury textiles and tapestry (for example, the factory of Gobelins in Paris) was established, and Olivier Serres introduced silkworms during the reign of Henri IV (1589–1610).

98. Rebecca Zorach, "Desiring Things," in *Other Objects of Desire: Collectors and Collecting Queerly*, ed. Michael Camille and Adrian Rifkin (Oxford: Blackwell, 2001), 205.

99. Nicolay's source for the four "types of religion" is Giovanni Antonio Menavino, *Trattato de' costumi et vita de' Turchi* (Florence: Lorenzo Torrentino, 1548). Only two of these groups are identifiable confraternities: the camiler (a sect founded by Ahmad Namikiyy-i Djami in the twelfth century whose followers drank wine and played music) and the Kalandriyya (calandar, a spiritual movement of Hindu and Buddhist origins, whose followers shaved their face and head, practiced chastity, and rejected private property). We may also note that Nicolay adds many details that transform Menavino's sympathetic description into a condemning portrait of Islam. For a historical study, see Ahmet T. Karamustafa, *God's Unruly Friends: Dervish Groups in the Islamic Later Middle Period 1200–1550* (Salt Lake City: University of Utah Press, 1994).

100. Nicolay, *Dans l'Empire de Soliman le Magnifique*, 187–197.

101. Postel translates "dervish" as "saint" or "fool" ("sont appellés *Deauff*, ou saints: & des autres, fols"), both of which had religious and mystical meanings, and describes their clothing and ornaments as "of an indescribable variety." He calls those that walk around naked "most foolish" and admits that there are many kinds, surpassing his understanding. Postel, *De la Republique des Turcs*, 108.

102. Pierre Belon, *Voyage au Levant* (1553), ed. and intr. by Alexandra Merle (Paris: Chadeigne, 2001), 482.

103. Nicolay, *Dans l'Empire de Soliman le Magnifique*, 192.

104. Crouzet shows that in the late 1560's French Catholics describe Protestants as bad blood corrupted by the abundance of bad humors in the body politic of the kingdom. Crouzet, *Les Guerriers de Dieu*, 2:24.

105. Nicolay, *Dans l'Empire de Soliman le Magnifique*, 83.

106. Nicolay, 143.

107. Nell Irvin Painter, *The History of White People* (New York: Norton, 2011), 43.

108. Belon, *Voyage au Levant*, 293. Similarly, Jean Palerne, a French traveler to the Levant, whose journal I discuss in the coda, claims that some Moorish women are quite beautiful "in spite of being black" ("encores qu'elles soyent noires, si est ce qu'il y en a de fort belles"). Jean Palerne, *D'Alexandrie à Istanbul. pérégrinations dans l'Empire Ottoman, 1581–1583*, ed. Yvelise Bernard (Paris: L'Harmattan, 1991), 75.

109. By the seventeenth century, some groups of non-Europeans were sometimes promoted to the allegedly higher status of having white skin. Pierre Boulle shows that, in a 1684 article attributed to the traveler and medical doctor François Bernier, Egyptians (along with Indians) are described as essentially White and their skin is seen as darker only because it has been burned by the sun. Pierre H. Boulle, *Race et esclavage dans la France de l'Ancien Régime* (Paris: Perrin, 2007), 68.

110. Larry Wolff, *Inventing Eastern Europe: The Map of Civilization on the Mind of the Enlightenment* (Stanford, Calif.: Stanford University Press, 1994).

111. Nicolay, *Dans l'Empire de Soliman le Magnifique*, 213.

112. Nicolay, 273.

113. Belon, *Voyage au Levant*, 310.

114. Belon, 310.

115. The Roma and the Sinti came into the Balkans and, later, into other parts of Europe with the conquering Ottoman armies, either by participating as auxiliary soldiers and craftsmen or accompanying them. Elena Marushiakova and Vesselin Popov describe the spotty records in Ottoman archives of the Roma and the Sinti, where they are often referred to as "Kibts" (i.e., Copts) or "Chingene" (i.e., "Turkish from China"). Moreover, Ottoman authorities often made both Christian and Muslim Roma and Sinti pay taxes, unlike other Muslim groups. Elena Marushiakova and Vesselin Popov, *Gypsies in the Ottoman Empire* (Hatfield: University of Hertfordshire Press/Centre de recherches tsiganes, 2001), 26, 29, 32–34.

116. Belon admires the cosmopolitan culture of Jews in the Ottoman Empire, noting their occupations as merchants, doctors, and pharmacists, as well as their ability to speak many languages and operating printing presses that print in Spanish, Latin, Italian, Greek, and German. He credits Jews with educating Turks. Yet he also interprets them as menacing, noting that they appropriate the revenues of the Ottoman Empire, and paints their resourcefulness as malevolent (noting, for example, that they are prone to disguising themselves as Turks, by wearing white turbans, instead of yellow ones prescribed by Ottoman authorities, when they travel to Italy). Belon, *Voyage au Levant*, 466–467.

117. Belon considers Greeks ignorant, weak, and inclined to adopt the culture of the conqueror, Ottomans or Venetians. In his description of the Greek Orthodox monasteries on Mount Athos, he underscores that most monks are illiterate and that the reading of any books outside of theology is forbidden. André Thevet also labels Greeks as "hypocrites." Belon, *Voyage au Levant*, 66–67, 140. Thevet, *Cosmographie de Levant* (Lyon: Jean de Tournes: 1554), 37, 95–100.

118. Through an analysis of the charters of Haseki Hürrem's charitable foundations, Leslie Peirce shows that she engaged in conspicuous giving, endowing mosques, schools, soup kitchens, hostels, Sufi lodges and hospitals, and used this and other means to wield considerable influence on court decisions and policies. See Peirce, *Empress of the East: How a European Slave Girl Became Queen of the Empire* (New York: Basic Books, 2017). On the public persona that Haseki Hürrem Sultan was able to create for herself through the promotion and financing of

charitable foundations and architectural projects as well as for a reproduction of Matteo Pagano's portrait of her, see the first part of Chapter 7 ("Queens: Wives and Mothers of Sultans") in Gülru Necipoğlu, *The Age of Sinan: Architectural Culture in the Ottoman Empire* (London: Reaktion Books, 2005), 268–280.

119. Nicolay, *Dans l'Empire de Soliman le Magnifique*, 66.

120. Zorach cites Leo Steinberg on the "slung legs" and frontal portrayal that designate lesbians in Renaissance art. This woman, like Zorach's "artificial lesbian," serves as an object of desire for men, but here her function is not to kindle but to mediate that desire—to direct it straight into the scene, pointing to a place, elsewhere, from which to desire. In addition, in sixteenth-century France, lesbians were wielders of artifice and cunning, for example, through the use of dildos as described by the seigneur of Brantôme. Zorach, "Desiring Things," 206, 209.

121. Sara Ahmed, *Queer Phenomenology: Orientations, Objects, Others* (Durham, N.C.: Duke University Press, 2006), 105.

122. An archival note erroneously attributes the images to Titian: "Les quatre premiers livres des navigations et pérégrinations orientales de Nic. De Nicolay d'Arfeville Dauphinois. Lyon; Roville 1667, in-fol. fig. Première édition de cette ouvrage. Les estampes dont elle est ornée sont en bois, mais gravées sur un dessein du Titien, et coloriées, ce qui donne un très grand prix à ce volume." *Notice sur la bibliothèque publique de le ville de Moulins*, [R. A. K.] (Moulins: Place-Bujon, 1839), 39.

5. Distancology and Universalizing French Masculinity

1. Florimond de Raemond, *L'Anti-christ, L'anti-Papesse Édition seconde reveue, corrigée et de beaucoup augmentée par l'autheur* (Paris: L'Angelier, 1607 [first printed in 1599]), 638–639; translation mine here and elsewhere in the book unless otherwise noted

2. Raemond, *L'Anti-christ*, 634–637.

3. Noailles reported to Charles IX on April 27, 1572, that all five hundred French captives in Algiers had been freed. BN ms 16142, f. 138 r.; cited in Géraud Poumarède, "La France et les barberesques: police des mers et relations internationales en Méditerranée (XVIe-XVIIe siècles)," *Revue d'histoire maritime* 4 (2005): 117–146.

4. Ernest Charrière, ed., *Négotiations de la France dans le Levant*, 4 vols. (Paris: Imprimerie nationale, 1848–1860), 3:lx.

5. The *honnête homme* was defined as a well-read gentleman, a man of letters who was skilled in reading and writing in the seventeenth century. Warren Boutcher shows that this ideal was later rekindled by historical and philological traditions in the positivistic decades of the late nineteenth and the early twentieth centuries, at which point the image of Montaigne as an educated private person became a convenient tool for raising the status of studying history and literature within the positivist systems of university education in France. Warren Boutcher, "Villey and the Making of the Modern Critical Reader," in *The School of Montaigne in Early Modern Europe*, 2 vols. (Oxford: Oxford University Press, 2017).

6. The linear narrative of Montaigne's intellectual development from Stoicism to Skepticism and Lucretian thought has been questioned, especially by scholars who have shown the complications of the self-portrait metaphor for the *Essays* including, notably, Erich Auerbach, Michel Beaujour, and James Helgeson. See Erich Auerbach, *Mimesis: The Representation of Reality in Western Literature*, trans. Willard R. Trask, with Introduction by Edward Said, Fiftieth Anniversary edition (Princeton, N.J.: Princeton University Press, 2002), 285–311; Michel Beaujour, *Miroirs d'encre* (Paris: Seuil, 1980); James Helgeson, *The Lying Mirror: The First-Person Stance and Sixteenth-Century Writing* (Geneva: Droz, 2012).

7. Lescalopier intended to travel from Istanbul to the Holy Land, but after arriving in Constantinople, he was asked by the French ambassador to travel to Transylvania as an envoy with the task of negotiating on behalf of the French crown. Lescalopier, *Voyage fait par moy Pierre Lescalopier l'an 1574 de Venise à Constantinople par mer jusques à Raguse et le reste par terre et le retour par Thrace, Bulgarie, Walachie, Transilvanie ou Dace, Hongrie, Allemagne, Trieste, et Marche Trevisane jusques à Venise*, 35v–36r, 37v–38r. The manuscript is held at Bibliothèque de la faculté de Médicine, Montpelier, H. 385. fol. 40–41v, 48v–64.

8. Philippe Desan speaks here specifically about the last third of the sixteenth century, when ambassadors typically came from the ranks of middle-level nobility and legal professionals. Philippe Desan, *Montaigne: A Life*, trans. Steven Rendall and Lisa Neal (Princeton, N.J.: Princeton University Press, 2017), 319.

9. Ronsard's poem appears in a later edition, Nicolas de Nicolay, *Discours et Histoire Veritable des Navigations, peregrinations et voyages* (Antwerp: Arnould Conix, 1586), np.

10. The theories of resistance elaborated in the Middle Ages, taken up by the reformers at the end of the sixteenth century and during the French Revolution, are examples of elaborations of compelling reasons for collective political engagement. Alin Fumurescu, "The Dialectic of the Individual and the Paradox of French Absolutism," *European Legacy* 16, no. 6 (September 2011): 717–734.

11. Hampton discusses the assassination by the Duke of Sforza of the Milanese merchant Maraviglia, who was sent to Naples by Francis I on a secret mission; a case that shed light on the entangled public and private persons of the ambassador and was widely discussed in diplomatic literature, and upon which Montaigne, too, commented. Timothy Hampton, *Fictions of Embassy: Literature and Diplomacy in Early Modern* Europe (Ithaca, N.Y.: Cornell University Press, 2013), 41–42.

12. On Montaigne's remarkable loyalty to Catholicism and the monarch, which was only complicated by his loyalty to his patrons, see Alain Legros, "Montaigne on Faith and Religion," in *The Oxford Handbook of Montaigne*, ed. Philippe Desan (Oxford: Oxford University Press, 2016), 525–543.

13. On Montaigne's documented career as a diplomat, mediating between the court and the Protestant faction, see Daniel Ménager, *L'Ange et l'ambassadeur. Diplomatie et théologie à la Renaissance* (Paris: Garnier, 2013), 185–197.

14. Michel de Montaigne, *The Complete Essays*, trans. M. A. Screech (London: Penguin, 1987), 122; *Les Essais*, ed. Marcel Conche, Verdun-Louis Saulnier, and

Pierre Villey (Paris: Presses Universitaires de France 2004), 108–109. The story is discussed as a theme for a moral essay in Quintilian's *Institutio oratoria: Books 1–3*, trans. H. E. Butler, Loeb Classical Library 124 (Cambridge, Mass.: Harvard University Press, later printing edition, 1980), 158. It was cited by humanists, including Erasmus.

15. Dufourmantelle emphasizes the disturbing quality of gentleness, which comes both before and after violence, along with the closeness of gentleness and animality. Anne Dufourmantelle, *Power of Gentleness: Meditations on the Risk of Living*, trans. Katherine Payne and Vincent Sallé, with Foreword by Catherine Malabou (New York: Fordham University Press, 2018), 24.

16. Dufourmantelle, *Power of Gentleness*, 25.

17. Louisa Mackenzie, "La masculinité itinérante du *Journal de voyage* de Montaigne," in *Théories critiques et littérature française. Mélanges offerts à Laurence D. Kritzman*, ed. David LaGuardia and Todd Reeser (Paris: Garnier, 2020), 155–175.

18. Charrière, *Négotiations de la France dans le Levant*, 3:183n.

19. Matthieu Gellard, *Une reine épistolaire. Lettres et pouvoirs au temps de Catherine de Médicis*. Bibliothèque histoire de la Renaissance (Paris: Garnier, 2015).

20. Charrière, *Négotiations de la France dans le Levant*, 3:289.

21. Gellard, *Une reine épistolaire*, 295.

22. Charrière, *Négotiations de la France dans le Levant*, 3:324n.

23. Gabriel Naudé, *Considérations politiques sur les coups d'état* ([sl]:[sd], 1673).

On the gradual development of absolutism, first as an idea, then as a political principle that was put into effect in the seventeenth century, see two studies by Arlette Jouanna, *Le Pouvoir absolu. Naissance de l'imaginaire politique de la royauté* (Paris: Gallimard, 2013) and *Le Prince absolu. Apogée et déclin de l'imaginaire monarchique* (Paris: Gallimard, 2014).

24. Charrière, *Négotiations de la France dans le Levant*, 3:373.

25. Charrière, 3:368n.

26. Charrière, 3:373.

27. Charrière, 3:354n.

28. Philippe de Fresne-Canaye, *Le Voyage du Levant de Venise à Constantinople, l'émerveillement d'un jeune humaniste* (1573), ed., trans., M. H. Hauser, with Preface by Olivier Cèbe (Fontrieu: Éditions de Poliphile, 1986), 69–70.

29. In the second half of the sixteenth century, there occurred an increased codification of courtly ceremonies in the Ottoman Empire, which withdrew the sultan into silent detachment in the hidden inner sphere of the third courtyard of the Topkapı Palace and rendered him invisible in harmony with changes in the representations and understanding of Ottoman sovereignty. See Gülru Necipoğlu, *Architecture, Ceremonial, and Power: The Topkapı Palace in the Fifteenth and Sixteenth Centuries* (Cambridge, Mass.: MIT Press, 1992); Leslie Peirce, *The Imperial Harem: Women and Sovereignty in the Ottoman Empire* (Oxford: Oxford University Press, 1993).

30. In the play, Rose, the sultan's wife, plots to have Mustapha killed and insults him as "vulgar" and "son of the earth" because of his Ottoman birth while elevating

herself as both foreign born (Bounin falsely attributes "Armenian" origin to her) and "royal" because she is wedded to the sultan. Gabriel Bounin, *La Soltane* (Paris: Guillaume Moral, 1561). See also Antónia Szabari, "The Crescent Moon and the Orb: Political Allegory and Cosmographic Detour in Gabriel Bounin's *La Soltane*," *French Forum* 40, no. 2–3 (2015): 1–16.

31. Nicolay notes in his *Navigations et pérégrinations* that there was some confusion in France about the term: "The Sophies, who are the Persians, wear red. The Sophy is not the name of the Persian king, as many think, for this name denotes one of their religious sects, which commands them not to wear anything richer on their head than cotton, by humility." Nicolas de Nicolay, *Dans l'Empire de Soliman le Magnifique*, ed., intr. M.-C. Gomez-Géraud and S. Yérasimos (Paris: Presses du CNRS, 1989), 199.

32. Fresne-Canaye, *Le Voyage du Levant*, 165–79.

33. Alison Calhoun, "Redefining Nobility in the French Renaissance: The Case of Montaigne's 'Journal de Voyage,'" *Modern Language Notes* 123, no. 4, French Issue: Christian Delacampagne: Philosopher of Modern Times/Philosopher dans les temps modernes (September 2008): 836–854, esp. 839, 846.

34. Montaigne, *Complete Essays*, 1200; Montaigne, *Les Essais*, 1058;

35. Montaigne, *Complete Essays*, 1173; Montaigne, *Les Essais*, 1037.

36. Montaigne, *Complete Essays*, 1203; Montaigne, *Les Essais*, 1061.

37. Montaigne, *Complete Essays*, 1203–1205; Montaigne, *Les Essais*, 1061–1062.

38. Michel de Montaigne, *Oeuvres complètes*, ed. Albert Thibaudet and Maurice Rat, with Introduction by Maurice Rat (Paris: Gallimard, 1962), 1395–1396.

39. See Antónia Szabari, "Montaigne's Plants in Movement," in *Early Modern Écologies: Beyond English Ecocriticism*, ed. Pauline Goul and Phillip John Usher, Environmental Humanities in Pre-Modern Cultures, ed. Gillian Overing, Heide Estes, Philip Slavin, and Steve Mentz (Amsterdam: University of Amsterdam Press, 2020), 263–285.

40. Montaigne, *Complete Essays*, 288; translation slightly modified; Montaigne, *Les Essais*, 258.

41. Montaigne, *Complete Essays*, 288; Montaigne, *Les Essais*, 259.

42. Montaigne, *Complete Essays*, 297, translation slightly modified; Montaigne, *Les Essais*, 265–266.

43. Montaigne, *Complete Essays*, 290; Montaigne, *Les Essais*, 260.

44. Montaigne, *Complete Essays*, 295; Montaigne, *Les Essais*, 264.

45. Serge Gruzinski, *The Mestizo Mind: The Intellectual Dynamics of Colonization and Globalization*, trans. Deke Dusinberre (New York: Routledge, 2002), 26; Gruzinski, *La pensée métisse* (Paris: Pluriel, 2012), 47.

46. Montaigne, *Complete Essays*, 1100; *Les Essais*, 973.

47. Dorine Rouller describes Montaigne's cosmopolitanism as "chameleon-like"; that is, activated in certain relations. See Dorine Rouller, "Le caméléon et le hérisson: cosmopolitisme et élargissement des horizons géographiques à la Renaissance (Montaigne, Charron)," *Bibliothèque d'Humanisme et Renaissance* 76, no. 3 (2015): 559–572.

48. Montaigne, *Complete Essays*, 253; Montaigne, *Les Essais*, 225.
49. Montaigne, *Complete Essays*, 254; Montaigne, *Les Essais*, 225.
50. Montaigne, *Complete Essays*, 254; Montaigne, *Les Essais*, 226.
51. Montaigne, *Complete Essays*, 254; Montaigne, *Les Essais*, 226.
52. Montaigne repeats this point in a more general way when he compares the devotion of Christians to that of Muslims and Pagans, arguing that the latter are more devout. Montaigne, *Complete* Essays, 493; *Les Essais*, 442.
53. Montaigne, *Oeuvres complètes*, 1387.
54. George Hoffmann examines Michel de Montaigne's more than half a dozen *a secco* paintings of mythical scenes with nude bodies of Mars, Venus, and others, which decorated the walls of a chamber adjacent to his famous library. He suggests that the essayist used them to entertain elite guests in the interest of promoting his ambitions at the court. George Hoffmann, "Montaigne's Nudes: The Lost Tower Paintings Rediscovered," *Yale French Studies* 110, "Meaning and Its Objects: Material Culture in Medieval and Renaissance France" (2006): 122–133, esp. 126.
55. Montaigne, *Oeuvres complètes*, 210; Montaigne, *Les Essais*, 187.
56. Rebecca Zorach discusses eroticization of the relationship between master and servant in *Blood, Milk, Ink, and Gold: Abundance and Excess in the French Renaissance* (Chicago: University of Chicago Press, 2005), 186.
57. Montaigne, *Complete Essays*, 223; Montaigne, *Les Essais*, 198.
58. Montaigne, *Complete Essays*, 223; Montaigne, *Les Essais*, 197.
59. Todd W. Reeser underscores the importance of moderation in the development of early modern masculinity, and we can add also Christian and European identity. Todd W. Reeser, *Moderating Masculinity in Early Modern Culture* (Chapel Hill, N.C.: University of North Carolina Press, 2006), 12–13.
60. Montaigne, *Complete Essays*; Montaigne, *Les Essais*, 198.
61. Lyndan Warner, *The Ideas of Man and Woman in Renaissance France: Print, Rhetoric, and Law* (London: Routledge, 2019).
62. Historical records show that the sixteenth century's most famous French (Basque) peasant, who became the lackey of a Spanish aristocrat, was able to manipulate the world of male bonds to move outside his geographic and social milieu into the world of important people and matters, but he returned to his wife when he lost a leg in battle. In her microhistory of peasants in the Pyrenean village of Artigat, Natalie Zemon Davis analyzes these gendered differences between the two rival men, Martin Guerre and Arnaud du Tilh, who are able to establish their social and geographic mobility, commit acts of betrayal, and make claims of authenticity, on the one hand, and Guerre's wife Bertrande de Rols, who is described as carefully protecting her honor and social status but lacks the same mobility, on the other. Natalie Zemon Davis, *The Return of Martin Guerre* (Cambridge, Mass.: Harvard University Press, 1983), 27–34, 72, 82–83, 111.
63. Montaigne, *Complete Essays*, 225; Montaigne, *Les Essais*, 199.
64. Montaigne, *Complete Essays*, 225; Montaigne, *Les Essais*, 200.
65. See also Louisa Mackenzie, "La masculinité itinérante," 172.

66. Susan A. Skilliter, "Catherine de' Medicis's Turkish Ladies in Waiting: A Dilemma in Franco-Ottoman Diplomatic Relations," *Turcica* 7 (1975): 188–204, esp. 194.

67. On the racial normativizing power of conversion in the Middle Ages, which "could wash a black person white" as attested by numerous conversion narratives that hinged on the passage back and forth between crusader narratives (in which dark skin tone marked the other to be defeated) and the need for spiritual examination (evoking one's own "Blackness"), see Cord J. Whitaker, *Black Metaphors: How Racism Emerged from Medieval Race-Thinking* (Philadelphia: University of Pennsylvania Press, 2019), 20.

68. Also mentioned in Suraiya Faroqhi, *The Ottoman Empire: A Short History*, trans. Shelley Frisch (Princeton, N.J.: Markus Wiener Publishers, 2009), 133.

69. Charrière, *Négotiations de la France dans le Levant*, 2:764–765n; cited in Skilliter, "Turkish Ladies in Waiting," 196–197.

70. Charrière, 2:459–460n; cited in Skilliter, 195–196.

71. Skilliter, "Turkish Ladies in Waiting," 202.

Coda: Race and Self-Discovery

1. Palerne began traveling sometime around Hercule-Francis's ceremonial entry into the Netherlands on February 19, 1582 and returned just months before the duke's early death.

2. Jean Palerne, *D'Alexandrie à Istanbul. Pérégrinations dans l'Empire Ottoman, 1581–1583*, ed. Yvelise Bernard (Paris: L'Harmattan, 1991), 54–55.

3. Palerne, *D'Alexandrie à Istanbul*, 54.

4. Palerne, 153–154.

5. Palerne, 156.

6. Palerne, 84–86, 104–105.

Using the Library of Congress Romanization guide, I re-transcribed the Arabic words that Palerne inserts in his text. I thank Sarah Ouwayda for helping me with the transcription of Arabic words.

7. Palerne shifts everything, from the political to the physical world, through the lens of the personal freedom of the French traveler. He gives a fantastic definition of the term "Frank" (the designation of Western Christians in the Ottoman Empire) as "free from servitude to the sultan." Palerne, *D'Alexandrie à Istanbul*, 60.

8. Palerne, 94.

9. Palerne, 170–171.

10. Palerne, 66.

11. On the cultural values of the dark skin of European peasants, see Paul Freedman, *Images of the Medieval Peasant* (Stanford, Calif.: Stanford University Press, 1999), 139. On the racialization of skin color in Lisbon in the fifteenth through eighteenth centuries, see Catherine Coquery-Vidrovich, *Les routes de*

l'esclavage. Histoire des traites africaines, VIᵉ–XXᵉ siècle I (Paris: Albin Michel, 2021 [2018]), 95.

12. Toni Morrison, *Playing in the Dark: Whiteness and the Literary Imagination* (Cambridge, Mass.: Harvard University Press, 1992), 107.

13. Cord J. Whitaker, *Black Metaphors: How Racism Emerged from Medieval Race-Thinking* (Philadelphia: University of Pennsylvania Press, 2019), 20, 26.

14. Morrison, *Playing in the Dark*, 107.

15. Palerne, *D'Alexandrie à Istanbul*, 70.

16. In late medieval and Renaissance Europe, slaves were often branded on the face to mark them as possessions of the owner or as punishment, so Europeans often misrepresented facial tattoos as "badges of dishonor" in enslaved Africans taken to Europe. Kate Lowe, "The Stereotyping of Black Africans in Renaissance Europe," in *Black Africans in Renaissance Europe*, ed. T. F. Earle and K. J. P. Lowe (Cambridge: Cambridge University Press, 2005), 17–47, 22.

17. Palerne knows the sartorial rules and, in his *Pérégrinations*, remarks that "now that it [the turban] is prohibited to Christians," Muslims can wear all colors except for green, but they prefer white. This manuscript of Palerne's poetry was found in the nineteenth century by Auguste Benoit. See Palerne, *D'Alexandrie à Istanbul*, 275; and Jean Palerne, *Poésies*, intr. and notes by Auguste Benoit (Paris: Pillet et Dumoulin, 1884; repr. Geneva: Slatkine Reprints, 1971), 9.

18. Marcel Detienne and Jean-Pierre Vernant, *Cunning Intelligence in Greek Culture and Society*, trans. Janet Lloyd (Sussex: Harverster Press, 1978), 14.

Works Cited

Primary Sources

Aristotle, *The Nicomachean Ethics*, trans. H. Rackham, Loeb Classical Library 73 (Cambridge, Mass.: Harvard University Press), 117–153.

———. *Politics*, section 1254b, trans. H. Rackham, Loeb Classical Library 264. Cambridge, Mass.: Harvard University Press, 1932.

Augustine, *The City of God Against the Pagans*. Cambridge: Cambridge University Press, 1998.

Bassano, Luigi. *I costume, et i modi particolari de la vita de' Turchi*. Ristampa fotomeccanica dell' edizione originale (Roma, Antonio Blado, 1545) corredata da una introduzione, note biobibliografiche ed un indice analitico. Edited by Franz Babinger. Leiden: Brill, 1963.

Belon, Pierre. *L'histoire de la nature des oyseaux, avec leurs descriptions, & naifs portraicts retirez du naturel*. Illustrated by Pierre Gaudet. Paris: Guillaume Cavellat, 1555. [hand colored copy]

———. *Voyage au Levant (1553). Les Observations de Pierre Belon du Mans*. Edited and Introduction by Alexandra Merle. Paris: Chandaigne, 2001.

Borderie, Bertrand de la. *Le Discours du voyage de Constantinoble (1542)*. Edited by Christian Barataud and Danielle Trudeau. Paris: Champion, 2003.

Bounin, Gabriel. *La Soltane*. Paris: Guillaume Moral, 1561.

Boyvin, René, engraver. *Histoire de Jason et de la conquête de la toison d'or*. 26 plates. Paris: Jean de Mauregard, nd. [ca. 1563].

Brantôme, Seigneur de. *Oeuvres complètes de Pierre de Bourdeille, seigneur de Brantôme*. 11 vols. Edited by Ludovic Lalanne. Paris: Jules Renouard, 1868.

Caron, Antoine, artist. "Les Présents échangés entre Clément VII et François Ier à Marseille," ca. 1562. Ink and brown wash on paper. Musée de Louvre, Paris, Département des arts graphiques.

Champier, Symphorien. *Le fondement et origine des tiltres de noblesse et excellens estatz de tous nobles et illustres, quant à la différence des empires, royaulmes, duchez, contez et aultres seigneuries. Petit dialogue de noblesse auquel est déclaré que c'est de noblesse et les inventaires d'icelle*. Paris: D. Janot, 1544.

Charrière, Ernest, ed. *Négotiations de la France dans le Levant ou correspondances, mémoires et actes diplomatiques des ambassadeurs de France à Constantinople et des ambassadeurs, envoyés ou résidents à divers titres à Venise, Ragouse, Rome, Malte, et Jérusalem en Turquie, Perse, Géorgie, Crimée, Syrie, Égypte, etc. et dans les états de Tunis, d'Alger, et de Maroc*. 4 vols. Paris: Imprimerie nationale, 1848–1860.

Chesneau, Jean. *Le Voyage de Monsieur d'Aramon, ambassadeur pour le roy en Levant, escript par le noble homme Jean Chesneau*. Edited by Charles Schefer. Paris: E. Leroux, 1897.

Cotgrave, Randle. *Dictionarie of the French and English Tongues*. London: James Howell, 1611.

Dassonville Michel, ed. *La tragédie à l'époque d'Henri II et de Charles IX*, vol. 1: 1550–1561. Florence-Paris: Olschki-PUF, 1986.

De Testa, Ignace, ed. *Recueil des traités de la Porte Ottomane, avec les puissances étrangères, depuis les premier traité conclu, en 1536, entre Suléyman I et François II, jusqu'à nos jours*. 11 vols. Paris: Amyot, Muzard & Leroux, 1864–1911.

Diogenes Laertius, *Lives of Eminent Philosophers*. 2 vols. Translated by R. D. Hicks, Loeb Classical Library 185. Cambridge, Mass.: Harvard University Press, 1959.

Du Bellay, Jean. "Memoire des principaulx poinctz et propoz que le cardinal du Bellay aura a tenir de la part du Roy a nostre Sainct-Pere." In *Correspondance du Cardinal Jean du Bellay*. Edited by Rémy Scheurer. 2 vols. Paris: Klincksieck, 1973, 2: 2–9.

Du Bellay, Joachim. *Les Regrets suivis des Antiquités de Rome et du Songe*. Edited by François Roudaut. Paris: Livre de poche, 2002.

Du Bellay, Martin. *Les Mémoires de Messire Martin du Bellay, Seigneur de Langey. Contenans le discours des choses memorables advenues au Royaume de France, depuis l'an M.D.XIII jusques au trespass du Roy Francois premier, ausquels l'Autheur a inseré trois livres, & quelques fragmens des Ogdoades de Messire Guillaume du Bellay, Seigneur de Langey son frere*. Jacques Chouet, 1594.

Dürer, Albrecht. *Les quatre livres d'Albert Durer, Peinctre et Geometrien Tres excellent, De la Proportion des parties & pourtraicts des corps humains, Traduicts par Loys Meigret*. Paris: Charles Perier, 1557.

Erasmus, Desiderius. *Collected Works of Erasmus: Spiritualia 66*. Edited by John W. O'Malley. Toronto: Toronto University Press, 1988.

Estienne, Charles, and Jean Libault. *L'agriculture et la maison rustique*. Paris: Jacques Dupuys, 1583.

Ficino, Marsilio. *Commentary on Plato's Symposium of Love by Marsilio Ficino*. Translated with Introduction and notes by Sears Jayne. Dallas: Spring Publications, 1985.

Fresne-Canaye, Philippe de. *Le Voyage du Levant de Venise à Constantinople, l'émerveillement d'un jeune humaniste* (1573). Edited and translated by M. H. Hauser, with Preface by Olivier Cèbe. Fontrieu: Éditions de Poliphile, 1986.

Gilles, Pierre. *The Four Books of the Antiquities of Constantinople.* Translated by John Ball. New York: Italica, 1986.

———. *Itinéraires byzantins.* Edited and translated by Jean-Pierre Grélois. Paris: Association des amis du Centre d'histoire et civilization de Byzance, 2007.

Giovio, Paolo. *Dialogue des devises d'armes et d'amours.* Lyon: Guillaume Rouillé, 1561.

Henriët, Henk, artist. "Drinkende reus, twee figuren, een gezicht met een vogel in het haar en het gezicht van een man," ca. 1936–c. 1940. ["A study of a drinking giant, two figures, a face with a bird in the hair, and the face of a man."] Rijksmuseum, Amsterdam.

Hieroglyphica sive de sacris aegyptiorum literis commentarii, Joannis Pierri Valeriani Bolzanii Bellunensis. Basel: [s.n.], 1556.

Jodelle, Étienne. *Les Amours, Contr'amours, Contre la riere-Venus.* Edited by Emanuel Buron. Publications de l'Université de Saint-Étienne, 2003.

———. *Les Oeuvres & meslanges poetiques d'Estienne Jodelle, sieur du Lymodin.* Paris: Nicolas Chesneau, 1574.

———. *Oeuvres complètes,* 2 vols. Edited by Enea H. Balmas, NRF. Paris: Gallimard, 1965.

———. "Préface." In *L'histoire palladienne, traitant des gestes et généreux faitz d'armes et d'amours de plusieurs grandz princes et seigneurs, spécialement de Palladien, filz du roy Milanor d'Angleterre, et de la belle Sélerine, soeur du roy de Portugal. Nouvellement mise en nostre vulgaire françoys, par feu Cl. Colet.* Paris: J. Dallier, 1555.

———. *Le recueil des inscriptions, 1558: A Literary and Iconographical Exegesis.* Edited by Victor E. Graham and W. McAllister Johnson. Toronto: University of Toronto Press, 1972.

La Boétie, Étienne de. *Le discours de la servitude volontaire.* Edited by Pierre Léonard. Followed by essays by Félicité Lamennais, Pierre Leroux, Auguste Vermorel, Gustav Landauer, Simone Weil, Miguel Abensour, Marcel Gauchet, Pierre Clastres, and Claude Lefort. Paris: Payot, 1976.

Le Pois, Antoine. *Discours sur les medalles et les graveures antiques, principalement romaines.* Paris: Mamert Patisson, 1579.

Lescalopier, Pierre. *Pierre Lescalopier utzása Erdélybe (1574).* Translated and notes by Lajos Tardy and Kálmán Benda. Budapest: Bibliotheca Historica, 1982.

———. *Voyage fait par moy Pierre Lescalopier l'an 1574 de Venise à Constantinople par mer jusques à Raguse et le reste par terre et le retour par Thrace, Bulgarie, Walachie, Transilvanie ou Dace, Hongrie, Allemagne, Trieste, et Marche Trevisane jusques à Venise.* Unpublished manuscript held at Bibliothèque de la faculté de Médicine, Montpelier. H. 385. fol. 40–41v, 48v–64.

Markham, Grevase. *Cauelarice, or The English horseman containing all the arte of horse-manship, as much as necessary for any man to vnderstand, whether he be horse-breeder, horse-ryder, horse-hunter, horse-runner, horse-ambler, horse-farrier, horse-keeper, coachman, smith, or saddler. Together, with the discouert of the subtil trade or mystery of horse-coursers; & an explanation[n] of the excellency or horses understa[n]ding, or how to teach them trickes like Bankes his curtall: and that horses may be able to drawe drie-foot like a hound. Secrets before vnpublished, & now carefully set down for the profit of this whole nation.* London: Edward White, 1607.

M. Ménard, ed. *Pièces fugitives pour servir à l'histoire de France, Avec des notes historiques et géographiques.* Paris: Chaubert, 1749.

Menavino, Giovanni Antonio. *Trattato de' costumi et vita de' Turchi.* Florence: Lorenzo Torrentino, 1548.

Monbart, Joséphine de. *Lettres tahitiennes.* Modern Humanities Research Association Critical Texts 36. London: The Modern Humanities Research Association, 2012.

Monluc, Jean de. *Commentaires, 1521–1576.* Edited by Paul Corteault. Paris: Gallimard, 1964.

Montaigne, Michel de. *The Complete Essays.* Translated by M. A. Screech. London: Penguin, 1987.

———. *Les Essais.* Edited by Marcel Conche, Verdun-Louis Saulnier, and Pierre Villey. Paris: Presses Universitaires de France, 2004.

———. *Oeuvres complètes.* Edited by Albert Thibaudet and Maurice Rat, with Introduction by Maurice Rat. Paris: Gallimard, 1962.

Naudé, Gabriel. *Advis pour dresser une bibliothèque présenté à Mgr. le président de Mesme.* Paris: F. Targa, 1627.

———. *Considérations politiques sur les coups d'état* ([sl]:[sd], 1673).

Nicolay, Nicolas de. *Discours et Histoire Veritable des Navigations, peregrinations et voyages, faicts en la Turquie par Nicolas de Nicolay Daulphinois, Seigneur d'Arfeuille, Valet de chambre & Geographe ordinaire du Roy de France, contenans plusieurs singularitez que l'Auteur à veu & observez.* Antwerp: Arnould Conix, 1586.

———. *Dans l'Empire de Soliman le Magnifique.* Edited and with Introduction by M.-C. Gomez-Géraud and S. Yérasimos. Paris: Presses du CNRS, 1989.

———. *Les quatre premiers livres des navigations et pérégrinations orientales de N. de Nicolay daulphine, Valet du chambre et géographe ordinaire du Roy.* Lyon: Guillaume Rouillé, 1567.

Notice sur la bibliothèque publique de le ville de Moulins. R. A. K. Moulins: Place-Bujon, 1839.

Palerne, Jean. *D'Alexandrie à Istanbul. Pérégrinations dans l'Empire Ottoman, 1581–1583.* Edited by Yvelise Bernard. Paris: L'Harmattan, 1991.

———. *Poésies.* With Introduction and notes by Auguste Benoit. Paris: Pillet et Dumoulin, 1884; repr., Geneva: Slatkine Reprints, 1971.

Paradin, Claude. *Les Devises héroiques par M. Claude Paradin, Chanoine de Beaujeu.* Lyon: Jean de Tournes and Guil Gazeau, 1557.

Paré, Ambroise. *Discours d'Amroise Paré, Conseiller et Premier Chirurgien du Roy, A Sçavoir de la mummie, des venis, de la licorne et de la peste.* Paris: Gabriel Buon, 1582.

———. "Le voyage d'Ambroise Paré à Metz"-1552. *L'Austrasie* 2 (1906–1907): 231–238, 369–375.

Pasquier, Étienne. *Les Oeuvres d'Étienne Pasquier, contenant ses recherches de la France, son Plaidoyer pour M. le duc de Lorraine; celuy de M. Versois pour les Jesuites, Contre l'Université de Paris, Clororum virorum ad Steph. Pasquierium carmina, Epigrammatum libri sex, Epitaphiorum liber, Iconum liber, cum nonnullis Theod. Pasquierii, In Francorum Regum Icones Notis, Ses Lettres, Ses Oeuvres meslées, et les Lettres de Nicolas Pasquier, Fils d'Estienne.* 2 vols. Amsterdam: Les libraires associéz, 1723.

Péruse, Jean de la. *Médée, Tragédie et autres diverses poésies, Par J. de la Péruse.* Poitiers: Marnefs & Boutsetz frères, sd.

Pico della Mirandola, Giovanni. *Oration on the Dignity of Man: A New Translation and Commentary.* Edited by Francesco Borghesi, Michael Papio, and Massimo Riva. Cambridge: Cambridge University Press, 2016.

Plato, *Timaeus, Critias, Cleitophon, Menexenus, Epistles.* Translated R. G. Bury. Loeb Classical Library 234. Cambridge, Mass.: Harvard University Press, 1929.

Pliny. *Natural History* X. Books 36–37. Translated by D. E. Eichholz. Loeb Classical Library 419. Cambridge, Mass.: Harvard University Press, 1962.

Plutarch. "On Exile," In *Moralia* VI. Book 526. Translated by Phillip H. de Lacy and Benedict Einarson. Loeb Classical Library 405. Cambridge, Mass.: Harvard University Press, 1959: 513–571.

———. *Lives* IX. Translated by Bernadotte Perrin, Loeb Classical Library 101. Cambridge, Mass.: Harvard University Press, 1920.

———. *Roman Lives: A selection of Eight Roman Lives.* Translated by Robin Waterfield, with Introduction and notes by Philip A. Stadter, Oxford World's Classics. Oxford: Oxford University Press, 1999.

Postel, Guillaume. *Des histoires orientales et principalement des Turkes ou Turchikes et Schitiques ou Tartaresques et aultres qui en sont descendues oeuvre pour la tierce fois augmenté. Et divisé en trois parties avec l'indice des choses les plus memorables y continues par Guillaume Postel cosmopolite deux fois de là retourné et veritablement informé.* Paris: Jérôme de Marnef, 1575.

———. *Des histoires orientales et principalement des Turkes ou Turchikes et Schitiques ou Tartaresques et aultres qui en sont descendues oeuvre pour la tierce fois augmenté. Et divisé en trois parties avec l'indice des choses les plus memorables y continues par Guillaume Postel cosmopolite deux fois de là retourné et veritablement informé.* Modernized and with Introduction by Jacques Rollet. Istanbul: Isis, 1999.

———. *Linguarum duodecim characteribus differentium alphabetum introductio ac legendi modus longe facilimus.* Paris: Pierre Vidoue, 1538.

———. *De Phoenicum literis, seu de prisco latine et graece lingue, charactere ejusque origine et usu commentatiuncula.* Paris: Martinus Juvenis, 1552.

———. *De la Republique des Turcs: & là ou l'occasion s'offrera, des moeurs & loy de tous Muhamedistes* par Guillaume Postel cosmopolite. Poitiers: Enguibert de Marnef, 1560.

———. *Le Thrésor des Prophéties de l'Univers.* Manuscript published with Introduction by François Secret. Archives Internationales des histoire des Idées. The Hague: Nijhoff, 1969.

Quintilian. *Institutio oratoria: Books 1–3.* Translated by H. E. Butler. Loeb Classical Library 124. Cambridge, Mass.: Harvard University Press, later printing edition, 1980.

Rabelais, François. *Les cinq livres.* Edited by Jean Céard, Gérard Defaux, and Michel Simonin. Paris: Livre de Poche, 1994.

———. *The Complete Works of François Rabelais.* Translated by Donald M. Frame. Berkeley: University of California Press, 1999.

———. *Oeuvres complètes.* Edited by Mireille Huchon and François Moreau. Paris: Gallimard, 1994.

———. *Pantagruel.* Lyon: Claude Nourry, nd.

———. *Pantagruel.* François Juste, Lyon, 1534.

———. *Pantagruel.* [sl], 1537.

Raemond, Florimond de. *L'Anti-christ, L'anti-Papesse. Édition seconde reveue, corrigée et de beaucoup augmentée par l'autheur.* Paris: L'Angelier, 1607 [first printed in 1599].

Refik, Ahmed. *Ononcu asr-ı Hicrīde İstanbul Hayatı (1495–1591).* Istanbul: Enderun Kitabevi, 1988.

Ribier, Guillaume, ed. *Lettres et mémoires d'état.* 2 vols. Blois: J. Hotot, 1666.

Ronsard, Pierre de. *Oeuvres complètes.* Edited by Jean Céard, Daniel Ménager, and Michel Simonin. 2 vols. Paris: Gallimard, 1993–1994.

Rouillé, Guillaume. *La première partie du promptuaire des medalles des plus renommees personnes qui ont esté depuis le commencement du monde.* Lyon: Guillaume Rouillé, 1553.

———. *La seconde partie du promptuaire des medalles des plus renommees personnes, commençant à la nativité de nostre Sauveur Jesus Christ.* Lyon: Guillaume Rouillé, 1553.

Royal order of May 12, 1519, Bibliothèque nationale de France, manuscript fr. 5756.

Sagon, François. *Apologye en defense pour le Roy, fondée sur texte d'evangile, contre ses ennemys & calumniateurs.* Paris: Denys Janot, 1544.

Sainte-Marthe, Scévole de. *Eloges des hommes illustres. Qui depuis un siècle ont fleury en France dans la profession des lettres.* Translated by G. Colletet. Paris: Sommaville et Courbé, 1644.

Scholasticus, Zacharias. *Vie de Sévère d'Antioch, par Zacharie le scholastique.* Edited by Marc-Antoine Kugener. 2 vols. Paris: Patrologia Orientalis, 1907.

Thevet, André. *Cosmographie de Levant.* Lyon: Jean de Tournes, 1554.

———. *Cosmographie de Levant. Revue & augmentée de plusieurs figures.* Lyon: Jean de Tournes, 1556.

---. *Cosmographie de Levant*. Edited by Frank Lestringant. Geneva: Droz, 1985.

---. *Les singularitez de la France antarctique, autrement nommée Amérique, & de plusieurs terres & isles découvertes de nostre temps: par F. André Thevet, natif d'Angoulesme*. Anvers: Christophle Palantin, 1558.

Valbelle, Honorat de. *Histoire journalière d'Honorat de Valbelle (1498–1539). Journal d'un bourgeois de Marseille au temps de Louis XII et François Ier*. Edited by V. L. Bourilly, Lucien Gaillard, and Charles Rostaing. Aix-en-Provence, Marseille: J. Laffitte, 1985.

Villegagnon, Nicolas Durand de. *Le discours de la guerre de Malte, contenant la perte de Tripolis & d'autres fortresses faulsement imposée aux Français*. Lyon: Jean Temporal, 1553.

Secondary Sources

Ahmed, Sarah. *Queer Phenomenology: Orientations, Objects, Others*. Durham, N.C.: Duke University Press, 2006.

Andrews, Walter G., and Mehmet Kalpaklı. *The Age of Beloveds: Love and the Beloved in Early-Modern Ottoman and European Culture and Society*. Durham, N.C.: Duke University Press, 2005.

Antonioli, Roland. "Rabelais et la médicine." In *Études rabelaisiennes*. Geneva: Droz, 1976.

Asad, Talal. *Formations of the Secular: Christianity, Islam, Modernity*. Stanford, Calif.: Stanford University Press, 2003.

Aubert, Guillaume. "'The Blood of France': Race and Purity of Blood in the French Atlantic World." *The William and Mary Quarterly* 61, no. 3 (July 2004): 439–478.

Auerbach, Erich. *Mimesis: The Representation of Reality in Western Literature*. Translated by Willard R. Trask, with Introduction by Edward Said. Fiftieth Anniversary edition. Princeton, N.J.: Princeton University Press, 2002.

Balmas, E. H. *Un Poeta del Rinascimento francese, Étienne Jodelle. La sua vita, il suo tempo*. Preface by M. Raymond. Florence: Olchiski, 1962.

Barkan, Leonard. *Unearthing the Past: Archeology and Aesthetics in the Making of Renaissance Culture*. New Haven, Conn.: Yale University Press, 1999.

Barroux, Robert. "Nicolaï d'Arfeuille, agent secret, géographe et dessinateur (1517–1583)." *Reveue d'histoire diplomatique* 51 (1937): 81–109.

Barthe, Pascale. "Du Turc au traître: Les chevaliers de Saint-Jean-de-Jérusalem, les Ottomans et la France de François I dans *L'oppugnation* de Jacques de Bourbon." *French Historical Studies* 30, no. 3 (2007): 427–449.

---. *French Encounters with the Ottomans, 1510–1560*. London: Routledge, 2016.

Bartlett, Robert, *The Making of Europe: Conquest, Colonization, and Cultural Change, 950–1350*. Princeton, N.J.: Princeton University Press, 1993.

Beaujour, Michel. *Miroirs d'encre*. Paris: Seuil, 1980.

Bennassar, Bartolomé, and Lucile Bennassar. *Les chrétens d'Allah. L'histoire extraordinaire des renégats.* Paris: Perrin, 2001.

Bensoussan, Nicole. *Casting a Second Rome: Primaticcio's Bronze Copies and the Fontainebleau Project.* Dissertation, Yale University, 2009. ProQuest Dissertations and Theses.

Biller, Peter. "Black Women in Medieval Scientific Thought." *Micrologus* 13 (2005): 477–492.

Bloch, Ernst. *The Spirit of Utopia.* Translated by Anthony A Nassar. Stanford, Calif.: Stanford University Press, 2000.

Boulle, Pierre H. *Race et esclavage dans la France de l'Ancien Régime.* Paris: Perrin, 2007.

Bourrilly, Victor-Louis. "La première ambassade d'Antonio Rincón en Orient (1522–1523)." *Revue d'histoire modern et contemporaine* 2, no. 1 (1900): 23–44.

———. "Les diplomates de François Ier. Antonio Rincón et la politique orientale de François I. (1522–1541)." *Revue historique* 113, no. 2 (1913): 268–308.

Boutcher, Warren. *The School of Montaigne in Early Modern Europe.* 2 vols. Oxford: Oxford University Press, 2017.

Bouwsma, William. *Concordia mundi: The Career and Thought of Guillaume Postel, 1510–1581.* Harvard Historical Monographs. Cambridge, Mass.: Harvard University Press, 1957.

Bowen, Willis. *Jacques Gohory.* PhD dissertation, Harvard University, 1935. *ProQuest Dissertations and Theses.*

Brach, Jean-Pierre. "Illicit Christianity: Guillaume Postel, Kabbalah, and a 'Transgender' Messiah." *Téma* 27, no. 1 (2019): 3–15.

Brancher, Dominique. "Dégeler Rabelais." In *Christian Prigent: trou(v)er sa langue,* edited by B. Gorillot and F. Thumerel, 227–244. Paris: Hermann éditeurs, 2017.

Braudel, Fernand. *La Méditerranée et le monde méditerranéen à l'époque de Philippe II.* 3 vols. Paris: Armand Colin, 1949.

Calhoun, Alison. "Redefining Nobility in the French Renaissance: The Case of Montaigne's 'Journal de Voyage.'" *Modern Language Notes* 123, no. 4, French Issue: Christian Delacampagne: Philosopher of Modern Times / Philosopher dans les temps modernes (September 2008): 836–854.

Casala, Giancarlo. *The Ottoman Age of Exploration.* Oxford: Oxford University Press, 2010.

Certeau, Michel de. *La Fable mystique XV^{Ie}–XVIIe siècle.* Paris: Gallimard, 1982.

———. *The Mystic Fable.* Edited by Luce Giard. Translated by Michael B. Smith. Chicago: University of Chicago Press, 2015.

———. *The Practice of Everyday Life I.* Translated by Steven F. Rendall. Berkeley: University of California Press, 2011.

Chen, Mel Y. "Perverse Modernities." In *Animacies: Biopolitics, Racial Mattering, and Queer Affect.* Edited by Jack Halberstam and Lisa Lowe. Durham, N.C.: Duke University Press, 2012.

Cockram, Sarah. "Interspecies Understanding: Exotic Animals and Their Handlers at the Italian Renaissance Court." *Renaissance Studies* 31, no. 2. Special Issue: The Animal in Renaissance Italy (April 2017): 277–296.
Cohen, Jeffrey Jerome. "Monster Culture (Seven Theses)." In *Monster Theory: Reading Culture*, edited by Jeffrey Jerome Cohen, 3–25. Minneapolis: University of Minnesota Press, 1996.
Conley, Tom. *Errant Eye: Poetry and Topography in Early Modern France*. Minneapolis: University of Minnesota Press, 2010.
———. *The Self-Made Map: Cartographic Writing in Early Modern France*. Minneapolis: University of Minnesota Press, 2010.
———. "A Space-Event: The 'Apologie' in the *Essays* of 1595." *Montaigne Studies* 8 (October 1995): 113–115.
Connor, Steven. *The Book of Skin*. Ithaca, N.Y.: Cornell University Press, 2004.
Constantinou, Costas M. *States of Political Discourse: Words, Regimes, Seditions*. London: Routledge, 2004.
Cooper, Richard. *Rabelais et l'Italie. Études rabelaisiennes* 24. Geneva: Droz, 1991.
Coquery-Vidrovitch, Catherine. *Les routes de l'esclavage. Histoire des traites africaines, VIe-XXe siècle*. Paris: Albin Michel, 2021.
Crouzet, Denis. *Les Guerriers de Dieu: La violence au temps des troubles de religion vers 1525–vers 1610*. 2 vols. Paris: Champ Vallon, 1990.
Crowley, Martin. *Accidental Agents: Ecological Politics beyond the Human*. New York: Columbia University Press, 2022.
Cuneo, Pia F. "Just a Bit of Control: The Historical Significance of Sixteenth- and Seventeenth-Century German Bit-Books." In *The Culture of the Horse: Status, Discipline, and Identity in the Early Modern World*. Edited by Karen Raber and Treva J. Tucker. New York: Palgrave Macmillan, 2005.
Cunnally, John. *Images of the Illustrious: The Numismatic Presence in the Renaissance*. Princeton, N.J.: Princeton University Press, 1999.
Damroch, David. "World Literature in a Postcanonical, Hypercanonical Age." In *Comparative Literature in an Age of Globalization*, edited by Haun Saussy, 43–53. Baltimore: Johns Hopkins University Press, 2006.
Dannenfeldt, Karl H. "Egyptian Mumia: The Sixteenth Century Experience and Debate." *The Sixteenth Century Journal* 16, no. 2 (Summer 1985): 163–180.
Davis, Natalie Zemon. *The Gift in Sixteenth-Century France*. Madison: University of Wisconsin Press, 2000.
———. "Publisher Guillaume Rouillé: Businessman and Humanist." In *Editing Sixteenth-Century Texts*, edited by Richard J. Schoeck, 72–112. Toronto: University of Toronto Press, 1966.
———. *The Return of Martin Guerre*. Cambridge, Mass.: Harvard University Press, 1983.
De Groot, Alexander H. *The Historical Development of the Capitulatory Regime in the Ottoman Middle East from the Fifteenth to the Nineteenth Centuries*. Oriente

Moderno. Nuova serie Anno 22, vol. 3, no. 3. *The Ottoman Capitulations: Text and Context* (2003): 575–604, 578.

Defaux, Gérard. *Pantagruel et les sophistes. Contribution à l'histoire de l'humanisme chrétien au XVIe siècle.* International Archives of the History of Ideas Archives internationales d'histoire des idées. Book 63. New York: Springer, 1973.

———. "Rabelais et les cloches de Notre Dame." *Études rabelaisiennes* 9 (1971): 1–28.

Deleuze, Gilles. *Cinema 1: The Movement Image.* Translated by Hugh Tomlinson and Barbara Habberjam. Minneapolis: University of Minnesota Press, 1986.

Demerson, Guy. *Rabelais.* Paris: Fayard, 1991.

Demonet, Marie-Luce. "Rabelais et l'utopie de l'ermitage." In *VII Jornadas sobre el pensamiento utópico. Religoón en Utopía,* Madrid, November 2010, edited by Iveta Nakládalová, 71–96. Berlin: Akademia Verlag, 2013.

Der Derian, James. *On Diplomacy: A Genealogy of Western Estrangement.* Oxford: Blackwell, 1987.

Desan, Philippe. *Montaigne: A Life.* Translated by Steven Rendall and Lisa Neal. Princeton, N.J.: Princeton University Press, 2017.

Despret, Vinciane. *Our Emotional Make-Up: Ethnopsychology and Selfhood.* Translated by Marjolijd de Jager. New York: Other Press, 2004.

Detienne, Marcel, and Jean-Pierre Vernant. *Cunning Intelligence in Greek Culture and Society.* Translated by Janet Lloyd. Sussex: Harvester Press, 1978.

Devyver, André. *Le Sang épuré. Les préjugés de race chez les gentilhommes français de l'ancien régime (1520–1720).* Brussels: Éditions de l'Université de Bruxelles, 1973.

DeVun, Leah. *The Shape of Sex: Nonbinary Gender from Genesis to Renaissance.* New York: Columbia University Press, 2021.

Dewerpe, Alain. *Espion, une anthropologie historique du secret d'État contemporain.* Paris: Gallimard, 1994.

Dufourmantelle, Anne. *Power of Gentleness: Meditations on the Risk of Living.* Translated by Katherine Payne and Vincent Sallé, with Foreword by Catherine Malabou. New York: Fordham University Press, 2018.

Duval, Edwin. *The Design of Rabelais's* Pantagruel. New Haven, Conn.: Yale University Press, 1991.

Dyer, Richard. *White: Twentieth Anniversary Edition.* With a new introductory essay "Looking into the Light: Whiteness, Racism and Regimes of Representation" by Maxime Cervulle. London: Routledge, 2017.

Ehrman, Jean. *Antoine Caron, peintre des fêtes et des massacres.* Paris: Flammarion, 1986.

Elliot, Matthew. "Dress Codes in the Ottoman Empire: The Case of the Franks." In *Ottoman Costumes: From Textile to Identity,* edited by Suraiya Faroqhi and Christophe K. Neumann, 103–124. Istanbul: Eren, 2004.

Erickson, Peter. "The Moment of Race in Renaissance Studies." *Shakespeare Studies* 26 (1998): 27–36.

Escamilla, Michèle, and María José Bertomeu Masiá. "Antonio Rincón: Transfuge, espion, ambassadeur et *casus belli* à temps de Charles Quint." In *Ambassadeurs, apprentis espions et maîtres comploteurs*, edited by Béatrice Perez, 87–171. Sorbonne, Paris: PUPS, 2010.

Faroqhi, Suraiya. "Introduction, or Why and How One Might Want to Study Ottoman Clothes." In *Ottoman Costumes: From Textile to Identity*. Edited by Suraiya Faroqhi and Christoph K. Neumann. Istanbul: Eren, 2004.

———. *The Ottoman Empire: A Short History*. Translated by Shelley Frisch. Princeton, N.J.: Markus Wiener Publishers, 2009.

Fiorenza, Giancarlo. "Penelope's Web: Francesco Primaticcio's Epic Revision at Fontainebleau." *Renaissance Quarterly* 59 (2006): 795–827.

Foucault, Michel. *Courage of Truth: The Government of Self and Others II*. Translated by Graham Burchell. "Michel Foucault: Lectures at the Collège de France." Book 8. London: Picador, reprint, 2012.

———. *The History of Sexuality, vol. 2: The Use of Pleasure*. Translated by Robert Hurley. New York: Vintage, 1990.

Fraser, James G. "The Inauguration of Semitic Epigraphy and Paleography as Scientific Disciplines." In *Perspectives on Language and Text: Essays and Poems in Honor of Francis I. Andersen's Sixtieth Birthday*, edited by Edgar W. Conrad and Edward G. Newing, 19–33. University Park, Penn.: Eisenbrauns, 1987.

Freccero, Carla. "Early Modern Psychoanalytics: Montaigne and the Melancholic Subject of Humanism." *Qui parle* (Winter 1999): 89–114.

———. "Queer Rabelais?" In *Approaches to Teaching the Works of François Rabelais*, edited by Floyd Gray and Todd W. Reeser, 182–191. New York: MLA, 2011.

Freedman, Paul. *Images of the Medieval Peasant*. Stanford, Calif.: Stanford University Press, 1999.

Fumurescu, Alin. "The Dialectic of the Individual and the Paradox of French Absolutism." *European Legacy* 16, no. 6 (September 2011): 717–734.

Gellard, Matthieu. *Une reine épistolaire. Lettres et pouvoirs au temps de Catherine de Médicis*. Bibliothèque histoire de la Renaissance. Paris: Garnier, 2015.

Goul, Pauline. "Pointless Ecology of Renaissance Cynicism." *The Comparatist* 43 (October 2019): 159–172.

Goul, Pauline, and Phillip J. Usher, eds., *Early Modern Écologies: Beyond English Ecocriticism*. Amsterdam: Amsterdam University Press, 2021.

Grodecki, Catherine. "Le graveur Lyon Davent, illustrateur de Nicolas de Nicolay." *Bibliothèque d'Humanisme et Renaissance* 36, no. 2 (1974): 347–351.

Grogan, Jane, ed. *Beyond Greece and Rome: Reading the Ancient Near East in Early Modern Europe*. Oxford: Oxford University Press, 2020.

Gruzinski, Serge. *The Mestizo Mind: The Intellectual Dynamics of Colonization and Globalization*. Translated by Deke Dusinberre. New York: Routledge, 2013.

———. *La pensée métisse*. Pluriel, 2012.

Habib, Imtiaz. *Black Lives in the English Archives, 1500–1677: Imprints of the Invisible*. London: Routledge, 2008.

Hall, Kim E. *Things of Darkness: Economies of Race and Gender in Early Modern England*. Ithaca, N.Y.: Cornell University Press, 1996.
Hampton, Timothy. *Fictions of the Embassy: Literature and Diplomacy in Early Modern Europe*. Ithaca, N.Y.: Cornell University Press, 2013.
———. *Literature and Nation in the Sixteenth Century: Inventing Renaissance France*. Ithaca, N.Y.: Cornell University Press, 2000.
———. "'Turkish Dogs': Rabelais, Erasmus, and the Rhetoric of Alterity." *Representations* 41 (1993): 58–82.
———. *Writing from History: The Rhetoric of Exemplarity in Renaissance Literature*. Ithaca, N.Y.: Cornell University Press, 1990.
Haraway, Donna. *Cyborg Manifesto: Science, Technology, and Socialist-Feminism in the Late Twentieth Century*. Minneapolis: University of Minnesota Press, 2016 [originally published in 1985].
Heath, Michael J. "Foolish or Fearsome Franks? The Supposed Ottoman View of European Christians in the Sixteenth Century." In *Conceptions of Europe in Renaissance France: Essays in Honour of Keith Cameron*, edited by David Cowling, Faux Titre 281, 153–176. Amsterdam: Rodopi, 2006.
Helgeson, James. *The Lying Mirror: The First-Person Stance and Sixteenth-Century Writing*. Geneva: Droz, 2012.
Heng, Geraldine. *The Invention of Race in the European Middle Ages*. Cambridge: Cambridge University Press, 2018.
Hennepe, Mieneke Te. "Of the Fisherman's Net and Skin Pores: Reframing Conceptions of the Skin in Medicine 1572–1714." In *Blood, Sweat, and Tears: The Changing Concepts of Physiology from Antiquity into Early Modern Europe*, edited by Manfred Horstmanshoff, Helen King, Claus Zittel, 523–548. Leiden: Brill, 2012.
Hirai, Hiro. "*Logoi Spermatikoi* and the Concept of Seeds in the Mineralogy and Cosmogony of Paracelsus." *Revue d'histoire des sciences* 61, no. 2 (2008): 245–264.
Hock, Jessie. *The Erotics of Materialism: Lucretius and Early Modern Poetics*. Philadelphia: University of Pennsylvania Press, 2021.
———. "Waging Loving War: Lucretius and the Poetry of Remy Belleau." *The Romantic Review* 104, no. 3–4 (May 2013): 275–291.
Hoffmann, George. "Montaigne's Nudes: The Lost Tower Paintings Rediscovered." *Yale French Studies* 110 "Meaning and Its Objects: Material Culture in Medieval and Renaissance France" (2006): 122–133.
Holmes, Brooke. "The Body of Western Embodiment Classical Antiquity and the Early History of a Problem." In *Embodiment: A History*, edited by Justin E. H. Smith, 18–50. Oxford: Oxford University Press, 2017.
Huon, Antoinette. "Le Thème du Prince dans les entrées parisiennes au XVIe siècle." In *Les fêtes de la Renaissance I*. Edited by Jean Jacquot. Paris: CNRS, 1956.
Ibbett, Katherine. *Compassion's Edge: Fellow-Feeling and Its Limits in Early Modern France*. Philadelphia: University of Pennsylvania Press, 2018.

Isom-Verhaaren, Christine. *Allies with the Infidel: The Ottoman and French Alliance in the Sixteenth Century.* London: I. B. Tauris, 2013.
Jackson, Zakiyyah Iman. *Becoming Human: Matter and Meaning in an Antiblack World.* New York: New York University Press, 2020.
Janson, H. W. *Apes and Ape Lore in the Middle Ages and Renaissance.* London: The Warburg Institute, 1952.
Jensen, De Lamar. "The Ottoman Turks in Sixteenth-Century French Diplomacy." *Sixteenth-Century Journal* 16, no. 4 (Winter 1985): 451–470.
Jones, Ann Rosalind, and Peter Stallybrass. *Renaissance Clothing and the Materials of Memory.* Cambridge: Cambridge University Press, 2000.
Jouanna, Arlette. *L'idée de race en France au XVIe siècle (1498–1614).* 3 vols. Lille: Atelier reproduction des thèses, 1976.
———. *Ordre social. Mythes et hierarchies dans la France du XVIe siècle.* Paris: Hachette, 1977.
———. *Le Pouvoir absolu. Naissance de l'imaginaire politique de la royauté.* Paris: Gallimard, 2013.
———. *Le Prince absolu. Apogée et déclin de l'imaginaire monarchique.* Paris: Gallimard, 2014.
Juall, Scott. "Early Modern Franco-Ottoman Relations: Utopian Mapping of Imperialist Encounters in François Rabelais's *Pantagruel.*" *Études rabelaisinennes* 44 (2006): 79–110.
Karamustafa, Ahmet T. *God's Unruly Friends: Dervish Groups in the Islamic Later Middle Period 1200–1550.* Salt Lake City: University of Utah Press, 1994.
Keller, Marcus. "Nicolas de Nicolay's *Navigations et peregrinations* and the Domestic Politics of Travel Writing." *L'Esprit créateur* 48, no. 1 (2008): 18–31.
Kemper, Rachel H. *Costume.* New York: Newsweek Books, 1977.
Kenny, Neil. *The Uses of Curiosity in Early Modern France and Germany.* Oxford: Oxford University Press, 2004.
Klemettilä, Hannele. *Animals and Hunters in the Late Middle Ages.* London: Routledge, 2015.
Kłosowska, Anna. "The Etymology of *Slave.*" In *Disturbing Times: Medieval Pasts, Reimagined Futures*, edited by Catherine E. Karkov, Anna Kłosowska, and Vincent W. J. van Gerven Oei, 151–217. Santa Barbara, Calif.: Punctum Books, 2020.
Komaroff, Linda, ed. *Gifts of the Sultan: The Arts of Giving at the Islamic Courts.* Edited by Los Angeles County Museum of Art. New Haven, Conn.: Yale University Press, 2011.
La Charité, Claude. "Rabelais et le *De contemptu rerum fortuitarum* (1520) de Budé." *Revue d'histoire littéraire de France* 108, no. 3 (July–September 2008): 515–527.
Lacore-Martin, Emmanuelle. "'Encores me frissonne et tremble le coeur dedans sa capsule': Rabelais's Anatomy of Emotion and the Soul." *Renaissance and Reformation/Renaissance et Réforme* 39, no. 3 (Summer/ÉTÉ 2016): 33–58.

LaGuardia, David P. *Intertextual Masculinity in French Renaissance Literature: Rabelais, Brantôme, and the Cent nouvelles nouvelles*. London: Routledge, 2009.
Latour, Bruno. *The Pasteurization of France*. Translated by Alan Sheridan and John Law. Cambridge, Mass.: Harvard University Press, 1988.
Leal, Pedro Germano. "Reassessing Horapollon: A Contemporary View of the Hieroglyphica." *Emblematica* 24 (2014): 37–75.
Lebègue, Raymond. *Études sur le théâtre François 1. Moyen Âge, Renaissance, Baroque*. Paris: Éditions A.-G. Nizet, 1977.
———. *La tragédie religieuse en France*. Paris: Honoré Champion, 1923.
Leblanc, P. *Les écrits théoriqes et critiques français des années 1540–1561 sur la tragédie*. Paris: Seuil, 1972.
Legros, Alain. "Montaigne on Faith and Religion." In *The Oxford Handbook of Montaigne*, edited by Philippe Desan, 525–543. Oxford: Oxford University Press, 2016.
LeGuin, Elisabeth. "Man and Horse in Harmony." In *The Culture of the Horse: Status, Discipline, and Identity in the Early Modern World*, edited by Karen Raber and Treva J. Tucker, 175–196. New York: Palgrave Macmillan, 2005.
Lewis, John. "From *Gargantua* to the *Tiers livre*: Rabelais's Quiet Years?" *The Modern Language Review* 107 (July 2012): 729–755.
Long, Kathleen P., *Hermaphrodites in Renaissance Europe*. London: Routledge, 2016.
Long, Kathleen P., ed. *High Anxiety: Masculinity in Crisis in Early Modern France*. Philadelphia: Penn State University Press, 2002.
Longino, Michèle. *Orientalism and French Classical Drama*. Cambridge: Cambridge University Press, 2002.
Loskoutoff, Yvan. "Magie et tragédie. La *Cléopâtre captive* d'Étienne Jodelle." *Bibliothèque d'Humanisme et Renaissance* 53, no. 1 (1991): 65–80.
Lowe, Kate. "The Stereotyping of Black Africans in Renaissance Europe." In *Black Africans in Renaissance Europe*, edited by T. F. Earle and K. J. P. Lowe, 17–47. Cambridge: Cambridge University Press, 2005.
Mackenzie, Louisa. "La masculinité itinérante du *Journal de voyage* de Montaigne." In *Théories critiques et littérature française. Mélanges offerts à Laurence D. Kritzman*, edited by David LaGuardia and Todd Reeser, 155–175. Paris: Garnier, 2020.
Malabou, Catherine. *Plasticity at the Dusk of Writing: Dialectic, Destruction, and Deconstruction*. Translated by Carolyn Shread. New York: Columbia University Press, 2010.
Mandrou, Robert. *La France au XVIIe et XVIIIe siècles*. Paris: Presses Universitaires de France, 1967.
Margócsy, Dániel. "The Camel's Head: Representing Unseen Animals in Sixteenth-Century Europe." *Netherlands Yearbook of Art History* 61 (January 2011): 63–85.
Martel, Marie-Thérèse de. "La Mission de Jean Yversen à la Porte du Grand Seigneur (mai–juin 1559)." *Revue d'histoire diplomatique* 93 (1983): 5–53.

Marushiakova, Elena, and Vesselin Popov. *Gypsies in the Ottoman Empire*. Hatfield: University of Hertfordshire Press/Centre de recherches tsiganes, 2001.

Massing, Jean Michel. "Black African Slaves in Renaissance Spanish Literature." In *Black Africans in Renaissance Europe*, edited by T. F. Earle and K. J. P. Lowe, 48–69. Cambridge: Cambridge University Press, 2005.

Mastnak, Tomaz. *Crusading Peace: Christendom, the Muslim World and Western Political Order*. Berkeley: University of California Press, 2001.

McNay, Lois. "Agency." In *The Oxford Handbook of Feminist Theory*, edited by Lisa Disch and Mary Hawkesworth, 39–57. Oxford: Oxford University Press, 2016.

Ménager, Daniel. *L'Ange et l'ambassadeur. Diplomatie et théologie à la Renaissance*. Paris: Garnier, 2013.

Miglietti, Sara. "Climate Theory: An Invented Tradition?" In *Spreading Knowledge in a Changing World*, edited by Charles Burnett and Pedro Mantas-España, 205–224. Córdoba and London: UCO Press and the Warburg Institute, 2019.

Miller, Michelle. "Constrained Friendship: Rabelais and the Status of Friendship in Evangelical Humanism." *Renaissance and Reformation/Renaissance et Réforme* 33, no. 1 (Winter 2010): 31–54.

Morrison, Toni. *Playing in the Dark: Whiteness and the Literary Imagination*. Cambridge, Mass.: Harvard University Press, 1992.

Mukerji, Chandra. "Costume and Character in the Ottoman Empire: Dress as Social Agent in Nicolay's *Navigations*." In *Early Modern Things: Objects and Their Histories, 1500–1800*, edited by Paula Findlen, 151–169. London: Routledge, 2013.

Muñoz, José Esteban. *Cruising Utopia: The Then and There of Queer Futurity*. Sexual Cultures, 50. New York: New York University Press, 2019.

Nájera, Rafael. "Scholastic Philosophers on the Role of the Body in Knowledge." In *Embodiment: A History*. Edited by Justin E. H. Smith. Oxford: Oxford University Press, 2017.

Naya, Emmanuel. *Rabelais, une anthropologie humaniste des passions*. Paris: PUF, 1998.

Nealon, Jeffrey T. *Plant Theory: Biopower and Vegetable Life*. Stanford, Calif.: Stanford University Press, 2015.

Necipoğlu, Gülru. *The Age of Sinan: Architectural Culture in the Ottoman Empire*. London: Reaktion Books, 2005.

———. *Architecture, Ceremonial, and Power: The Topkapı Palace in the Fifteenth and Sixteenth Centuries*. Cambridge, Mass.: MIT Press, 1992.

———. "Süleyman the Magnificent and the Representation of Power in the Context of Ottoman-Hapsburg-Papal Rivalry." *The Art Bulletin* 71, no. 3 (September 1989): 401–427.

Noël, Érick, editor. *Dictionnaire des gens de couleur dans la France moderne. Paris et son basin*. Geneva: Droz, 2011.

———. *Dictionnaire des gens de couleur dans la France moderne. La Bretagne*. Geneva: Droz, 2013.

———. *Dictionnaire des gens de couleur dans la France moderne. Le midi*. Geneva: Droz, 2017.
Nussbaum, Arthur. *A Concise History of the Law of the Nations*. Revised Edition. New York: Macmillan, 1961.
Nutton, Vivian. "Epidemic Disease in a Humoral Environment: From *Airs, Waters, and Places* to the Renaissance." In *Holism in Ancient Medicine and Its Reception*, edited by Chiara Thumiger, 357–376. Leiden: Brill, 2021:
Olsthoorn, Johan. "Grotius and Pufendorf." In *The Cambridge Companion to Natural Law Ethics*, edited by Tom Angier, 51–70. Cambridge: Cambridge University Press, 2019.
O'Malley, John W. "The Council of Trent (1545–63) and Michelangelo's 'Last Judgment' (1541)." *American Philosophical Society* 156, no. 4 (December 2012): 388–397.
Painter, Nell Irvin. *The History of White People*. New York: W. W. Norton, 2011.
Paris, 1553: audaces et innovations poétiques. Colloque international organisé avec le concours de la Bibliothèque nationale de France (April 3–4, 2008). Audio recording, Bibliothèque nationale de France.
Peabody, Sue. *"There Are No Slaves in France": The Political Culture of Race and Slavery in the Ancien Régime*. Oxford: Oxford University Press, 1997.
Peirce, Leslie. *Empress of the East: How a European Slave Girl Became Queen of the Empire*. New York: Basic Books, 2017.
———. *The Imperial Harem: Women and Sovereignty in the Ottoman Empire*. Oxford: Oxford University Press, 1993.
———. *A Spectrum of Unfreedom: Captives and Slaves in the Ottoman Empire*. Budapest-New York: Central European University Press, 2021.
Peralta, Dan el-Padilla. "Barbarians Inside the Gate." Part I. *Eidolon* (November 9): 2015.
Petris, Loris. "Entre implication et distanciation: Pouvoir et écriture dans la correspondance du Cardinal du Bellay." *Seizième siècle* 6 (2010): 165–184.
Pirillo, Diego. *The Refugee-Diplomat: Venice, England, and the Reformation*. Ithaca, N.Y.: Cornell University Press, 2018.
Pomata, Gianna. "Observation Rising: Birth of an Epistemic Genre, 1500–1650." In *Histories of Scientific Observation*, edited by Lorraine Daston and Elizabeth Lunbeck, 45–80. Chicago: University of Chicago Press, 2011.
Pomian, Krzysztof. *Collections and Curiosities: Paris and Venice, 1500–1800*. Translated by Elizabeth Wiles-Portier. Cambridge: Polity Press, 1990.
Poumarède, Géraud. "La France et les barberesques: police des mers et relations internationales en Méditerranée (XVIᵉ–XVIIᵉ siècles)," *Revue d'histoire maritime* 4 (2005): 117–146
———. "Justifier l'injustifiable. L'aliance turque au miroir de la chrétienté." *Revue d'histoire diplomatique* 111 (1997): 216–246.
Prawer, Joshua. *The Crusaders' Kingdom: European Colonialism in the Middle Ages*. Essex, V.T.: Phoenix, 2001.

Randall, Michael. *The Gargantuan Polity: On the Individual and the Community in the French Renaissance*. Toronto: University of Toronto Press, 2008.
Rawles, Stephen, and Michael Andrew Screech, eds., *A New Rabelais Bibliography*. Geneva: Droz, 1987.
Reeser, Todd W. *Moderating Masculinity in Early Modern Culture*. Chapel Hill: University of North Carolina Press, 2006.
———. *Setting Plato Straight: Translating Ancient Sexuality in the Renaissance*. Chicago: University of Chicago Press, 2016.
Renouard, Ph. "Notes sur le Lymodin et les créanciers d'Étienne Jodelle." *Revue de l'histoire littéraire de la France* (November–December 1922): 484–488.
Rigolot, François. "Rabelais, Misogyny, and Christian Charity: Biblical Intertextuality and the Renaissance Crisis of Exemplarity." *PMLA* 109, no. 2 (March 1994): 225–237.
———. "Tolérance et condescendence dans la littérature francaise du XVIe siècle." *Bibliothèque d'humanisme et Renaissance* 62, no.1 (2001): 25–44.
Robertson, Kellie. *Nature Speaks: Medieval Literature and Aristotelian Philosophy*. Philadelphia: University of Pennsylvania Press, 2017.
Rollet, Jacques, Introduction to *Des histoires orientales et principalement des Turkes ou Turchikes et Schitiques ou Tartaresques et aultres qui en sont descenduies oeuvre pour la tierce fois augmenté. Et divisé en trois parties avec l'indice des choses les plus memorables y continues par Guillaume Postel cosmopolite deux fois de là retourné et veritablement informé*, by Guillaume Postel. Modernized and edited by Jacques Rollet, ix–xxxiii. Istanbul: Isis, 1999. Facsimile edition of book printed in Paris, by Guillaume Caveillat, in 1575.
Rosolato, Guy. *Essais sur le symbolique*. Paris: Gallimard, 1969.
Rouillard, Clarence Dana. *The Turk in French Thought, History, and Literature (1520–1660)*. Paris: Boivin & cie, 1941.
Rouller, Dorine. "Le caméléon et le hérisson. cosmopolitisme et élargissement des horizons géographiques à la Renaissance (Montaigne, Charron)." *Bibliothèque d'Humanisme et Renaissance* 76, no. 3 (2015): 559–572.
Sameth, Mark. *The Name: The History of the Dual-Gendered Hebrew Name for God*. Eugene, Ore.: Wipf and Stock, 2020.
Schiebinger, Londa. *Plants and Empire: Colonial Bioprospecting in the Atlantic World*. Cambridge, Mass.: Harvard University Press, 2007.
Scott, Joan W. "Gender: A Useful Category of Historical Analysis." *The American Historical Review* 91, no. 5 (December 1986): 1053–1075.
Screech, Michael Andrew. "Some Further Reflections on the Dating of *Gargantua* (A) and (B) and on the Possible Meaning of Some of the Episodes." *Études rabelaisiennes* 13 (1976): 79–111.
———. "Some Reflexions on the Problem of Dating *Gargantua*, 'A' and 'B.'" *Études rabelaisiennes* 11 (1974): 9–56.
Sedgwick, Eve Kosofsky. *Between Men: English Literature and Male Homosocial Desire*. Thirteenth Anniversary Edition. New York: Columbia University Press, 2015.

Skilliter, Susan A. "Catherine de' Medici's Turkish Ladies in Waiting: A Dilemma in Franco-Ottoman Diplomatic Relations." *Turcica* 7 (1975): 188–204.
Smith, Ian. *Race and Rhetoric in the Renaissance: Barbarian Errors*. New York: Palgrave Macmillan, 2009.
Smith, Justin E. H. *Nature, Human Nature, and Human Difference: Race in Early Modern Philosophy*. Princeton, N.J.: Princeton University Press, 2015.
Szabari, Antónia. "The Crescent Moon and the Orb: Political Allegory and Cosmographic Detour in Gabriel Bounin's *La Soltane*." *French Forum* 40, no. 2–3 (2015): 1–16.
———. "Montaigne's Plants in Movement." In *Early Modern Écologies: Beyond English Ecocriticism*, edited by Pauline Goul and Phillip J. Usher, 263–285. Environmental Humanities in Pre-Modern Cultures, edited by Gillian Overing, Heide Estes, Philip Slavin, and Steve Mentz. Amsterdam: University of Amsterdam Press, 2020.
Thumiger, Chiara, ed. "Holism, Parts, Holes." In *Holism in Ancient Medicine and Its Reception*, edited by Chiara Thumiger, 25–46. Leiden: Brill, 2021.
Tillich, Paul. *The Courage to Be*. New Haven, Conn.: Yale University Press, 2000.
———. *Der Mut Zum Sein*. Stuttgart: Steingrüben, 1953.
Tinguely, Frédéric. "L'*alter sensus* des turqueries de Panurge." *Études rabelaisiennes* 42 (2003): 57–73.
———. *L'écriture du Levant à la Renaissance. Enquête sur les voyageurs français dans l'empire de Soliman le Magnifique*. Geneva: Droz, 2000.
———. "Éros géographe. Bertrand de la Borderie et le Discours du voyage de Constantinoble." In *La Génération Marot. Poètes français et néo-latins (1515–1550)*, Actes du Colloque International de Baltimore (December 5–7, 1996), edited by Gérard Defaux, 471–486. Paris: Champion, 1997.
Tolan, John V. *Saracens: Islam in the Medieval European Imagination*. New York: Columbia University Press, 2002.
Ursu, J. *La Politique orientale de François I, 1515–1547*. Paris: Honoré Champion, 1908.
Usher, Phillip John. *Exterranean: Extraction in the Humanist Anthropocene*. New York: Fordham University Press, 2019.
———. "Prudency and the Inefficacy of Language: Re-politicizing Jean de la Péruse's *Médée* (1553)." *Modern Language Notes* 128, no. 4 (September 2013): 868–880.
———. "Walking East in the Renaissance." In *French Global: A New Approach to Literary History*, edited by Christie McDonald and Susan Rubin Suleiman, 193–206. New York: Columbia University Press, 2010.
Van Orden, Kate. "Female *Complaintes*: Laments of Venus, Queens, and City Women in Late Sixteenth-Century France." *Renaissance Quarterly* 54, no. 3 (Autumn 2001): 801–845.
Veyne, Paul. "*Humanitas*: Romans and Non-Romans." In *The Romans*, edited by Andrea Giardina, translated by Lydia G. Cochrane, 342–369. Chicago: University of Chicago Press, 1993.
Vicary, Grace Q. "Visual Art as Social Data: The Renaissance Codpiece." *Cultural Anthropology* 4, no. 1 (February 1989): 3–25.

Vidal-Naquet, Pierre. *The Black Hunter: Forms of Thought and Forms of Society in the Greek World*. Translated by Andrew Szegedy-Maszak. Baltimore: Johns Hopkins University Press, 1986.

Vigarello, Georges. *Concepts of Cleanliness: Changing Attitudes in France since the Middle Ages*. Translated by Jean Birrell. Cambridge: Cambridge University Press, 1988.

Warner, Lyndan. *The Ideas of Man and Woman in Renaissance France: Print, Rhetoric, and Law*. London: Routledge, 2019.

Watbled, Ernest. "Aperçu sur les premiers consulats dans le Levant et les états barbaresques." *Revue africaine* 16 (1872): 20–34.

Weiss, Gillian Lee. *Captives and Corsairs: France and Slavery in the Early Modern Mediterranean*. Stanford, Calif.: Stanford University Press, 2011.

Welch, Ellen R. *A Theater of Diplomacy: International Relations and the Performing Arts in Early Modern France*. Philadelphia: University of Pennsylvania Press, 2017.

Whitaker, Cord J. *Black Metaphors: How Racism Emerged from Medieval Race-Thinking*. Philadelphia: University of Pennsylvania Press, 2019.

Whitford, David Mark. *The Curse of Ham in the Early Modern Era: The Bible and the Justifications of Slavery*, 101–102. Farnham: Ashgate, 2009.

Williams, Alison. "Sick Humour, Healthy Laughter: The Use of Medicine in Rabelais's Jokes." *The Modern Language Review* 101, no. 3 (July 2006): 671–681.

Williams, Wes. *Pilgrimage and Narrative in the French Renaissance: "The Undiscovered Country."* Oxford: Clarendon Press, 1999.

Wolfe, Jessica L. "The Cosmopolitanism of the Adages: The Classical and Christian Legacies of Erasmus' Hermeneutics of Accommodation." In *Cosmopolitanism and the Middle Ages*, edited by John M. Ganim, Shayne Aaron Legassie, 207–230. New York: Palgrave Macmillan, 2013.

Wolff, Larry. *Inventing Eastern Europe: The Map of Civilization on the Mind of the Enlightenment*. Stanford, Calif.: Stanford University Press, 1994.

Wynter, Sylvia. "Unsettling the Coloniality of Being/Power/Truth/Freedom: Towards the Human, After Man, Its Overrepresentation—An Argument." *CR: The New Centennial Review* 3, no. 3 (September 2003): 257–337.

Zechner, Carla. "The çengî: Descriptions of Professional Female Performers in French and Italian Accounts of Travel to the Middle East, 1550–1650." *L'Esprit créateur* 60, no. 1 (Spring 2020): 148–158.

Zerner, Henri. *The School of Fontainebleau: Etchings and Engravings*. New York: Harry N. Abrams, 1969.

Zinguer, Ilana. "Narration et témoignage dans les *Observations* . . . de Pierre Belon (1553)." *Nouvelle Revue du seizième siècle* 5 (1987): 25–40.

Zorach, Rebecca. *Blood, Milk, Ink, Gold: Abundance and Excess in the French Renaissance*. Chicago: University of Chicago Press, 2005.

———. "Desiring Things." In *Other Objects of Desire: Collectors and Collecting Queerly*. Edited by Michael Camille and Adrian Rifkin. Oxford: Blackwell, 2001.

Index

NOTE: The Ottoman Empire is sometimes abbreviated as "OE" in this index. Page numbers in *italics* denote illustrations.

Africa: Blackness as "shimmering," 53, 193, 202n15, 215n67; Blackness, Old World anxieties of the self and fascination with, 193; conditional acceptance of persons from, 39; facial tattoos of, branding of slaves confused with, 193–194, 248n16; humoral racism and the negative marking of black people, 35–36; Islamic conquest of, 200n2; North Africa (*see* Egypt; Ethiopians; French liberation of captive persons; piracy and privateering). *See also* black skin and racism; black skin associated with slavery; race

agency: animality of natural bodies and, 24–26, 49–51, 66, 185; of artists, 101, 104; disrespecting conventions of diplomacy as, 33, 138–139, 173; distributed agency, 8–9, 13–14, 21, 25–26, 103, 208nn73,75–76; diversity of the OE and dynamic scale of, 27; humanist metaphor of slavery as loss of, 11, 20–21, 26, 192, 206n57; and the humoral body, perfection of, 35, 39–40, 41; of the humoral body, through appetite, 5, 54–56, 64; of the humoral body, through mourning, 90–91, 92, 93–94, 101, 107, 118, 225–226n14; and importance of cultural models, 195; of matter as an excess both threatening and productive, 25–26, 208nn76–77; of nature, 63–65, 101, 112, 129; of the nonhuman, 8–9, 168; and plasticity of humanity, 26–27, 72, 170,

208nn78–79; tied to testing, 26, 79–81, 179; transgressive animality as, 21, 59. *See also* mixed agency of agents; moral agency

agents of the French crown: overview, 10–11; as crossing boundaries, 53–54, 58, 62, 71, 88, 142, 157; *curiosité* as term referencing spy activities of, 51, 71, 164; held captive by pirates, 72, 129, 138–139; numismatic spoils of, 110–114, *111*, *113*; and people on the margins of OE society as more "like" themselves, 71, 87, 142, 157; rivalries among, 129; skills required of, 164, 243n8. *See also* agency; diplomacy; Franco-Ottoman Alliance; French empire, projected by agents; humanism; mixed agency of agents; Ottoman Empire and agents of the French crown; spying and spies; travel writing about the Ottoman Empire; *specific people*

Agrippa von Nettesheim, Cornelius, 96

Ahmed, Sarah, *Queer Phenomenology: Orientations, Objects, Others*, xi, 69, 90, 157, 199–200n5

Aimars, Antoine Escalin des (aka Captain Polin de la Garge), 43–44, 213n42

Albany, Duke of (John Stuart), 46

alchemy: alchemical Jesus, 84; animality and, 25; mourning as, 91, 93–94, 118; and the nonbinary body, 84, 223–224n77; seeds and, 101, 228n41

Alençon, Duke of (Hercule-Francis, "le Monsieur"), 189, 247n1
Alexander VI (pope), 203n25
Alexandria, 105, 107, 112, 171
Algeria, 38, 138–139
Algiers, 138, 142, 162, 242n3
Americas. *See* Indigenous peoples of the Americas; New World
Amurat III (sultan), 190
Andrews, Walter G., *The Age of Beloveds*, 84, 223n75
androgyny. *See* queerness
animality: *anima mundi*, 24–25; and artistic agency, 101; Belon on the agency of (Bird-Man), 66–67, 68; and ceremonial rituals of submission in the OE, 173–174, 175; the Cynics and, 55–56, 57, 216n87; definition of, 63; gentleness as delicate dance with that of the other, 85; Grotius's natural voluntarism and transcendence of, 209–210n7; Jodelle's *Cléopâtre captive* as tying to race, 92, 97–99, 101, 104, 110; and modern subjectivity, 216n87; Montaigne's story of the young woman holding a calf, 168–170, 244n15; ontological bias of ancient Greek and Roman holism to, 24–25; and *physis*, 24; plasticity of the human and, 26–27, 49, 208–209nn78–79; Rabelais on the agency of, 49–51, 54, 59; as representation of conquering people, 232n99; and susceptibility of the will to pressure, 26; as term in the text, 24–25; transgressive, as resistance to loss of autonomy, 21, 59; and violence (Dufourmantelle), 244n15
animals: aping as metaphor, 211n25; envoy of Hayreddin Pasha bringing to Francis I, 43, 212n38; exotic animal handling, 62, 218n11; Francis I as taming, 61–62, 217n7; horses, 62, 179, 217–218nn8–9; as hunting companions with humans, 62, 77, 78, 161, 179, 217–218nn8–9; Montaigne on subjectivity (nobility) of, 178, 179, 180; "noble races" of, 62, 179, 180; in Rabelais, 38, 40, 52, 53, 54, 55; racial slurs of Muslim based in, 52–53, 215nn66–67; spirit attributed to, 63; as symbol of appetite, 38; as symbol of human mimicry, 38, 211n25; taming/domestication of, 61–62, 211n26. *See also* birds; dogs; lions
Anjou, Duke of (later Henri III), 17, 162, 173
antiquarianism, 112–114
anti-sensualist tradition: overview, 203n22; enslavement linked to the passions and desires of the body, 11, 20, 180, 184–185, 206n55; humanism and, 23–24; as not accounting for sensualist and moral claims of French agents, 12; sublimation of personal interest to the state, 11–12; susceptibility of the will to pressure, 26. *See also* Foucault, Michel
Antony and Cleopatra: and Egypt's conquest by the Roman Empire, 90; Jodelle's allegory, 108; in numismatic collections, 110–114, *111*, *113*; Plutarch's "Life of Antony," 77, 91–92, 96, 97, 106, 110; statue of Cleopatra, controversy on, 226n19. *See also* Jodelle, Étienne: *Cléopâtre captive*
aping, 211n25
appetite: agency of the humoral body through, 5, 54–56, 64; Belon and agencies of, 64, 69, 71; of the body, Orientalism and, 69, 71; as index for moral agency, 39, 41, 54–55; Rabelais's *Gargantua* and, 34, 38–39, 41, 172; Rabelais's *Pantagruel* and agencies of, 4, 5–8, 7, 51–55
Arabs ("Turks"): as colonizable people, 153; humoral racism of, 210n19; skin color of, 91, 106–107, 151–152, 241n109
Aragon, 38
Aramon, Gabriel de Luels d': as ambassador to the OE, 132–135, 137, 138, 139–141, 142, 232n92, 236nn29,34–35,39,42, 238nn61,68; appointed ambassador to the OE by Francis I, 43, 129, 130, 132; biographical information, 130; Nicolay's rivalry with, 130, 134, 154; Titian portrait of, 130, 132, 133
Argo, Jean, 115
Aristotle: analogical classification, 6; animality, 24, 25; birds, 219n24; duality of matter and form, 25, 34, 38, 62, 128, 208n77; enslavement to the body, 58; ethnic bias of, 8; human agency, 8, 9; legitimate political power, 39; medieval revival through Arabic commentaries, 218n13; physics of, 62–63, 77–78, 218nn13–14; subconscious acts, 8; wholeness and rationality as privileged in, 5. Works: *Nicomachian Ethics*, 8; *Peri psuchēs*, 24
Armagnac, Georges d,' 72, 129
Armenians, 153
art: aesthetic of privileging the natural over the artificial, 145–146; ambivalence about, as morally suspect as well as desirable, 146; both beautiful and difficult as expectation for, 110; the enjoyment of art as confirming the privileged status of those with access to it, 89–90, 157–159;

INDEX

the French and European male gaze and, 157, 242n120; lesbian desire, representation of, 155–157, 156, 242n120; transgressive yet conservative powers of, as symbolic glue of the state, 104. See also Fontainebleau art; Nicolay, Nicolas de, Les Quatre premiers livres des navigations et pérégrinations; nudity; prints (cheap reproductions)
Asad, Talal, 17
Aubert, Guillaume, "'The Blood of France'," 203–204n27
Aubigné, Agrippa d,' Les tragiques, 239n93
Auerbach, Erich, 243n6
Augustinian physics, 62
Avicenna, 227n38

Balkans: peoples of, as colonizable, 153–154, 241n115; as zone of rivalry with other empires, 152
barbarians: Nicolay's relentless narrative of the Ottomans as, 138, 139, 140, 141; as term, 137–138, 237n56
Barbarossa ("Red Beard"). See Hayreddin Pasha (Hayreddin Barbarossa)
Barkan, Leonard, 226n19
Barroux, Robert, 239n88
Barthe, Pascale, 53–54, 58, 215n72
Bartlett, Robert, 139
Bassano, Luigi, costume book of, 115
bathing culture: Belon on the OE, 79, 81–82, 222n65; European cultures with, 78, 79; Greek and Roman as basis of comparison of OE, 79; humoral medicine view of the skin and dangers of, 77–79; Palerne on the OE, 191–192; as pleasure, 79, 81–83; Postel on the OE, 81–82; Thevet on the OE, 79, 80, 81–82
Báthory, Stephen, 117, 163
beard: grooming of as Orientalist gesture adopted by French men, 79, 81, 118–119; as symbol of Ottoman male identity, 45
beauty: and moral agency (Montaigne), 176; skin color and racist norms of, 151–152, 192–193, 240n108
Belleau, Remy: as actor in Jodelle's Cléopâtre captive, 90, 94; Les pierres, 217n7; poems of, 103, 229n53
Belon, Pierre: overview, 60–61; agency sought by, 64–65; as agent, 61–62, 68–69, 72, 99; biographical information, 61, 72, 218n10; clothing of the OE worn by, 73–74, 75; on colonizable groups of people, 153–154, 241nn116-117; and community, desire for,

70, 72, 166; and the cosmopolitan turn, x–xi, 237n58; René du Bellay as patron of, 218n10; Gilles's conflict with, 129; as humanist "hero," x, 199n2; and the numismatic spoils for agents, 112; as Palerne influence, 189–190; and people on the margins of OE society as more "like" himself, 71, 87; as pirate captive, 72; on skin color and beauty norms, 151–152; as spy, 61, 71, 72, 220n43; on spying networks to protect against pirates, 71–72; utopian visions of, 61, 70–71, 127–128. Works: L'histoire de la nature des oyseaux, 61–63, 65, 67, 67–68, 77, 219n24; Observations, 64, 65, 99, 99–101, 112, 149, 153, 189, 211n26, 218n10; Voyage au Levant (modern edition of Observations), 220n43, 222n65, 227n35, 228nn39,41, 241nn116–117
—AS NATURAL HISTORIAN: ancient authorities, desire to correct, 65, 218n24; on appetitive bodies, 64, 69; on the bathing culture of OE, 79, 81–82, 222n65; on bird migration, 65–66, 219n24; birds, identification of Belon with, 66–67, 68, 69; on bird skeleton similarities with human, 66, 67; on civets, 211n26; on dervishes, 147–148, 149; on Egyptian drug "mummy," 100–101, 228n39; on Egyptian flora and fauna, 69, 101, 228n41; on Egyptian pyramids and Sphinx of Giza, 99–100, 227n35; on Francis I taming animals, 61–62, 65; on goshawks, 77, 78; on imitative rivalry of humans with animals, 64, 65; nature as a separate realm of autonomy and sovereignty, 62–64, 69, 70–71, 130, 218nn13–14; on nature's pleasure, 63–64, 70–71; on observation and the spirit of the observer, 65, 68–69; on observation as pleasure, 69–71; on peasants and relation with animals, 62, 64, 65; on pigeons used to send messages, 58, 217n94; as Rabelaisian project, 62; on the rock snail as figure of nature's pleasure, 70–71, 220n36; throwing bread in the river for Egyptian boys, 69–70; on transplanting of trees, 62; on women in the OE, 74, 75, 151–152
Bennassar, Bartolomé, 239n79
Bennassar, Lucile, 239n79
Bennett, Jane, 25, 208n73
Berbers, 38
Bernier, François, "The New Division of the Earth," 152, 202n16, 241n109
Béthencourt, Jean de, 38

birds: as automata, 219n23; aviary of Francis I, 61; "facial features" of humans as etymologically connected to, 77, 78; migration of, 65–66, 219n24; as noble hunting companions of humans, 62, 77, 78, 161; pigeons, 58, 59, 217n94; of prey, human imitative rivalry with, 64, 65; skeletons as similar to human, 66, 67; as undoing the binary of human and animal (Deleuze), 66, 67–68
Blackness: Old World anxieties of the self and fascination with, 193; as "shimmering," 53, 193, 202n15, 215n67
black skin and racism: beauty norms, 151–152, 192–193, 240n108; biblical "curse of Ham," 2, 200n2, 229–230n62; conflation of climate and temperament and, 106–107, 229–230nn62–3; conversion to Christianity as washing black person white, 247n67; the humoral body and marking of, 35–36; as marker of low status, 192–193; Thomas More and, 35–36; Old World anxieties of the self and, 193; Shakespearean references to, 200n7, 201n14; status of white skin as preferable, 152, 240n109. See also race; skin color
black skin associated with slavery: early modern Europe, 193; European slave trade and, 200n2; the Ham narrative and, 200n2; and hierarchizing of the plasticity of the human and the animal, 26–27, 208–209n79; in the Ottoman Empire, 192–193, 200n2. See also slavery; unfree persons in France
the body: control of, in ancient Greece, 207–208n71; noble spirit and, no longer tied to aristocracy (Nicolay), 128–129, 144–145; sōma, 49–50; suppleness of, as not contaminating the spirit, 161, 163, 167; testing of and care for, nobility as the product of (Montaigne), 175–180, 181–184. See also emotions; facial features; humoral body; nudity; pleasure; skin
Boétie, Étienne de la, De la servitude volontaire, 19–20, 167, 171, 180
Bomberg, Daniel, 84, 224n78
books, and spying, 237n54. See also print and printing
Borderie, Bertrand de la: overview, 60–61; as agent, 75, 221n54; Discours du voyage à Constantinoble, envoyé à une damoyselle françoyse ("The Story of a Voyage to Constantinoble, Epistle Sent to a Young French Lady"), 75–77, 221–222nn55–56, 58, 60
Bosnian delis, 142–145, 143, 147, 153
Boulle, Pierre, 3, 201n6, 241n109
Bounin, Gabriel, La Soltane (play), 174, 244–245n30
Bourg, Charles du, 19, 170–171
Bourg, Claude du, 19
Boutcher, Warren, 163, 242n5
Bouwsma, William, 82
Boyvin, René, Livre de la conquette de la toison d'or, 119, 119, 233nn108–109
Brahmans, 57
Brancher, Dominique, 201n8
Brantôme, seigneur of (Pierre Bourdeille), 44, 114, 115, 116–117, 213n42, 242n120
Braudel, Fernand, 236n39
Brazil, French colonies in, 139
Buda, Ottoman siege of, 212–213n39
Budé, Guillaume, 31, 32, 209n4; De contemptu rerum fortuitarum, 209n5
Bulgaria, peoples of, as colonizable, 153–154, 241n115
Buron, Emanuel, 226n20

Cairo, Ottoman conquest of, 14–15, 203n25, 204n32
Calhoun, Alison, 175–176
Canary Islands, 38
cannibals and cannibalism: by Christians in the Crusades, 238n65; Montaigne on, xi, 168, 183, 184, 223n72; origin of term, 54; as term of dietary transgression, 53–54; of Western melancholic masculinity, 223n72
Caribes, 54
Caron, Antoine: biographical information, 121, 233–234n3; drawing, 121–124, 122, 233–234nn3–5
Casala, Giancarlo, The Ottoman Age of Exploration, 203n25
Casas, Bartolomé de las, 12, 204n28
Castella, Henri, 60
Cateau-Cambrésis, Treaty of, 123, 125
Catherine of Aragon, 36, 45
Catholic Church: Council of Trent decree banning nude and lascivious print content, 124, 234n8; Index of Prohibited Books, 211–212n31; papal court and ceremonialism, 161. See also Christianity; French Catholicism; specific people
Céard, Jean, 29
censorship: of the Cynics, 55, 56, 57; Index of Prohibited Books, 211–212n31; of Rabelais, 211–212n31

ceremonial customs: molding the body to conform to, and the "spirit" remaining immutable, 161, 163, 167; the Ottoman Empire and importance of, 43, 44–45, 160–161, 173–174, 244n29; papal, 161; unfree persons and costumes featured in the French court, 18, 116–117, 233nn94,99. *See also* custom

Certeau, Michel de, 71, 83, 142, 220n39, 223n72

Chambord, Treaty of, 90

Champier, Symphorien, *Le fondement et origine des tiltres de noblesse*, 201n5

Charité, Claude la, 31, 209n5

charity, in Rabelais, 31. *See also* compassion

Charles IX: and cooling of the Franco-Ottoman Alliance, 125–126; copy of Nicolay's *Navigations et pérégrinations*, 157; Noailles as agent for, 162, 242n3; and Postel's universal empire, 224n84

Charles V (Holy Roman Emperor): assassination of Rincón and Fregoso, 50, 212–213n39; crown of, 103–104, 229n54; election of, 107; entry to Rome, 46; Francis I imprisoned by, 15, 22; Francis I's envoys promised safe conduct by, 50; the Franco-Ottoman Alliance and intention to counter the power of, 14, 15, 26, 43–44, 107–108, 132, 236n34. *See also* Holy Roman Empire; Spain

Charrière, Ernest, 162–163

Chen, Mel Y., 25

Chesneau, Jean, 129, 132, 236n42

Christian Cynicism. *See* Erasmus of Rotterdam, Desiderius

Christianity: *adiaphora* (applied to gestures and clothing), 161; conversion as washing black person white, 247n67; conversion of unfree Muslims to, 186–187; converts to Islam, 141, 142, 144, 147, 192, 239n79; dietary restrictions of, 7; early universalism of, 16; evangelical rule ("render onto Caesar"), 16; the Franco-Ottoman Alliance justified as protection of, 15, 17, 76, 123, 222n58; the immortal soul, 34; martyrdom, 54, 216n75; Montaine on reason of, as source of moderation and agency, 184, 185–186; natural law and, 16; rationality attributed to non-Christians, 16; spiritual countertradition of nonbinary sex as divine and human ideal, 82–83, 84–85, 224n78. *See also* Catholic Church; Christian narratives; compassion; Crusades; French Catholicism; medieval narratives; Middle Ages (European); Protestants

Christian Kabbalists, 82, 83, 84–85

Christian narratives: Adam and Eve, 2, 11, 128; androgyne Adam, 84, 223–224n77; Cain and Abel, 1, 2, 4, 5, 6, 10; gap between body and soul, 204n28; of God as "other," 22; Ham, 2, 200n2, 229–230n62; Noah, 2, 200n2; Samaritan parable, 22–23; Sara/Ishmael origin of "Saracen" as threat, 10, 202n19

Christian-Platonist rationale for Franco-Ottoman Alliance, 15, 17, 76, 123, 222n58

Cicero, 31, 73, 205n41, 211n25

Circassians, 202n18

classical Greek and Roman philosophy: Cicero, 31, 73, 205n41, 211n25; and control of the body, 207–208n71; eating and appetite as natural, 215n73; Epicureanism, 18, 25, 106, 209n5; Galen of Pergamon (Aelius Galenus), 34, 79, 210n19, 218n14; Hippocrates, 5, 25, 79; New World exploration and epistemological shift from authorities of, 218n14; ontological holism, 24–25; pre-Socratic hylozoism, 24–25, 228n41; Seneca, 18, 103; Sophists, 57, 58. *See also* Aristotle; classical mythology; Cynics/Cynicism; humoral body; Plato; Socrates; Stoics/Stoicism; *other specific people*

classical mythology: Aeneas, 178; Bacchus, 105, 118; Hercules, 100, 230–231n69; Jason and the Argonauts, 101–103, 108, 110, 230–231n69; Odysseus, 215n73; Pan, 24, 49–51, 148–149; Phoebus, 95, 105–106; Priapus, 2, 24, 148–149, 150; Prometheus, 103, 229n53; rape of Europa, 152; Ulysses, 135–136, 138, 144, 230–231n69; Venus, 237n50; Victory, 142. *See also* Medea

Clement VII (pope), 31, 43, 45, 229n54; in Caron drawing of Henri II's wedding, 121–123, 122; gift exchange with Francis I, 43, 121–122, 122, 233n2

Cleopatra. *See* Antony and Cleopatra; Jodelle, Étienne: *Cléopâtre captive* (play)

climate, conflation of temperament and skin color and, 106–107, 229–230nn62–3

clothing: androgynous gendering produced by, 87; Borderie as agent anxious about Levantine clothing, 75–77, 221–222nn55–56,58,60; the *braguette* (codpiece), 73, 87–88, 221n46, 222n60; breeches, 222n60; chastity belt, 88; costumes used in theater, 116, 231nn77–78; exotic costumes and unfree persons incorporated in the French court, 18, 232n94; French textile industry and demand for luxury, 240n97;

clothing *(continued)*
    as gendered privilege, 73, 75; livery of servants, 123, 234n5; mobility and agency granted agents in Levantine attire, 73–74, 75, 87, 194; Montaigne on, as consciously chosen self-representation, 182; Montaigne on, as custom and not a need, 181–182; Ottoman sartorial laws, agents satisfying, 73–74; as socially and legally codified, 73; travel writing not emphasizing changes in, 74; viewed as envelope for the body, 73, 78; women and veiling in the OE, 74–75, 157, 222n64; women of the OE and, 74–75, 87, 88. *See also* crowns; headpieces; headpieces— turbans; Nicolay, Nicolas de, *Les Quatre premiers livres des navigations et pérégrinations*
Code noir, 202n16, 203–204n27
Codignac, Michel de, 204n30
Cohen, Jeffrey Jerome, 201n10
Colbert, Jean-Baptiste, 237n54
collecting: of ambivalent objects of abundance, 146; numismatics and antiquarianism, 110–114, *111, 113*
colonialism: denigration of indigenous knowledge, 218n14; globalism of, and the Franco-Ottoman Alliance, 107–108; medieval Christian version, 16–17; multiple identities of colonized peoples, 141, 142, 154, 239n79; Old World anxieties of the self and reflexive fascination with Blackness, 193; studies of representation as project of, x, 199n3. *See also* French colonialism
Columbus, Christopher, 54
community (French): conformism in the *forum externum* and, 166, 243n10; and French individualism, 165–166; imperial fantasies of agents as stemming from desire for, 166; and private space, creation of, 166–167; rational model of the common good and Christian *universitas*, 41, 166
compassion: humanist argument for Muslim moral agency, 22–23; the king as "Compassioner-in-Chief," 22, 206–207n63
Condé, Prince of, 19, 177–178
Conley, Tom, 66, 219n23, 222n56
Constantinople, Ottoman conquest of, 10
Constantinou, Costas M., 238n66
Constant, Jean-Marie, 220n43
Cooper, Richard, 213n45
Corbett, Jean-Baptiste, 203–204n27
Corneille, Pierre, *Médée* (play), 232n97

cosmology, and animality, 25
cosmopolitanism: Cynic, 16, 23–24, 205nn41,44; early Christianity and, 16; Epicurean, 18; etymology of term, 23–24, 207n69; Roman, and integration vs. expulsion of specific groups, 16, 205n44; Stoic, 16, 18, 19, 174, 205n44
—FRENCH TURN TO: overview, x–xi, 199–200n5; aristocratic families employing non-French service people, 18, 116–117, 186–187; and the centralization and expansion of the French state, 17–18; and civilized rationality, failure of, 19; colonizing attitudes arising from, 17, 32, 126–128, 164–165, 194, 205n47; definition of, 126; and failure to create an inclusive polity for French Protestants, 18–19, 175; and the Franco-Ottoman Alliance, 15–16, 161; Montaigne and, x–xi, 24, 168, 180, 181, 245n47; and the New World, xi; Nicolay's totalizing universalist version of, 126–128, 138, 142, 144, 152, 179, 237n58; readers of travel writing not attuned to, 74; resistance to the Roman Empire as symbol in, 18, 95, 116; unfree persons and costumes featured in French court, 18, 116–117, 233nn94,99; universalist frame of, 16. *See also* theater; travel writing about the Ottoman Empire
Cotgrave, Randle, *Dictionarie of the French and English Tongues*, 235n20
Crates of Thebes, 205n41
Crouzet, Denis, 235n15, 240n104
Crowley, Martin, *Accidental Agents*, 208n73
crowns: diadem given to Cleopatra by Antony, 112; of Suleiman I, and rivalries, 103–104, 229n54. *See also* headpieces
Crusades: Christian brotherhood in blood, 139, 140–141, 238n65; and increased contact between Muslims and Christians, 205n45; and Muslims conceived as evil, 4, 10, 202–203n20; Rabelais as cutting across cultural boundaries drawn by, 6–7; as shifting the economic balance toward Europe, 16–17. *See also* Catholic Church; Christianity; medieval narratives; Middle Ages (European)
cultural relativism: Montaigne and, 168, 170, 185; "when in Rome" (Raemond), 161, 170
curiosity *(curiosité)*: and ennobling pleasure of observation, 69–70; as marker of cosmopolitan attitude, 164; as reference to spying, 51, 71, 164. *See also* spying and spies

custom: defined as synonym for political institutions and power, 167; gendered as feminine, 170; and the need for private space, 165–166; of Ottoman caravansaries, 165; Palerne and acceptance of differences in, 191–192; Raemond on the soul as uncontaminated by the body's submission to, 161, 163, 167; tyranny of (Montaigne), 167, 168–170, 181–184; violence of, gentleness as power to resist (Montaigne), 168–170, 244n15. See also ceremonial customs

Cynics/Cynicism: animality and, 55–56, 57, 216n87; asceticism of, 23–24, 55–57, 179; censorship and marginalization of, 55, 56, 57; cosmopolitanism of, 16, 23–24, 205nn41,44; dogs as model taken by, 55; Foucault on, 24, 55–57, 216nn80,87; humanist references to, 23–24; human needs as defined by animals, 56, 181; and the necessity of breaking laws and rules to discover the self, 56; paradox of, 56–57; Rabelais as referencing, 55, 58–59, 217n95; Renaissance revivals of, 57, 216n87, 217n95; self-as-other, 23; as speaking truth to power, 46; universalizing of, 56–57

dark skin. See black skin and racism; black skin associated with slavery; skin color
Davent, Léon ("Lyon Davent"): biographical information, 125; drawings for Nicolay's Navigations et pérégrinations, 125, 131, 143, 146–147, 148–149, 151, 155, 157–160, 158, 234nn10–12, 242n122
Davis, Natalie Zemon, 236n32, 246n62; The Gift in Sixteenth-Century France, 29, 209n1
Defaux, Gérard, 213n41; Pantagruel et les sophistes, 57, 212n32
De Groot, Alexander H., 204n32
Deleuze, Gilles, 66, 67–68
Demonet, Marie-Luce, 47, 49, 214n56
Derian, James der, 127, 235n19
dervishes: Belon on, 147–148; Montaigne on, 168, 183–184; Nicolay on, 124, 147–151, 148–149, 192, 240n99; Palerne on, 192; Postel on, 147, 240n101; universalist claims and, 24
Desan, Philippe, 164, 168, 243n8
Descartes, René, 34, 63, 66
Despret, Vinciane, Our Emotional Make-Up, 57
DeVun, Leah, 223–224n77
Diascorides, 218n14, 227n38
Diogenes Laertius, 24, 207n69

Diogenes the Cynic, 23, 24, 56, 57, 58–59, 148–149, 205n41, 217n95
diplomacy: anti-diplomatic attitude to, 127, 130, 134, 154, 235n19; "communication" as code word in, 22; European legal framework for autonomy of diplomats, 18–19, 206n52; French privileges inhering to the Franco-Ottoman Alliance, 17–18; immunity of ambassadors, 212–213n39; private and public lives of diplomats, 166–167, 243n11; sixteenth-century conflation of servitude with enslavement, 11, 19–22, 26, 187, 206n57; systematic collection of correspondence of, 237n54; theater as metaphor for, 171–172, 173; theater of, seventeenth-century, 45, 213n44. See also agents of the French crown; Franco-Ottoman Alliance; spying and spies; specific people
dogs: Cynics taking as model for human needs, 55; as noble hunting companions of humans, 62, 179, 180; in Rabelais, 40, 52, 53, 54, 55, 57; as slur against Muslims, 52–53, 215nn66–67; training of, 62, 217n8; as universal insult, 191. See also animality; animals
Dolu, François, 125
Dorat, Jean, 90
du Bellay, Guillaume, 49–51, 214nn48,57
du Bellay, Jean, 20, 21, 45–46, 214nn48,50
du Bellay, Joachim, x–xi, 20–21, 89, 171, 229n51; Antiquitez de Rome, 226n19
du Bellay, Martin, 50
du Bellay, René, 218n10
Duchêne, Roger, 117
Dudley, Henry, 134
Dufourmantelle, Anne, The Power of Gentleness, 85, 160, 169, 244n15
Dürer, Albrecht, Four Books on Proportion, 36, 37
Dutch Calvinist Church, 18–19
Dyer, Richard, White, 202n18

Eastern Christians, as colonizable people, 153–154, 241nn115,117
Eastern Europe: division of Europe into Western and, 152; peoples viewed as colonizable, 153–154; as zone of rivalry with other empires, 152
Edict of Nantes, 206–207n63
Edirne, 142
Egypt: Belon's description of flora and fauna of, 69, 101, 228n41; Belon's descriptions of ruins and mummification, 99–101, 227n35, 228n39; Belon's pleasure in

Egypt *(continued)*
throwing bread in the river for peasant boys, 69–70, 190; as destination of French agents, 90; Egyptomania of the Renaissance, 96–99, 98, 110, 226nn19,23; Franco-Egypt commercial agreement, 14–15, 90; mummification, mummies, and "mummy drug," 99, 100–101, 227–228nn38–40; Ottoman conquest of, 14; Palerne's description of, 190–194; pyramids of Giza, 99–100, 190–191, 227n29; religion of, and cosmopolitanism of the French crown, 18; religion of, in Jodelle's *Cléopâtre captive*, 95, 96–97; religion, suppression of, 96–97; Roman conquest of, 90; skin color of Egyptians, 151, 241n109; Sphinx of Giza, and copies, 100, 191, 227n35

Ehrman, Jean, 233–234nn3–4
Elizabeth I, 161, 189
Elliot, Matthew, 221n48
emotions: the anti-sensualist tradition linking lack of control of passions to metaphorical slavery, 11, 20, 180, 184–185, 206n55; Aristotle on the emotions as enslavement, 58; excessive, agency denied to (Montaigne), 178, 180, 184–185, 187; excessive, as barbarism (Nicolay), 138, 147–149, 151; freedom as product of moderation of, 184–185, 249n59; inconstancy of (Jodelle), 95, 105–106; Platonic view of the tripartite soul and control of, 57–58; Rabelais and boundary crossing of, 58. *See also* body, the; pleasure

empire. *See* colonialism; French colonialism; French empire; Holy Roman Empire; Ottoman Empire; Roman Empire
the Enlightenment, and Europe as civilized "West" and backward "East," 152
Epictetus, 23
Epicureanism, 18, 25, 106, 209n5
Erasmus of Rotterdam, Desiderius, 3–4, 23, 31, 57, 209n4, 211n25; "The Complaint of Peace," 215n63; "Handbook of the Christian Soldier," 23; tracts on the Turkish question, 52, 215n63; on war, self-defense as justified, 52, 215n63
Erickson, Peter, 201n14
erotic pleasure: in the artificial or overly material foreign, 146, 239n95; in combination with zealous moralizing as key to success of Nicolay's work, 124, 154; and construction of French masculinity, 136, 237n50; cuckolded husband, 157; erotic knowledge mixed with political knowledge, 135–136, 221n55, 229n51; images forbidden by the Catholic Church, 124, 234n8; triangulation with the reader, 154–155. *See also* queerness; sexual pleasure

Escalopier, François, 117
Estissac, Geoffroy d,' 46–47
Ethiopians, as term, 192. *See also* Africa; Blackness; black skin
European identity: the aquiline nose and, 77; Christian brotherhood of blood, 139, 140–141, 238n65; formation of, as ethnicization of Christianity, 139; moderation in, 246n59. *See also* Whiteness
exemplarity, logic of, 30–31, 75, 209nn4–5
existentialism, 55–56

facial features: the aquiline nose and European identity, 77; and the civilizing effect of countenance, 177–178; as humoral hardening, 77
Ferdinand (ruler of Spain), 224n84
Ficino, Marsilo, 92, 225n6
firearms, 128, 129
Foix, Germain Gaston de, 167
Fontainebleau art: aesthetic of privileging the natural over the artificial, 145–146; ambivalent objects of abundance, and desire to collect, 146, 239n95; engravings of interiors (Lyon Davent), 125; *Galérie d'Ulysse* (Primaticcio), 135–136, 135; lesbian desire in, 155; nudity in, 237n50. *See also* art
Fontainebleau, school of, 25–26, 119, 146
Forest, Jean de la, 15–16, 42, 43, 76, 82, 83, 86
Foucault, Michel: anti-sensualist genealogy of modernity, 11, 203n22, 206n55; on Belon's misidentification, 70; and biopower, 182, 202n16; on the Cynics, 24, 55–57, 216nn80,87
Francis I: animals tamed by, 61–62, 217n7; art commissioned by, 100; in Caron drawing of Henri II's wedding, 121–123, 122; crowns and, 103–104, 229n54; diplomatic relationship with Hayreddin Pasha, 43–44; diplomatic relationship with Sultan Suleiman I, 14–16; failed attempt to acquire title of "Holy Roman Emperor," 107; Hayreddin Pasha's gift of lion to, and re-gifted to Pope Clement VII, 43, 121–123; and iconography of the Argonauts, 230n69; imprisonment by Charles V, 15, 22; and the islands of Hyères as refuge for those outside the law, 47, 49, 214n56; and

the Knights of Malta, 139; and Primaticcio's *Galérie d'Ulysse*, 135; splitting military forces, 46; and the Stoic's natural reason, 15–16, 31; tithes received from the pope, 46. *See also* Franco-Ottoman Alliance; French crown
Francis II, 174
Franco-Ottoman Alliance: overview as realpolitik, 14; *ahidnâme* of (1536), 15, 83; arrows as symbol of military alliance, 132; captive OE women held in France during, 186–187; and the centralization of the French state, 17; ceremonial and ritual aspects, importance of, 43, 44–45, 160–161, 173–174, 244n29; consular outposts in OE, 125, 235n13; containment of Spain as motive for, 14, 15, 26, 43–44, 107–108, 132, 236n34; cooling of French enthusiasm for, 125; cooling of French enthusiasm for, Noailles's efforts to dissuade, 171–173; as coup d'état of the Valois kings, 172; diplomatic privileges of, 17–18; Franco-Egypt commercial agreement as legal precedent for, 14–15; as "friendship" ("amitié"), 42; history of commercial agreements preceding, 14–15, 204n32; joint military campaigns against Spain, 15, 43, 83, 132–134, 236n39; justified as community of compassion (with motive of conquering the OE), 22–23; justified as French self-defense, 14, 132; justified as protection of European Christianity (Christian-Platonist rationale), 15, 17, 76, 123, 222n58; justified via natural reason, 15–16, 31; the lion-gift as symbol of, 122–123; Ottoman–Venetian peace treaty, 173; Rabelais as referencing, 6–7, 42–43, 44, 45, 47, 213n44; renewals of, 15, 170–171, 190; the rights of French subjects due to, 15; trade as secondary concern of, 14, 204n30. *See also* French liberation of captive persons; gift economy
Franks (Western Christians), 74, 247n7
Freccero, Carla, 41, 88, 212n32
freedom: as acquired through death, 18, 92, 93–95, 104–105, 117; as internal vs. granted by law, 185; as mirrored in the unfreedom of others, 118–120, 126; as the product of moderated passions, 184–185, 249n59. *See also* libertines and libertine freedom; slavery as metaphor
free soil principle: overview, 26–27; Brantôme invoking, 114, 115, 116–117; civilization as signaled by, 115; exceptions to rule abolishing slavery, 115–116, 117, 186–187; galley slaves as exception to, 115; invoked to differentiate France from the OE or Spain, 116, 117; medieval origins of, 115, 231n89; prisoners of war as exception under, 115; serfs and, 115, 231n89. *See also* French liberation of captive persons; slavery; unfree persons in France
Fregoso, Cesar, 50
French Catholicism: Henri III's devotion to penitential rituals, 184; Montaigne's respect and loyalty to the institution of, 167–168; Nicolay's ideology of colonial mission of, 127–128, 235n20. *See also* Christianity; French civil wars (Wars of Religion); French Protestants
French civil wars (Wars of Religion): overview, 165, 235n15; as context of Nicolay's *Navigations et pérégrinations*, 125–126, 151, 235n15; and cooling of the Franco-Ottoman Alliance, 124–126; Lescalopier's disappointment with French institutional inability to resolve, 165; Malcontents as faction in, 165, 189; Massacre of St. Bartholomew's Day, 18, 165, 172–173, 175; the Massacre as coup d'état of the Valois kings, 172; Noailles on Ottoman perception of, 172, 173; and vulnerability of agents, 99, 172, 175, 176
French colonialism: agents as seeing peoples as colonizable, 126, 152–154, 241nn115–117; centralized policies of cultural and religious assimilation, 203–204n27; *Code noir*, 202n16, 203–204n27; cosmopolitanism as giving rise to colonizing attitudes, 17, 32, 126–128, 164–165, 194, 205n47; French cultural superiority rhetoric, 127, 235n21; Nicolay as training the inner eye of the reader to see the world as colonizable, 13, 145, 146–147, 152–155, 157–159, 195; Nicolay on the human as colonizer, 128; Nicolay's ideology of Catholic mission of, 127–128, 235n20; Old World anxieties of the self and appetite for, 1, 27, 193, 194–195; spying as opening the New World to, 194–195. *See also* French Empire; Indigenous peoples of the Americas; New World
French crown: increasing absolutism of, 21; as increasingly self-defined as Christian, 17; loyalty to, moral value of, 104; loyalty to the royal person required of agents, 43, 161, 162, 164, 166–168, 167, 171, 174–175; "pleasure of," and absolute right, 63, 70;

French crown (continued)
realpolitik of, 14, 125, 171; as relying on Platonic and Christian notions of transcendence, 14; unfree persons and costumes featured in ceremonies of, 18, 116–117, 233nn94,99. See also agents of the French crown; cosmopolitanism—French turn to; diplomacy; Fontainebleau art; Francis I; Franco-Ottoman Alliance; French colonialism; French empire; French liberation of captive persons; Henri II; nobility; spying and spies; *specific people, places, and events*

French empire: overview, xi; the crown as projecting, 107–108; liberation of captive persons as state-building method and rationale for, 17, 18, 114, 115, 116, 205n20; natural historians as destructive agents of, 64. See also French colonialism
—PROJECTED BY AGENTS: overview, xi–xii; agency of agents as aided in, 164; agency of readers and, 165; barbarian/civilized narrative and, 137–138; belief that France was destined to conquer the OE, 23, 85, 86, 88, 107, 108–110, 164, 207n65, 224n84; conquerable, colonizable groups of people and, 126, 152–154, 241nn115–117; French cultural superiority and, 127–128, 235n21; French individualism and community and, 166; gentleness and, 34, 85, 126–127; the Holy Roman Empire as object of, 95, 107–108; as imitative rivalry with the OE, 152–154; shift to the OE as object of, 107–108

French language: *captif*, 116, 118; *chétif*, 118; *douceur*, 85; *esclave*, 21, 116, 206n57; *esclaver*, 118, 233n107

French liberation of captive persons: cooling of the Franco-Ottoman Alliance and intensification of efforts for, 125, 154, 235n14; as expression of Christian charity and protection of Christianity, 17, 114; as Franco-Ottoman Alliance agreement, 17, 115, 232n92; Franco-Ottoman Alliance violations, 232n92; Noailles and, 162, 242n13; population growth due to, 115; *racheter* (buy back) as term for, 154; as routine duty of French diplomats, 115; selective politics of as reinforcing French identity, 154; as state-building method and rationale for empire, 17, 18, 114, 115, 116, 205n20; unfree status of liberated persons, 116–117. See also free soil principle; slavery; unfree persons in France

French Protestants: and Boétie's *De la servitude volontaire*, 19; Calvinists, 18; "Conjuration of Amboise," 174; cosmopolitanism as failing to create an inclusive polity for, 18–19; diplomatic missions of, 19, 173–174; the king as "Compassioner-in-Chief" as failing to include, 206–207n63; Moldavian settlement of, proposal for, 17–18, 19; Montaigne and association with, 167–168; Rabelais appropriated by, 40–41, 211–212n31; repression against, 17, 184; and selective liberation of captives in the OE, 154. See also French civil wars (Wars of Religion)

French studies (sixteenth-century), and distinction between modern and sixteenth-century notions of "race," ix–x

Fresne-Canaye, Philippe du, 19, 173–175

Fumel, François de, 99

Fumurescu, Alin, 166, 243n10

Galen of Pergamon (Aelius Galenus), 34, 79, 210n19, 218n14. See also humoral body

Garde, Baron de la, 134

Gellard, Matthieu, 171

gender: assignment of roles in theater, 225–226n14; clothing flexibility as privilege of, 73, 75; the feminine, masculinity defined by the appropriation and effacement of, 170; mobility as privilege of, 185, 246n62; as signifying relationships of power, 214n61. See also masculinity; queerness; women

Genoa: French claim on, 14; privateers and merchants, 38

Gentili, Alberico, 18

gentleness: animality and, 85, 244n15; etymology of term, 85; kindness in animal training, discovery of, 217n8; as power to resist violence of custom (Montaigne), 168–170, 244n15; and projection of French Empire by agents, 34, 85, 126–127; and projection of superior agency, 60–61; as virtue, 22

geography: conflation of climate, temperament, and skin color, 106–107, 229–230nn62–3; in medieval racializing narratives, 11

Georgijević, Bartolomej, 237n58

German bathing culture, 78, 79

German Protestants, 19, 90

German racial "science," 202n18

Germigny, Jacques de, 190

gift economy: animals in, as province of ruling elites, 62; d'Aramon as ambassador

and, 132, 137, 138, 140; Francis I exchange with Pope Clement II, 43, 121–122, 122, 233n2; and the Franco-Ottoman Alliance, generally, 44, 132, 137, 138, 236n32; Hayreddin Pasha's gift of lion to Francis I, 43, 121–123; and the Indigenous peoples of the Americas, 236n32; interpretation of Rabelais in terms of, 29, 209n1; Nicolay on, 137, 138, 140
Gilles, Pierre, 129–130, 132, 175
Ginés de Sepúlveda, Juan, 204n28
Giovio, Paoblo, 230n67
God: as androgyne, 82–83, 84–85, 223–224nn77–78; as other, 22
Gohory, Jacques, 109n109
Goldenberg, David M., 200n2
Gomez-Géraud, Christine, 125, 236nn29,35
Goul, Pauline, 58, 217n95
Grandchamp, Guillaume de, 19, 170–171
Greece, ancient: barbarians (non-Greeks), 137, 237n56; bathing culture, 79; funeral practices, 99; gentleness associated with civilization, 85; homosexuality in, 184; Montaigne referencing, 182, 184; and skin color, 202n18. See also classical Greek and Roman philosophy; classical mythology; Roman Empire
Greek Orthodox people, as colonizable, 153, 241n117
Grélois, Jean-Pierre, 129
Grodecki, Catherine, 234nn10–11
Grotius, Hugo, 18, 209–210n7; "On the Law of War and Peace," 31
Gruzinski, Serge, 24, 180–181
Guise, Duke of (François de Lorraine II), 90, 114, 116–117
Guise, Duke of (Henri), 170

Habib, Imtiaz, 35–36, 117
hadiths, mocking citations of, 83, 223n71
Hall, Kim E., 201n14
Hampton, Timothy: *Fictions of Embassy*, 166–167, 206n52, 243n11; *Literature and Nation*, 52, 53, 215n62; *Writing from History*, 209n4, 239n93
Hapsburgs. See Spain
Haraway, Donna, 25
Hasan Pasha, 134, 138, 238n61
Haseki Hürrem Sultan (aka Roxelana), 155, 241–242n118
Hatun, Humā, 186–187
Hayreddin Pasha (Hayreddin Barbarossa), 15, 42–45, 46–47, 48; lion as gift to Francis I, 43, 121–123

headpieces: adventurer's hat appropriate for the OE (Postel), 87; Bacchic garland as preferred adornment (Ronsard), 118; Sufi ("Sophy"), as sign of humility (Nicolay), 245n31. See also clothing; crowns
—TURBANS: among exotic costumes worn in the French court, 232n94; disparaged as "Oriental Excess," 112; as prop for Orientalist self-fashioning, 194; as prop in French theater, 116; used for cross-dressing (Postel), 83–84; wear of prohibited to Christians in OE (Palerne), 194, 248n17; white color authorized only for Muslims in OE, 221n48
Helgeson, James, 243n6
Heng, Geraldine, *The Invention of Race in the European Middle Ages*, 9–10, 39, 201n14, 202n19, 215n66, 216n75, 230n65, 238n65
Henriët, Henk, 5, 6
Henri II: and d'Aramon's attempts for a joint military campaign with the OE, 132–134, 140–141; death of, 123; exotic costume spectacles and, 232n94; failure to pay his agents, 129, 134236n42; *impresa* of, 108, 230n67; Jodelle's works addressed to, 90, 95, 108–110, 109; and the Knights of Malta, 139; and Metz, 90; Postel's appeal to, 84; repression of French Protestants, 17; and trade, 204n30; wedding of, Caron drawing depicting, 121–124, 122, 233–234nn3–5
Henri III, 184
Henri IV (formerly king of Navarre), 167–168, 173, 175, 240n97
Henry III (Castilian king), 38
Henry VIII, 45, 134
hermaphrodites. See queerness
Hermes Trismegistos, 96
heroism tropes, 144, 239n93
Hesiod, 53
Hippocrates, 5, 25, 79. See also humoral body
Hitchcock, Alfred, *The Birds*, 67
Hock, Jessie, 103, 217n7, 229nn51–53
Hoffman, George, 246n54
Holmes, Brooke, 207–208n71
Holy Roman Empire: Francis I's failed attempt to acquire title, 107; the Franco-Ottoman Alliance and turn from, 107–108; humanist attacks on, via critiques of ethnocentrism and imperialism, 14; medieval universalism as basis of, 107; projection of French conquest of, 95, 107–108. See also Charles V (Holy Roman Emperor); Spain

Homedes y Coscón, Juan de, 139, 140
Homer, 23, 35, 53
homosexuality: homosociality and, 212n33; lesbian desire, representation of, 155–157, 156, 242n120; Montaigne as rejecting, 184
homosociality (male bonding): autonomous agency as residing in, 184, 185, 246n62; in construction of French masculinity, 136; exclusion and control of women and, 41–42, 185–186; and homosexuality, 212n33; Rabelais and, vs. the law, 32–33, 41–42, 212nn32–33; triangulation of erotic desire and competition in, 151, 154–155
Horapollon, *Hieroglyphica*, 96, 97, 98, 226n23
horses, 62, 179, 217–218nn8–9
Hotman, François, 167
humanism: the anti-sensualist tradition and, 23–24; and the critique of imperialism, 14; Egyptomania and, 96–99, 98, 110, 226nn19,23; the Ham narrative and, 200n2; heroic narratives of, x, 199n2; male bias ("manism") of, x; and man as the measure of all things, x; Thomas More and negative marking of black bodies, 35–36; overrepresentation of Man (Wynter, "Man 2"), 11–12; pigmy references and humoral racism in, 35–36, 37; and slavery as metaphor for loss of autonomy, 11, 20–21, 26, 192, 206n57; spy culture and turn from the erudition of, 137, 138, 237n34; and the Stoic critique of ethnocentrism, 14; and sublimation of personal interests to the interests of the state, 11–12. *See also* cosmopolitanism—French turn to; universalist claims of humanism
humanity (*humanitas*): critique of imperialism in the name of, 14; defined as colonizer, 128; definition of, 16; exclusion of those deemed without virtue, 16; the Franco-Ottoman Alliance justified in terms of, 15–16. *See also* cosmopolitanism
humoral body: overview, 5; agency achieved via perfection of, 35, 39–40, 41; agency through appetites of, 54–56, 64; agency through ritualized mourning by, 90–91, 92, 93–94, 101, 107, 118, 225–226n14; conflation of climate, temperament, and skin color, 106, 230n63; control of the body, 207–208n71; French male bodies as privileged, 35, 39–40; Hippocratic-Galenic model, 5, 25; implicit hierarchy of, 38; of noble animals, 63; of the observer, 65; proportionate vs. disproportionate bodies, 5, 8, 10, 36; and purging of the body, 35; quintessence, 5–6, 35, 40; in Rabelais, 5, 8, 10, 35–36, 39–40, 41; Rabelais and knowledge of, 34–36, 49, 210n13; the skin as hardening of the humors, 77; the skin as porous and dangerously open, clothing as protection for, 77–79, 181; and the soul, 34. *See also* humoral racism

humoral racism: Arabic, 210n19; in Dürer, 36, 37; in More, 35–36; pigmy references and the negative marking of black people, 35–36; Rabelais and, 35–36, 39
Hungary, 15, 212–213n39, 222n58; slave girl in Tripoli market, 124, 151, 152, 154, 155
Hyères islands, 47, 49, 214n56

Ibbet, Katherine, 206n63
Ibrahim Pasha, 43, 212–213n39
Iman Jackson, Zakiyyah, *Becoming Human*, 26, 208–209n79
imitative rivalry: of agents seeking agency, 64–65; of humans with animals, 64, 65; in observation, 64; of the OE, projection of French Empire by agents as, 152–154; viewing peoples as colonizable, 145
Indigenous peoples of the Americas: gift economy and, 236n32; knowledge of, 218n14; labeled "barbarians," 237n56; labeled "cannibals," 53, 54; "savage" as term for, 51; status in the Spanish Empire, 12, 204n28; universalizing European fantasies of, 24. *See also* New World
individualism (French): and *forum internum/forum externum* distinction, 166; and the need for private space, 165–166. *See also* community (French)
Ioannes Annius of Viterbo, 229–230n62
Isis, temple of, 96–97
Islam: Christian converts to, 141, 142, 144, 147, 192, 239n79; Nicolay's condemnation of, 147; Postel's syncretic mysticism and, 82; Western tradition of studying via derisive stereotypes, 83, 86, 223n71. *See also* Muslims
Isom-Verhaaren, Christine, 220n43

Jensen, De Lamar, 14
Jerusalem, 15
Jews: as colonizable people, 153, 154, 241n116; expulsion from Rome, 205n44; and Ottoman apparel laws, 116n116; in the Ottoman Empire, 74, 75, 116n116, 171; piracy and the slave trade and, 38; racialization of, 10; in the Samaritan fable, 22
Jodelle, Étienne: agency of artists/agents advanced by, 89–91, 94, 95, 104–105, 108, 110, 112, 119–120; and the cosmopolitan

turn, x–xi; "écriture rapportée" phrasing of, 95, 226n20; Henri II addressed in works of, 90, 95, 108–110, 109; poetry as symbolic glue of political regimes, 104; projection of French conquest of the Holy Roman Empire, 95, 108; and projection of French conquest of the OE, 90, 104, 107, 108, 109, 110. Works: Antony and Cleopatra allegory, 108; city of Paris commission (*mascarades* and allegories), 108–110, 112, 231nn73–74,77–78; Jason and Medea allegory, 108, 110; *Recueil des inscriptions*, 108, 109, 110, 112

— *Cléopâtre captive* (play): overview, 13, 89–91; agency of artists advanced in, 90–91, 94, 104–105; and agency of the humoral body through ritualized mourning, 90–91, 92, 93–94, 101, 107, 118, 225–226n14; alchemy in, 91, 93–94, 118; animacy of Cleopatra as serpent-like quality, 92, 97–99, 101, 104, 110; as art, 89–90, 95, 104, 110; and the artist-artisan's place in the new political equilibrium, 103–104; the audience as socially and personally elevated by, 89; Bacchic celebration following productions (cast party), 105; *captive* as pejorative term in title, 118; captive persons featured in, 114–115, 116, 117–119; as directing the Western male gaze toward the Orient, 104; Egyptian cult of the Renaissance and, 96–99, 98, 110, 226nn19,23; Egyptian religion evoked in, 95, 96–97; as first classical tragedy in France, 90; freedom acquired through death, 18, 92, 93–95, 104–105, 117; freedom as mirrored in the unfreedom of others, 118–119; Greek religion evoked in, 95; Henri II addressed in, 95, 108; inconstancy of passion in, 95, 105–106; magic in, 91, 92, 96, 225n6; Medea references in, 102, 106, 107, 118; as Orientalist play, 90–91, 104, 105–107; Péruse's *Médée* as mutually referencing and commenting with, 103; pity toward the unfree woman, 118; plot of, 91–95, 225–226nn14,16; Plutarch's "Life of Antony" as basis of, 77, 91–92, 96, 97, 106, 110; productions of, 89–90; projection of French conquest of the Holy Roman Empire in, 95, 164; projection of French conquest of the OE in, 90, 104, 107, 108, 109; skin color evoked in conjunction with captivity, 116; the Stoics referenced in, 95; *translatio imperii* staged in, 95, 108; whitening of Cleopatra, 91, 105, 106–107, 151

John Sigismund Zápolya (Transylvanian prince), 19, 212–213n39
Jones, Ann Rosalind, and Peter Stallybrass, *Renaissance Clothing and the Materials of Memory*, 123, 234n5
Jouanna, Arlette, 3, 200–201n4
Julius II (pope), 226n19

Kalpaklı, Mehmet, *The Age of Beloveds*, 84, 223n75
Karamians, 153
Keller, Marcus, 125–126
Klemettilä, Hannele, 217n8
Knights of St. John, 38, 133, 139, 140–141, 142, 186, 238n66

Lacore-Martin, Emmanuelle, 34
Latour, Bruno, 25, 208n73; articulation, 12–13, 70–71, 72
Leal, Pedro Germano, 226n23
Lebègue, Raymond, 228n42, 232n96
Leonardo da Vinci, 121, 233n2
Leo X (pope), 226n19
Lepanto, battle of, 162, 171, 172
Le Pois, Antoine, *Discours sur les medalles*, 112–114, 113, 194
lesbian desire, representation of, 155–157, 156, 242n120
Lescalopier, Pierre, 163–164, 165, 243n7
Lestringant, Frank, 227n29
liberation of captives. *See* French liberation of captive persons
libertines and libertine freedom: René Boyvin's image of Medea as spectacle of, 119–120, 120; exclusion of non-French, non-White, female, and non-Christian subjects from, 119–120; "Family of Love" spiritual sect, 233n109; individualist *forum internum* as basis of, 166; Rabelais appropriated by, 40–41, 211–212n31
Linnaeus, Carl, *Systema naturae*, 65
lions: in Caron's drawing of wedding of Henri II, 121, 122, 123, 234n4; Hayreddin Pasha's gift to Francis I, and regift of to Pope Clement VII, 43, 121–123; as symbol of the Franco-Ottoman Alliance, 122–123; tamed by Francis I, 61
literary studies (sixteenth-century), distinction made between modern and sixteenth-century notions of "race," ix–x, xii, 200n7
Longino, Michèle, 232n97, 235n21
Long, Kathleen P., 223–224n77
Loskoutoff, Yvan, 96
Louis X, 231n89
Louis XI, 63, 230n65

Louis XII, 204n32
love, "fascination," 92, 225n6
Lowe, Kate, 248n16
Lucretius, *De rerum natura*, 103, 229nn51–52

Mackenzie, Louisa, 170
McNay, Lois, 25
Mahdia, Spanish conquest of, 132, 133, 139–140, 236n34, 238n68
Malabou, Catherine, 26, 208n73, 208n78
Malcontents, 165, 189
male bonding. *See* homosociality
male gaze (French and European): cheap prints and access for, 157; economy of, 144–145; lesbian desire represented for, 157, 242n120; network of, and construction of masculinity, 136, 237n50
Malta, 38, 136, 139
Mandou, Robert, 21
Maraviglia (Milanese merchant), as secret envoy for Francis I, 243n11
Marc Antony. *See* Antony and Cleopatra
Marchant, Olivier, 208n73
Marchetti, Rafaele, 208n73
Marcus Aurelius, 205n41
Margócsy, Dániel, 70, 220n36
Marliani, Bartolomeo, *Topographia antiquae Romae*, 45
marriage: as lawful captivity of unfree women, 186–187; Montaigne on sexual immoderation in, 185–186; Montaigne on social equality as absent from, 184; Rabelais's Panurge character on, 71
Marseille, 235n13
Marushiakova, Elena, 241n115
masculinity: Aristotelian form as gendered masculine, 25; and bathing culture of the OE, 79, 81–82; the beard as sign of in France and OE, 79; clothing flexibility as privilege of, 73, 75; competitive (Postel), 87–88; and femininity, appropriation and effacement of, 170; moderation as gendered solely masculine, 184–185, 246n59; of Montaigne, 170, 184; Montaigne on Henri III's as failing, 184; the network of the male gaze and construction of, 136, 237n50; in Rabelais, 41, 51, 73; Western, melancholic mold of, 83, 223n72; and the "wild man" archetype, 148–149. *See also* gender; homosociality (male bonding); male gaze (French and European)
Massacre of Saint Bartholomew's Day, 18, 165, 172–173, 175
Al-Mas'udi, Bagdad, 210n19

materialism: matter as an excess both threatening and productive, 25–26, 208nn76–77; new, and ontological egalitarianism, 25, 26, 208n73; old, and ontological holism, 25–26
Matignon, Jacques Goyon de, 168, 177–178, 183
matter: Aristotelian duality of form and, 25, 34, 38, 62, 128, 208n77; as excess both threatening and productive, 25–26, 208nn76–77
Medea: Boyvin's images of as spectacle of libertine freedom, 119–120, 119; contemporary readings as outsider/woman of color, 116; Pierre Corneille's *Médée* (play), 232n97; Jodelle's allegory of Jason and, 108, 110; Jodelle's *Cléopâtre captive* and, 102, 106, 107, 118; in numismatic collections, 112; Seneca's play, 103. *See also* Péruse, Jean de la: *Médée* (play)
Medici, Ippolito de,' 121
Médicis, Catherine de: Caron drawing depicting wedding to Henri II, 121–124, 122, 233–234nn3–5; commissioning Nicolay as cartographer, 124; commissioning *Sophonisbe* (play), 18, 116, 232n96; female courtiers ("the flying squadron"), 186; and Francis II, attempt to kidnap, 174; lady-in-waiting (Renée de Rieux), 163; Noailles and, 171
medieval narratives: Rabelais as rewriting, 4, 6–8; study of Islam using derisive stereotypes, 83, 223n71; *translatio imperii*, 95, 108; universality claimed for European culture, 11, 107. *See also* medieval racializing narratives; Middle Ages (European)
medieval ontological order (Great Chain of Being), 8, 11
medieval racializing narratives: overview, 9–10, 201n14; Blackness as "shimmering," 53, 202n15, 215n67; conversion to Christianity and, 247n67; enslavement as legacy of Adamic fall, 11; geography and, 11; geopolitical boundaries and, 9; Muslim "Saracens" as incapable of moral agency, 4, 10, 52–53, 202–203nn19–20, 205n45, 215nn63,66–67; overrepresentation of Man (Wynter, "Man 1"), 11; race as strategic essentialism, 9; racial slurs of Muslims, 52–53, 215nn66–67; religion and, 2, 9, 200n2, 229–230n62; skin color and, 9
Medina, Pedro de, 141
Mehmed (Ottoman prince), 190
Mehmet Pasha, 163–164, 165

Menavino, Giovanni Antonio, *Trattato de' costumi et vita de' Turchi*, 147, 240n99
Merle, Alexandra, 62, 220n43
Merleau-Ponty, Maurice, 199–200n5
Metz, 90, 114, 225n3
Middle Ages (European): Aristotelian-Thomist physics, 62–63, 218–219nn13–14,16; birds as automata, 219n23; distinction between *forum internum* and *forum externum* (private conscience and social roles), 166; Franco-Egypt commercial agreement, 14–15, 90; history of commercial agreements preceding the Franco-Ottoman Alliance, 14–15; kindness in animal training, 217n8; the knight's representative power (*ius gentium*) as superceded by the spy, 141; "noble animals" and the ruling elites, 62, 217–218nn8–9; self-as-other, 39; White slavery ("luxury slaves"), 151, 152. *See also* Christianity; Crusades; humoral body; medieval narratives
Miglietti, Sara, 106, 230n63
Mignon, Jean, 155
mirrors, 192–193
mixed agency of agents: overview, xi; and the attraction of allying agency with human and nonhuman others, 9; conflation of service with enslavement and, 11, 19–22, 26, 187, 206n57; definition of, 164; the French civil wars and vulnerability of agents, 99, 172, 175, 176; lack of money, 129, 134, 236n42; loyalty to the royal person required of agents, 43, 161, 162, 164, 166–168, 167, 171, 174–175. *See also* ceremonial customs; custom; Ottoman laws
—ASSERTION OF AGENCY: devotion to service as, 183, 187; fictions of community and, 166–167; freedom as mirrored in the unfreedom of others, 118–120, 126; the fruits and richness of the Ottoman Empire as metaphor of, 128, 129–130; imitative rivalry and seeking of, 64–65; Jodelle aggrandizing the artist and agents, 89–91, 94, 95, 104–105, 108, 110, 112, 119–120; Montaigne and gentle resistance to institutions of monarchy, 168–179; by Nicolay, 126, 128–129, 130, 134, 136, 141–142, 154; by Noailles, 171, 172, 173, 187; others of the OE viewed as models for, 21–22, 27, 75, 120; by de la Péruse, 102, 104; projection of French empire and, 164; travel as test of, 26; viewing peoples as colonizable, 126, 152–154, 241nn115–117

modern notion of race: overview, ix; and miscegenation, prevention of, 202n16; and the plantation economy, 193, 202n16; sixteenth-century French studies and distinction between protocolonial notions and, ix–x; sixteenth-century literary studies and distinction between protocolonial notions and, ix–x, xii, 200n7; and Whiteness, reproduction of, 202n16
monarchy: absolute right of, 21, 63, 70; distributed sovereignty, 41. *See also* French crown
Monbart, Joséphine de, *Lettres Tahitiennes*, 1, 17, 205n47
Monluc, Blaise de, 132
Monluc, Jean de, 132
Montaigne, Michel de: overview, 13, 162; actors denied agency by, 180; Aeneas referenced by, 178; as agent and informant, 168, 170, 187; on animal (and plant) subjectivity (nobility), 178, 179, 180; on beauty, 176; biographical information, 163, 167–168, 176–178, 182; and the cannibal, xi, 168, 183, 184, 223n72; Catholicism, loyalty to the institution of, 167–168, 184; Christian reason as basis of moderation and agency, 184, 185–186; on clothing as consciously chosen self-representation, 182; on clothing as custom and not a need, 181–182; and the cosmopolitan turn, x–xi, 24, 168, 180, 181, 245n47; cultural relativism and, 168, 170, 185; and the dervish, 168, 183–184; on devotion as virtue, 183–184, 246n52; devotion of service by, 183, 187; as "distancologist" (measuring the distance to be traversed between self and other), 13, 178–180; femininity, appropriation and effacement of, 170; and the French civil wars, 168, 176; on the gentleman (*honnête homme*), 163, 180–181, 182, 183, 242n5; and gentleness as resistance to violence of custom, 169–170, 244n15; gestural language as agency, 176, 178, 184; and God as other, 22; on habit, 168–169; homosexuality as excessive passion, 184; as humanist "hero," x, 199n2; immoderation projected to deny agency to others, 178, 180, 184–185, 187; as loyal royalist, 168, 181; as loyal servant, 183; masculinity of, 170, 184; the "mob" denied agency by, 180; national ties subordinated to universal ones, 181; on nobility as product of testing of the body, 175–180, 181–184; not publishing de la Boétie, 19; nude

Montaigne, Michel de *(continued)*
paintings in home of, 246n54; on nudity as test conferring nobility, 27, 181–184; and private space of reflection (*arrière-boutique*), 162–163, 166–167, 170; and Protestants, connections with, 167–168; respect for institutions, 167–168; on risk of being a self, 182; and the self-as-other, 168; on "service" of authors to readers, 228–229n48; on the tyranny of custom, 167, 168–170, 181–184; universal persona/self-portrait metaphor of, 162–163, 167, 168, 242nn5–6; women denied agency by, 184–186. Works: *Journal de voyage*, 170; letters to Matignon, 177–178, 183
—*The Essays*: overview, 13, 162; "On Friendship," 184; "On Moderation," 184–186, 187; "On Physiognomy," 176–177; "On the Custom of Wearing Clothes," 181–184; "On the Inequality There Is between Us," 179; "On Vanity," 181
Moors: as colonizable people, 153; as term, 44
moral agency: of actors, as denied, 95, 180; ambiguity of, 32, 39, 126, 146; appetite as index for, 39, 41, 54–55; aristocrats calling on purity of blood to assert, 21; Aristotle as the basis of Western notions of, 8, 39; Aristotle's ethnic bias in, 8; in the ascetic tradition, 23, 203n22; beauty and (Montaigne), 176; the capacity for, extended to all bodies (Rabelais), 2, 4–5, 8–9, 10, 57–59; cosmopolitan, x, 16, 29; of Cynics, 55–57, 179, 217n95; distributed, 2; and embodiment, 2, 4–5, 8, 24, 36, 40; gentleness and civilized conduct and possibility of, 85, 127; gentleness as resistance to the violence of custom against, 168–170, 244n15; gestural language and, 124, 141, 176, 178, 184; humanist ontological hierarchy of, 8, 11; imperialism of, 88, 108–110, 126–128; loyalty to the crown, 104; nobility as the product of testing the body (Montaigne), 175–180, 181–184; numismatics and moral reflection, 112–114; personal bias elevated to, 57, 180; Plato's tripartite soul, 57–58; race entwined with, 1–6; universally claimed, xi, 57, 166–167, 174, 184; of women, as denied, 184–187, 246n62. *See also* agency; mixed agency of agents; Muslims—moral agency of; plasticity of the human
More, Thomas: model of nature, 62–63, 219n16; negative marking of black people, 35–36; *Utopia*, 36

Morocco, as pirate state, 38
Morrison, Toni: *Beloved*, 26; *Playing in the Dark*, on reflexive fascination with Blackness in classical American novels, 1, 193
Mothe, Charles de la, 90
Mother Giovanna (or Jeanne), Postel's syncretic mysticism of, 82–83, 84–85
Muhammad the Prophet: derisive depictions of, 86; mocking citations of hadiths, 83, 223n71; racial slurs of Muslims based on the name of, 52, 215n67
multiple identities: of colonized peoples in the OE, 141, 142, 154, 239n79; of Montaigne's gentleman, 180–181
Murad III (sultan), 186
Murat Aga, 141–142
Muret, Marc-Antoine, 89
Muslims: derided as pagan idolaters, 223n71; dietary restrictions on, 54, 55, 86; Rabelais and literalization of racial slurs against, 52–53, 215nn66–67; represented as seeking to transgress their own laws, 60. *See also* Islam
—MORAL AGENCY OF: medieval racializing narratives and denial of, 4, 10, 52–53, 202–203nn19–20, 205n45, 215nn63,66–67; Montaigne as crediting, 185, 246n52; Rabelais rewriting medieval racializing narratives of, 4, 6–8, 29, 32; the Samaritan fable and compassion narratives of, 22–23
Mustafa (Ottoman prince), 174–175, 244–245n30

naming: Christian names given to non-Christians, 184, 185–186; of unfree people, after their master or mistress, 186
Naples, 14, 134, 141
Nasi, Joseph, 171
Native Americans. *See* Indigenous peoples of the Americas
natural goodness, 31, 32, 33–34
natural historians: curiosity as ennobling of, 69–70; as destructive agents of empire, 64. *See also* Belon, Pierre—as natural historian
naturalism, and constructions of race, 202n16
natural law: and rationality attributed to non-Christians, 16; and the universalist Church, 16
natural needs of the body: Cynics as indexing to animal needs, 56, 181; Montaigne as indexing to animal needs, 181; the Ottoman law and customs as recognizing, 165

natural reason: the Franco-Ottoman Alliance justified via, 15–16, 31; Grotius on natural voluntarism in, 31–32, 209–210n7

nature: agency of, 63–65, 101, 112, 129; animal breeding and race, 179; Aristotelian-Thomist physics, 62–63, 218nn13–14, 219n16; Belon's conception as separate realm of autonomy and sovereignty, 62–64, 69, 70–71, 130, 218nn13–14; capacity of change through accidents, Rabelais and the plasticity of the physical world, 4–5, 9, 24, 130; Cartesian rationalist model, 63; control of, in statecraft, 61–62, 217n7; modern conception as "mere rationality," 218n14; Montaigne's articulation of the powers of the nude body and, 181–182; the OE as imaginary space of matter and, 27, 76, 129–130; Orientalism and, 69, 71

Naudé, Gabriel, 172, 237n54; *Considérations politiques sur les coups d'état*, 172

Navarre, king of (later Henri IV), 167–168, 173, 175, 240n97

Navigations et pérégrinations. See Nicolay, Nicolas de, *Les Quatre premiers livres des navigations et pérégrinations*

Naya, Emmanuel, 34

Nealon, Jeffrey T., *Plant Theory*, 216n87

new historicism, heroic narratives of early modern travel literature, x, 199n12

New World: overview, xi; and barbarian/civilized distinction, 237n56; exploration of, and epistemological shift from ancient authorities, 218n14; "great forest" myth, 24; Old World anxieties of the self and appetite for dreams of, 1, 27, 193, 194–195; self-reinvention and, 27; spying by Frenchmen as opening colonialism in, 194–195. *See also* colonialism; Indigenous peoples of the Americas

Nice, siege of, 15, 132, 134

Nicolay, Nicolas de: agency of the agent asserted by, 126, 128–129, 130, 134, 136, 141–142, 154; as agent and spy, 125, 128–129, 130, 134–142, 238–239nn78,88; antidiplomatic attitude to diplomacy, 127, 130, 134, 154, 235n19; biographical information, 125; capture by pirates, 138–139; as cartographer, 125, 141; as Catholic loyalist, 127; and the cosmopolitan turn, 23–24; "lawless space" of romance claimed by, 136; and people on the margins of OE society as more "like" himself, 157; Spanish language fluency of, 141; Ulysses referenced by, 135–136, 144

—*Les Quatre premiers livres des navigations et pérégrinations*: overview, 13, 124–125; and ambivalence about the bodies of others, 124–125; anatomical depictions as analogy with artistic images, 146–147; on Christian brotherhood in blood, 139, 140–141; on the colonial mission of French Catholicism, 127–128; the cooling of Franco-Ottoman Alliance as context of, 125; as costume book, 124; economy of the gaze and, 144–145; erotic and political desires for dominance as blended in, 135–136; erotic desire and the construction of French masculinity, 136; erotic pleasure combined with zealous moralizing as key to success of, 124, 154; etchings by "Lyon Davent"/Léon Davent, 125, 131, 143, 146–147, 148–149, 151, 155, 157–160, 158, 234nn10–12, 242n122; excessive passions as barbarism, 138, 147–149, 151; on the fallacy of trusting, 141, 238–239n78; on the gift economy, 137, 138, 140; hand-colored special copies of, 157–160, 158; images in, becoming stereotypes, 151; imitation of aristocratic culture of consumption, 126, 145, 146, 157, 240n97; Menavino as source for, 147, 240n99; noble spirit and body as no longer tied to the aristocracy, 126, 128–129, 144–145; noble status, as mirrored in the unfreedom of others, 126; the OE as relentlessly vilified in, 125–126, 137–138, 139, 140–141, 147, 153, 155; as Palerne influence, 189–190; on the pleasure of reading his book as ennobling, 146, 240n96; popularity of, 124; projection of exclusive Christian community in, 154; projection of French empire in, 126, 127–128, 152–154, 164–165; the Protestant-Catholic conflict as context of, 125–126, 151, 235n15; publication and editions of, 125, 234–235nn7,12; and reliance on non-French actors, 141–142, 239n88; Ronsard poem prefixing, 164–165, 243n9; skin color and racialization in, 125, 156, 157–159, 158; on the Sufis ("Sophies"), 174, 245n31; Terence's dictum of universalism of the human referenced by, 128, 142, 179; as training the inner eye of the reader to see a colonizable world, 13, 145, 146–147, 152–155, 157–159, 195; universalist cosmopolitanism and limitation of the human in, 126–128, 138, 142, 144, 152, 179, 237n58; women commodified in, 154–157

—illustrations and descriptions: dervishes, 124, 147–151, 148–149, 192, 240n99; grand Turkish lady, 154–155; Hungarian slave girl, 124, 151, 152, 154, 155; Slavic delis, 142–145, 143, 147, 153; Turkish cook, 130, 131; women on the island of Chios, 124; wrestlers, 157–159, 158

Noailles, François de: agency of the agent asserted by, 171, 172, 173, 187; as ambassador under Charles IX, 19, 160–161, 162–163, 164, 167, 170–173; household in Constantinople, 165; and the Massacre of St. Bartholomew's Day, 172–173; as not respecting Ottoman ceremonial etiquette, 160–161, 167; on spying, 163, 164; theater as diplomatic and political metaphor, 171–172, 173; as writer, 162–163

nobility: newly minted through royal grants, and "race" as bloodline and upbringing, 3, 201nn5–6; newly minted through royal grants, and tension with old nobility, 200–201n4; as no longer tied to the aristocracy (Nicolay), 126, 128–129, 144–145; old bloodlines and concept of "race," 2, 3, 21, 179, 200n4; as product of testing the body (Montaigne), 175–180, 181–184; purity of blood and agency of, 21

nonbinary gender. See queerness

North Africa. See Egypt; Ethiopians; French liberation of captive persons; piracy and privateering

nudity: as ambivalent, 123–124, 183–184; in Caron drawing, 123–124; Catholic Church's decree against lascivious content and, 124, 234n8; circulation of popular images in cheap print formats, 124; in Fontainebleau and private art collections, 124, 237n50, 246n54; Montaigne on, as conferring nobility, 27, 181–184; as noble artistic taste, 183–184, 246n54; of slaves in the market, 151. See also bathing culture

numismatics and the spoils of being an agent, 110–114, 111, 113

observation: overview as term, 65; Belon on, and the spirit of the observer, 65, 68–69; Belon on, as pleasure, 69–71; distance implied by, 65; and freedom and status, search for, 64–65; and the humoral body, 65; imitative rivalry in, 64

Octavian. See Jodelle: Cléopâtre captive; Plutarch: "Life of Antony"

ontological ambiguity, 9, 10

ontological egalitarianism, 25, 208n73

ontological holism, 24–25

Oporin, Jean (aka Johannes Herbst), 88

Orden, Kate van, "Female Complaintes," 225–226n14

Orientalism: and the appetitive body, 69, 71; and communities of compassion argument for the Franco-Ottoman Alliance, 23; decline of the Orient and projection of French conquest of the OE, 106, 107–108; of Erasmus, 23; Jodelle's Cléopâtre captive as first Orientalist play, 90–91, 104, 105–107; the Orient as extension of the Western self, 69, 118; de la Péruse's Médée as Orientalist play, 91, 104

Orthodox Christians, 74, 153, 241n117

Ottoman Empire: caravansary lodgings, 165; ceremonial customs, importance of, 43, 44–45, 160–161, 173–174, 244n29; conquest of Constantinople, 10; distinctions made between non-Muslims and Muslims in, 74; imperialistic dreams of conquest of (see French empire); the lion as symbol of, 122–123; multiple identities of colonized peoples in, 141, 142, 154, 239n79; Ottoman-Spanish peace treaty, 132, 238n68; Ottoman–Venice peace treaty, 173; polygynous dynasty tradition, 155; and the Roma and Sinti peoples, 153–154, 241n115; "savage" as term used to discuss, 51; status demonstrated by retinues of servants and slaves, 74–75; universalist claims of, 12, 203n25; as world in the world, xi. See also Franco-Ottoman Alliance; Hayreddin Pasha (Hayreddin Barbarossa); Ottoman laws; slavery—in the Ottoman Empire; Suleiman I (sultan); women—in the Ottoman Empire; specific people and places

Ottoman Empire and agents of the French crown: diversity in the OE and a dynamic scale of agency, 27; "greed" projected onto Ottomans, 26, 42, 55, 107, 138, 141, 145, 146, 171–172, 173; as imaginary space of nature and matter, 27, 76, 129–130; as representing a world of excess both threatening and productive, 26; richness of the fruits and natural resources of, as metaphor for the agency of agents, 128, 129–130; richness of, viewed as evidence of moral corruption, 138; as space of self-reinvention, 27; travel as test of agency, 26. See also clothing; mixed agency of agents; travel

Ottoman laws: agents and travelers perceiving as fair and applying equally to all, 165, 192; agents as generally bound to, 136; cleanliness and bathing, 79, 222nn64–65; Nicolay as rewriting himself into a "lawless space" of romance, 136; for non-Muslims, 191, 194, 221n48, 248n17; as regulating peaceful coexistence of different social groups, 165, 166; sartorial, agents and dressing for, 73–74; sartorial, and Jews, 241n116; travel writers and the "disembodied eye" perspective on, 69; women and clothing, 74–75

Painter, Nell Irvin, *The History of White People*, 151–152, 202n18
Palerne, Jean: biographical information, 189–190, 247n1; *Poesies*, signature with turban drawing in, 194, 248n17
—*Pérégrinations*: overview, 189–190; "Frank" defined by, 247n7; Nicolay, Belon, and other travel writers as influences on, 189–190; and Ottoman law, 191, 194, 248n17; the personal freedom of the French traveler as lens of, 190–192, 194, 195, 247n7; and racist norms of beauty, 192–193, 240n108; on the slave market in Cairo, 193–194
Paradin, Claude, 230n67
Paré, Ambroisé, 101, 114, 225n3, 228n40
Parmigianino, Francesco, 125
Pasquier, Étienne, 89, 90, 91, 115, 116, 117, 167, 228n42; *Recherches de la France*, 115
passions. *See* emotions
Paul III (pope), 15, 214n50
Pavia, battle of, 15, 22, 46, 107–108
Peabody, Sue, 115, 231n89
peasants: agency as male purview, 246n62; imitative rivalry with birds of prey, 64; Montaigne's story of the young woman holding a calf, 168–170, 244n15; taming and domestication of animals, 61, 62
Peirce, Leslie, 74, 241–242n118
Pellicier, Guillaume, 50, 130, 212–213n39
Penni, Luca, 125
people of color: absence from the archive, 116, 117, 186–187, 233n105; hypersexualization of, 13, 36, 55, 106–107, 203–204n27; as rendered invisible without agency, 117–118. *See also* black skin; skin color; unfree persons in France
Peralta, Dan el-Padilla, 205n44
Persia: defeat of the Ottomans, 46–47, 132; Montaigne on male sexual moderation in, 185; in Nicolay, 153
Péruse, Jean de la: as actor in Jodelle's *Cléopâtre captive*, 90, 94; biographical information, 91, 228n42; and poetry as symbolic glue of political regimes, 104
—*Médée* (play): overview, 13, 91; aggrandizement of the artist in, 102, 104; and the artist-artisan's place in the new political equilibrium, 103–104; captive persons featured in, 116, 118; Jodelle's *Cléopâtre captive* as mutually referencing and commenting with, 103; mirror in, 192–193; as Orientalist play, 91, 104; pity toward the unfree woman in, 104, 118; plot of, 101–103; projection of French conquest of the OE in, 104; script as unfinished at first performance, 101, 228n42; serpent-like quality of Medea in, 104
Peter the Venerable, 202–203n20
Petremol, François, 125, 186, 235n14
Philip II (king of Spain), 170
Pico della Mirandola, Giovanni, 84, 96; *Oration on the Dignity of Man*, 8, 11
piracy and privateering: agents held captive by, 72, 129, 138–139; Belon on, 72; Belon on spying networks and communications of coast peoples to protect against, 71–72; French privateers in the slave trade, 115; geography of, 38; Knights of St. John, 238n66; in Rabelais, moral agency of, 29, 32
Piton, Pierre de, 43
pity: exclusion implied by, 154; as Hebrew-Christian virtue, 22; in Jodelle, 118; in Nicolay, 154; in de la Péruse, 104, 118; in Rabelais, 33, 154, 210n11
plasticity of the human: animality and, 26–27, 49, 208–209nn78–79; Belon on agency and, 72; birds as representing, 69; cultural relativism, 161, 170
Plato: ideal of unity and peace, 126; primacy of the eye over hearing, 137; the skin, 78; the soul as tripartite, 57–58. Works: *Republic*, 57–58; *Symposium*, 225n6; *Timaeus*, 24–25. *See also* Socrates
Platter, Thomas, 167
pleasure: as absolute right of kings, 63, 70; bathing culture of the OE as, 79, 81–83; Belon on, 63–64, 69–71; of curiosity, 69–70; distributed pleasure, 69–71; as fortuitous outcome of nature, 64; Montaigne on immoderacy as forfeiting agency, 178, 180, 184–185, 187; nature's pleasure, 63–64, 69, 70–71; Nicolay on ennobling pleasure of viewing his book, 146, 240n96; observation as, 69–71; Palerne as traveling for, 190; political hierarchies of, 70, 71; Postel on the gentle pleasures of communal eating and entertainments, 83–84, 85, 86; Rabelais and, 31, 209n5. *See also* erotic pleasure; nudity; sexual pleasure

Pléiade group, 25, 90, 91, 103, 112, 229n51, 233n109
Pliny the Elder, 35, 100, 218n14, 227nn35,38
Plutarch: overview, 91; and "cosmopolitanism" as term, 207n69; "Life of Antony," 77, 91–92, 96, 97, 106, 110; "The Obsolescence of Oracles," 49
poetry: gender roles assigned in, 225–226n14; as symbolic glue of the state, 104. *See also* theater
Poitiers, Diane de (Duchesse de Valentinois), 233–234n3
Poland, 181; Duke of Anjou as king of, 17, 162, 173
Popov, Vesselin, 241n115
Portugal: dark skin as marker of low status in, 192, 193; privateers and merchants, 38; slave trade of, 38, 115; universalist claims of, 203n235
Postel, Guillaume: overview, 60–61; as agent, 23, 83, 88; on bathing culture, 81–82; biographical information, 61, 82, 88; and Daniel Bomberg, 84, 224n78; on clothing, 87–88; on colonizable groups of people, 153; and the cosmopolitan turn, x–xi, 23–24, 237n58; dark skin as curse of Ham, 229–230n62; on dervishes, 147, 240n101; on the gentleness and sweetness in the OE, 85, 127; Gilles's conflict with, 129; on the hospitality of Anatolian Turks, 86–87; as humanist, 82; on imperial order of the OE court, 86; on Islam via derisive stereotypes, 83, 86, 223n71; and the numismatic spoils of being an agent, 112; and people on the margins of OE society as more "like" himself, 87; on the pleasures of eating and sharing meals and entertainments, 83–84, 85, 86; queer/androgynous gendering and, 83–85, 87–88, 224n78; syncretic mysticism of, 82–83, 84–85, 224n78; utopian Christian empire sought by, 23, 61, 82–83, 84, 85, 86, 88, 127, 166, 224n84; and wine, psychosomatic indigestion due to lack of, 86; and the *Zohar*, 84, 224n78. Works: *De la Republique des Turcs*, 81, 83, 84, 86, 153, 183, 224n84; *De Orbis terrae concordia*, 88; *De Phoenicum literis . . . commentatiuncula*, 224n78; *Le Thrésor des Prophéties de l'Univers*, 224n78; *Linguarum duodecim characteribus*, 207n64
Primaticcio, Francesco, 125, 233–234n3; *Galérie d'Ulysse*, 135, 135
print and printing: books and spying, 237n54; Jews and, 241n116; market for travel books, 124, 145; proliferation of, 25–26, 43, 124. *See also* art; prints (cheap reproductions)
prints (cheap reproductions): desire to collect and demand for, 146, 151; as generative matter getting "out of control," 25–26; image as making its own medium visible, 151; as model of promiscuity, 147; nude images circulating via, 124; and the repeatedly viewing male gaze, 157
profit making: Belon's curiosity (pleasure of observation) as spiritual profit, 69–70; collectors of coins making moral claim superior to, 112–114; Nicolay's "mutual exchange" of French Catholic colonizing mission as distinguished from, 127–128
prostitutes. *See* sex work and sex workers
Protestants: Calvinists, 18–19, 40; critique of papal ceremonies, 161; critique of Stoic universalism, 18–19; Metz ruled by, 90. *See also* French Protestants
protocolonial notions of race in France: conflation of climate, skin color, and temperament, 106–107, 229–230nn62–3; dietary racism, 51–55, 60; excessive or stunted growth of the body or body parts, 36, 37, 55; hypersexualization of people of color, 55, 106–107; martyrdom of Christians in, 54, 216n75; and the need to justify the Franco-Ottoman Alliance, 12; nobility as product of testing the body (Montaigne), 175–180, 181–184; notions of race, 2–3; self-reinvention of agents and, 27; sixteenth-century French studies and distinction between modern notion and, ix–x; sixteenth-century literary studies and distinction between modern notion and, ix–x, xii, 200n7; skin color and beauty norms, 151–152, 240–241n109; skin color and status, 152, 241n9; spying as changing French culture, 194–195. *See also* black skin and racism; black skin associated with slavery; humoral racism; medieval racializing narratives
"public women." *See* sex work and sex workers

Qansuh al-Guri (sultan), 204n32
queerness: androgynous clothing, 87; androgynous *köçek* and *çengī* dancers and harp players in the OE, 83–84, 223n75; binary patriarchal erotic culture in contrast to nonbinary, 84, 223n75; "hermaphrodites" and other classificatory terms, 223–224n77; lesbian desire, representation of, 155–157, 156, 242n120; in Postel, 83–85,

87–88, 224n78; in Rabelais, 41–42, 88, 212nn32–33; spiritual countertradition of nonbinary sex as divine and human ideal, 82–83, 84–85, 224nn77–78

Quran, Latin translation of, 202–203n20

Rabelais, François: overview, 12; agency defined by visible bodies, 39–41; on the agency of animality, 49–51, 54, 59; as agent in the Mediterranean, 4, 49, 213n45; anti-Platonic models in, 57–58; and the aquiline nose, 77; biographical information, 4, 45–47, 49, 90, 214n56; censorship of, 211–212n31; Cicero referenced in, 73; on clothing, 73; and the cosmopolitan turn, x–xi, 24; established interpretations as humanist fictions about ideal government, 3–4, 29, 201nn7–8, 209n1; the Franco-Ottoman Alliance referenced in, 6–7, 29, 42–43, 44, 45, 47, 213n44; and gentleness, 34, 127; on his patron, Guillaume du Bellay, 49–51, 214nn48,57; on his patron, Jean du Bellay, 45–46, 214n48; as humanist "hero," x, 199n2; the humoral body in, 5, 8, 10, 35–36, 39–40, 41; and humoral medicine, knowledge of, 34–36, 49, 210n13; hybridity in, 9; medieval racializing narratives as rewritten by, 4, 6–8, 9, 10; opposition to princely use of religious tithes, 46; people on the margins of OE society as more "like" Pantagruel, 87; political community as universalist and imperialist, 42, 55, 57, 88, 166; and the political effects of sudden emotions, 35; and print, proliferation of, 43; queerness in, 41–42, 88, 212nn32–33; as rejecting Western exceptionality of human agency, 9; on self-defense, 46–47; and Sophism, 57, 58; utopian visions of, 12, 29, 32, 41, 88, 127–128. Works: letter to Geoffroy d'Estissac, 46–47; letter to Guillaume Pellicier, 49; *Quart livre*, 33, 49, 214n57; *Stratagemata* (lost), 214n48; *Tiers livre*, 49, 73, 210n11

—*Gargantua*: animals as symbols in, 38, 211nn25–26; and appetite, 34, 38–39, 41, 172; on Christian exemplarity, 30–31, 209nn4–5; crying/important tears in, 33, 154, 210n11; dating of, 43, 213n41; ennobling of Panurge, 40, 41, 211n30; and the humoral body, perfection of, 35, 39–40, 41; humoral racism in, 35–36, 39; moral agency granted to Muslim pirates, 29, 32; and More's *Utopia*, 36; and natural goodness, 31, 32, 33–34; personal (male) bonds vs. the law in, 32–33, 41–42, 212nn32–33; and pleasure, 31, 209n5; and self-reinvention, 27; and servitude, 20; splitting military forces, 46; voluntary self-subjection of the Canarrian pirates in, 31–32, 33–34, 36, 38–39, 72, 172

—*Pantagruel*: agencies of appetite in, 4, 5–8, 7, 51–55; agency extended to the nonhuman realm in, 8–9; Alcofrybas Nasier as pseudonym and anagram of Rabelais, 58; animality in, 57, 59; Belon's work described in reference to, 62; on Black persons, 36; the capacity for moral agency extended to all bodies, 2, 4–5, 8–9, 10, 57–59; on clothing, 73; the Cynics in, 55, 58–59, 217n95; dietary racism and, 51–55, 60; differences, ambivalence toward, 5, 6, 8–9, 201n10; differences as due to nature's capacity for change through accidents, 4–5, 9, 24, 130; the humoral body as proportionate vs. disproportionate, 5, 8, 10, 36; Panurge's tale of captivity and escape, 51–55, 57, 58, 59, 88; race entwined with agency in, 1–2, 3–4

race. *See* humoral racism; medieval racializing narratives; modern notion of race; protocolonial notions of race in France; "race" (as term in sixteenth-century texts); race in sixteenth-century European culture; race, transhistorical constructions of

"race" (as term in sixteenth-century texts): new nobility and tensions of, 200n4; the nobility (*lignée*, bloodline) as most privileged, 2, 3, 21, 179, 200n4; parody of, as allowing supplementary significance, 2; quotation marks used for term, 199n1; Rabelais's destabilization through accidents of nature and violent events, 3; as rank and place in society, 3, 179, 200n4; "razza" as term, 2–3. *See also* protocolonial notions of race in France; race in sixteenth-century European culture

race in sixteenth-century European culture: overview, 201n14; and the *Code Noir*, 202n16, 203–204n27; enslavement justified through metaphysical gap between body and soul, 204n28; in François Bernier, 202n16. *See also* medieval racializing narratives

race, transhistorical constructions of: Blackness as "shimmering," 53, 193, 202n15, 215n67; false racial category of "Caucasians," 152; naturalism as enabling, 202n16

Raemond, Florimond de, *L'Anti-Christ*, 160–161, 163, 165–166, 167, 169, 170
Ragusans, 153
Randall, Michael, *Gargantuan Polity*, 41
readers: agency of, and projections of French empire, 165; and the male sense of orientation in the world, 190; Montaigne on "service" to, 228–229n48; Nicolay on the ennobling pleasure of his book for, 146, 240n96; as not attuned to the cosmopolitanism of the French court, 74; pleasure of, 69; "service" of authors to, 102, 228–229n48; trained to see the world as colonizable, 13, 145, 146–147, 152–155, 157–159, 195; and triangulation of erotic desire, 154–155. *See also* travel writing about the Ottoman Empire
Reeser, Todd W., 246n59
Rieux, Renée de, 163
Rigolot, François, 211n30
Rincón, Antonio, 15, 43, 50, 212–213n39
risk: constitutive of the holistic conception of the body, 2, 35, 81–82, 146, 161; dangers to agents, downplayed, 72, 79, 166–167, 170, 190; presented as testing, 162, 182–184
Rollet, Jacques, 82
Roma, 74; as colonizable people, 153–154, 241n115
Roman Empire: bathing culture, 79; conquest of Egypt, 90 (*See also* Jodelle: *Cléopâtre captive*; Plutarch: "Life of Antony"); cosmopolitanism of, and integration vs. expulsion of specific groups, 16, 205n44; funeral practices, 99; gentleness associated with civilization, 85; integration of non-Romans, 16; Montaigne referencing, 182. *See also* classical Greek and Roman philosophy; classical mythology; Greece, ancient
Romano, Giulio, 125
Ronsard, Pierre de, 105; "Ode to Vulcan," 118–119, 233n107; poem prefixed to Nicolay's *Navigations et Pérégrinations*, 164–165, 243n9
Rouillard, Clarence Dana, *The Turk in French Thought, History, and Literature (1520–1660)*, 199n3
Rouillé, Guillaume, 47, 48, 200n2; *Promptuaire des medalles*, 110–112, 111; as publisher of Nicolay's *Navigations et pérégrinations*, 125
Rouller, Dorine, 245n47
Rumi, 174
ruse: characteristic of the absolutist state, 237n54; enabling mobility and ennobling, 12–13, 128; recognized as transnational sign of agency, 64, 75, 88, 142, 144

Sagon, François, *Apolygye* (1544), 22–23, 127, 207n64
Saint Andrews (Scottish fortress), French siege of, 134
St. Bernard, *De Laude Novae Militiae*, 202–203n20
Saint-Blancard, Baron of (Bertrand d'Ornesan), 44–45, 75, 117, 221n54
Sainte-Marthe, Scévole de, 116
Saint-Gelais, Mellain de, 232n96
St. Maurice, 39
St. Michel (knightly order), 132
Saracens: origin of term, 10, 202n19. *See also* Muslims
"savage" as term, 51
Savoy, Louise de, 15
Schiebinger, Londa, *Plants and Empire*, 218n14
Scottish fortress, French siege of Saint Andrews, 134
Scott, Joan, 214–215n61
Screech, Michael Andrew, 213n41
Sedgwick, Eve Kosofsky, *Between Men*, 41, 212n33
self: agents and reinvention of, 27; projection of anxieties onto the other, 60
self-as-other: Belon, 66, 77; the Cynics, 23–24; as divine (Postel), 84; medieval identification with the other's valued qualities, 39; Montaigne and, 168, 178; Nicolay, 128; and the Old World fascination with Blackness in the New World, 1, 193; in theater, 91
self-interest, humanist subordination to the interests of the state, 11–12
self-knowledge, the Cynics and need to break laws and rules to produce, 56
Selim I (sultan), 204n32
Selim II (sultan): ceremonies of reception and, 173–174, 175; release of French captives under, 186
Semsi Ahmet Pasha, 190
Seneca, 18; *Medea*, 103
serfs: bondage of tithe-paying, 115; liberation (for a fee), 115, 231n89
Serres, Olivier, 240n97
servants, livery worn by, 123, 234n5. *See also* free soil principle; French liberation of captive persons; slavery; unfree persons in France
Severus, 97

INDEX

sexual pleasure: hypersexualization of others, 13, 36, 55, 106–107, 203–204n27; Montaigne as denying agency to immoderate expression of, 185. *See also* erotic pleasure; sex work and sex workers
sex work and sex workers: described by Nicolay, 155; described by Palerne, 190, 192; as informants for Nicolay, 239n88; as models for drawing of high-ranking women in Nicolay, 155; Persian Shahs deemed to practice sexual moderation with, 185; "public women" as pejorative for, 155; in Rabelais, as rendering assistance, 51–52, 55; White slavery ("luxury slaves"), 151, 152
Seyssel, Claude de, *La grant monarchie de France*, 41
Sforza, Duke of, 243n11
Shakespeare, William: racial (anti-Black) codes in, 200n7, 201n14. Works: *Hamlet*, 21; *Othello*, 201n14
Sicily, 132, 134, 141
Sinan Pasha, 134, 137, 139–140, 142, 238n68
Sinti, as colonizable people, 153–154, 241n115
Skilliter, Susan A., 186
skin: as envelope, and bathing culture, 77, 79, 81; as hardening of the humors, 77; humoral medicine view as open and porous, clothing needed to protect, 77–79, 181; as protective barrier rendering clothes unnecessary, 27, 181–184. *See also* skin color
skin color: conflation of climate and temperament and, 106–107, 229–230nn62–3; hypersexualization of people with dark skin, 13, 36, 55, 106–107, 203–204n27; Nicolay and racialization of, 125, 156, 157–159, 158; racist norms of beauty based on light vs. dark, 151–152, 192–193, 240n108; and viewing peoples as colonizable, 157–159; whitening of Cleopatra, 91, 105, 106–107, 151. *See also* black skin and racism; black skin associated with slavery; Whiteness
slavery: and barbarian/civilized distinction, 137–138, 237n56; capture and trade of Eastern European women tied to male erotic desire, 154, 155; corporal punishment, 117; *esclave* as term, 21, 116, 206n57; facial tattoos as adornment, vs. branding of slaves, 193–194, 248n16; in medieval racializing narratives, 11; and race as transhistorical construct, 202n16; White ("luxury slaves"), as defining racist norm of beauty and skin color, 151, 152. *See also* black skin associated with slavery;

colonialism; free soil principle; French liberation of captive persons; slavery as metaphor; unfree persons in France
— IN THE OTTOMAN EMPIRE: black skin and, 192–193, 200n2; Hungarian slave girl, 124, 151, 152, 154, 155; White slavery ("luxury slaves"), 151, 152. *See also* French liberation of captive persons
— SLAVE TRADE OF EUROPE: black skin and, 200n2; French privateers in, 115; Portuguese, 38, 115; Spanish, 115
slavery as metaphor: the anti-sensualist tradition linking lack of control of passions to, 11, 20, 180, 184–185, 206n55; Aristotle on the emotions as, 58; blackening of humanity and the plasticity of the human and the animal, 26–27, 208–209n79; sixteenth-century conflation of service with servitude and, 11, 19–22, 26, 187, 206n57; as "spiritually inflicted," 118; of the will (*esclaver*), 118, 233n107
Slavs: as colonizable people, 153, 154; delis, 142–145, 143, 147, 153; *esclave* as referring to, 21, 116, 117
Smith, Ian, *Race and Rhetoric in the Renaissance*, 200n7
Smith, Justin E. H., *Nature, Human Nature, and Human Difference*, 137, 202n16, 204n28, 218n14, 237n56
Socrates: and "cosmopolitanism" as term, 207n69; Erasmus on, 23; rejection of the Sophists, 57
Sokollu Mehmed Pasha, 175
sōma, 49–50
Song of Roland, 52, 215n66
soul: enslavement justified through Christian narrative of gap between body and, 204n28; the humoral body and, 34; mind-body dualism, 34; Platonic tripartite soul, 57–58
Spain: conquest of Mahdia, 132, 133, 139–140, 236n34, 238n68; the Franco-Ottoman Alliance as counterbalance to, 14, 15, 26, 43–44, 107–108, 132, 236n34; joint Franco-Ottoman military campaigns against, 15, 43, 83, 132–134, 236n39; Ottoman-Spanish peace treaty, 132, 238n68; privateers and merchants, 38; siege of Metz, 90, 114; slave trade of, 115; Treaty of Cateau-Cambrésis, 123, 125; universalist claims of, 12, 203n235. *See also* Charles V (Holy Roman Emperor); Holy Roman Empire
spirit: attributed to animals, 63; definition of, 63; of the observer (Belon), 65, 68–69

spying and spies: Belon's description of coastal people's networks of communication to prevent piracy, 71–72; Belon's role in, 61, 71, 72, 220n43; books and, 237n54; *curiosité* as term referencing, 51, 71, 164; firearms as increasing the necessity of, 129; the French ruling elite as commonly employing, 72, 107, 163–165, 239n83, 243n11; the knight's representative power (*ius gentium*) as superceded by, 141; by Catherine de Médicis's "flying squadron" of courtiers, 186; the modern state and rise of, 239n83; the New World opened to colonialism due to, 194–195; Nicolay's role in, 125, 128–129, 130, 134–142, 238–239nn78,88; Ottoman perspective on, 163–164; professional class of spies, 137; and secrets, 142

Stallybrass, Peter, and Ann Rosalind Jones, *Renaissance Clothing and the Materials of Memory*, 123, 234n5

Steinberg, Leo, 242n120

Stoics/Stoicism: and agents' construction of autonomy, 14; as alternative to the ruthless logic of political necessity, 29; antisensualist tradition of, 20, 206n55; *apathea*, 209n5; awakening the individual will, 21; cosmology of, 25, 106, 129; cosmopolitanism of, 16, 18, 19, 174, 205n44; critique of ethnocentrism, 14; freedom as internal vs. granted by law, 185; interpretation of Rabelais in light of, 29; Jodelle's *Cléopâtre captive* referencing, 95; natural reason, 15–16, 31–32; the seed as creative force and origin, 101, 228n41

Sublime Porte. *See* Ottoman Empire

Sufis ("Sophies"), 174, 245n31

Suleiman I (sultan): *ahidnâme* of 1536, 15; crown of, 103–104, 229n54; death of, 170–171; execution of Prince Mustafa, 174–175, 244–245n30; and the Franco-Egypt commercial agreement, 14–15; Haseki Hürrem Sultan (aka Roxelana), wife of, 155, 241–242n118; Guillaume Pellicier and, 212–213n39; pious turn of, 17; splitting military forces, 46. *See also* Franco-Ottoman Alliance; Ottoman Empire

Supúlveda, Gené de, 12

Swiss bathing culture, 78, 79

Tatars (Turkic people), 53, 155
Téligny, Charles de, 19

Templars, 202–203n20
Terence, 128, 142, 179
theater: actors denied agency, 95, 180; as art, 89–90, 95, 104, 110; the audience visualizing the self onstage, 13, 91; captive foreigners involved in, 116, 117–119, 232nn94,99; cost of, borne by the poet, 110, 231n78; costumes, 116, 231nn77–78; diplomacy of (seventeenth century), 45, 213n44; gender roles assigned in, 225–226n14; Jodelle's failures of staging, 110, 231nn73,77–78; as metaphor for diplomacy and politics, 171–172, 173; negative value given to, 171; transgressive yet conservative powers of art as symbolic glue of the state, 104. *See also* Jodelle, Étienne; Péruse, Jean de la

Thevet, André: on bathing culture of the OE, 79, 80, 81–82; on colonizable groups of people, 153, 241n117; conflation of climate, temperament, and dark skin, 229–230nn62–63; on the drug "mummy," 101; as humanist "hero," x, 199n2; spoils of being an agent, 114. Works: *Cosmographie de Levant*, 79, 80, 153; *Les singularitez de la France antarctique*, 218n13, 229–230nn62–63

Thiery, Leonard, 119, 233n108
Thomas of Aquinas, 16
Thumiger, Chiara, 24
Tinguely, Frédéric, 69, 221–222nn55,64
Titian: erroneously attributed the images in Nicolay, 242n122; portrait of d'Aramon, 130, 132, 133
Tolan, John Victor, 223n71
Tordesillas, Treaty of, 203n25
Tournon, André, 72
Touteville, Nicolas de, 19
transgender. *See* queerness
Transylvania, 19, 117, 163, 212–213n39, 243n7
travel: Nicolay on the noble spirit and body of the agent, 128–129, 144–145; Ottoman caravansaries and customs for, 165; and Ottoman laws, 73–74, 165, 192, 221n48; by pilgrims, 60; risks of, 190; as test of agency, 26
travel writing about the Ottoman Empire: adoption of Ottoman clothing as glossed over in, 74; conflation of climate, temperament, and skin color, 106, 230n63; cosmopolitanism extended to broader audiences via, 124; "disembodied eye" rhetorical technique, 68–69; impact on the male sense of orientation in the

INDEX 293

world, 190; market for, 124, 145; Nicolay as training the inner eye of the reader to see the world as colonizable, 13, 145, 146–147, 152–155, 157–159, 195; Palerne as influenced by, 189–190. *See also* agents of the French crown; print and printing; readers; *specific authors*

Tripoli: siege of, 133–134, 139–142, 238n68; slave market of, 151, 152

Trissino, Gian Giorgino, *Sophonisbe* (play), 18, 116, 232n96

Tunis, 43, 44, 45, 47

Tunisia, as pirate state, 38

"A Turkish Woman Making Love" (print), 155–157, 156, 242n120

Turnebus, Adrianus, 89

unfree persons in France: adoption by French parents, 117; corporal punishment of, 117; court ceremonies and theater featuring, 18, 116–117, 233nn94,99; definition of, 115–116; freedom as mirrored in the unfreedom of others, 118–120, 126; liberated captive persons retaining unfree status, 116–117; named after their master or mistress, 186; pity toward, 118; as rendered invisible in French society, 117–118; as rendered invisible in the archives, 116, 117, 186–187, 233n105. *See also* free soil principle; French liberation of captive persons; slavery; women

universalist claims: as anti-diplomatic attitude to diplomacy, 127, 235n19; early Christian aspirations, 16; of medieval culture, 11, 107; of the Ottoman Empire, 12, 203n125; Roman Stoicism, 16, 17, 18; of Spain, 12, 203n235; of the Valois Court, 16, 17, 18, 19; virtue and, 16

universalist claims of humanism: of agents of the crown, 21, 23; and the Cynics, 24; and the "dervish" and other Ottoman exemplars, 24; European ethnocentricity as masked by, 11, 21; of morality, 174; and the New World, 24; and the "wild man" archetype, 24, 148–151

Usher, Philip John: "Prudency and the Inefficacy of Language," 102; "Walking East in the Renaissance," 60

utopian visions of agents: overview, xi–xii; and anti-diplomatic attitude to diplomacy, 235n19; Belon, 61, 70–71, 127–128; Postel, 23, 61, 82–83, 84, 85, 86, 88, 127, 166, 224n84; in Rabelais, 12, 29, 32, 41, 88, 127–128

Valbelle, Honorat, *Histoire journalière d'Honorat de Valbelle (1498–1530)*, 117, 212n38, 221n54

Valeriano, Piero, illustrated *Hieroglyphica* translation, 96, 97, 98

Valla, Pietro, *Hieroglyphica* translation, 96

Vallier, Gaspar de, 140–141

Valois court. *See* French crown

Valois, Marguerite de, 19

Véga, Jean de, 44, 117

Vély, Claude Dodieu de, 46

Venice: envoys to, 50; French interest in vying with, 204n30; Ottoman–Venetian peace treaty, 173; Postel exposed to mysticism in, 82; printers and booksellers, 125; White slavery practice of, 151, 152

Veyne, Paul, 16

Vidal-Naquet, Pierre, 215–216n73

Villegagnon, Nicolas Durand de, 139, 140

Villey, Pierre, 163

violence of custom, gentleness as resistance to, 169–170, 244n15

virtue: Cynics as shortcut to, 57; devotion as (Montaigne), 183–184, 246n52; gentleness as, 22; universalist claims and, 16; as visible in the body (Montaigne), 179

warfare, firearms and transformation of, 129

the weak, intelligence of, 71–72, 220n39

Weiss, Gillian Lee, *Captives and Corsairs*, 17, 114, 205n50, 235n13

Whitaker, Cord J., *Black Metaphors*, 53, 193, 202n15, 215n67

White French men, as empowered by humanism, x

Whiteness: "Caucasians," represented as embodiment of, 152; development as subject position, 9–10, 107, 202n118, 230n65; non-Europeans "promoted" to, 241n109; and racist beauty norms of skin color, 151–152, 240–241n109; "white" as color of European skin, 10, 107, 230n65; whitening of Cleopatra in Jodelle's play, 91, 105, 106–107, 151

"wild man" archetype, 24, 148–149, 163–164. *See also* Bosnian delis; dervishes

will: free, 219n16; metaphorical slavery of the (*esclaver*), 118, 233n107; susceptibility to pressure, 26

Williams, Wes, 199n2

wine: as cultural boundary separating Christians and Muslims, 4, 86; and dietary racism of Rabelais, 54, 55; Muslim ban on, 54, 55; Postel's "spiritual indigestion" for

wine *(continued)*
    lack of, 86; representations of Muslims drinking, 60
Wolff, Larry, 152
women: décolleté worn by, 183–184; homosocial bonding and exclusion/control of, 41–42; as invisible as historical subjects, 117, 186, 214n61; lamentation norms for, 94, 225–226n14; as "leaky vessels," 93–94; moral agency denied to, 185–187, 246n62; Postel's syncretic mysticism of (Mother Giovanna), 82–83, 84–85. *See also* gender; marriage; queerness; sexual pleasure; sex work and sex workers; theater; unfree persons in France
—IN THE OTTOMAN EMPIRE: and bathing culture, 222n64; capture and trade of, as tied to the erotics of male desire, 154, 155; captured and held in service to Catherine de Médicis, 186–187; chastity belts, 88; clothing of, 74–75, 87, 88; concubines, 155; Haseki Hürrem Sultan (aka Roxelana), 155, 241–242n118; lesbian desire, representation of, 155–157, 156, 242n120; Nicolay's commodification of, 154–155; patriarchal erotic culture and binary sexual roles of, 84, 88, 223n75; queer and gender bending roles of, 83–84, 223–224nn75,77; skin color and racist beauty norms, 151–152, 192–193, 240n108; status of, 74–75; veiling, 74–75, 157, 222n64; as vendors in the marketplace, 74
Wynter, Sylvia, "Unsettling the Coloniality of Being/Power/Truth/Freedom," 11–12, 17, 66–67

Yates, Francis, 233n109
Yérasimos, Stéphane, 125, 236nn29,35
Yverson, Jean d,' 232n94

Zeno of Citium, 205n41
Zinguer, Ilana, 62
Zorach, Rebecca: *Blood, Milk, Ink, Gold*, 25–26, 57, 94, 110, 145–146, 147, 232n99, 233n109, 239n95; "Desiring Things," 147, 242n120
Zoroastrianism, 101

Antónia Szabari is professor of French and comparative literature at the University of Southern California. Her interests include early modern literature and political culture, interspecies ethics, plant ontology, and speculative fiction, both old and new. She is the author of *Less Rightly Said: Scandals and Readers in Sixteenth-Century France* (Stanford University Press, 2009) and co-author, with Natania Meeker, of *Radical Botany: Plants and Speculaive Fiction* (Fordham University Press, 2019), winner of the 2019 Science Fiction and Technoculture Studies book prize.

www.ingramcontent.com/pod-product-compliance
Lightning Source LLC
Chambersburg PA
CBHW020356080526
44584CB00014B/1039